David J. Galbreath

NATION-BUILDING AND MINORITY POLITICS IN POST-SOCIALIST STATES

Interests, Influence and Identities in Estonia and Latvia

With a foreword by David J. Smith

ibidem-Verlag
Stuttgart

Bibliographic information published by the Deutsche Nationalbibliothek
Die Deutsche Nationalbibliothek lists this publication in the Deutsche Nationalbibliografie; detailed bibliographic data are available in the Internet at http://dnb.d-nb.de.

Bibliografische Information der Deutschen Nationalbibliothek
Die Deutsche Nationalbibliothek verzeichnet diese Publikation in der Deutschen Nationalbibliografie; detaillierte bibliografische Daten sind im Internet über http://dnb.d-nb.de abrufbar.

ISSN: 1614-3515

ISBN-13: 978-3-89821-467-4

Printed in the United States of America

oviet and Post-Soviet Politics and Society (SPPS)

SSN 1614-3515

Soviet and Post-Soviet Politics and Society (SPPS)

ISSN 1614-3515

Founded in 2004 and refereed since 2007, SPPS makes available affordable English-, German-, and Russian-language studies on the history of the countries of the former Soviet bloc from the late Tsarist period to today. It publishes between 5 and 20 volumes per year and focuses on issues in transitions to and from democracy such as economic crisis, identity formation, civil society development, and constitutional reform in CEE and the NIS. SPPS also aims to highlight so far understudied themes in East European studies such as right-wing radicalism, religious life, higher education, or human rights protection. The authors and titles of all previously published volumes are listed at the end of this book. For a full description of the series and reviews of its books, see www.ibidem-verlag.de/red/spps.

Editorial correspondence & manuscripts should be sent to: Dr. Andreas Umland, DAAD, German Embassy, vul. Bohdana Khmelnitskoho 25, UA-01901 Kyiv, Ukraine. e-mail: umland@stanfordalumni.org

Business correspondence & review copy requests should be sent to: ***ibidem*** Press, Leuschnerstr. 40, 30457 Hannover, Germany; tel.: +49 511 2622200; fax: +49 511 2622201; spps@ibidem.eu.

Authors, reviewers, referees, and editors for (as well as all other persons sympathetic to) SPPS are invited to join its networks at
www.facebook.com/group.php?gid=52638198614
www.linkedin.com/groups?about=&gid=103012
www.xing.com/net/spps-ibidem-verlag/

Recent Volumes

114 Ivo Mijnssen
The Quest for an Ideal Youth in Putin's Russia I
Back to Our Future! History, Modernity and Patriotism according to *Nashi*, 2005-2012
With a foreword by Jeronim Perović
ISBN 978-3-8382-0368-3

115 Jussi Lassila
The Quest for an Ideal Youth in Putin's Russia II
The Search for Distinctive Conformism in the Political Communication of *Nashi*, 2005-2009
With a foreword by Kirill Postoutenko
ISBN 978-3-8382-0415-4

116 Valerio Trabandt
Neue Nachbarn, gute Nachbarschaft?
Die EU als internationaler Akteur am Beispiel ihrer Demokratieförderung in Belarus und der Ukraine 2004-2009
Mit einem Vorwort von Jutta Joachim
ISBN 978-3-8382-0437-6

117 Fabian Pfeiffer
Estlands Außen- und Sicherheitspolitik I
Der estnische Atlantizismus nach der wiedererlangten Unabhängigkeit 1991-2004
Mit einem Vorwort von Helmut Hubel
ISBN 978-3-8382-0127-6

118 Jana Podßuweit
Estlands Außen- und Sicherheitspolitik II
Handlungsoptionen eines Kleinstaates im Rahmen seiner EU-Mitgliedschaft (2004-2008)
Mit einem Vorwort von Helmut Hubel
ISBN 978-3-8382-0440-6

119 Karin Pointner
Estlands Außen- und Sicherheitspolitik III
Eine gedächtnispolitische Analyse estnischer Entwicklungskooperation 2006-2010
Mit einem Vorwort von Karin Liebhart
ISBN 978-3-8382-0435-2

120 Ruslana Vovk
Die Offenheit der ukrainischen Verfassung für das Völkerrecht und die europäische Integration
Mit einem Vorwort von Alexander Blankenagel
ISBN 978-3-8382-0481-9

121 Mykhaylo Banakh
Die Relevanz der Zivilgesellschaft bei den postkommunistischen Transformationsprozessen in mittel- und osteuropäischen Ländern
Das Beispiel der spät- und postsowjetischen Ukraine 1986-2009
Mit einem Vorwort von Gerhard Simon
ISBN 978-3-8382-0499-4

For the women in my life:
Jolene, Lee and Pat

List of Contents

List of Tables

List of Abbreviations

CEC	-Central Executive Committee
CPE	-Communist Party of Estonia
CPE-CPSU	-Communist Party of Estonia on the Platform of the Communist Party of the Soviet Union
CPL	-Communist Party of Latvia
CPSU	-Communist Party of the Soviet Union
CoE	-Council of Europe
CSCE	-Conference for the Security and Co-operation in Europe
DPFSU	-Democratic People's Front of the Soviet Union
EDM	-Estonian Democratic Movement
ENF	-Estonian National Front
ENIP	-Estonian National Independence Party
EP	-European Parliament
ESSR	-Estonian Soviet Socialist Republic
EU	-European Union
EUPP	-Estonian United People's Party
FCPNM	-Framework Convention for the Protection of National Minorities
FF	-Fatherland and Freedom
FHRUL	-For Human Rights in a United Latvia
HCNM	-OSCE High Commissioner on National Minorities
ILCP	-Independent Latvian Communist Party
KGB	-Committee of State Security
KMU	-*Koonderakonna ja Maarahva Uhendus*
LDDP	-Latvian Democratic Labour Party
LNIM	-Latvian National Independence Movement
LPA	-Latvian Privatisation Agency
LPF	-Latvian People's Front
LSDWP	-Latvian Social Democratic Worker's Party
LSSR	-Latvian Soviet Socialist Republic
LW	-Latvia's Way

LZS	-Latvian Green Party
MFA	-Ministry of Foreign Affairs (Russian)
MRP	-Molotov-Ribbentrop Pact
MRP-AEG	-Estonian Group for the Publication of the Molotov-Ribbentrop Pact
MVD	-Ministry of Internal Affairs
NATO	-North Atlantic Treaty Organisation
ODIHR	-OSCE Office for Democratic Institutions and Human Rights
OSCE	-Organisation for Security and Co-operation in Europe
OSTK	-United Council of Work Collectives
PFE	-Popular Front of Estonia
RDM	-Russian Democratic Movement
RPE	-Russian Party in Estonia
SLAT	-Harmony for Latvia – Revival for the Economy
UN	-United Nations
UNDP	-United Nations Development Project
USSR	-Union of Soviet Socialist Republics
UWC	-Union of Work Collectives
VAK	-Environmental Protection Club (Estonia)

Acknowledgements

As Bo Petersson wrote, 'to write an academic book is quite different from experiencing the loneliness of a long distance runner.' Indeed, this book is a product of both the support of the academic community and home. In the academic community, numerous friends, colleagues and acquaintances have contributed to its improvement. Although I am solely responsible for the thesis, I wish to thank everyone who has contributed to the process, even though I am only able to mention a few.

I would like to thank Universities UK, the University of Leeds and the International Institute for Education's J. William Fulbright Research Fund for their financial support. Furthermore, without the support of many individuals in the field, this book would not have been feasible. Most especially, I would like to thank Vello Pettai at the University of Tartu for his early advice and direction. Furthermore, I would like to thank Janis Ikstens, Brigita Zepa, Daunis Auers, Artis Pabriks, and Nils Muiznieks. I give a special thank you to historian Kaspars Ozolins at the University of Latvia for his informative seminar series on Latvian history. I would also like to thank Vadim Poleshchuk at the Legal Information Centre for Human Rights in Estonia and Alexei Dimitrov at the Latvian Human Rights Committee. I also show gratitude to my Latvian language instructor, Arija Smildzina, for her constant good spirits and imparting her knowledge.

Closer to home, I would like to thank Hugo Radice for his advise, direction, and support. Furthermore, I would like to thank Neil Winn for his comments and overall support as well as Clive Jones for his comments and support early in the process. I would also like to thank Susan Paragreen, Caroline Wise, Tess Hornsby Smith, Preethi Sukumaran, and Dorne Greensmith for their continued support at POLIS. I hold a great deal of appreciation to all of my former colleagues at the University of Sheffield, especially Tony Paine and Mike Kenny.

Finally, I would like to thank friends and family. I give a special thank you for those individuals that kept me company in dark, cold Latvia such as

Iain Murdoch, Astrid Krumins, Liz Galvin, John Leopold, Rachelle Harrison and Mara Pelece. I also thank Maria and Frans Slothouber for their continued support. And last but not least, I thank my wife who has shown great patience and offered unlimited support during this process. I only hope that I will have returned it in kind.

Foreword

The question of how to reconcile civic equality with the ethno-cultural dimension of collective identity has figured prominently on the agenda of those organisations at heart of the post-Cold War new Europe. At a time when the management of multiculturalism was already becoming increasingly important to projects of governance in the longer-established western nation-states, the end of the Cold War again brought minority politics to the forefront of developments in central and eastern Europe. As was case following the collapse of multinational empires in 1918, the territorial rearrangements accompanying the demise of the USSR singularly failed to resolve what is often termed the 'nationality question'. Many would claim that they simply exacerbated it: each of the new states that replaced the Soviet Union contained significant minority populations, while economic collapse and a tendency by titular elites to view post-soviet nation-building through the prism of decolonisation inevitably inflamed nationalist tensions. Extrapolating from events in the former Yugoslavia, many commentators at the start of the 1990s predicted a similar wave of violent conflict across the former Soviet space. Thankfully such violence has proved to be the exception rather than the rule, though it took a while for western social science, steeped in essentialist portrayals of the region, to actually recognise this fact and seek to explain it.

This comparative study of Estonia and Latvia 1991-2001 usefully illuminates what Rogers Brubaker has famously termed the triadic nexus – the interplay of nationalising states, national minorities and external national homelands which continues to frame nationalist politics in the region. In both cases, the presence of a large, mainly Russian-speaking population of Soviet-era settlers and their descendents, coupled with accumulated bitterness at Soviet nationalities policy, meant that democracy and the nation-state were portrayed as 'conflicting logics' – to use Linz and Stepan's phrase - in the aftermath of the 1991 restoration of independence. This reasoning informed the establishment of a system of hegemonic control by the titular nationality, founded on the denial of automatic citizenship rights to Soviet-era settlers and their descendents. The breaking of the zero option citizenship rule applied elsewhere in the former Soviet Union has evoked discontent on the part of the affected population, but more especially on the part of Moscow, whose frequent verbal interventions have often proved akin to pouring oil on troubled waters. Yet, despite the relentlessly bleak assessments emanating from this quarter, Estonia and Latvia have both proved remarkably successful in maintaining ethno-political stability over the past decade and a half: the 'Moldovan road', which many claimed awaited them in the early 1990s, has not been followed.

The explanation for this must be sought first and foremost in the domestic sphere: alongside the divide-and-rule logic inherent in the political system, one can cite the startling diversity of the putative 'Russian-speaking population', which is more akin to a loose network group than a politically mobilised national minority in Brubaker's sense of the term. Furthermore, widespread perceptions of discrimination have not prevented the Estonian and Latvian states from acquiring a growing legitimacy in the eyes of their non-titular, non-citizen residents, a fact which rests upon their relative economic success and ability to secure rapid integration into the European Union. This takes us on neatly to the external dimension. The importance of international organisations to the evolution of minority politics has always been clear in the Baltic case. In this regard, it would be more appropriate to speak of a four-way relational nexus rather than the triadic framework discerned by Brubaker. In this work covering the period 1991-2001, David Galbreath presents a detailed study of this four-way identity-political nexus, combining new empirical findings with a comprehensive treatment of the already extensive theoretical and case-specific literature on this question.

As part of their process of accession to the European Union, Estonia and Latvia have both been required to make major changes to their laws on citizenship. Legislative amendments granting automatic citizenship to children of non-citizen permanent residents born after 1992 mean that at least there will be no more new non-citizens created in the two countries. At the same time, new EU-sponsored programmes have marked the start of more intensive efforts to integrate the remaining adult population of non-citizens. Yet the entry of the two countries to the EU has not drawn a line under this issue. In many ways, it has simply moved things to a new level, especially now that Baltic relations with Russia have become subsumed within the broader framework of EU-Russian relations. As the author indicates here, a number of intriguing questions remain: will the salience of ethno-cultural identities give way to more civic-based understandings as citizenship becomes more widely available? Will EU minority rights policy ever evolve beyond the current minimalist framework and, if so, what are the implications of this? Will state sovereignty retain its primacy within the EU project of governance, or is there scope – as some Hungarian commentators have suggested – for a Europe of nationalities alongside a Europe of nation-states? Similar questions were posed back in the 1920s, an era when the nationalities question stood at the centre of efforts to achieve a lasting European peace. Far from being passive 'policy-takers' guided League of Nations strictures, actors from central and eastern European states (and from Estonia and Latvia in particular) were instrumental at that time in advancing innovative liberal approaches to minority rights such as non-territorial cultural autonomy. It remains to be seen whether the region will play a similar role in today's Europe.

David J. Smith
Convenor, Glasgow Baltic Research Unit
Editor, *Journal of Baltic Studies*
Department of Central and East European Studies
University of Glasgow

Chapter 1 Introduction

1.1 Research Subject and Objectives

Where the Soviet Union once stood, there are now fifteen multi-ethnic states. Of these states, Estonia, Latvia and Lithuania have shown the most promise for democratisation and market development. The histories of the Baltic states are closely connected.[1] Geographically located on the eastern shores of the Baltic Sea, they have often shared occupiers. The most notable of these are German vassals, the Russian Empire, and the Soviet Union. From 1917 to 1939, all three nations experienced independent statehood. However, during the chaos of the Second World War, the Baltic states were absorbed by the Soviet Union through the controversial Molotov-Ribbentrop Pact of 1939 between Hitler and Stalin. During the Soviet period, all three 'republics' experienced high rates of development. With this came a high rate of migration, mostly Russians and Russian-born Balts that were regarded by the Soviet regime as appendages of Moscow. Estonia and Latvia experienced the largest demographic shift during this period with a rise of minorities from 8 per cent to over 30 per cent and 33 per cent to 48 per cent, respectively. In the 1980's, the Baltic states were in the vanguard of the nationalist uprisings in the Soviet Union, driven by the experience of independent statehood earlier in the century. In fact, the Baltic experiences with confronting the Soviet centre were highly regarded by dissident groups throughout the USSR.[2] The culmination of these uprisings was the desire by many in the Baltic states to join the West in developing a market economy and re-establishing independence.

---

1 Dreifelds, Juris. 1996. *Latvia in Transition.* Cambridge: Cambridge University Press.; Taagepera, Rein. 1993. *Estonia: Return to Independence.* Boulder, CO: Westview Press.; and Smith, Graham. 1996. The Resurgence of Nationalism. In *The Baltic States: The National Self-Determination of Estonia, Latvia, and Lithuania.*, edited by Graham Smith. New York: St. Martin's Press.

2 Dreifelds 1996, 53.

After the 1991 August Coup in Moscow and the subsequent dissolution of the Soviet Union, the Baltic states found themselves experiencing the growing pains of transitioning from an authoritarian, state-socialist regime to a civic democracy that was vulnerable to the ebb and flow of the market. Within democratic societies, there are always competing groups as both democracy and capitalism are based on the principle of mitigated competition. Often, democratic states are galvanised along ethnic lines, and like many other states in the post-Soviet area, ethnicity has played a large role in politics in Estonia and Latvia.

After the collapse of the Soviet Union, those who were appendages of the centre, found themselves stranded. Thus, in the new states, this left the titular nationalities and the settler communities. As titular ethno-nationalism was among the primary factors leading to the collapse of the Soviet Union, state-building has been greatly influenced by continued nationalist policies. A fitting example is the stringent citizenship laws initially adopted by Estonia and Latvia. In particular, legislation had excluded much of the Russophone community from citizenship, although there has been ever-increasing change to the naturalisation laws in both states since 1997 and 1998, respectively. Given these nations' status as prospective new EU and NATO member-states, the domestic minority issues in Estonia and Latvia have a larger international context.

It is necessary to point out here that the 'Russian' label so often placed on the minority groups in Estonia and Latvia is largely misleading and ultimately incorrect. Although Russians predominate, the minority group also consists of Belarusian, Ukrainian, and other smaller ethnic groups. Despite this diversity, non-titular nationalities were equally affected by the nation-building policies employed by Tallinn and Riga in the early nineties. Keeping this in mind, how do we refer to the two minority communities at hand? Graham Smith and Andrew Wilson offer an initial approach to post-Soviet ethnic relations.[3] They state that self-identification will differ in post-Soviet states over how much titular nationalities believe they should be entitled to cultural

3 Smith, Graham and Andrew Wilson. 1997. Rethinking Russia's Post-Soviet Diaspora: The Potential for Political Mobilization in Eastern Ukraine and North-East Estonia. *Europe-Asia Studies* 49 (5):845-864.

and political dominance. Furthermore, they argue that scholars should not overstate the minority identities as they may be 'multiple and fragmented.' This may be especially the case in urban areas, where lifestyles encourage individuals within the community to have a 'hybridity' of identities. Therefore, 'the symbolic constitution of social solidarity amongst the [minority community] is likely to be defined by the actual practice of mobilization and the process of competition between group spokespeople to define the [minority community's] status, rather than being a pre-determined given.'[4]

Indeed, the evidence of a definable group is debatable. Neil Melvin uses the term 'Russified settlers' instead of simply Russian in an effort to avoid confusion and controversy.[5] In justification, he gives several reasons that help characterise the minority community at hand. First, as stated above, various ethnic groups were represented as vestiges of the socialist regime after the Soviet era. Those within this group use Russian as their first language and tend to have assimilated into Russian culture. Second, Russified communities were not only organised around ethnicity, but were part of the Soviet structure. Third, the nature of the Russian community is made more complex by the concentration of cultural features such as language. Fourth, the partisan nature of the Russian community serves various political interests. In particular, the Russian government can use them as leverage in borderland politics. In addition, this then tends to generate a reaction from the nationalising elites. Finally, since the transition, many in the 'settler' community have become class conscious, as many Russian jobs became redundant during the move away from heavy industry. Melvin argues that use of the Russian language as the sole indicator is thus misleading.

In an earlier work, Melvin focuses on the way in which the Russian Federation defined the Russophone communities throughout the former Soviet Union.[6] As will be discussed further in chapter seven, Moscow's definitions play a significant role in the way the minority communities see them-

4 Smith and Wilson 1997, 845.

5 Melvin, Neil J. 1995. *Russians Beyond Russia: the Politics of National Identity.* London: Royal Institute of International Affairs, 50.

6 Melvin, Neil J. 1994. *Forging the New Russian Nation: Russian Foreign Policy and the Russian-Speaking Communities of the Former USSR.* London: Royal Institute of International Affairs.

selves. He states that since the dissolution of the Soviet Union 'large sections of the Russian-speaking settler communities have, for the first time, begun to think of themselves as members of the Russian nation and of the Russian Federation as their homeland.' David Laitin argues that Melvin's conclusions are inconsistent with his own findings, in which Melvin offers several variations of the definition of the Russian community.[7] Nevertheless, Laitin's claim that Melvin is inconsistent is flawed. Laitin fails to recognise Melvin's effort to characterise the Russian community from the perspective of the Russian Federation. Included in his essay are various characterisations that change from 1991-1994. Thus, we should expect the outcome of Melvin's analysis to contain not simply one definition of the minority community, but rather several: a 'Russian' self-identity as well as several definitions that have been formed over time.[8]

Most importantly, Russia has classified the Russians outside Russia as a 'diaspora', implying that the Russian Federation is the external homeland rather than having imperial ambitions to recapture the tsarist or Soviet lands.[9] Nikolai Rudensky offers a more detailed account of the characteristics of the Russian diaspora throughout the post-Soviet states.[10] First, much of the diaspora lives in urban areas such as Tashkent in Uzbekistan and Narva in Estonia. Second, as stated earlier, a high percentage of Russians in the periphery were employed in heavy industry and the larger state apparatus. However, the move towards a market economy subject to international competition and prices, not to mention the breakdown of the Soviet political apparatus, has made the Russian diaspora extremely vulnerable. Furthermore, Rudensky argues that there were three main currents in the Russian diaspora from 1988-1991. Many Russians actually supported the national fronts as a way

7 Laitin, David D. 1998. *Identity in Formation: the Russian-speaking populations in the near abroad.* Ithaca London: Cornell University Press, 298.

8 See especially Poppe, Edwin and Louk Hagendoorn. 2001. Types of Identification among Russians in the 'Near Abroad'. *Europe-Asia Studies* 53 (1):57-71.

9 Smith, Graham, Vivien Law, Andrew Wilson, Annette Bohr, and Edward Allworth, ed. 1998. *Nation-Building in the Post-Soviet Borderlands: The Politics of National Identity.* Cambridge: Cambridge University Press, 12.

10 Rudensky, Nikolai. 1994. Russian minorities in the newly independent states. In *National Identity and Ethnicity in Russia and the New States of Eurasia*, edited by Roman Szporluk. New York: M. E. Sharpe, 61-64.

towards democratic change, while others formed non-political groups geared towards saving aspects of the Russian culture such as the prevalence of the Russian language. Finally, others were active opponents of the popular national fronts. Specifically, they wanted to maintain the republic's ties to the Soviet system. Again, this movement generally coalesced into the *interfront* movements that are discussed in chapter four.

Overall, Russians became a new minority group spread amongst a multitude of states. The use of the Russian language is a clear example of the principle of isomorphic organisation. An ethnic group may revolve around the use of a common language and the culture that generally accompanies it. Therefore, this book asserts that although loosely tied together, the Russophone community constitutes an ethnic group, which has been made more the case by developments both within and outside Estonia and Latvia. Furthermore, ethnicity has become the basis for a number of civic, social and business networks.

An analysis of the current situation finds that the Russophone communities have been represented in the post-Soviet period in different ways, even though, as shown above, the Baltic states have begun from a largely similar position. In particular, while Estonia has incorporated many of the Russophone intellectuals into the traditional political sphere, including the development of various Russian parties over time, Latvia's Russophone community is best represented in the economic sphere with many individual Russians becoming successful entrepreneurs. As previously stated, both Estonia and Latvia implemented exclusive citizenship policies after independence, relegating many Russophones in both spheres to something of a second-class status in society. On the other hand, Lithuania instituted an inclusive policy on citizenship after independence although it too had a similar starting point. Lithuania's demographic dimensions are more complex, as it also has a significant Polish community. At the time of independence, minorities were less than 20 per cent and have reduced since. Differences in state policy and the existence of a third ethnic group (Poles) have led ethnic interactions in Lithuania toward different policies from the beginning. Furthermore, the relationship between Lithuania and Moscow has been different in that it has revolved far less around the issue of the Baltic state's Russophone minority. Finally, regional organisations have not insisted on monitoring the ethnic situation in Lithuania, while both Estonia and Lithuania were under close scrutiny. However, it is important not to understate the role ethnicity plays in Lithuania, for ethnic identities remain important social identities, even if they affect the political process far less.[11] Although the question of why Lithuania chose a different course from that of its fellow Baltic states would be interesting, it falls outside the scope of this research. Thus, given the use of a multi-level analysis of minority politics, this research project will be a comparative examination of socio-political developments in Estonia and Latvia.

Within these states, two ethno-nationalisms, one titular and one minority, are acting and reacting in the political sphere. These nationalist movements are facilitated through collective action on behalf of each group. These social movements have been represented by everything from political parties to religious organisations and protests. In fact, the growth of civil society under a new democratic regime should lead to this result. Despite the negative connotations associated with nationalisms, these social movements are a natural part of democratic societies and continue to shape the future of the state.

In addition to the majority and minority groups, several external actors have attempted to affect changes in the state policies not only regarding language, but other aspects of cultural life. As alluded to above, one of the most important has been the Russian Federation. Often used as domestic political capital, the Russophone communities in Estonia and Latvia have maintained significant cultural links to the Russian state. In addition, regional and international organisations have also played an important part. Such organisations include the OSCE, the EU, the Council of Europe and the United Nations. Although other actors have been involved, namely individual states such as Finland and the United States, their participation in minority politics is insignificant in comparison. Overall, this book will analyse the process of minority politics in Estonia and Latvia within both a domestic and an international context.

---

11 See Smith 1996, 138; and Lane, Thomas. 2002. *Lithuania: Stepping Westward.* London: Routledge.

The book looks at the process of minority politics in Estonia and Latvia from 1991-2001. This time period begins with the reestablishment of independent states and ends with the withdrawal of the permanent OSCE Missions to Estonia and Latvia. The conclusion of the OSCE long-term missions is significant since it signalled the recognition of a normalisation of majority-minority relations in both states. Although, this is not to say that the issues of citizenship and language have not remained important, minority policy evolution has practically stopped since the OSCE missions' withdrawals.

Keeping this in mind, the book addresses several questions. How do we go about analysing minority politics in the current European system? What actors play a significant part in shaping minority policy? How have the minority communities been able to preserve their perceived cultural rights during this time of nation-building? What role have traditional actors, such as the Russian Federation, and non-traditional actors, such as the EU, played in affecting policy changes? What does the importance of regional actors say about the changing state of minority politics in post-socialist states? Finally, how have the minority policy processes in Estonia and Latvia differed from 1991-2001? The answers to these questions can further our understanding of minority politics.

1.2 Minority Politics

The East European transitions have been an important litmus test for many theories of democratisation, regime transition, ethnicity and nationalism, and international relations. Today, minority politics is an important inter-disciplinarian issue that crosses all of these political sub-divisions. *By minority politics, I mean the complete political process relating a minority community to the larger political establishment traditionally controlled to a large extent by the majority community.* In order to analyse post-Soviet minority politics, we must investigate several key debates that have arisen with the collapse of the Soviet Union. Chapter Two focuses on democratic transitions and the comparative debate in which one views all such transitions as the same process despite whether the country lies in Latin America or Eastern Europe. This regionalism is important to many other scholars, whereby each individual case should be taken as a process unto itself. From this view, we have witnessed the rise of post-Soviet theories of transition. Inherent in these theories is that the experience of having been a part of the Soviet Union has greatly affected the nationalist movements, independence, and post-Soviet politics and foreign policy.

A primary feature of the East European transitions is that they have included an ethnic dimension with which traditional theories of ethnicity have had to cope. As we shall see in Chapter Three, ethnic heterogeneity and politics often exist together. However, exclusion is highlighted when ethnicity becomes politicised. Primordialism had increasingly lost favour as a theory of ethno-nationalism. With the breakdown of the socialist bloc and the rise of many ethnic tensions (if not conflict), primordialism once again became a viable theory. In addition, primordialism along with constructivism, structuralism, and elite determinism were provided a plethora of new case studies through which they would need to explain why conflict happened as well as why it did not occur.

Furthermore, the breakdown of the bi-polar international system provided a new test for traditional theories of international relations. In Chapter Four, we see that the aftermath of the breakdown of authoritarian regimes in Central and Eastern Europe brought about a growth in regional and international organisations as well as increased responsibilities for these institutions. Almost from the very beginning, those states not already sovereign entered the Organisation for Security and Co-operation in Europe as well as the United Nations. Additionally, almost all of the post-socialist countries set a path for membership in the Council of Europe, European Union, and North Atlantic Treaty Organisation. With this seemingly renewed importance placed on international organisations, traditional theories of international relations and foreign policy have had to explain the relationship between the state and these institutions. While realist theories offer a realpolitik explanation, liberal theories interpret this relationship as growing interdependence, in which nations are more likely to manoeuvre via diplomatic bargaining rather than flexing muscles. With these theories, we must attempt to gauge the importance of international organisations and their effects on the state.

Indeed, the questions posed by each inter-disciplinarian field, whether it is democratic transitions, ethnicity and politics, or international institutions, require answers. In reality, these issues are related and thus the situation is even more convoluted. This book looks at the cases of Estonia and Latvia within this complex relationship. By themselves, the theories within these academic fields are only able to expound on these case studies to a certain degree. Therefore, this book attempts to build on what Rogers Brubaker has metaphorically referred to as a 'nexus' in order to explain the events between 1991-2001.[12] He maps out the relationships inherent in minority politics. In particular, he addresses those nationalisms that were produced by a redrawing of political institutions, lending his work to post-Soviet case studies. Brubaker posits a triadic nexus that represents the relationships between national minorities, the newly nationalising state in which the minorities live, and the external national homeland.[13]

Brubaker argues that contentious relationships are based on nationalising nationalisms, in which policies are made in the newly nationalising state on behalf of the core nationality (i.e. Estonians and Latvians). The new nationalism is spurred on by the perception of the core nationality that they are culturally, economically, and demographically weak because of their past subjection to colonial rule. Brubaker argues that this nationalism is an effort to compensate for the past. However, it can be argued that all nationalisms, whether post-colonial or not, are based on grievances of the past.[14]

In response to the nationalism of the new state, the external national homeland feels that it is their right and obligation to support the minority community. For this reason, the national homeland can negatively affect nationalist policies in the nationalising or host state. The process whereby a state becomes an external national homeland is when elites within that state define ethno-national kin in other states as members of one and the same nation. They may assert that the condition of the minority must be monitored, protected, and promoted by the state. Between the minority community and the external national homeland, the perception of a nationalising state that

---

12 Brubaker, Rogers. 1996. *Nationalism Reframed: Nationhood and the National Question in the New Europe*. Cambridge: Cambridge University Press.

13 See also Smith and Wilson 1997, 846.

threatens the minority group is what is necessary for reaction. This is the case regardless of whether or not the state is truly acting nationalistically. Furthermore, both the minority community and the nationalising state have a large impact on the relations in this metaphorical nexus. The minority has its own form of nationalism that is also an attempt to secure its cultural, economic, and demographic future.

The case studies presented here also fit within this analytical structure. However, it overlooks key influential actors that constantly intrude on domestic politics: international institutions and foreign governments. Nevertheless, the importance of international actors in relation to domestic policy is well known, as we shall see in Chapter Four. By comparing Estonia and Latvia, this book can add to the empirical work that demonstrates clear linkages between international actors and domestic policy. In this way, we need to ground this project in a comparative theoretical framework.

1.3 Theoretical Framework and Methods

Why does comparison assist in the testing and elaboration of empirical proofs of the hypothesis? Rarely in social research do scholars get the opportunity to have such similar conditions as we have in Estonia and Latvia. Although later politics deviated somewhat, the starting points of these states are the closest conditions political science can get to laboratory settings. Specifically, both states are roughly the same geographical size along with similar population sizes. In addition, both states have experienced similar histories as demonstrated. Furthermore, Russian migration to the Baltic states has been similar and currently Russians make up a significant part of the population.

Before going any further, it is necessary to cover some basic methodological terms. In this research project, we are relying on two case studies. What is the general role of case studies in the development of theories concerning political phenomena? Harry Eckstein defines a 'case' as a phenomenon for which we report and interpret only a single measure on any pertinent

---

[14] See also Brubaker 1996, 79.

variable.[15] He argues that case studies are valuable at all stages of the theory-building process. However, they are most important in testing the validity of theories. King, Keohane, and Verba argue that case studies are essential for adding a descriptive component to theories.[16] Furthermore, case studies lend themselves most securely to the field of comparative politics. Since the crux of this research project is the comparison of like political processes, we need an adequate definition of comparative methods. Eckstein defines comparative study "as the study of numerous cases along the same lines, with a view to reporting and interpreting numerous measures on the same variables of different 'individuals'."[17] Many scholars have discussed the importance of comparative case studies in political research. Przeworski and Teune sum up the relationship between comparative case studies and theoretical development:[18]

> In our view the formulation of general theories is possible if and only if these theories take into account what appears to us to be a pervasive property of social reality: social phenomena are not only diverse but always occur in mutually interdependent and interacting structures, possessing a spatiotemporal location. If stable, these patterns of interaction can be treated as systems. Social systems are composed of interacting elements, such as individuals, groups, communities, institutions, or governments. What is important for comparative inquiry is that systems with which we ordinarily deal, such as societies, nations, and cultures, are organized in terms of several levels of components and that the interactions within these systems are not limited to any particular level but cut across these levels.

Additionally, David Collier writes:

> Comparison is a fundamental tool of analysis. It sharpens our power of description, and plays a central role in concept-formation by bringing into focus suggestive similarities and contrasts among cases. Comparison is routinely used in testing hy-

---

15 Eckstein, Harry. 1975. Case Study and Theory in Political Science. In *Handbook of Political Science: Strategies of Inquiry*, edited by Fred I. Greenstein and Nelson W. Polsby. Reading, Mass: Addison-Wesley Publishing Company, 75.

16 King, Gary; Robert O. Keohane; and Sidney Verba. 1994. *Designing Social Inquiry*. Princeton, New Jersey: Princeton University Press, 44.

17 Eckstein 1975, 75.

18 Przeworksi, Adam and Henry Teune. 1970. *The Logic of Comparative Social In-*

> potheses, and it can contribute to the inductive discovery of new hypotheses and to theory-building.[19]

Overall, I have tried to fit within this framework of social inquiry. Given the nature of the comparison as well as the domestic and international scope of this project, the book relies heavily on sources that can be easily compared and represent this multi-level analysis.

For this reason, the core empirical chapters (6-9) rely on several sources. First, data collection was done through a day-by-day review from January 1991 to December 2001 through the Radio Free Europe – Radio Liberty *Report, Newsline* and *Baltic States Report*. As an international media source, RFE/RL has a far less partisan nature than does the local press. However, the author freely acknowledges that this media source itself contains a certain level of bias that is rooted in its manufacture for Western consumption. Ideally, the RFE/RL services allow us to analyse a region where three main language groups converge, of which only two of three are at least partially known by the author. Second, additional data collection was derived from several Russian-language sources primarily published in the Russian Federation. Russian-language newspapers and other publications used are *Izvestia, Nevazisimaya Gazeta, Pravda, Sevodnya, Kommersant Daily,* and *Rossiiskaya Gazeta*. In this way, the book can balance the bias of RFE/RL with an equally divergent Russian bias. Third, primary sources are used as we discuss international institutions including the OSCE High Commissioner on National Minorities letters to the Estonian and Latvian Governments, European Commission Regular Reports from the EU and Council of Europe documents including the Framework Convention for the Protection of National Minorities. Finally, the book relies on a small number of interviews carried out between 2001-2004 (see appendix). While the interviews can answer several specific questions and bring colour to the overall discussion, this book combines all of these sources to provide an in-depth analysis of minority politics in Estonia and Latvia.

---

quiry. Malabar, FL: Robert E. Krieger Publishing, 12.

19 Collier, David. 1993. The Comparative Method. In *Political Science: The State of the Discipline II*, edited by Ada W. Finifter. Washington, DC: APSA, 105.

1.4 Book Structure

Overall, this analysis aims first and foremost to provide an in-depth analysis of events in Estonia and Latvia from 1991-2001. It will also hopefully provide wider lessons about minority politics in democratising states. The purpose here is not to overstate such a scheme but rather to test the conditions under which we may best be able to understand minority politics. With this in mind, the book is laid out as follows. As discussed earlier, Chapter Two reviews the approaches to democratic transition in general and post-Soviet transitions specifically. In addition, we also discuss the definition of consolidated democracy and the role of democratic institutions in managing ethnic relations. Chapter Three focuses on the relationship between ethnicity and politics. More specifically, the chapter looks at ethnicity as an identity, the politicisation of ethnicity and the ethnic group dynamics. Chapter Four reviews the theoretical approaches to international relations, domestic sources of foreign policy and international institutions. This chapter constructs a framework on which to analyse the relationship between institutions and affected states.

In order to understand the post-Soviet situation in Estonia and Latvia, Chapter Five contextualises the study by looking at the historical conditions that make the former Soviet region a unique space. The chapter presents a brief history of the two Baltic states from colonialism to independence, occupation and then to independence again. The chapter is also largely concerned with the development of titular-minority relations in the Gorbachev era. Specifically, the liberalisation period is divided into three phases. In particular, the book approaches these phases using a broad social movement theory as a means of comparing and contrasting the different movements. As many of the naturalisation and language policies are rooted in the late Soviet period, it is important to understand the context in which these policies were made.

Two chapters are dedicated to the politics and policies in Estonia and Latvia. Chapter Six focuses on the domestic process within the time period of 1991-2001 and analyses the political systems and the policy-making process in the case studies. This chapter looks at the issue of ethnicity was used in the political system and how this filtered into the policy-making process. Special detail is given to the influence of political parties on policy-making. In this way, we may be able to see how majority and minority groups affect the policy-making process. Next, Chapter Seven looks at minority policies in-depth. In particular, the chapter focuses on the citizenship, language, and education laws in both Estonia and Latvia. More specifically, this chapter analyses the influences on and evolution of these minority policies.

Likewise, two chapters are dedicated to the external influences on the domestic policy-making process. Chapter Eight examines the actions of the Russian Federation in relation to the Russian-speaking community in the Baltic states. Special attention is given to the relationship between the 'human rights' issue and the border and troop withdrawal issues. Chapter Nine largely focuses on the influence of international institutions. The chapter specifically details the relationship between Estonia and Latvia with the OSCE, EU, Council of Europe and other actors such as the United Nations, NATO and Western governments.

Finally, Chapter Ten concludes the book with an overall summation of the general hypothesis and the results of its application to the case studies. Furthermore, the experience of Estonia and Latvia is contrasted and compared. In the end, we should have the answer to several questions. What role has history played in establishing the post-Soviet political structure in Estonia and Latvia? What effect did the independence movements have on the post-restoration nation-building policies? How did domestic politics shape the policy process? How did minority policies evolve over time? As the external national homeland, what role did Russia play in affecting the policy process? Likewise, how did regional and international organisations shape minority policies? Finally, what do the experiences in Estonia and Latvia tell us about the process of minority politics?

Chapter 2 Democratic Transitions

With the beginning of the 'third wave' of democratic transitions in 1974, a new focus on the process of democratisation arose in scholarly literature.[20] While the path to democratisation was the object of much of this analysis, a paucity of the literature actually identified 'democratisation'. Eventually, a process approach to democratisation helped identify the key characteristics. Typically in political studies, the process of democratisation has been conceived along a continuum from a minimal to a maximalist position, whereby the end-point is a 'consolidated' liberal democracy. In this sense, consolidation is meant by democracy as the 'only game in town'.[21] A process or transition approach to democratisation can be dated back to Rustow's classic critique of the modernisation school.[22] Rustow's three stages of democratisation came to be known as liberalisation, transition and consolidation. With this conceptual model in mind, this chapter looks at democratisation in general and in Eastern Europe specifically.

While we can define democratisation as a redefinition of the nation-state, there may indeed be circumstances where the democratisation process and nation-building project disagree. In *Problems of Democratic Transition and Consolidation*, Linz and Stepan examine Estonia and Latvia with the view that this relationship is illogical. This brings about the question of how do states consolidate when there is a question of national integrity or a 'stateness' issue. On the one hand, democratisation is a renewed time of political, economic and social competition that favours that largest group. On the other hand, liberal democracy demands that state institute safeguards that protect the rights of minorities. However, given the often historical animosities be-

20 Huntington, Samuel P. 1991. *The Third Wave*. Norman: University of Oklahoma Press.

21 Linz, Juan J. and Alfred Stepan. 1996. *Problems of Democratic Transition and Consolidation: Southern Europe, South America, and Post-Communist Europe*. Baltimore: Johns Hopkins, 5.

22 Rustow, Dankwart. 1970. Transition to Democracy: Toward a Dynamic Model. *Comparative Politics* 2 (3).

tween ethnic groups, majority groups may be willing set aside some democratic standards as a means of redressing history or even controlling the state. This is currently the case in Estonia and Latvia, although significant changes have been made. After looking at democratic transitions in Eastern Europe, this chapter will concentrate on ways in which to manage majority-minority relations as well as apply them to our particular case studies.

2.1 Democratic Transition in Eastern Europe

The collapse of the Soviet Union had a large affect on the psyche of the 25 million Russophones living outside Russia. Valerie Bunce defines *state collapse* as the reduction and eventual collapse of the state's coercive and spatial monopoly.[23] The policies of Gorbachev, aimed at regenerating the Soviet Union, actually facilitated this coercive and spatial breakdown of the state.[24] Bunce argues that the ever-increasing contradictions of the Soviet system, maintained by the 'burdens of empire', brought about the collapse. In particular, Bunce offers three inherent characteristics of the Soviet empire that were catalysts for collapse.[25] First, she states that policy and personnel changes in the Soviet Union spread quickly into Eastern Europe. These changes were different in form and intensity than was the case in the Soviet Union. This she terms as 'elite sensitivity'.

Second, the Soviet bloc contained 'transmission belts' that ran from party to public and also from the CPSU to Eastern European parties. However, these belts were capable of operating in the opposite direction, causing the regime to lose some control over politics. Finally, economic and political problems tend to 'bunch' in domestic socialism. Therefore, as the problems continued to mount, the manoeuvrability of the socialist governments became

---

23 Bunce, Valerie. 1999. *Subversive Institutions: The Design and the Destruction of Socialism and the State*. Cambridge: Cambridge University Press, 11.

24 Take note of the differences between the two liberalising policies of Gorbachev in the Soviet Union and Deng Xiopeng in the People's Republic of China. While Gorbachev focused on political liberalisation under the guise of *perestroika* and *glasnost*, Deng Xiopeng focused on economic liberalisation under the guise of the 'four modernisations'.

25 Ibid., 41-45. Bunce is referring to the entire region.

impaired. For example, problems within a command economy would have been echoed throughout the system. 'The bloc, therefore, proved to be the perfect host for communicating the diseases of [East] European socialism.'[26] Overall, given the inherent tendencies towards crisis in economics and the growth of a new civil society within Eastern Europe and the Soviet Union, the burdens of empire were greater than the system could handle.

In the post-Soviet era, the former Soviet Republics have been going through a triple transition: from colonialism to de-colonisation, from authoritarianism to democracy, and command to market economy.[27] Both Estonia and Latvia have been going through democratic transitions at least since 1991. The debate in democratic transition literature throughout the 1990's focused on the significance of regional comparisons. While some scholars believe that something can be gained by comparing democratic transitions in the post-communist world and Latin America, others argue that the difference in histories and culture preclude the usefulness of comparison. By reviewing this debate here, it not only tells us something about transition studies but also about important characteristics about East European transitions. Specifically, the post-communist area and Latin America have had completely different experiences in the twentieth century. At the beginning of the century, Eastern Europe was split amongst various empires, while the Soviet Union was itself an empire. On the other hand, the majority of Latin American countries had been independent since the beginning of the previous century.

While the post-communist area suffered through two world wars and the elimination of civil society, Latin America was a main source of primary goods that helped fuel the post-war industrial boom. The Soviet Union had seen little if any democracy in the twentieth century. Eastern Europe experienced limited democratic governments before 1940. On the other hand, most Latin American states encountered various forms of populist regimes, eventually replaced by bureaucratic authoritarian regimes. Overall, Latin America has

---

26 Ibid., 43.

27 Smith, Graham. 1996. The Resurgance of Nationalism. In *The Baltic States: The National Self-Determination of Estonia, Latvia, and Lithuania.*, edited by Graham Smith. New York: St. Martin's Press. See also Brubaker, Rogers. 1996. *Nationalism Reframed: Nationhood and the National Question in the New Europe*. Cambridge: Cambridge University Press.

had a much stronger democratic tradition, albeit limited compared to Western Europe or North America. Now, many of the current regimes of Eastern Europe and the former Soviet Union are attempting to install democratic governments as much of Latin America has done in the 1980's and 90's.

Terry defines democratic transitions as the dismantling of the pre-existing structures of authoritarian rule.[28] Democratic transitions also encapsulate the task of creating the new structures to take their place. Linz and Stepan call this 'the need to reach an agreement on the specific institutional arrangement for producing democratic government.'[29] They also guard against what has been called the 'electoral fallacy.' This is the phenomenon in which some governments assume that having free elections is enough reform to be regarded democratic. When regimes in transition make this assumption, the transition generally goes no further. The further Eastern Europe and the post-Soviet states come away from authoritarian rule, the more salient become the differences when compared to Latin America.[30] Terry gives five challenges confronting Eastern Europe that distinguish it from Latin America. First, Eastern Europe has to reform on a 'dual track.' Terry defines this process as the simultaneous attempt to construct both democracy and capitalism. The pressures put upon society by economic hardships cause political instability. In general, this crisis slows institutional infrastructure and foreign investment. As seen in the Russian Federation, the economic crisis has been a major factor in the chaotic politics of the Russian *Duma*.

Second, Eastern European countries have a much higher level of socio-economic and industrial development. The initiation of reform strategies is much harder to implement in more developed levels of industrialisation. Terry argues that Latin American economies are less developed, thus making the transition much easier. This implies that it is better to start 'from scratch' than overhaul the current system. Along these same lines, post-Soviet states may find it easier to develop a fully functioning civil society, an integral part of democracy, than Latin America. Furthermore, Schmitter and Karl state that the former 'monopolistic fusion' of political and economic power into a party-state

[28] Terry, Sarah Meiklejohn. 1993. Thinking about Post-Communist Transitions: How different are they. *Slavic Review* 52 (2): 337.

[29] Linz and Stepan 1996, 4.

apparatus divides Eastern Europe from much of Latin America (the predominance of the Institutional Revolutionary Party in Mexico being an exception).[31] Overall, the previous regimes of Eastern Europe were bureaucratically complex, which means that it has been far more difficult for the current governments to overhaul the old system.[32]

Third, Latin American transitions have not involved the same degree of ethnic complexity. Terry states that nationalism is incompatible with democracy and that it prohibits the emergence of an authentic civil society. On the other hand, Valery Tishkov argues that nationalism is a key part of democratic states.[33] In particular, consolidated democracies are strong governments. Based on this, Tishkov argues that the establishment of a civic nationalism is the only sure way to create a strong centre. In addition, I would argue that race is still important in Latin America, not to mention the larger problem with political and economic polarity. The polarisation of politics in particular can cause a break down in democratic consolidation as seen in Nicaragua and El Salvador.[34]

Fourth, the level of international involvement in the form of ideology in the post-communist region is far lower than in Latin America. Much of Latin America's democratising experience occurred during the realpolitik of the Cold War. Since the West was willing to offer material benefits to 'friendly' states, many Latin American countries were able to initiate democratic reforms without a breakdown of the traditional patronage system. However, this is not to say that all 'friendly' states were inclined to democratise or that the West consistently encouraged reform. Yet, in the post-Cold War era, the West has been even more unlikely to invest or interact given the lack of clear benefits for the Western governments or economies (even in the case of

30 Terry 1993, 334.

31 Schmitter, Philippe C. with Terry Lynn Karl. 1994. The Conceptual Travels of Transitologists and Consolidologists: How far to the East should they attempt to go? *Slavic Review* 53 (1):173-185.

32 Terry 1993, 335.

33 Tishkov, Valery. 1997. *Ethnicity, Nationalism, and Conflict in and after the Soviet Union: The Mind Aflame*. London: Sage Publishers.

34 Barnes, William A. 1998. Incomplete Democracy in Central America: Polarization and Voter Turnout in Nicaragua and El Salvador. *Journal of Interamerican Affairs* Fall:63-79.

American intervention, democratic reforms seem far removed from the foreign policy agenda.) Without an overt ideological reasoning, the international community will have a limited interest in democratic transitions in the post-communist area, although the relatively recent war on terrorism may give a new impetus for democratic change. However, this has yet to be seen.

Finally, and most importantly, Latin American post-authoritarian transitions had a more substantial civil society. The lack of interaction within an established institutional framework creates obstacles for what Terry calls a 'real' civil society. A 'real' civil society is made distinct because an etatisation of society can occur when the government has the resources to maintain control. Terry argues that at best, post-communist states had an embryonic form of civil society during the years of authoritarian governance. Schmitter and Karl argue that Eastern European transitions are negatively affected because of the region and many years of policy measures designed to suppress class and sectoral distinction, promote material equality, and eliminate property rights.[35] After the socialization of society, those structures of civil society that did exist were decimated. Terry argues that socialist governments used a considerable amount of resources to repress civil society. The lack of resources led to an implosion in Eastern European regimes. According to Karl, Latin America had imposed top-down transitions, as this region did not experience significant social movements.[36] The case can be made for the occurrence of top-down transitions in Eastern Europe as well as the Former Soviet Union, with some exceptions. In these situations, traditional rulers remain in control. In addition, they successfully use strategies of compromise and force, if needed, to retain a portion of power. This type of transition must have strong elite actors in order for reform to work.

Overall, there are many differences between the transitions of Eastern Europe and Latin America. The starting points of the two regions have had a great effect on the progress of transition. Although there are some commonalities, students of democratisation should be aware of the differences that make comparison more difficult. On the whole, these scholars have helped

---

35 Schmitter, et al. 1994, 180-182.

36 Karl, Terry Lynn. 1990. Dilemmas of Democratization in Latin America. *Comparative Politics* (October):8-9.

put into perspective the difficulties faced by democratising states. Finally, this discussion has highlighted the complex paradox that arises with democracy and ethnic heterogeneity. With this in mind, we need to address what it is we mean by consolidated democracy and then how can democratic institutions manage multi-ethnic states.

2.2 Defining Consolidation

The first stage of democratisation is the initial liberalisation of the *ancien regime*. As Przeworksi noted in 1991, this liberalisation does not ensure further reform, but there is the possibility that the process may continue.[37] This next stage has been referred to as the 'transition.' The last stage of consolidation denotes the regime's transformation into a liberal democracy. The last part of the process is often the most contentiously discussed in the scholarly literature. By examining this debate, we can construct an in-depth description of democracy. Robert Dahl's study of 'polyarchy' is the most notable work on the characteristics of a fully functioning democracy, and many scholars have used Dahl's definition as a starting point to define consolidated democracies.[38] Based on these works, I present the following criteria for defining democratic consolidation:

First, the concept of democracy usually conjures up images of individuals at the ballot box voting in a fair election.[39] With this in mind, it is not surprising that one of the primary characteristics of democracy is that rulers must be freely elected. In turn, these elected officials cannot infringe on the constitution or violate the rights of the 'citizenry'. Under no circumstances should non-elected officials restrict these elected officials. Finally, elected officials should not be arbitrarily dismissed from their posts before their term has expired. However, as in much of Central America, elections are used as a

37 Przeworksi, Adam. 1991. *Democracy and the Market: Political and Economic Reforms in Eastern Europe and Latin America*. Cambridge: Cambridge University Press.

38 Dahl, Robert A. 1989. *Democracy and its Critics*. New Haven: Yale University Press.

39 Ibid., 221.

means to justify stalled reforms. This has been referred to as the 'electoral fallacy'. Democracy is about more than elections. For those Central and East European countries that have entered the European Union, elections have been relatively 'free and fair'.

Second, consolidation should include associational autonomy.[40] A deeply entrenched civil society should be present in a democratic state. Freedom of expression should be assured in order to facilitate the existence and continuation of civil society. Likewise, individuals should be able to access alternative sources of information. Finally, so that the regime may reflect the will of the people, individuals must be able to participate in politically driven collective action. This condition too is not uncontested. The concentration on civil society was invigorated by Putnam's continuation of the 'social capital' hypothesis, where civic association leads to better democracy. However, Hardin as well as Dowley and Silver show that not all mobilisation is good for democracy especially when based on racial or ethnic lines.[41] Nevertheless, there is a need for society to participate in an organised fashion in the political process so that a democratic government can continue to articulate the interests of the people.

Third, consolidated democracy requires exclusive democracy.[42] Political actors within the new regime should view democracy as the only possible political process, or 'the only game in town', as discussed earlier. Schedler argues that this is best done through the infusion of democratic ideals in society. Through a democratic civil society and political collective action, a democratic regime may be sustained. At the same time, we have to bear in mind that democratic regimes must prevent groups with non-democratic goals from entering into the democratic process.

Fourth, the elimination of all authoritarian blocs is a fundamental characteristic of democratic governance.[43] The power used to repress democratic

40 Ibid., 221; O'Donnell, Guillermo. 1996. Illusions about Consolidation. *Journal of Democracy* (April):34-51.

41 Hardin, Russell. 1995. *One for All.* Princeton: Princeton University Press; and Dowley, Kathleen M. and Brian D. Silver. 2002. Social Capital, Ethnicity and Support for Democracy in the Post-Communist States. *Europe-Asia Studies* 54 (4):505-527.

42 Schedler, Andreas. 1998. What is Democratic Consolidation? *Journal of Democracy* (April):91-107.; and Karl 1990.

43 Schedler 1998, 91-92; Karl 1990, 2.

groups within the authoritarian bloc is most often associated with a policing organisation. Thus, the strong arm of the government, whether it be the military or police, must be placed in civilian hands. However, this is an especially difficult objective for a new democratic regime. As seen in the most successful democratisation projects in South America, Argentina, Brazil and Chile, elite-pacts have allowed security organisations to remain quite influential, often preventing further reform.[44]

Finally, one of the most difficult characteristics to fulfil for reformers is the criterion that there must be a state accepted by all participants as the only legitimate set of government institutions.[45] This is known as either national integrity or stateness. Simply, there can be no questions as to the authority and domain of this state because of significant competing identities and loyalties that exist within the nation. The voting population should be clearly defined by an uncontested national territory. The concept of the state is important to the idea of democracy in that democratic regimes require strong societies and strong states. This is the most important condition for consolidated democracy in multi-ethnic states. As this and other studies indicate, democratisation is about redefining the nation. Democratisation is a nation-building project. However, this begs the questions that Linz and Stepan have asked previously: 'Are there circumstances when democracy and nation-state are conflicting legacies? If so, what can be done to achieve an inclusive democracy?'[46] The latter question we shall deal with further on, but let us engage with Linz and Stepan's comments specific to our case studies.

Linz and Stepan state that Estonia and Latvia most reconcile the logic of a nation-state and democracy in order to become consolidated democracies. However, as the book indicates, the consolidation process has gone much further in both cases without reconciling these logics. Nevertheless, what has been described before as the 'Baltic Model' of democratisation depends upon the potential for multiple identities. That is, if Russian-speakers

44 See Higley, J and R. Gunther, ed. 1992. *Elites and Democratic Consolidation in Latin America and Southern Europe*. Cambridge: Cambridge University Press.

45 Rustow 1970, 350; Linz and Stepan 1996, 14-15; and Schedler 1998, 91-92

46 Linz and Stepan 1996, 401. See also Stepan, Alfred. 1994. When Democracy and the Nation-State are Competing Logics: Reflections on Estonia. *European Journal of Sociology* 35:127-41.

can perceive themselves to be both Russophonic and Estonian or Latvian, consolidation will be completed. Yet, this has not happened. Each state has continually propagated an exclusive discourse that creates 'polar' identities, which 'work against the multiple complementary identities that make possible democratic life in a de facto multinational state.'[47] At the same time, the discussion of identities in the first chapter gave us some indication of the latest work done on multiple identities in Estonia and Latvia. In a survey of Russian-speakers across the post-Soviet space, Poppe and Hagendoorn found that while few individuals are likely to have both 'Russian' and 'titular' identities, the greatest number are likely to have 'republican' identities.[48] This allows individuals to be culturally 'Russian', while politically 'titular'. Thus, Linz and Stepan's conclusions regarding polar identities may still be true to some degree, but Poppe and Hagendoorn show that an inclusive 'republican' identity is the most prevalent amongst the Russian-speaking communities.

Estonia and Latvia have had significant success with elections, civil society, eliminating authoritarian institutions and working within the confines of the rule of law. However, the question of national integrity remains. As we shall see in the book, the definition of the 'nation' was of primary importance to governments and the minority communities. While Estonia and Latvia have implemented exclusivist policies, the programmes of 'integration' continue to redefine the 'nation'. Let us turn our attention to Linz and Stepan's second question of how inclusive democracy can be established in a multi-ethnic state.

---

47 Ibid., 417.

48 Poppe, Edwin and Louk Hagendoorn. 2001. Types of Identification among Russians in the 'Near Abroad'. *Europe-Asia Studies* 53 (1):57-71.

2.3 Democracy and Institutions

With the collapse of the Soviet Union, former Soviet Republics were required to build, or rebuild in the case of the Baltic states, a nation.[49] Nation-building can best be understood as the (re)negotiation of authority.[50] Bendix poses the question of whether or not nation-building experiences can be compared. Is there a common evolution of states? Bendix suggests that there are three ways in which social change occurs: industrialisation, modernisation, and development. For this reason, Bendix is able to find common characteristics of nation-building which allow us to compare processes. In particular he writes:

> To maintain this balanced approach, comparative studies should not only highlight the contrasts existing between different human situations and social structures, but also underscore the inescapable artificiality of conceptual distinctions and the consequent need to move back and forth between the empirical evidence and the benchmark concepts which Max Weber called 'ideal types'.[51]

Therefore, this comparative case study should allow us to focus on similarities and differences between Estonian and Latvian nation-building. In particular, we must identify those 'contingencies' on which the legitimacy of political authority rests.

Democratic transitions, a particular form of nation-building, are the establishment of institutions theoretically grounded in democratic norms and values. This does not mean we should expect democratic political systems to be free of contention. Democracy *is* mitigated competition.[52] Donald Horowitz

---

49 For a general discussion on the concept of nation and nation-building see Weber, Max. 1947. *The Theory of Social and Economic Organization.* Translated by A. M. Henderson and Talcott Parsons. New York: The Free Press; Gellner, Ernest. 1983. *Nations and Nationalism.* Oxford: Blackwell Publishers; Geertz, Clifford, ed. 1963. *Old Societies and New States the Quest for Modernity in Asia and Africa.* London: Free Press of Glencoe Collier-Macmillan; and Nagel, Joane and Susan Olzak. 1982. Ethnic Mobilization in New and Old States: An Extension of the Competition Model. *Social Problems* 30 (2):127-141.

50 See Weber, Max, 1947 and Bendix, Reinhard. 1996. *Nation-Building and Citizenship.* Enl. ed. London: Transaction Publishers.

51 Bendix 1996, 22.

52 For discussions on the relationship between democratic transitions and ethnic heterogeneity, see Diamond, Larry and Marc F. Plattner. 1994. *Nationalism, Ethnic*

writes, 'democracy is about inclusion and exclusion, about access to power, about privileges that go with inclusion and the penalties that accompany exclusion.'[53] The fundamental problem of democracy in ethnically heterogeneous states is the assurance of 'decent' treatment of minorities. As Horowitz points out, democracy often facilitates majority rule. Assuming (and this is a large assumption) that individuals will vote exclusively based on the issue-axis of ethnicity, democracies tend to protect the majority group while relegating the minority group to second-class citizenship. The case is made even more complicated when groups determine political legitimacy through group competition. Overall, the goal of democratic nation-building in ethnically heterogeneous states is to devise institutions that will lead politicians to accommodate rather than exclude the out-group.

Institutions matter when managing ethnicity in democratic states. Grugel argues that 'institutional arrangements have distributional consequences. So the institutional decisions made during the transition tend to reflect the balance of power between groups at the time (of transitions).'[54] As we shall see in later chapters, institutions have been constructed in post-restoration Estonia and Latvia to address the lack of power during the Soviet era. While the titular communities built institutions to protect their interests, they have also needed to construct institutions to address minority rights. This has been the major area of concern for the OSCE High Commissioner on National Minorities and Council of Europe.

In modern state systems, especially in Estonia and Latvia, existing ethnic structures are often re-enforced by institutional design. Ethnic democracies relegate collective political and civil rights to specific groups, while denying the same to the remaining groups in society. They are referred to as democracies because they do have all of the characteristics of liberal democra-

---

Conflict, and Democracy. London: Johns Hopkins University Press; Evans, Geoffrey. 1998. Ethnic Schism and the Consolidation of Post-Communist Democracies. *Communist and Post-Communist Studies* 31 (1):57-74; Smith, 1996; and Smooha, Sammy. 1990. Minority Status in Ethnic Democracy: the status of the Arab minority in Israel. *Ethnic and Racial Studies* 13 (3):389-413.

53 Horowitz, Donald L. 1994. Democracy in Divided Societies. In *Nationalism, Ethnic Conflict, and Democracy*, edited by Larry Diamond and Marc F. Plattner. London: Johns Hopkins University Press., 35-36

54 Grugel, Jean. 2002. *Democratization: a Critical Introduction*. London: Palgrave, 71.

cies, but limit full democratic rights and powers to a specific portion of the population. There are moderate and extreme types of ethnic democracies. The most severe type is a 'Herrenvolk' democracy.[55] The most obvious example, and the one from which it gets its name, is apartheid South Africa. In this case, democracy was limited to individuals of the 'master race.' These regimes are extremely unstable due to their blatant double standards. Their ability to contain and repress the pressure to reform also depends in part on the 'master race's' share of the entire population. Similarly, by denying African-Americans many civil liberties, the United States was also faced with this dual governance. Although there was a plethora of factors at work in this case, the relative size of the black population played a large part in allowing the white majority to sustain such a system.

Needless to say, not all ethnic democracies are as harsh as 'Herrenvolk democracies.' In other transitioning states, the privileged ethnic group(s) receives full democratic rights while the other groups are denied specific rights, and this denial is institutionalised into law according to majoritarian rules. This discrimination can range anywhere from the denial of job opportunities to forced cultural assimilation.[56] There are four areas of conflict in such societies; the first involves the features of public domain (e.g., language, symbols, emblems, holidays). A second area of contention involves ethnic groups contending over individual rights and duties (e.g., job opportunities and social status). A third area of contention involves the minority group's collective rights (e.g., the right to form groups, the degree of ethnic autonomy). Finally, contention exists over the minority's access to the power structure (e.g., voting, running for office, access to civil service positions). Within ethnic democracies, minorities are disadvantaged in all of these areas of contention. However, unlike 'Herrenvolk democracies,' disadvantaged groups can avail themselves of democratic institutions to negotiate better terms. Ideally, democracy gives minorities the opportunity to increase their political influence.

Graham Smith defines ethnic democracy in the Baltic states as when 'the titular nation has secured an institutionally superior position and status for

---

55 Smooha 1990, 390.

56 Mueller, John. 1995. Minorities and the Democratic Image. *East European Politics and Societies* 9 (3):513-522.

itself – in the political legislature, education, the law courts and in public administration – in part by successfully depriving the Russian settler communities of particular political rights and through state language policies.'[57] On the other hand, Vello Pettai argues that Estonia and Latvia cannot be classified as ethnic democracies as policy does not specify by ethnic group but rather citizenship.[58] There is some validity to this argument given that, as time goes on, more Russophones will become citizens and be able to influence policy-making more without a need for the reformulation of the rules of the game. However, this 'constitutional neutrality' allows government to favour those groups in society that are already benefiting from the social structure. As we shall see below, constitutional neutrality is not necessarily the best model for multi-ethnic democracies.

On the whole, only liberal-democracies are able to avert internal challenges to the state. Since one of the fundamental criteria for consolidated democracies is that democratic means are the only possible route through which citizens can pursue their interests and redress grievances, these types of governments are the best equipped to deal with conflict caused by ethnic competition. However, if democracy can be described as mitigated competition, politicised ethnicity becomes an inherent problem for states wishing to consolidate democracy since it challenges the state's 'national integrity' or level of stateness. To the extent that society is polarised along ethnic lines, ethnic groups must compete against one another for political and economic resources. Competition between ethnic groups often precludes the creation of a political system based on other forms of identity. If a state is divided ethnically, then a zero-sum game emerges between the groups in the competition over control of political offices. As one group wins additional seats in the legislature or the executive, the other group sees this as their loss. Thus, elites of the group suffering losses in democratic competition can enhance their own support among their constituents by framing the losses as grievances. They can depict the losses as representing an 'ethnic security dilemma,'

57 Ibid., 80. See also Smooha 1990.

58 Pettai, Vello. 2000. Competing Conceptions of Multiethnic Democracy: Debating Minority Integration in Estonia. Paper read at European Consortium for Political Research, Joint Sessions Workshop on 'Competing Conceptions of Democracy in the Practice of Politics', April 14-19, Copenhagen, Denmark.

whereby the rival group's gains pose a threat to the security of their own group. Taken as a whole, this exemplifies the volatile nature of multi-ethnic democratising states. However, ethnic relations can be managed through democratic institutions, given that these institutions address the specific nature of the 'ethnic system' within the state.

Within multicultural polities, the persistence of good governance depends upon the loyalty of the various groups within the state. Needless to say, this is not a simple task. Plural societies produce multiple (often competing and overlapping) loyalties that, as Richard Bellamy argues, 'unsettle[s] the theory and practice of politics.'[59] Looking at democracy as a process of mitigated competition, we can see why the 'rules of the game' may cause some members of a common polity to feel that they are no longer bound by shared purposes, thus affecting 'national integrity'. A typical response is to simply grant autonomy to competing ethnic groups. However, as Bellamy points out, granting autonomy may displace the problems that come with multiculturalism but will not resolve these issues outright. In general, there are four forms of democratic institutional design that we might provide policy prescriptions for Estonia and Latvia.

Constitutional neutrality establishes the boundary of politics through an agreement on a set of basic political liberties and rights.[60] The basis for its legitimacy comes from the document's overall neutrality, which removes justifiable grounds for grievance. In particular, when conflicts do arise, third parties (i.e. the government, as it has been made neutral by the constitution) steps in to relieve grievances. Although this model does have some relevance to Estonia and Latvia, general problems may arise with its application. Specifically, historical events such as titular nationalist movements before the end of 'Soviet Occupation' make it impossible to remove the nationalist tendencies of nation-building policies since independence. Both constitutions specifically call for the protection and advancement of the titular cultures. Therefore, the government is unable to play the part of mediator as it has sacrificed its third-party position. Although there is the theoretical possibility

59 Bellamy, Richard. 2000. Dealing with Difference: Four Models of Pluralist Politics. *Parliamentary Affairs* 53 (1):199.

60 Rawls, John. 1993. *Political Liberalism*. New York: Columbia University Press.

that institutional design may be re-directed towards neutrality, this is realistically not possible, nor should it be expected given the circumstances of post-Soviet rule. This model's primary contribution comes from the concentration on third-party positions. Various international organisations, such as the OSCE, EU, and the Council of Europe, have attempted to fill this role since independence.

The second model of pluralist politics is *interest group pluralism*. In this case, each group has the ability to control another group's actions. In order to protect its own interests, a minority group need only participate in politics. The availability of various types of competing political resources lends to a group being in a position to bargain or trade. The competition over these political resources dictates no consistent majority, but rather ever-shifting coalitions across groups depending on the issue at hand. Individuals will be more willing to compromise and 'keep things fair' because of her/his multiple identities and interests mentioned above.

Based on the characteristics of the group, bargaining may or may not be a reasonable outcome. In addition, we cannot assume that the government will be neutral in its relationship with these bargaining groups. Bellamy argues that, 'ethnic and cultural minorities have often found that their worries are ignored or rejected on the grounds that they fail to fit the established political morality.'[61] This is exactly the problem we have in the two northern Baltic states. In effect, the Russophonic community has been relegated to a lower bargaining position than that of the titular nationalities. Although this seems to be less the case in Latvia than Estonia, this flaw still exists. Nevertheless, as the nation-building process continues, we should expect minority bargaining positions to improve. This is exemplified by the changes in the 1989 Estonian Language Law.

The third model of pluralist politics is *consociationalism*.[62] This model attempts to produce a mixture of autonomy and power-sharing amongst ethnic groups. This allows groups to retain as many components of their culture as possible. The key elements of consociationalism revolve around ethnic

---

61 Bellamy 2000, 204.

62 Lijphart, Arend. 1984. *Democracies: Patterns of Majoritarian and Consensus Government in Twenty-one Countries*. Westford, Mass: Yale University Press.

self-determination enshrined in the structure of power-sharing (i.e. federalism). Through group autonomy, as well as checks within the political process to maintain this autonomy, competing ethnic groups may be able to co-exist within the same state. Furthermore, consociationalism applies best to groups who are geographically concentrated. In the case of Latvia, the Russophonic community is not geographically concentrated, although there is a high proportion in the district of Latgale. Rather, Russophones primarily reside in the major urban areas, especially in Daugavpils and Riga. Thus, power-sharing by allocating group rights through semi-autonomous regional institutions is unavailable in this case. Furthermore, as Kymlicka points out, the problem with self-government lies with maintaining the balance between centralisation and de-centralisation.[63] For reasons that will be discussed further below, it is unrealistic to expect the national governments and the titular communities to tolerate devolution to suit the Russophonic communities, nor is this particularly useful in such small states.

Initially, consociationalism lends itself to the Estonian case. In particular, Russophones are the overwhelming majority in the district of Ida-Virumaa in Estonia's northeast. Estonia's capital, Tallinn, also has a large Russophonic community, lying within the district of Harjumaa. Overall, the geographic concentration of Estonia's primary minority ethnic group in the northeast would be able to suit collective rights under a single administrative district that already exists (i.e. Ida-Virumaa). It is in such cities as Narva and Sillamae where Russophones feel the most alienated from the political process, as opposed to much of the Russophonic community in Tallinn that has influence over policy-making through voting in local and national elections, running for public office, and participating in business. Russophones in Ida-Virumaa, on the other hand, have been hurt most by the transition to a market economy. For the most part, the Soviet heavy industry that existed in the northeast experienced a gradual decline, along with the rest of the Soviet economy. The local governments in Ida-Virumaa are already cushions between the sometimes-harsh nationalising policies of the Estonian government

63 Kymlicka, Will. 1995. *Multicultural Citizenship: A Liberal Theory of Minority Rights*. Oxford: Clarendon Press.

and the Russophonic community. However, local governments have been largely ineffective in influencing policy in Tallinn.

Another logical key element of this model is the concentration on collective rights. A legitimate criticism levelled at consociationalism, for this reason, is that it institutionalises ethnic boundaries. In fact, since independence, both Estonian and Latvian governments have constantly attempted to maintain the hegemony of the titular ethnic group through favouring the titular languages and excluding the majority of the respective Russophonic communities from voting in national elections via an exclusionary citizenship policy.[64] Rather than protecting group rights, Estonia and Latvia have attempted to reaffirm the titular cultures while allowing individuals in the Russophonic communities to participate in the larger political process through assimilation (integration) alone. There is no doubt that the titular cultures were constantly under threat during the Soviet period through mass deportations, Russification, and Russophonic migration. Needless to say, Estonians and Latvians see an independent state as an assurance of maintaining the existence of the titular cultures. On the other hand, by requiring the Russophonic community to integrate, at least to the point of learning titular history and language, we cannot see that the Russian culture is under threat given the existence of Estonia and Latvia's largest neighbour: the Russian Federation. However, this does not mean that Baltic Russophonic communities feel that being Russian (or Ukrainian or Belorussian) is any less important than being Estonian or Latvian. Not to mention that much of the minority communities do not see a difference between integration and assimilation.

Kymlicka argues that the process whereby a minority group abandons its own cultural heritage for the existing norms and values of the dominant group is no longer a viable argument for assimilation.[65] Rather, minority groups living within a state based on liberal norms and values tend to reserve their individual rights to preserve their own cultural heritage. However, this desire to maintain cultural aspects such as language, dress, and gender customs derives from belonging to a group. In this way, cultural maintenance has the greatest opportunity to resist assimilation, whether forced or not. Never-

---

64 Note that in Estonia, permanent residents are allowed to vote in local elections.

65 Kymlicka 1995, 30. He refers to this process as 'Anglo-conformity'.

theless, it is this group identification that may be most volatile in a situation where groups compete for access to policy making via inter-group and intra-group relations. In this first case, an ethnic group may need to shield itself from the policies of a government controlled by the dominant ethnic group. In a democratic sense, this requires that the minority ethnic group will need in some way to bargain with the dominant ethnic group for relief, possibly through a polyethnic discourse.

In the second case, groups intent on maintaining their own cultural heritage must reduce internal pressures. As Laitin argues, where maintaining group boundaries are a choice made by the group as a whole, assimilation is an individual action.[66] Assuming that partial or complete assimilation brings with it some benefits, individuals are likely to gain the access that comes with assimilating while at the same time gaining from the group's efforts to maintain its own boundaries from external pressures. In essence, this fits a simple collective action problem where a rational actor will seek the option with the greatest pay-off rather than make the sacrifices needed to bring the group's efforts to fruition. This is based on the actor's knowledge that he or she is unlikely to make a large enough impact in the movement to make the difference between winning and losing. The optimal outcome for individuals is to individually assimilate while at the same time supporting group rights.

In the case of Estonia and Latvia, language is a key issue. Laitin describes the benefits of individual assimilation regarding language specifically.[67] Overall, he sees the payoff function of linguistic assimilation being a combination of three distinct calculations of expectation: economic returns, social mobility, and external acceptance. The greater the expected benefits, the more likely that individual assimilation will be a problem for boundary maintenance. Russophones who are willing to assimilate into the titular cultures can expect greater economic mobility as well as political and titular acceptance. However, 'hardline' elites in the Russophonic communities will attempt to stop individual assimilation as it reduces the strength of the call for

66 Laitin, David D. 1993. The Game Theory of Language Regimes. *International Political Science Review* 14 (3):227-239 and 1998. *Identity in Formation: the Russian-Speaking Populations in the Near Abroad.* Ithaca London: Cornell University Press.

67 Laitin 1993, 232.

cultural rights. These elites must then use selective incentives.[68] Negatively, members of the ethnic group may punish those who attempt to assimilate with violence or isolation. Alternatively, individuals may be positively treated as to give them a greater investment of group interest. Either way, the costs of assimilation become too great and boundary breakdown is avoided. However, given the economic and political incentives to assimilate individually, we should not expect the push for group rights to be at full capacity. Furthermore, the elites themselves have an incentive to integrate into titular society as it holds the potential for widening their dimensions for political representation.

There are additional problems with collective rights. As stated before, by relying on group rights the state locks itself into the current characterisation of ethnic boundaries. For the most part, Estonians and Latvians are trying to blur the lines in a way as to encourage integration into the titular communities. An additional problem with group rights is that there may be the possibility that the minority group does not approve of the way that it is being described. Furthermore, this may even be a way for the dominant group to impose their characterisation of minorities. Overall, whether the ethnic groups seek individual or group rights, it is through political action that policy-making is affected. Although consociationalism would seem a good fit for Latvia, given its consensual nature, and for Estonia, given its stress on group rights based on semi-autonomous regions, it seems unlikely that the titular majorities will allow Russophones in Riga, Daugavpils, or Ida-Virumaa to have what amounts to a minority veto over policy nor become power-sharing autonomous regions based ethnicity alone.

Following constitutional neutrality, there is *democratic liberalism* where differences are negotiated through compromise.[69] Reciprocity and mutual acceptability is the key to this style of negotiation. In essence, this model assumes that liberal rights are intrinsic to, and products of, the democratic process rather than preconditions for them. This gives us hope when discussing new democracies that have not experienced a significantly liberal past. Bellamy argues that this system is relies on a reflexive mentality; *audi alteram*

---

68 Kymlicka actually prescribes internal restrictions, giving this action a negative connotation. However, it seems that positive selective incentives may likely as well. See Kymlicka 1995.

partem or 'hear the other side'.[70] Democratic liberalism seems the best fit for Estonia and Latvia. As the Baltic states continue to experience liberal governance, the polity will be continually infused with liberal values. In this way, trimming, trading, and segregation must give way to negotiation.

Theoretically, this is done in three ways. First, voting systems must encourage as many voices as possible while encouraging reciprocity. The creation of single-issue parties can militate society and can make matters worse. Estonia and Latvia have only witnessed single-issue parties on the left, which have never made it into government. It seems that as time goes on and more Russophones become citizens (or are born as citizens) of their respective state, their voices also will be heard in national elections (and local elections in Latvia). Rather than the expected proportional representation system, this model requires the single transferable vote. In this case, voters cast votes by expressing a preference order. The most favoured (or rather least disfavoured) candidate wins. 'The electorate can converge once they realise that not everyone can secure his or her ideal preference', thus negotiation is necessary.

Second, power sharing should be spread amongst as many different voices as possible. Spreading power among semi-autonomous political units can give minorities a voice and an element of control. By sending representatives to a territorial based legislature, minority groups can feed into policy-making. However, it is at this point that democratic liberalism begins to resemble consociationalism most. Devolution is not a viable option in the Baltic states, especially when it is conceived on an ethnic basis.

Finally, rather than spreading power away from the national government (vertical power-sharing), we should encourage power-sharing within the national government (horizontal power-sharing). In liberal democracies, we have a constant critique of the government's efficacy and efficiency of the political system. In ethnically diverse societies, the rules of the game are constantly being criticised. Rather than this being a legitimacy problem, this criticism could be institutionalised and lead to the process of negotiation overall. Possibly the 'transmission belts' of political culture will help Estonians and Latvi-

---

69 Weale, Albert. 1999. *Democracy*. London: MacMillan Press.

70 Bellamy 2000, 211.

ans learn from their Finnish and Scandinavian regional neighbours. Overall, in applying these four models of pluralist politics to Estonia and Latvia, we see that democratic liberalism goes the furthest in fostering a civic nationalism. It is this civic nationalism that will give Estonia and Latvia a strong sense of 'national integrity' that is so crucial for successful consolidation.

Of these four systems of ethnic control/management, Estonia and Latvia have chosen to institute what has been called the 'Baltic model'.[71] Overall, chapters five and six elaborate in detail. In general, however, Estonia and Latvia have used state-sponsored integration programmes as a way of management. At the same time, non-governmental organisations like the Open Society Foundation and international organisations like the OSCE and EU have preferred linguistic integration as solution to the contentious relationship between democracy and nation-state in the Baltic countries. Having said this, the integration programmes are relatively new coming only in the late 1990's in Estonia and in 2000 in Latvia. Thus, the full effect of the integration programme, that is whether or not they have actually solved this particular relationship, is yet to be seen. Nevertheless, Estonia and Latvia have largely been able to satisfy both domestic and international actors, although unsurprisingly not their large Eastern neighbour. As Baltic commentators continually stress, the Baltic states require specific solutions to the unique problems of Estonia and Latvia. Chapter five will elaborate on the argument of historical uniqueness. On the whole, this chapter has illustrated that traditional institutional approaches are not particularly suited to our case studies.

In conclusion, we have seen many challenges of democratisation within multi-ethnic states in general. Specifically, we have seen the characteristics of the democratisation process in Eastern Europe. In addition, the chapter established a definition of consolidated democracy that will allow us to continue with the discussion of minority politics in Estonia and Latvia. Finally, we have

71 See Pettai, Vello. 2000. Competing Conceptions of Multiethnic Democracy: Debating Minority Integration in Estonia. Paper read at European Consortium for Political Research, Joint Sessions Workshop on 'Competing Conceptions of Democracy in the Practice of Politics', April 14-19, at Copenhagen, Denmark; and Pettai, Vello and Klara Hallik. 2002. Understanding Processes of Ethnic Control: segmentation, dependency and co-operation in post-communist Estonia. *Nations and Nationalism* 8 (4):505-529.

seen four trajectories of institution-building that attempt to manage ethnic relations in democratic states; the result of which signals the difficulty of catering for all groups in society. The way that ethnic groups behave is key to our understanding of democratisation in multi-ethnic states and we therefore now turn our attention to 'ethnicity and politics'.

Chapter 3 Ethnicity and Politics

3.1 Ethnicity and Identities

To begin with, we need to answer two fundamental questions regarding the nature of ethnicity. What is ethnicity as an identity construct and how does it apply to the group? Rather than define ethnicity and then draw a definition of ethnic groups around it, I will instead begin with defining the group and then discussing the identity construct. Ethnicity becomes most important when it affects group dynamics, whereby there exists an ingroup and an outgroup.[72] Groups make their decisions based on the actions of other groups. For many scholars, ethnic boundaries are the key to explaining ethnic group relations.[73] Ethnic boundaries represent those characteristics that are different between groups, but not necessarily the entire cultural characteristics of a group. Thus, the continuity of the group depends on the maintenance of the ethnic boundary. Anthony Smith defines an 'ethnic group' in six characteristics:[74]

1) a collective proper name of the group;
2) a myth of common ancestry;
3) shared historical memories;
4) one or more differentiating elements of common culture, e.g. language;
5) an association with a specific 'homeland', and;

72 See especially, Tajfel, Henri and John C. Turner. 1986. The Social Identity Theory of Intergroup Behavior. In *Psychology of Intergroup Relations*, edited by William G. Austin and Stephen Worchel. Chicago: Nelson-Hall Publishers.

73 Banton, Michael. 1983. *Racial and Ethnic Competition.* Cambridge: Cambridge University Press. Banton, Michael. 1998. *Racial Theories.* 2nd ed. Cambridge: Cambridge University Press; Barth, Fredrik. 1969. *Ethnic Groups and Boundaries: The social organization of culture difference.* London: Allen & Unwin; Barth, Fredrik and Donald Noel. 1972. Conceptual Frameworks for the Analysis of Race Relations: an evaluation. *Social Forces* 50:333-348; Hannan, Michael T. 1979. The Dynamics of Ethnic Boundaries in Modern States. In *National Development and The World System: Education, Economic, and Political Change 1950-1970*, edited by J. W. Meyer and M. T. Hannan. Chicago: University of Chicago Press; and Olzak, Susan. 1992. *The Dynamics of Ethnic Competition and Conflict.* Stanford: Stanford University Press.

74 Smith, Anthony. 1991. *National Identity.* London: Penguin Books.

6) a sense of solidarity for significant sectors of the population.

According to Smith, these characteristics allow for treating ethnic groups as another social unit. Following this, groups are continually re-evaluating their status in society in terms of their hierarchical positioning relative to other groups. Richard Jenkins argues that this evaluation is based on internal and external definitions of the group's status in relation to the other group(s).[75] Internal definitions are characteristics that define the 'self.' Alternatively, external definitions are characteristics that define the 'other.'

In times of dramatic changes in-group status, we should expect two outcomes. Anna Triandafyllidou argues that as aspects of the outgroup ethnicity become threatening to the ingroup, re-evaluation leads to an ethnically based nationalism.[76] In this circumstance, Triandafyllidou states that the in-group is most likely to reaffirm their ethnicity in order to further differentiate themselves from the out-group. However, this is not always the case. Rasma Karklins argues that in the case of economic migrants, as opposed to political migrants, individuals focus on economic gains rather than political opportunities.[77] From this, we can say that members of the threatened group may attempt to 'blend in' or assimilate rather than reaffirm their own ethnicity.

'Ethnicity' is a part of every person's identity construct and defines the 'permissible constellations' of statuses an individual may have.[78] Jenkins argues that ethnicity is situationally defined rather than being assigned a strict definition.[79] Therefore, the salience of the ethnicity among a particular group is variable. This may even be the case within the same ethnic system.[80] In most cases, ethnicity is subordinate to most other statuses such as class, tribal, or familial. To more fully explain the concept of salience, I rely on Don-

75 Jenkins, Richard. 1994. Rethinking Ethnicity: Identity, Categorization and Power. *Ethnic and Racial Studies* (April):198-201.

76 Triandafyllidou, Anna. 1998. National Identity and the 'Other'. *Ethnic and Racial Studies* (July):601.

77 Karklins, Rasma. 1994. *Ethnopolitics and Transition to Democracy: The Collapse of the USSR and Latvia*. Washington D.C.: The Woodrow Wilson Centre Press.

78 Barth 1969.

79 Jenkins 1994, 198.

80 By this, I simply mean the environment in which two or more ethnic groups find themselves reacting to each other.

ald Horowitz's discussion of ethnic markers.[81] He defines ethnic markers as those shared characteristics that exist amongst the group. These can range anywhere from language to dress.

Combined with Smith's model, ethnic markers are important in identifying specific ethnic groups. However, they do not necessarily determine the level of cleavage between groups. Rather, it is during times of conflict that these markers become most important in differentiating between groups and even lend to the rhetoric of aggressive behaviour. Those markers that are more recognisable will induce ethnic groups to remain separated, such as skin colour or body modifications. On the other hand, those ethnic markers that are more easily changed, such as dress and language, allow members of one ethnic group to assimilate into the other. However, if the conflict conditions do become more acute, it becomes more important for members of a group to locate those cues that differentiate the largest number of members within their own group. As ethnic group dynamics vary, the salience of some markers is not necessarily common nor are they always static amongst groups. For example, the importance of skin colour in the U.S. today may not be as important as language in fifty years.

3.2 Politicised Ethnicity

Ethnicity has had its greatest effect on politics through nationalist movements.[82] There are four basic theories of ethno-nationalism. *Cultural constructionists* argue that there is a natural tendency to organise around certain cultural characteristics such as language.[83] On the other hand, *structuralists*

---

81 Horowitz, Donald L. 1985. *Ethnic Groups in Conflict.* Berkeley London: University of California Press.

82 See Connor, Walker. 1978. A Nation is a Nation. *Ethnic and Racial Studies* 1 (4):379-388.; Gellner, Ernest. 1994. *Encounters with Nationalism.* Oxford: Blackwell; and more recently Mason, T. David and David Galbreath. 2004. Ethnicity and Politics. In *Encyclopedia of Government and Politics*, edited by Maurice Kogan and Mary Hawkesworth. London: Routledge.

83 See especially, Anderson, Benedict R. 1991. *Imagined Communities Reflections on the Origin and Spread of Nationalism.* Rev. and extended ed. London: Verso; and Greenfeld, Liah. 1990. The Formation of the Russian National Identity: the role of

argue that the structure of the system dictates the level of salience an individual has for his or her ethno-nationalist identity.[84] Rather than a natural tendency to organise, structuralists claim that an individual's reaction to the system structure will cause him or her to seek security by attaching to someone similar in ethnic background. Third, *social-psychological* treatments of ethno-nationalism look at the psychology of the ingroup-outgroup dynamics.[85] In particular, proponents look at the natural tendency of the survival of the self by creating an ingroup and outgroup. Finally, *instrumentalism* or *elite determinism* suggests that elites instigate or suppress nationalism by framing their goals, grievances, and ideology in such a way as to justify a desired trajectory for the group.[86]

This book attempts to bolster the structuralist argument in that it focuses on Baltic political structures as designed by minority policy. Gellner argues that nationalism is the external manifestation of the relationship between the state and culture.[87] In the case of Estonia and Latvia, we will see that the change in the 'political opportunities structure' in the Soviet and post-Soviet eras have led from a greater sense of nationhood to a normalisation of politics.[88] In the post-Soviet era, we see that the political re-structuring of inde-

---

status insecurity and resentment. *Comparative Studies in Society and History* (32):549-591.

84 See Gellner, Ernest. 1983. *Nations and Nationalism.* Oxford: Blackwell Publishers; Hechter, Michael. 1978. Group Formation and the Cultural Division of Labor. *American Journal of Sociology* 84 (2):293-319; and Horowitz, Donald L. 1971. Three Dimensions of Ethnic Politics. *World Politics* 23:232-244.

85 For example, Haas, Ernest. 1986. What is Nationalism and Should We Study It? *International Organization* 40 (3):707-744; Wilder, A. 1986. Social Categorization: Implications for creation and reduction of intergroup bias. In *Advances in Experimental Social Psychology,* edited by Leonard Berkowitz. New York: Academic Press; and Tajfel and Turner 1986.

86 See Brass, Paul R. 1991. *Ethnicity and Nationalism: Theory and Comparison.* London: Sage Publications; and Breuilly, John. 1993. *Nationalism and the State.* Second ed. Manchester: Manchester University Press. For a review of the literature on 'framing' see Zald, Mayer N. Culture, Ideology, and Strategic Framing' In *Comparative Perspectives on Social Movements: Political Opportunities, Mobilizing Structures, and Cultural Framings,* edited by John D. McCarthy Doug McAdam, and Mayer N. Zald. Cambridge: Cambridge University Press.

87 Gellner 1983, 35.

88 See Tarrow, Sidney. 1998. *Power in Movement: Social Movements and Contentious Politics.* Second ed. Cambridge: Cambridge University Press; Tarrow, Sidney.

pendence has transferred Baltic nationalisms from nation-seeking to nation-building. Again, in our cases, nation-building, and thus defining the nation, has led to what some describe as a process of ethnic control.[89] This study looks at how the political structure has affected the minority community by paying special attention to the making and evolution of minority policy. The argument put forward here is that although culture, political elites, and basic group dynamics play a part in the larger majority-minority relationship, the structure of the system is the key determinant of minority politics.

Structure plays a large part in determining ethnic group behaviour. In particular, different structures will produce varied opportunities and constraints on collective action. The simplest possible structures of ethnic systems can be divided into 'ranked' and 'unranked'.[90] 'Ranked' systems exist when, as the term suggests, ethnic groups are hierarchically ordered. In this situation, social stratification is synonymous with ethnic membership. Opportunities for social mobility are restricted by group identity. In fact, the dominant group is usually completely prevailing over the subordinate group socially, economically, and politically.

Van de Berghe sees the 'ranked' structure as being the most likely and realistic.[91] Reactive ethnicity theory, primarily based on Hechter's study of the

---

1999. States and Opportunities: the political structuring of social movements. In *Comparative Perspectives on Social Movements: Political Opportunities, Mobilizing Structures, and Cultural Framings*, edited by John D. McCarthy, Doug McAdam, and Mayer N. Zald. Cambridge: Cambridge University Press.

89 See especially Lustick, Ian. 1979. Stability in Deeply Divided Societies: Consociationalism versus Control. *World Politics* 31 (3):325-44, but also Pettai, Vello and Klara Hallik. 2002. Understanding Processes of Ethnic Control: Segmentation, Dependency and Co-operation in Post-Communist Estonia. *Nations and Nationalism* 8 (4):505-529.

90 Daalder, Hans. 1966. The Netherlands: Opposition in a Segmented Society. In *Political Oppositions in Western Democracies*, edited by Robert A. Dahl. New Haven, Conn: Yale University Press; Furnivall, John Sydenham. 1944. *Netherlands India: A Study of Plural Economy*. Cambridge: University Press; Kuper, Leo and M. G. Smith, ed. 1969. *Pluralism in Africa*. Los Angeles: University of California Press; Rogowski, Ronald. 1985. Causes and Varieties of Nationalism: a rationalist account. In *New Nationalisms of the Developed West*, edited by Edward A. Tiryakian and Ronald Rogowski. Boston: Allen and Unwin; and Horowitz 1985.

91 Van de Berghe, Pierre. 1967. *Race and Racism: A Comparative Perspective*. New York: John Wiley.

'Celtic fringe' in Britain, makes several suggestions.[92] Hechter discusses both internal colonialism and cultural division of labour, as being part of a process whereby there is an increased opportunity for ethnic collective action in hierarchically ordered systems. At first glance, these terms seem to overlap. Thankfully, Nielson makes a distinction between the two concepts.[93] Internal colonialism is the situation in which ethnic boundaries and occupational cleavages coincide as with Gurr's *ethnoclass*.[94] A cultural division of labour is the mechanism whereby this overlap increases the solidarity of the ethnoclasses by heightening the consciousness of ethno-national identities. Theoretically, internal colonialism and cultural division of labour refer to the same circumstance. While the former refers to the structure itself, the latter refers to the catalyst for mobilisation as consciousness increases. Overall, the concept is based on the main tenet that cultural and economic discrepancies are mutually reinforcing. Hence, collective action may occur when an ethnic group is segregated into low-class occupations. Increased ethnic solidarity means increased ethnic political mobilisation and a further displacement of the outgroup.

Alternatively, in an 'unranked' system, groups are not hierarchically ordered but are evenly matched (e.g. resources). Each group is stratified internally, having its own social, economic, and political spheres. Horowitz argues that these systems have the potential for a high level of violence as both groups theoretically have an equal amount of resources.[95] Specifically, these systems characteristically lack a sufficient overarching authority to establish a high level of reciprocity. In addition, unlike ranked systems, unranked sys-

---

92 Hechter, Michael. 1974. The Political Economy of Ethnic Change. *American Journal of Sociology* 79 (5):1151-1178; Hechter, Michael. 1975. *Internal Colonialism: The Celtic Fringe in British National Development, 1536-1966.* London: Routledge and Kegan Paul; Hechter, Michael. 1978. Group Formation and the Cultural Division of Labor. *American Journal of Sociology* 84 (2):293-319. For more recent case studies using reactive ethnicity theory, see Medrano, Juan Diez. 1994. The Effects of Ethnic Segregation and Ethnic Competition on Political Mobilization in the Basque Country, 1988. *American Sociological Review* 59 (6):873-889.

93 Nielson, Francois. 1985. Toward a Theory of Ethnic Solidarity in Modern Societies. *American Sociological Review* 50 (2):133-149.

94 Gurr, Ted Robert. 1994. Peoples Against States: Ethnopolitical Conflict and the Changing World System. *International Studies Quarterly* 38:347-377.

95 Horowitz 1985, 28,31.

tems do not have a ritualised way of interacting. Therefore, relations between groups become unpredictable.

The ethnic system structures in Estonia and Latvia are somewhere in between these ideal types. In the case of Estonia, the geographic concentration and lower minority population proportion makes it a mixture of the two systems. On the one hand, being geographically concentrated allows the Russophonic community to remain isolated without the need for quick assimilation. In addition, with permanent residents allowed to vote in local elections, the community has some control over local policy-making. On the other hand, this isolation and lower population proportion also keeps the Russophonic community from reaching its full potential. In Latvia, the Russophonic population is close to the 50-percentile mark in addition to being spread throughout the country, although there are some traditional areas of high Russophonic concentration. Again, Latvia also is between the two types. Although political alienation may lead us first to consider these two states to be unranked systems, the economic conditions force us to re-evaluate. In fact, it may be something of a blessing to represent a little of both systems as the propensity for conflict is far less.

Besides these two simple types, ethnic systems can be broken down even further. John Furnivall refers to ethnically heterogeneous societies as 'poly-ethnic social systems.'[96] Relying on Furnivall, Fredrik Barth presents four forms of poly-ethnic social systems.[97] First, ethnic groups may control separate niches and have minimal competition for resources, both economic and political. Second, ethnic groups may monopolise separate territories and compete for resources. Third, there may be a symbiotic relationship between groups whereby they provide important goods and services for each other. However, they may also compete if the goods and services provided by each group are through the monopolisation of different means of production. Finally, ethnic groups may partially compete within the same niche. Over time, one group will displace the other or assimilation will occur.

---

96 Furnivall 1944.

97 Barth 1969.

3.3 Ethnic Group Dynamics

The key question, however, is what factors cause this situation to tip one way or the other. Displacement may be a response to the way in which ethnic groups respond to each other in the economy. Similar to reactive ethnicity theory, ethnic competition theory tries to explain ethnic relations in the case of niche overlap.[98] Here, these scholars argue that competition intensifies the salience of ethnic identities and promotes some forms of ethnic collective action. Due to changes in the system brought on by immigration, migration, economic contractions, and uneven economic growth, ethnic groups may increasingly find themselves competing for the same resources. While ethnic displacement is a group dynamic, assimilation most likely occurs on an individual level.[99] More specifically, group saliency relies on others within the group to act in the same fashion. However, assimilation is not done for the purpose of securing the group's cultural characteristics, such as language, religion, and customs. Rather, it is done on a more material and physical basis. In particular, assimilation occurs as individuals attempt to avoid the negative externalities of ethnic politics and seek benefits (security, material) in the other group. Needless to say, the systems presented thus far are theoretical constructs. The rise of the state system with the focus on strong national governments and regional stability complicates their applicability.

Where there are political parties representing a minority community, they must attempt to overcome the political structure that has been established to favour the majority community. Rothschild argues that there are four steps needed to do this.[100] First, elites must be able to frame the issues in such a way as to make the ethnic group aware. Second, elites must mobilise the ethnic group into collective action, using that group's repertoire of contention.[101] Third, the ethnic group must be sufficiently organised in order to par-

---

98 Barth et al. 1972; Hannan 1979; Olzak, Susan. 1989. Contemporary Ethnic Mobilization. *Annual Review of Sociology* 9:355-74; Ragin, Charles. 1977. Class, Status, and "Reactive Ethnic Cleavages: The Social Bases of Political Regionalism. *American Sociological Review* 42 (3):438-450; and Banton 1998.

99 Laitin 1998.

100 Rothschild, Joseph. 1981. *Ethnopolitics: A Conceptual Framework.* New York: Columbia University Press, 6.

101 Tilly, Charles. 1995. Contentious Repertoires in Great Britain 1758-1834. In *Reper-*

ticipate in collective action. Finally, the ethnic group must direct their attention on to the political arena using the developments of the earlier steps.

As the number of democratic states increases, ethno-nationalism can be a potential threat to regime survival since the number of ethnically homogenous states is few. There are two ways in which ethnicity can become the primary political issue axis in democratising states. First, one group may not be a sufficiently significant portion of the population to win policy-making positions through elections given majoritarian electoral rules. Consequently, they are relegated to a permanent minority status. This situation may cause the smaller of the parties to resort to extra-institutional (and even undemocratic) means, ranging from peaceful demonstrations to terrorism, in order to gain access to policymaking. Second, institutional structures may be established in a fashion that would preclude a group from participating in policy-making, as seen in Chapter Two. For example, if institutional rules apportion abilities to affect decision making to various groups based on population size, the smaller group will be automatically allocated the least amount of policy input. Likewise, this situation may cause the minority group to resort to undemocratic means to change the institutional structures. However, in both cases, the politicisation of ethnicity may not be a threat to the stability of the government nor may it turn into large-scale violence. Instead, this may lead minority groups to express their disenfranchisement by the regime in a series of social movements designed towards changing the 'rules of the game'.

Although ethnic and national identities can greatly affect politics, they are not the only personal identities an individual may have. In fact, multiple identities are nearly universal in social life. However, an individual can only have multiple identities when there are no necessary choices. On the one hand, ethno-nationalist systems rank individuals in the outgroup in a zero-sum fashion. Alternatively, class based systems assign position on an individual basis.[102] Having two theoretical system types does not bring us any closer to understanding ethnonational renewal. In other words, when will indi-

---

toires and Cycles of Collective Action, edited by Mark Traugott. Durham and London: Duke University Press.

102 See Marrett, Cora Bagley and Cheryl Leggon. 1979. Introduction. In *Research in Race and Ethnic Relations*, edited by C. B. Marrett and C. Leggon. Greenwich, Connecticut: JAI Press Inc.

viduals choose ethno-national identities over class identity? The simple answer is when ethno-national identities become more salient. However, it is this process of increased salience which is important. Barth argues that ethno-national identities arise when two things happen.[103] First, society begins to be compartmentalised into exclusive and imperative status categories. This may happen, as Triandafyllidou notes, during times of economic or political crisis.[104] Second, a large segment of society begins to believe that standards can be applied differently among groups. The greater the differences between these applied standards, the more constraints there are on inter-ethnic relations.

However, some scholars do not see increased ethnic salience as an identity shift. Van de Berghe argues that ethno-nationalist and class based systems are not autonomous theoretical concepts.[105] Within nearly every ethnically heterogeneous society, groups are almost always hierarchically ordered. Gurr refers to this as an ethnoclass.[106] Therefore, when ethno-national and class identities overlap, group salience is reinforced. In this case, the politicisation of ethnicity becomes even more likely, especially in democratic or democratising states.

As a state proceeds through a democratic transition, institutional design becomes a key determinant of the potential for conflict, cooperation, and collective action among groups. Arend Lijphart argues that less homogenous societies must play a different democratic game than many of the older democracies.[107] Within these states, the policies of the principal parties diverge to opposite poles. Lijphart states that loyalties within these groups will be much more stringent because of the importance placed on polarizing issues. In turn, this reduces the chances for consensus. Before the democratic transition, ethnic groups were more able to remain separate and thus exist as relatively autonomous social subsystems. Once the transition has begun, there is absent the flexibility necessary for majoritarian government because of the

---

103 Barth 1969.

104 Triandafyllidou, Anna. 1998. National Identity and the 'Other'. *Ethnic and Racial Studies* (July):603.

105 Van de Berghe 1967.

106 Gurr 1994.

107 Lijphart 1984.

possibility of a tyranny of the majority ethnic group. Lijphart argues that minorities will continually be denied policy-making privileges. This situation has the potential to cause the smaller group to feel excluded and reject the legitimacy of the new regime.

With the arrival of ethnic political parties, a democratic political situation can become increasingly hostile. Ethnic parties in particular revolve around one complicated issue axis, namely ethnicity, and have a key interest in institutional design. Parties become the organizational expression of the ethnic groups they represent. Horowitz points out ethnic parties operate within a segmented electorate.[108] Individual ethnic parties only have to compete for resources from within a single ethnic group. In this case, competition for votes stays within the ethnic group. However, ethnic collective action is focused on affecting policy-making. Ethnic parties are unable to diversify their electorate. As elites increase the salience of ethnic identity, the opportunity for parties to recruit members from other ethnic groups and for party elites to build multi-ethnic parties or coalitions both decrease. Thus, ethnic parties are limited to the resources they can obtain from the ethnic group they represent. Threats to the policies of an ethnic party may appear to be more than the usual policy bickering between competing elites when we consider the role of opportunities and threats in determining future action.

Furthermore, ethnic party systems are generally polarized, making consensus difficult. Two-party systems, where each party devotes resources to encouraging defections from the opposing party and to maintaining its core constituents, gravitate to the centre or the median voter. However, in ethnically based systems, where birth dictates your party preference, polarization is much more extreme. Ethnic parties are overwhelmingly supported by a specific ethnic group and therefore only serve the interest of that ethnic group. 'By appealing to electorates in ethnic terms, by making ethnic demands on government, and by bolstering the influence of ethnically chauvinist elements within each group, parties that begin by merely mirroring ethnic divisions help to deepen and extend them.'[109] Horowitz argues that there are

108 Horowitz 1985, 342.
109 Ibid., 291.

centripetal ties among ethnic groups that are created by fostering affinity and common interests within groups.

In conclusion, ethnic political parties in Estonia and Latvia have for the most part revolved around the minority communities. For example, Estonia has the Estonian United People's Party and the Russian Party in Estonia while Latvia has the Equal Rights Party as well as the Latvian Socialist Party. At the same time, titular political parties like *Isamaa* in Estonia and *Tēvzemei un Brīvībai* in Latvia also represent centre-right interests. These parties will be discussed in more detail in Chapter Six. We have seen that the issue of ethnicity has become ever less important in elections since independence, although it still remains an important mobilising resource. Recognising that the salience of ethnic identity has changed overtime, this discussion of ethnicity and politics gives a theoretical framework in which to analyse minority politics and policies since independence. In order to consider a more complete approach to minority politics, we need now turn our attention to the role of international institutions.

Chapter 4 International Institutions

By expanding on Brubaker's 'nexus' metaphor, we may look at international politics in respect of the relationship between the nationalising state and the external national homeland, along with their relationship with international organisations. While traditional international relations have concentrated on state-to-state relations, this book highlights the role of international organisations and the state. In particular, international and regional organisations have become far more substantial since the end of the Second World War. This has been especially the case in Europe. In the same way that powerful states have been able to affect domestic and foreign policies over the years, so do international institutions now.

4.1 Foreign Policy and IR Theory

Likewise, political elites find themselves playing a two-level game, whereby they are required to appease the electorate while satisfying their international commitments.[110] Of course, this assumes that the politicians' primary objective is to remain in power while wanting to avoid the negative consequences of behaving within an organisation's mandate. Indeed, democratic countries go through phases that can be represented by two extremes. At one point, politicians are willing to submit to the requirements of international organisations with the purpose of tying the country to the benefits of the organisation. The majority of countries that are proposed to be new EU members have experienced this end of the process. On the other hand, international organisa-

110 Putnam, Robert. 1988. Diplomacy and Domestic Politics: the Logic of Two-Level Games. *International Organization* Summer:427-461. See also, Elman, M. 1995. The Foreign Policies of Small States: Challenging Neorealism in its own backyard. *British Journal of Political Science* 25 (2):171-217; and Ugur, M. 1997. State-society interaction and European integration: a Political Economy Approach to the Dynamics and Policymaking of the European Union. *Review of International Studies* 23 (4):469-500.

tion requirements may be seen by the electorate, and thus by entrepreneurial politicians, as negatively affecting the nation. An example would be the rise of Haider in Austria, where a right-wing populist party became part of the ruling coalition as a result of resentment against greater Europeanisation. Within these extremes lie the majority of cases. In regard to the countries of East and Central Europe, the majority of electorates have continually placed governments in power that were seeking a greater role in Europe and thus regional organisations.

While the two-level game theory tells us something of the decisions of the politician, we need to know more about the relationship between the nationalising state and the external national homeland as well as their relationship with international organisations. Following this, there are two traditional paradigms within the study of international relations. They are realism and liberalism.

Realist theories of international relations centre on one key factor: power. Classical realism is embedded with a moralistic vision of the world (à la Hobbes). In essence, it is a state-eat-state world and the strongest survives. Following the demise of the inter-war system and the re-emergence of power politics, political scholars set about trying to explain the new bi-polar system.[111] Based on classical realism, Kenneth Waltz, among others, formulated a revised understanding of the international system.[112] Several main tenets underpin what came to be termed neo-realism. First, classical realism was made more parsimonious, meaning that the state became the primary unit of analysis rather than observing the behaviour of politicians or even alliances. In addition, every state would be considered to be the same, only distinguishable by its level of power. Second, the definition of power has four dimensions: political, economic, diplomatic, and propagandistic. Therefore, despite all other characteristics, a state should behave as determined by its

111 Carr, E. H. 1946. *The Twenty Years' Crisis, 1919-1939: An Introduction to the Study of International Relations.* Second ed. London: Macmillan.

112 Waltz, Kenneth N. 1959. *Man, the State and War: a Theoretical Analysis.* New York: Columbia University Press; and id., 1979. *Theory of International Politics.* New York: Random House. See also Morgenthou. Morgenthau, Hans J. 1962. *Politics in the Twentieth Century.* Chicago: University of Chicago Press; and id., 1967. *Politics Among Nations: the Struggle for Power and Peace.* Fourth ed. New York: Knopf.

level of power. The state will determine its actions based on a complex cost-benefit analysis. Finally, and fundamentally, the international system is itself anarchic. In the same way that firms struggle against one another in a free market, so do states in an anarchic system. Based on these basic tenets, primarily coming from Waltz, various forms of neo-realism have been developed in the study of international relations.

Criticisms of the realist paradigm in general began after the First World War but were cut short with the fall of the League of Nations and subsequent war. With the rise of super-power politics, realism seemed an obvious explanation of international relations. However, neo-realism often suffers from its own parsimony. First, there are a plethora of actors that affect international relations including politicians, pressure groups, alliances, and international organisations. By only looking at the actions of the state, surely only part of the picture is available. Second, states do not always act according to their level of power. In some cases, powerful states are willing to sacrifice a level of sovereignty for the sake of a larger collective good. Following this, what a state decides is its national interest is an extremely dubious factor of analysis. The ambiguity of such rational choice decisions makes it difficult to interpret the process of international relations. Finally, the international system does not always exhibit the characteristics of realism's state-eat-state system, although the latest middle-eastern conflict may show otherwise. Rather, international relations do work within a largely co-operative structure, though there is no overarching super-state. Typically states work within the confines of international institutions such as the United Nations, the Organisation for Security and Co-operation in Europe, or the World Trade Organisation.

In general, the collapse of the Soviet Union and post-Cold War world order has been a major challenge to the realist paradigm. Events sent many realist theorists looking for answers to such questions as why NATO still existed, much less still expanding, without a viable rival power base. Although critics of realism have been somewhat dismayed with the latter Bush administration and its vision of the world through realist spectacles, realism still has much to answer. In particular, realist theories lack significant explanatory power because of the disregard for the importance of international organisations. This book highlights this deficiency. Specifically, based on realist theories, we would expect the Russian Federation, as a much more powerful state, to be able to significantly affect Estonia and Latvia in a way that would be favourable to Moscow. However, this book indicates that this was not the case. Rather, regional organisations were much more influential. So, for this conclusion we turn to the traditional alternative to the realism paradigm: liberalism.

Born from the ideas of the enlightenment, liberalism takes on a different view of international relations. Like classical realism, traditional liberalism maintains a moralistic view of international relations. Basically, liberalism concentrates on internationally shared values such as human rights, democracy, and neo-liberal economics. Although it can be seen in French and British colonial structures, traditional liberalism underpinned Europe's (and America's) attempts to rebuild the world order after the First World War. Most definitely, President Woodrow Wilson's attempts to prevent such a devastating conflict from happening again were based on liberal notions of shared values. As a result, the League of Nations attempted to encapsulate these values. Of course, the League failed and realism once again seemed to become a viable theory.

From the cracks of neo-realism, a new liberalism began to emerge which would rid the traditional theory of much of its moralistic baggage, as had been done with classical realism. Primarily based on Robert Keohane and Joseph Nye, interdependence liberalism disputed the rule of power politics in the international system.[113] Rather, the world system had witnessed an increased degree of interdependence whereby it was in nearly every state's interest to work through co-operation rather than contention. For example, a state would be less likely to use extra-political means against another state because it too would be affected negatively by these actions. Thus, rather than power politics, interdependence liberalism explains international relations as a bargaining process whereby states link important issues as a way of either gaining advantage or avoiding a loss. For example, the Russian

113 Keohane, Robert and Joseph Nye. 1977. *Power and Interdependence: World Politics in Transition.* New York: Little Brown. See also Keohane, 1984. *After Hegemony: Cooperation and Discord in the World Political Economy.* Princeton, N.J.: Princeton University Press; and id., 1989. *International Institutions and State Power: Essays in International Relations Theory.* Boulder: Westview Press.

government attempted to link troop-withdrawals and border agreements to the status of Russian-speaking minorities in Estonia and Latvia, although with little success.

Furthermore, this bargaining process very often works within the responsibilities of an international organisation. In particular, interdependence institutionalism focuses on international organisations as important actors in international relations. International institutions are embedded within the shared interests of member-states and therefore play an important role in international relations. Overall, the international component of this book lies within the context of neo-liberalism. In relation to the minority issue in the Baltic States, the OSCE, EU, Council of Europe and, to a lesser extent, the United Nations were important international actors. Rather than simply rehash the realism-liberalism debate, the point here was to highlight the theoretical approaches that can be used to analyse the relationship between the nationalising state, external national homeland, and international organisations. On the part of the last set of actors, a minority protection regime exists to encourage policy implementation. Let us take a look at how this community works.

4.2 Regimes and Liberal Communities

Since the dissolution of the Soviet Union, Estonia and Latvia have consistently aimed towards European integration. Specifically, they needed to cooperate with the OSCE, EU and the Council of Europe. Their relationship with these organisations has been significantly affected by the legacies of its Soviet past. One such legacy is the considerable minority communities that we are focusing on in this study. Early citizenship and language laws placed the state firmly in the hands of the titular population, while politically alienating the largely Russian-speaking minority community. In response, regional organisations became concerned over the potential for conflict and the overall democratic nature of domestic governance. Given this, successive governments have had to reconsider these policies as a result of regional pressure. In Chapter Nine, we examine how these organisations have attempted to implement international norms and agreements within the body of Estonian and Latvian citizenship and language legislation. In order to appreciate the relationship between these international organisations and the Baltic states, we need to first engage with several key approaches of enlargement.

The dialogue of international relations theory has been dominated by the agent-structure problem. Since the 1980's, many authors have attempted to move beyond this conception of international politics towards a more holistic approach. Of primary importance is Alexander Wendt's discussion in *International Organization* where he challenges structural theories of international relations.[114] He argues that the agent-structure problem is based on two assumptions about social life.[115] He states a) 'human beings and their organisations are purposeful actors whose actions help reproduce or transform society in which they live;' and b) 'society consists of social relationships, which structure the interactions between these purposeful actors.' From this, we can see that both agency and structure matter in international politics.

The inclusion of both agency and structure as co-determinants of international politics was incorporated into structuration theory, although better known under the rubric 'constructivism'. This alternative approach 'conceptualises agents and structures as mutually constituted or co-determined entities.'[116] In the context of this study, we can assume that international institutions are products of state-interests. However, we may also assume that once institutions are created, they will in turn affect states. Not only will institutions affect a state's international relations, but also its domestic politics. Those who study European institutions readily acknowledge the give-and-take relationship between states and institutions. However, this has not always been the case in international relations literature.

If this is so, why do states allow institutions to impair their sovereignty? The answer to this question is not new by any means. A rationalist approach would suggest that the purpose of international co-operation is to reduce collective 'bads'.[117] On the other hand, constructivist would argue the interna-

---

114 Wendt, Alexander E. 1987. The Agent-Structure Problem in International Relations. *International Organization* 41 (3):335-369.

115 Ibid., 337.

116 Ibid., 350.

117 See Krasner, Stephen D. 1982. Structural Causes and Regime Consequences: Re-

tional co-results from shared norms and values. In the European context, co-operation is seen in association and co-operation agreements but most intimately in membership. Thus, we might ask why did European organisations, namely the EU, decide to expand to Central and Eastern Europe?[118] Again, a rationalist account would suggest that a material benefit for existing members would be required for enlargement.[119] However, there is little evidence to suggest that enlargement will bring material benefits to existing benefits, which has not been missed by the EU's poorer states.[120] Constructivists, on the other hand, have argued that shared norms and values make enlargement more likely.[121] This prospective is known as the 'liberal community hypothesis', where 'regional organisations represent international communities of values and norms. Correspondingly, their enlargement will depend on whether outside states identify themselves with, and adhere to, the constitutive values and norms of the community.'[122] There is no doubt that we have seen the spread of norms and values from West to East and from this seen policy convergence in Europe as a whole. However, as Hughes and Sasse point out, we should be sceptical as to the extent to which Central and East European States are actually 'learning' liberal governance as well as how serious the EU is in enforcing such change.[123]

In Chapter Nine, we look mainly at the OSCE, EU and Council of Europe. All of these organisations fit into this idea of a liberal community by fostering and enforcing the spread of ideas in existing and prospective member-states. There have been several types of enforcement mechanisms, as

gimes as Intervening Variables. International Organization 36:1-21.

118 Schimmelfenning, Frank. 2001. The Community Trap: Liberal Norms, Rhetorical Action, and the Eastern Enlargement of the European Union. *International Organization* 55 (1):47-80.

119 See Moravscik, Andrew. 1993. Preferences and Power in the European Community: A Liberal Intergovernmentalist Approach. *Journal of Common Market Studies* 31 (4):473-524.

120 For a discussion of how enlargement occurred despite many member-states reluctance, see Schimmelfenning 2001.

121 For example, see Schimmelfenning, Frank. 2002. Liberal Community and Enlargement: An Event History Analysis. *Journal of European Public Policy* 9 (4):598-626.

122 Ibid., 598.

123 Hughes, James and Gwedolyn Sasse. 2003. Monitoring the Monitors: EU Enlargment Conditionality and Minority Protection in the CEECs. *Journal of Ethnopolitics*

we shall see. Perhaps the most important, primarily used by the OSCE, is 'epistemic communities'.[124] Shortly defined, epistemic communities are simply knowledge-based communities.[125] James Sebenius offers a more in-depth definition.[126] He defines an epistemic community as a "special kind of de facto natural coalition of 'believers' whose main interest lies not in the material sphere, but instead in fostering the adoption of the community's policy project."[127] Sebenius was the first to apply this concept to the European Union, although briefly.[128] We can see that in many issue-areas of the EU, there is a 'community' that has focused on a 'preferred policy choice'. Such preferred policies can be seen, for example, in the *Lund*, *Hague* and *Oslo* Agreements. If epistemic communities do exist within a European community, we should see policy alternatives emerging in (prospective) member-state governments if 'these communities are successful in obtaining and retaining bureaucratic power domestically.'[129] In the case of European integration, we have seen epistemic communities at work with domestic support as Central and East European electorates have continually returned pro-integration governments. In the case of Estonia and Latvia, government support was consistent with the predominance of centre-right governments.

Although the theoretical role of institutions may seem straightforward, often the political realities are somewhat different. In this way, we need to ask why specifically Estonia and Latvia was willing to allow international institutions to shape its domestic policy. In an earlier study of international institu-

---

and Minority Issues in Europe (1).

124 See especially, Haas, Peter M. 1992. Introduction: Epistemic Communities and International Policy Coordination. *International Organization* 46 (1):1-34. For an application, see Hjorth, Ronnie. 1994. Baltic Sea Environmental Co-operation: The Role of Epistemic Communities and the Politics of Regime Change. *Cooperation and Conflict* 29 (1):11-31; and Gough, Clair and Simon Shackley. 2001. The Respectable Politics of Climate Change: the Epistemic Communities and NGOs. *International Affairs* 77 (4):329-345.

125 Haas, Peter M. 1989. Do Regimes Matter? Epistemic Communities and Mediterranean Pollution Control. *International Organization* 43 (3):377- 403.

126 Sebenius, James K. 1992. Challenging Conventional Explanations of International Cooperation: Negotiation Analysis and the Case of Epistemic Communities. *International Organization* 46 (1):323-365.

127 Ibid., 325.

128 Ibid., 333.

129 Haas 1989, 402.

tions and Latvia, Mark Jubulis offers three such reasons.[130] First, politicians and much of the titular populace see European integration, and thus membership, as the ultimate security guarantee. These security guarantees are particularly meaningful considering the national psyche, the result of which is a product of a history of relative subjugation. This has even led to a concentration on NATO to the detriment of EU ESDP (European Security and Defence Policy).[131] Second, Russian accusations of human rights abuses have put titular politicians on the defensive.[132] In fact, the Russian Government initially favoured EU membership since Moscow perceived that the integration process would require the Baltic states to radically change their citizenship and language laws.[133] Finally, Jubulis argues that Latvia's Soviet past meant that the government did not have experience in dealing with human rights issues. This, in turn, led Latvia to require greater expert assistance.

Haas argues that 'without the help of experts, they risk making choices that not only ignore the connections with other issues but also highly discount the uncertain future, with the result that a policy choice made now might jeopardise future choices and threaten future generations.'[134] Compliance through policy implementation is for the move to rejoin Europe. How do epistemic communities work? Put simply, they work through the transfer of ideas. Through international learning, we begin to see the convergence of state policies. Learning happens in two ways: persuasion and policy pre-emption.[135] Persuasion occurs as networks of policy-experts rely on established international standards to pressure actors within the foreign and related ministries to change state policy. Policy pre-emption occurs when the epistemic community usurps decision-making authority and promotes policies consistent with its own perspective. In relation to European integration, I argue that epistemic

---

130 Jubulis, Mark A. 1996. The External Dimension of Democratization in Latvia: The Impact of European Institutions. *International Relations* 13 (3):68.

131 See Galbreath, David 'Kurp tālāk? Recenzija par Latvijas ārpolitikas pamatvirzienu projektu (iepriekšējo projektu).' *Politika.lv*, April 2004. http://www.politika.lv/index.php?id=108515&lang=lv.

132 For example, see *Izvestia*, 2 July 1992 and *Sevodnya*, 13 July 1994.

133 For the most recent agreement between the EU and Russia regarding minority rights, see Lobjakas, Ahto. 2004. Baltics: EU, Russia Agree Compromise Text for Joint Minorities Declaration. *RFE/RL Special Report* 27 April.

134 Haas 1992, 13.

communities have largely worked through persuasion while in the future we will see policy pre-emption, as traditional domestic policies will be governed by decisions made in Brussels.[136]

One of the most important matters for post-socialist Europe has been and will be the management of majority-minority relationships. As democratisation is as much about redefining the nation as the character of governance, the protection of minorities has been an important issue of conflict prevention. In Chapter Nine, we shall see how Europe's institutions have used enforcement mechanisms to encourage policy convergence. Overall, Estonia and Latvia's experiences since 1991 can illuminate the relationship between institutions and states by concentrating on minority protection. Before we turn our attention to post-restoration politics, we should come to grips with the historical context of today's Estonia and Latvia.

---

135 Haas 1989.

136 For a discussion on the 'Brusselisation' of policy, see Muller-Brandeck-Bocquet, Gisela. 2002. The New CFSP and ESDP Decision-Making System of the European Union. *European Foreign Affairs Review* 7:257-282.

Chapter 5 Occupation and Independence

The Baltic peoples experienced a great deal of suffering during the early years of Soviet occupation. Despite their best efforts, resistance movements were brutally put down. Through collectivisation, deportation, and the subsequent largely Russian migration, the Baltic titular communities had significant reasons to hold grievances against the Soviet state. The popular movements that arose generally wanted three things. First, the Baltic people wanted Moscow to acknowledge that their inclusion into the Soviet Union was an illegal act. This inclusion was based on the secret Molotov-Ribbentrop Pact as well as the Red Army's push towards Berlin at the end of the Second World War. Second, Baltic peoples wanted greater self-determination in relation to observing their own cultural traditions, preserving their environment, and remembering the past. This drive for autonomy also included a greater say over the local economy. Eventually, full independence movements developed, which called for release from the Soviet Union. These independence movements were based on a restoration ideology whereby the inter-war states still existed outside the Soviet occupation.

Before the arrival of Gorbachev, there was very little opportunity for Soviet nationalities to express their grievances. While Sovietisation attempted to bring the many communities together, the nationalities policy maintained clear boundaries. Once political reforms had begun, ethno-nationalism was ready to be the rallying cry for the new (and sometimes old) elite. Initially, this chapter will discuss the reform policies of Gorbachev, including the necessities of reform and its eventual outcome.

On the other side of these movements were the pro-Soviet movements that were born of the Soviet administration such as Party officials and Union-wide industries. While the Baltic peoples strove for independence through pro-active nationalist movements, the largely ethnically Russian pro-Soviet forces attempted to halt the reforms through reactive nationalist movements. As history has shown, the pro-Soviet forces, given Gorbachev's reforms, were at a disadvantage. However, this was not so obvious at the time.

This chapter will analyse 20th Century Baltic history from independence to Soviet incorporation to independence again. In particular, we will also discuss the independence and pro-Soviet movements in Estonia and Latvia as a means of establishing a base from which to study post-Soviet nation-building. This will be done by looking at the pro-active and nationalist movements as traditional collective action, which will assist the comparative nature of this study. Also, by using a collective action discourse, this analysis will reinforce the importance of socio-political structure as a determinant of ethnic relations. First we start with initial Baltic independence.

5.1 Baltic Incorporation and History

David Laitin claims that it was the Soviet Union's denial of the differences of the elite-incorporation in the periphery that led to the increased politicisation of ethnicity.[137] He suggests that in the Soviet case, the pattern of peripheral incorporation matters. This process occurred within the Russian Empire and was inherited by the Soviet regime. Laitin offers the 'integralist' model of elite-incorporation to explain the Baltic states' absorption into the Russian Empire in the early eighteenth century. In this model, the periphery is ruled from the centre indirectly, as opposed to assimilation or colonial rule. The centre uses a third party to control the periphery, such as Germans in the Baltic states and Indians in Africa. Laitin claims that in this model, the centre is unable to undermine the cultural integrity of the periphery. Overall, the titular group may experience a complete cultural, professional, and social life without being required to assimilate into the centre.

While assimilation did occur on some level (e.g. exogamy), there were considerable differences between titulars and 'settlers'. There were two primary sociological differences between the Baltic societies and Russia. First, the agrarian system in the Baltics differed significantly from the Russian case.[138] While Russia still maintained a commune (*mir*) system, whereby re-

---

137 Laitin, David D. 1998. *Identity in Formation: the Russian-speaking populations in the near abroad.* Ithaca London: Cornell University Press, p. 66-67, 202-207.

138 White, James D. 1996. Nationalism and Socialism in Historical Perspective. In *The*

sources were allocated across households, this agricultural institution no longer existed in the Baltic area at the time of incorporation into the Russian Empire. Rather, the household was the basic unit of social organisation. In particular, this is highlighted because it exhibits a clear sociological difference with that of much of the rest of the empire.

A second difference that applied only to Estonia and Latvia was their Lutheran faith. However, this attachment to a specific denomination should be taken with some caution. White points out that when the Russian government was willing to withhold 'freedom and land' because of this difference in theology, Estonian and Latvian peasants 'converted en masse to Orthodoxy'.[139] Nonetheless, both of these characteristics played a part in encouraging a cultural awakening when the tsarist government applied pressure to 'Russify' the Balts. Such an occasion came about with the arrival of Alexander III (1881-1894) to the throne. In the 1880's, Russification of the Baltic provinces became a key social policy, aimed at full assimilation. Also, during this time, there was a large growth in urbanisation and foreign investment. Urbanisation was a result of landless peasants finding employment, while foreign investment was a result of foreign firms establishing branches within the Baltic region in response to high tariffs placed on imported goods. Threats to national cultures and increased urbanisation had the effect of encouraging a reactionary movement to save the titular cultures which played a large part in establishing independent nationhood after the First World War.[140]

After the Treaty of Brest-Litovsk (1918) was signed transferring the Baltic provinces from the Russian Empire to Germany, and the subsequent de-

---

Baltic States: the National Self-determination of Estonia, Latvia, and Lithuania, edited by Graham Smith. New York: St. Martin's Press.

139 Ibid., 16.

140 For further information on early Baltic national movements in general see Lieven, Anatol. 1993. *The Baltic Revolution: Estonia, Latvia, Lithuania and the Path to Independence*. London: Yale University Press. For a treatment of Latvia see Dreifelds, Juris. 1996. *Latvia in Transition*. Cambridge: Cambridge University Press; and Pabriks, Artis and Aldis Purs. 2002. *Latvia: the Challenges of Change*. London: Routledge. Also, for a study of early nationalism in Estonia see Taagepera, Rein. 1993. *Estonia: Return to Independence*. Boulder, CO: Westview Press; and Unwin, Tim. 1998. Rurality and the Construction of Nation in Estonia. In *Theorising Transition: the Political Economy of Transition in Post-Commmunist Countries*, edited by John Pickles and Adrian Smith. New York: Routledge.

feat of the Germans, the Soviets opened peace negotiations. Estonia gained *de jure* recognition on 2 February 1920 while Latvia signed a similar treaty on 1 August 1920. For the first time, the Baltic nations were independent entities. Unfortunately, this was a limited affair and within twenty years, the Baltic nations would be Soviet republics. However, it is worth mentioning that although the level of democracy differed between states as well as varied across time, the experience of some level of democratic governance means that the Balts have a collective memory of what it means to live in a liberal political system. Furthermore, the existence of the previous periods of independent statehood has been important in constructing the policy agendas of later nationalist movements and thus also post-Soviet ethnic relations.

The Baltic states found themselves in an uncomfortable position in the late 1930's like much of the rest of Central and Eastern Europe.[141] On the one hand, Stalin saw the Baltic region as being a strategic position for halting any Nazi advance, since it forms at a possible military front. Furthermore, uncooperative Baltic governments made the Soviet Union increasingly vulnerable to a German invasion. On the other hand, the Nazi government saw little utility in the Baltic states despite the fact that it would become the area where German forces were launched against Leningrad and later Moscow. While the Baltic governments were worried about falling victim to power politics, they were also sceptical of each other. This scepticism was the result of the nationalism of nation-building that had begun in the nineteenth century.

Eventually, the Baltic governments would work together but it would make little difference. Sensing a German attack, Stalin sought assurances from Berlin that it would not threaten the Soviet Union. While the Baltic governments were in discussions with the British and French, the Soviets and Nazis signed the Molotov-Ribbentrop Pact on 23 August 1939. This non-aggression pact divided the area between the two countries into Soviet and German spheres of influence. The Baltic states were allocated to the Soviet sphere.[142] Using collusion with the Western Allies as an excuse, the Soviets demanded greater co-operation. Finally, the Soviet government decided that

---

141 For an in-depth discussion on the political-military events during this time see Erickson, John. 1975. *The Road to Stalingrad.* Second ed. London: Cassell.

142 Originally, Lithuania was placed in the German sphere of influence but was trans-

the Baltic governments alone would not be able to defend their neutrality. Eventually, the Soviets demanded to station troops in the Baltic countries.

The events that followed are tragic. As was to be expected, when the Soviets moved troops into the Baltic states in 1940, fascist sympathisers were rounded up and special privileges were given to the communist parties. In all three countries, new Soviet-friendly governments were installed through corrupt elections. When the war came in June 1941, the fighting was ferocious and the Red Army was forced to give ground quickly. Similar to the Soviets, the Nazis established new Berlin-friendly regimes and killed any Soviet-sympathisers or representatives. Furthermore, Baltic SS Legions were established to fight against the Red Army. Following the Soviet invasion in 1940, it is easy to understand why the Nazis were seen as liberators despite the fact that they too ruled through intense barbarity. Life was made far worse as the Soviets began to beat back the Nazis and eventually re-occupy the Baltic states. Throughout the war, many men had fought on both sides of the war. Controversy over decisions made long ago still exists today. Desperate times required desperate decisions and the Baltic peoples were made to pay for their actions. In 1944, the Baltic states were forcefully incorporated into the Soviet Union.

The loss of sovereignty and the subsequent mass deportations and Stalinist terror had significant affects on the Baltic psyche. Although resistance movements lasted for some time, the characteristics of the Soviet regime, in particular the brutality of Soviet security services, made resistance impossible. During the Soviet occupation, the structure of the system as well as the titular cadre policy allowed the Balts to maintain a sense of national identity although the level of saliency varied over time. After the Hungarian uprising (1956), there was an increasing level of dissidence in the Baltic states, particularly in Estonia.[143] In the later years of Khrushchev's time in power, the Baltic republics experienced a period of cultural revival connected to a renewed sense of national identity. For example, a pro-reform movement in the

ferred in September 1939.

143 Smith, David J. 2002. *Estonia: Independence and European Integration*. London: Routledge.

Komsomol within Tartu University emerged in the 1960's.[144] However, Brezhnev's arrival into power in 1964 put an end to the limited autonomy of Khrushchev's policies. Furthermore, the crackdown after the Soviet invasion of Czechoslovakia in 1968 further impeded the growth of national movements.

In 1964, a mass immigration of Russophones began in order to fill jobs in the all-Union industrial sectors (e.g. military industry in Latvia). There is also evidence that the intentions of the Soviet regime were to dilute the Baltic population and bolster pro-Soviet loyalties.[145] Needless to say, this demographic change caused a large amount of discontent within the titular communities. For the most part, immigrants were industrial workers and technical personnel destined to move on once their jobs were completed.[146] Furthermore, Riga being the exception, Russophonic immigrants were predominantly proletarian in nature. For these reasons, there was little incentive for them to learn the titular language, a fact that would come back to haunt the Russophonic communities later. Although the typical immigrant worker intended to return to Russia once their job was completed, many remained. Most of the Baltic Russophones arrived there before 1970 or were born to parents who were living there before 1970.

Even in the Brezhnev era, a low level of dissent existed throughout the Soviet system.[147] Although the Prague Spring resulted in a Soviet invasion, it did influence events within the Union. The July 1968 dissident samizdat article, 'To Hope or To Act?', called for democratic reform and a change in aggressive foreign policy. In Estonia, the Estonian National Front (ENF) and the Estonian Democratic Movement (EDM) offered a joint memorandum to the United Nations General Assembly capitalising on the fact that the Baltic states were never recognised by the West as being a part of the Soviet Union. Surprisingly enough, ethnic tensions can already be seen in this act of dissent since the ENF disagreed with the EDM over the inclusion of Russian democrats residing in Estonia.[148]

---

144 See Taagepera 1993 and Dreifelds 1996.
145 Lieven 1993.
146 Smith 2002, 41.
147 Taagepera 1993.
148 Ibid., 102.

As the UN did nothing, the Soviet security apparatus acted quickly to repress dissidents. However, the response was a far cry from the days of Stalin or even Khrushchev, with prison sentences of five to six years. Another action took place in October 1980 with the first industrial strike since 1940 demanding better norms and premiums. Their terms were met. In Latvia, a cultural preservation group was created in 1976, called 'Skandinieki', an act that would set a precedent for further collective action. Union-wide dissident actions are evident with the Democratic People's Front of the Soviet Union's (DPFSU) silent half-hours in the summer of 1981, occurring on the first working week of the month. The DPFSU were calling for the return of troops from Afghanistan and for the Soviet Union to halt interference in Poland, halt the exporting of food, eliminate special stores for party officials, free political prisoners, reduce military service and respect human rights. These monthly events were repressed in December 1981 in response to the repression of *Solidarity* in Poland. These events do show that there was a pattern emerging regarding collective action in the USSR even before Gorbachev came to power.

Ironically, the Soviet nationalities policy helped provide the basis for the breakdown of the Soviet Union. Partly, this is the fault of Marxism's inability to address nationalism as a movement outside class conflict. Furthermore, the Soviet movement, as directed by Lenin, was heavily dependent on the nationalist struggles. The continuation of such a relationship was based on the centre's ability to control the mobilisational resources required for significant alternative social movements. This follows an instrumental discourse in which ethnicity/national identity is used as a means for political and economic objectives. Importantly, national elites were placed in control (within reason given the top-down system) of these mobilisational resources. In effect, this gave national elites the ability to remain in power while limiting the creation of alternative power bases. However, this system assumes that the national elites themselves would not be willing to challenge the centre for greater control over the community's interests.

In fact, this is what did happen. In the non-Russian republics, titular communist party members were often national communists. The popular appeal of the national communists combined with the grievances of the Sovietisation process. For most, Sovietisation resembled the process of Russification. As a result, titular national communists found themselves alienated from the centre by the nationalities policy and the continued predominance of the Russian language and ethnic Russians. In addition, the party system was based on territorial localities that were themselves often based on different national communities. The most obvious example of this was the Baltic Republics. Thus, while trying to reduce the importance of national identities in the Soviet Union, the centre continued to reinforce these same identities through its own party structure.

Eventually, as the policies of repression slowly declined, this federalised patronage system began to breakdown. This allowed for the opportunity of alternative political elites that often originated in the party system. In the Baltic republics, the breakdown of the Soviet federal system began nearly three and half decades before the restoration of independence. In particular, Khrushchev began to eliminate the most repressive elements of the Soviet system. Brezhnev did little to restore Stalinism and encouraged a policy of static political cadres. This policy allowed party elites to become far more powerful than before although those elites who went to far could be removed from power. On the back of this, Gorbachev's policies unleashed another national awakening.

As to be expected, many current political issues in the Baltic states are a result of their challenging history. Estonia and Latvia in particular have experienced almost unabated foreign occupation from the twelfth century. With the first national awakening in the nineteenth century, titular elites began to strive for autonomy and then independence. Ironically, it was the breakdown of Imperial Russia and the rise of the Soviet regime that gave the Baltic states their experience of independence. This sovereignty was only to be brutally taken away by power politics and the Second World War. Once incorporated, the Stalinist terror apparatus proceeded to break the resistance movement and any hopes of independence. From the arrival of Khrushchev, low levels of dissent were seen in the Baltic region. By the time of the Gorbachev era, national independence was once again a possibility.

5.2 From Gorbachev to Independence

The stagnation that came with the long years of the Brezhnev era meant that those who followed would be required to reform. Simply, the system in place was not working. Of course, the system would have either needed to become even more orthodox in its application of state-socialism or moderate away from Socialism. The reformers that followed took the latter course. Although some reforms were begun immediately after Brezhnev's death, the short reigns of Yuri Andropov and Konstantin Chernenko meant that little was changed. Afterwards, Gorbachev's rise to power was directly challenged by hard-liners in the Party. However, as Andropov's chief lieutenant and practically the Party leader under Chernenko's nominal position, Gorbachev succeeded in becoming leader. Once he assumed leadership, Gorbachev continued Andropov's initial reforms. These reforms became formulated as glasnost and perestroika. While the former was oriented towards opening the political system, the latter was focused on reorganising the economic system in the context of de-centralisation. Unlike the leadership in China, the logic behind the Soviet reforms was based on a successful new economic system being dependent on a larger role for civil society. Thus, in effect, both political and economic reforms were directed at decentralising the Soviet system.

In his attempt to change the system, Gorbachev made the mistake of attacking Marxism-Leninism and Soviet history. This action deprived the Union of legitimacy, since proletarian internationalism was the main reason for the Soviet Union to retain its size. The Soviet Union's failure to react to the *Solidarity* movement in Poland showed those in the Soviet bloc that dissent was possible without extreme repercussions. Gorbachev's actions lead some scholars to argue that he allowed organized dissent against the government in the hopes that society would help pressure hardliners into reforming the political and economic system.[149] However, the 'openness' created by Gorbachev's reforms overwhelmed the government's ability to address grievances. Finally, Gorbachev allowed open opposition to the communist party. Unfortu-

149 See Hough, Jerry F. 1997. *Democratization and Revolution in the USSR 1985-1991*. Washington D.C.: Brooking Institute Press; and Bunce, Valerie. 1999. *Subversive Institutions: The Design and the Destruction of Socialism and the State*. Cambridge: Cambridge University Press.

nately, the absence of civil society for such a long time did not prepare the population for organizing traditional challenges to the CPSU. On the other hand, ethno-nationalism was, for the reasons discussed in chapter three, ready to take advantage of these new opportunities.

Somewhat surprisingly, Bunce argues that there was a 'homogenisation' of society that had a large influence on public actions in socialist states during Gorbachev's reforms. 'Publics under socialism occupied a virtually identical structural location.'[150] This means that generally all individuals feel the same societal effects. When things are going well, nearly everyone reaps the benefits. However, in bad times, nearly everyone experiences the decline. This homogenisation has several consequences.[151] The first and most obvious consequence is the 'durable bonds' that existed among individuals. This could produce a sense of common determination and a willingness to change things for the better. Second, individuals shared common interests derived from similar experiences. Since all citizens, besides those in the *nomenklatura*, were experiencing everything from price controls to policy reforms, grievances were likely to be applicable to all. Third, homogenisation created a common definition of the 'enemy.' Not only were grievances identical, but also the source of those problems, the state, was also universally recognizable. Finally, homogenisation encouraged individuals to divide their personalities into a private and public conformist self.[152] This produced a situation where the government was unable to identify discontent.

Possibly this is why Gorbachev made such a miscalculation regarding the nationalities. On the other hand, Bunce's theory of homogenisation has its limits when related to the Soviet Union. Despite the efforts of Sovietisation policies, the nationalities policy prevented the homogenisation of Soviet society. Thus, ethno-nationalism was the key issue-axis by which a challenge to the CPSU control of power was based. Rather than a homogenisation of society, Soviet society was apt to break apart at the first available moment, though a repressive regime does not let go easily. As Joseph Nogee and

150 Bunce 1999, 29.

151 Ibid., 27-29.

152 For an earlier discussion on the development of private and public selves see Hough, Jerry F. and Merle Fainsod. 1979. *How the Soviet Union is Governed.* New York: Harvard University Press.

Judson Mitchell argue, 'the non-Russian nationalities turned out to be far more anti-Soviet than pro-[reform].'[153]

In addition to the rise of ethno-nationalism, the increasing economic difficulties of the Soviet system was arguably the most important factor leading to the collapse. Gorbachev began his political reforms with the hopes that it would produce a pseudo-market economy, instead of a moral obligation to give the citizens of the Soviet Union responsible democratic governance. As alluded to earlier, the economic breakdown began in the early 1960's in Czechoslovakia and later spread into the remaining part of the socialist bloc. Bunce argues that, 'the economic slowdown reflected the perverse incentives generated by state ownership, monopoly, fusion, and autarky.'[154] Generally speaking, the burdens on the Soviet economy included 'hidden inventories, captive consumers, low rates of technological innovation, the labour and capital hunger of enterprises, and the reliance on queues, connections, and corruption.'[155] Specifically, the economic system was burdened by heavy subsidies for housing, utilities, and food.[156] Similar to the inefficiency of the political system, the economic system was unable to cope with changes because of its ever-increasing complexity.

Since the entire economy was administered from the top, the budget had to be approved twelve months or more in advance. Hence, Gorbachev was delayed in influencing economic policy. The new general secretary could not begin reforms until the budget for 1987 was under construction. Unfortunately for the future of reforms in the Soviet Union, there was a great deal of resistance from hardliners. Overall, not only was the economic system inherently lacking in an efficient rationality, but also the over-planning characteristic of all socialist political systems prohibited Gorbachev from instituting reforms that may have helped alleviate the system from some of its many problems. Needless to say, economic problems on their own may have been enough to end the Soviet project. However, in the Baltic states, the primary factor was ethno-nationalism.

---

153 Nogee, Joseph L., and R. Judson Mitchell. 1997. *Russian Politics: The Struggle for a New Order*. Needham Heights, MA: Allyn & Bacon, 67.

154 Bunce 1999, 34.

155 Ibid.

156 Hough 1997, 112-114.

5.3 Pro-Active and Reactive Nationalism

As described in chapter two, ethno-nationalism is politicised ethnicity whereby groups collectively act to affect the policy-making process. The Soviet Union did not experience collective action until Gorbachev's rise to power in 1985. In order to place the events in both Estonia and Latvia into some type of comparative perspective, we need to employ a general scheme to analyse collective action. We can do this by looking at the changing mechanisms that determine the key characteristics of collective action, such as the opportunities for action, on what basis mobilisation occurs, how issues will be interpreted, and in what way groups attempt to affect policy-making. In other words, this is *attribution of opportunity and threat*, *social appropriation*, *social construction*, and *innovative collective action*.[157]

By combining the importance of opportunities and threats with the subjective way in which potential actors perceive them, we can more closely analyse the causal relationship between these structural factors with action and inaction. The level of opportunities and threats varied over time during the Soviet era. As mentioned in chapter three, the death of Stalin and rise of Khrushchev allowed some groups within Soviet society to perceive the opportunity for mobilisation, regardless of scale. However, the replacement of Khrushchev with Brezhnev eliminated many of those opportunities, although the level of repression was not to the same degree as during the Stalinist era. By the time Gorbachev came to power, the attribution of opportunity and threat had clearly changed.

A discussion of social appropriation allows us to explain why some groups were able to mobilise outside the traditional collective action monopoly held by the Party. Surely these groups lacked organisational resources required ordinarily to mobilise? Relying on traditional Resource Mobilisation Theory would have led us to predict the continuing dominance of the Party's ability to mobilise.[158] So, how were new groups able to overcome an organ-

---

157 McAdam, Doug, Sidney Tarrow, and Charles Tilly. 2001. *Dynamics of Contention.* Cambridge: Cambridge University Press, 45-49.

158 McCarthy, John D. and Mayer N. Zald. 1977. Resource Mobilization and Social Movements: A Partial Theory. *American Journal of Sociology* 82 (6):1212-1241; Jenkins, J. Craig. 1983. Resource Mobilization Theory and the Study of Social

isational deficit? The answer is ethno-national identities. For those who have studied the Soviet Union, this comes as little surprise. However, this does allow us to differentiate between mobilisation within the Russian republic and that within the peripheral republics. Also, it allows us to differentiate between movements for democratic change in much of the Soviet Union and Eastern Europe. This is not to say that ethno-nationalism did not play some part in the collapse of authoritarian regimes in East Europe. However, it was rarely the only organising source for democratic movements. As we will see regarding some Baltic groups, especially as radicalisation occurred, this became ever more the case.

Social construction not only allows us to see how issues are portrayed and used to mobilise support, but also to see how competing groups interpret events that define important issues. For example, it is in this way that a group perceives new opportunities and threats in relation to an emerging contentious episode. Within the larger process of social construction, strategic 'framing' processes occur when activists within contesting groups compete over the development of 'metaphors, images, and definitions of the situation' that support alternative programs.[159] In essence, framing translates grievances into something tangible aimed at those within the group. Not only does framing sustain mobilisation but it is also used to recruit new participants. In the Baltic case, it was the collective interpretation and attribution of new opportunities and threats by dissidents prior to the Gorbachev era that set the nationalist struggle in motion. The way in which the nationalist movement framed issues was partly a product of this earlier process of social construction.

Movements. *American Review of Sociology* 9:527-553; Kitschelt, Herbert. 1991. Resource Mobilization Theory: A Critique. In *Research on Social Movements*, edited by Dieter Rucht. Boulder, CO: Westview Press; and Klandermans, Bert. 1991. New Social Movements and Resource Mobilization: The European and the American Revisited. In *Research on Social Movements*, edited by Dieter Rucht. Boulder, CO: Westview Press.

159 For more on framing see, McAdam, Doug. 1999. Conceptual Origins, Current Problems, Future Directions. In *Comparative Perspectives on Social Movements: Political Opportunities, Mobilizing Structures, and Cultural Framings*, edited by John D. McCarthy Doug McAdam, and Mayer N. Zald. Cambridge: Cambridge University Press.

Innovative collective action highlights the shifts in focus, form, and meaning of collective action.[160] Forms of mobilisation have three dimensions.[161] First, 'particularism' refers to how specifically the forms of mobilisation attach to certain definable groups. Second, 'scale' refers to size. Finally, 'mediation' refers to the degree to which personal connections have an effect on the outcome of claims. These three dimensions will allow us to analyse the change in collective action in the Baltic states more clearly. In general and with reference to dissident activities in the Soviet Union, each new action was taken with the previous result of mobilisation in mind. For example, when acts of dissent began occurring in the 1970's and early 80's without a response of extreme repression, public demonstrations were used to address grievances.

By looking at the changing causal mechanisms of mobilisation in these terms, we can interpret actions of the nationalist movements, pro-Soviet movements, the republican leadership, and even the Soviet regime in the framework of collective action. An even closer look is taken here at collective action in the Soviet Union by examining at three somewhat overlapping phases of the last few years of Soviet Estonia and Latvia. These phases exhibit many common features found in other comparative social movements. The phases begin with the initial popular movements and end with the politicisation of ethnicity.

5.4 First Phase: Organised Dissent

The start of a renewed sense of national identity began with environmental and human rights movements. As Jane Dawson argues, the catastrophic events of Chernobyl opened the floodgates of 'green' protest, setting in motion a change in the political opportunity structure.[162] By focusing on such 'universal' issues, collective action could be initiated with groups attributing little threat to their mobilisation. At the same time, these issues allowed the movements to take on the largest size possible, allowing for a reduction in

---

160 McAdam et al. 1999, 48.

161 McAdam 1999, 141.

162 Dawson, Jane I. 1996. *Eco-Nationalism: Anti-Nuclear Activism and National Identity*

perceived possibilities of repression. Furthermore, this type of social appropriation allowed them to overcome the organisational deficit that was associated with the Party's control over mobilisational resources. In Latvia, protests began over plans to construct a hydro-electric dam on the Daugava close to Daugavpils in 1986. Not only were the ecological consequences on the mind of the protesters, but also there was a concern of an increase in non-Latvian immigration into the republic, again shifting the delicate demographic balance.

A further grievance was the failure of the Moscow planners to consult the local population before the decision to build.[163] Eventually, the USSR Council of Ministers cancelled the project. In Estonia, Moscow needed to increase the supply of phosphate (used for fertilisers) in order to meet industrial demand. This placed increasing pressure on the phosphate mines at Maardu, near Tallinn. After a call to create new mines in February 1987, Estonians reacted in mobilising demonstrations. The primary complaint came from the belief that the mines would cause an ecological disaster, leading to one of the first 'green' protests in the Soviet Union. By May Day, demonstrators were carrying green banners rather than red. An additional possibility of complaint could be that similar to Latvians in the hydro-electric dam case, Estonians also knew that an increase in construction and industry would lead to the further immigration of non-Estonians. The Latvian green movement was symbolised in the Environmental Protection Club (Vides Aizesardzibas Klubs – VAK) which equated 'thinking green' with 'thinking Latvian', while in Estonia it was the Estonian Naturalists Society that pressed for environmental reforms.

A survey of the human rights movements in the Baltic republics suggests that they mostly centred on the issue of forced incorporation into the Soviet Union and the subsequent purges and mass deportations. The Molotov-Ribbentrop Pact (MRP) of 1939 was a primary issue of contention.

---

in Russia, Lithuania, and Ukraine. London: Duke University Press.

163 Taagepera, Rein. 1993. *Estonia: Return to Independence*. Boulder, CO: Westview Press, 120-121. See also Furtado, Charles F. and Michael Hechter. 1992. The Emergence of Nationalist Politics in the USSR: A Comparison of Estonia and the Ukraine. In *Thinking Theoretically about Soviet Nationalities: History and Comparison in the Study of the USSR.*, edited by Alexander J. Motyl. New York: Columbia University Press; and Lievan 1993.

Agreed to in secret, the MRP protocols carried the details of the 'dirty' dealings between the Nazi and Soviet Regimes. A group in Estonia, the MRP-AEG (*Molotov-Ribbentropi Pakti Avalikustamise Eesti Grupp* or the Estonian Group for the Publication of the Molotov-Ribbentrop Pact), formed in 1987 to push for more dialogue over the illegal nature of the MRP. Likewise, Latvian dissidents formed Helsinki-86 in 1986 to protest the mass deportations in 1941. This increased focus on history followed Gorbachev's relaxation of the 'history debate'. Both the ecological and human rights groups were constantly under surveillance from the KGB. Although these movements were not purely nationalist in nature, dissidents learned how to organise, test the regime, and focus their resources on one specific issue. The lessons eventually transformed these movements into something else. This phase is also characteristic of low-level particularism, although such groups as the Estonian Heritage Society were formed at the same time. Both of the movements also exhibit a low amount of mediation, as it was the direct confrontation that forced the Soviet authorities to address both the ecological and historical problems.

5.5 Second Phase: Nationalism Reawakened

In 1988, collective action in the Baltic states became much more nationalist in nature. On the more moderate side, the Popular Front of Estonia (PFE) was created in order to represent the views of reformers, while in October, the moderate Latvian People's Front (LPF) was formed. In the beginning, both of the popular fronts pushed for greater autonomy and democratic reform, but did not call for complete independence. Greater autonomy over economic issues meant that titulars could control the means of production, have a greater control over how much left the republic, and limit the amount of new non-titular labour. Along with Gorbachev's policy of perestroika, the popular fronts represented the movements for democratic reform. In particular, PFE, LPF, and *Sajudis* (the Lithuanian equivalent) led the way for democratic reform across the Union.[164] Muiznieks refers to the relationship amongst the popular

164 Muiznieks, Nils R. 1995. The Influence of the Baltic Popular Movements on the Process of Soviet Disintegration. *Europe-Asia Studies* 47 (1):3-25.

movements in the Baltic republics and that between the republics and the other non-Russian republics as 'fraternal assistance'. Although specifically targeted at the titular communities, the popular movements applied the universal principle of national self-determination. Almost at their inception, the popular movements had established parallel institutions to liaise with other democratic movements across the Union. The limited nature of the nationalist influence in the Baltic popular movements is exhibited by their Russian language publications edited by Baltic Russians. Both of the popular movements exhibited characteristics of 'brokerage' whereby several groups band together under one umbrella organisation creating new collective action groups. Furthermore, it allowed for new connections to be made amongst the popular movements and the titular factions of the communist parties.

Going even further, the MRP-AEG disbanded and reformed as the Estonian National Independence Party (ENIP – *Eesti Rahvusliki Sõltumatuse Partei*) calling for the complete independence of Estonia. Demonstrations were held on 27 February 1988, the anniversary of the Estonian independence day of 1920. Over 10,000 protestors participated in Tallinn. In Latvia, the Latvian National Independence Movement (LNIM- *Latvijas Nacionalas Neatkaribas Kustiba*) performed a similar function as the ENIP in Estonia. Both organisations established 'Citizens' Committees' in order to register eligible voters in their move to elect an alternative government to the Supreme Soviets.[165] The Estonian Citizens' Committees were originally established in 1989, but began operating in 1990. The Latvian version was soon to follow. The role of the diasporas in North America and Australia are especially interesting during this time as increased communications allowed for Western influence to radicalise the nationalist movements. As can be seen in post-restoration politics, the returnees from the émigré community have been often more nationalist in their rhetoric than those who lived in the Soviet Union.

There was no doubt that defining the future 'selectorate' would be controversial and impact ethnic relations even after independence. In Estonia,

165 See Pabriks, Artis and Aldis Purs. 2002. *Latvia: the Challenges of Change*. London: Routledge, 57-58; Smith, David J. 2002. *Estonia: Independence and European Integration*. London: Routledge, 51; and Kionka, Riina. 1990. The Estonian Citizens' Committee: an opposition movement of a different complexion. *RFE/RL Report on the USSR* February 9:30-33.

registration mainly focused on those who were citizens in the Estonian state prior to July, 1940 and their descendants. Applications for citizenship were also accepted from post-1940 immigrants (sic) and Estonians living abroad. In Latvia, only those who were citizens before Soviet occupation were eligible to vote. Eventually, representatives would be chosen in the Congress of Estonia and the Latvian *Saeima*.[166] The establishment of the Committees forced the Popular Fronts to become more radical in their pursuit of independence. However, in doing this, the popular movements reinforced the issue of ethno-national identities.

In this phase, we can see the process of 'object shift' as mobilising groups shifted their claims from general universal grievances to specific claims that reduced the level of both particularism and scale. Furthermore, we saw a change in the way that grievances were framed, in that greater political freedoms (or independence) and economic autonomy took on the semantics of democratic reform.

5.6 Third Phase: From Autonomy to Independence

As ethnicity became more politicised, a natural fissure occurred in the republican communist parties along ethnic lines.[167] Despite the taint of being associated with the Party, the 'nationalist communists' joined the popular fronts in pressing for reforms. While the split in the communist parties can be seen in reform vs. conservative terms, it is no accident that the division fell upon ethnic lines. This split, however, was not an official break-up, but rather an attempt by some members of the governing elite to reach out to groups within society, as was happening in many Central and East European states during this time. Although most reforms were rather more ambiguous, the most prominent were the reforms to nationalise the symbols of state. For example, in June 1988, the presidium of the ESSR Supreme Soviet legalised the na-

166 Ilves, Toomas. 1990. The Congress of Estonia. *RFE/RL Report on the USSR* March 23:31-32; and Kionka, Riina. 1990. The Congress Convenes. *RFE/RL Report on the USSR* March 23.

167 For a general theory on the politicisation of ethnicity see Rothschild, Joseph. 1981. *Ethnopolitics: A Conceptual Framework*. New York: Columbia University Press.

tional flag of Estonia as that different from the red ESSR 'state flag'. Later that same year, the reformers in the CPE backed the longstanding demand of PFE and ENIP for Estonian becoming the official language of the Estonian republic. In September of that same year, Latvian was made the official language of the Latvian republic, and also the state symbols of Latvian independence were restored.[168] The new language law made Latvian the official language in all government and business. In both Estonia and Latvia, it was the reforms of the third phase, borne out of the growing relationships between the nationalist sections of the communist parties and the popular fronts that cause the Russophonic communities to finally stand up and take notice of how politics was changing around them.

For the most part, the nationalist movements throughout the 1980's had bypassed the Russophonic communities. Although the enclave nature of the Russophonic community in Estonia accounts for why they failed to mobilise resistance to change earlier, being somewhat cut off from the titular community, this does not explain the same occurrence in the much more metropolitan Latvia. Possibly another explanation is centred on the belief in the maintenance of the status quo as was pressed onto the population by Brezhnev. Furthermore, on some level there was a belief that Moscow would only allow reforms to go so far before reining in the nationalist tendencies of the titular groups. Finally, what the Russophonic populations were truly lacking were leaders that could frame the situation in such a way as to mobilise group resistance. However, it has to be said that some Russophones actually saw a benefit for themselves in reform and even independence. In particular, non-titulars had been participating in the ecological and democratic movements in addition to some of the popular fronts. Taagepera argues that about a third of the Russophonic population in Estonia actually identified with the titular community.[169] Likewise in Latvia, the LPF had the support of many non-Latvians. Nevertheless, we shall discuss this in more detail after completing a review of the events that occurred at the end of the Soviet Union.

---

168 Rudenshiold, Eric. 1992. Ethnic Dimensions in Contemporary Latvian Politics: Focusing Forces for Change. *Soviet Studies* 44 (4):609-639.

169 Taagepera 1993, 141.

There were many in both the Russophonic and titular communities that wished to see the Soviet Union continue. In particular, those who were serving in or retired from the military saw the independence movements as a threat. Also, resistance came from those who depended on employment in the all-Union industrial sectors, including workers and managers. The first line of resistance to reforms was the pro-Soviet factions of the communist parties that were made up of communists from both communities, although predominantly non-titular. In Estonia, the communist party fractured in 1988 with the rise of Arnold Rüütel as Chair of the Estonian Supreme Soviet. On his arrival, Rüütel began to push the nationalist agenda. The official split would come in 1990, when the pro-independence faction of the CPE became *Free Estonia* and pro-Soviet faction of the CPE became the CPE-CPSU (The Communist Party of Estonia on the Platform of the Communist Party of the Soviet Union). In Latvia, the LCP also split in 1988 into reform and conservative wings. Like Rüütel, the rise of Anatolijs Gorbunovs as the Chair of the Latvian Supreme Council led the LCP to begin pressing for the nationalist agenda in competition and co-operation with the LPF. Led by Alfreds Rubiks, the primary responsibility of the conservative faction of the LCP was to keep Latvia in the USSR. By 1990, the LCP had officially split with the reform faction, by this time calling for the independence of Latvia, calling itself the Independent Communist Party of Latvia (ILCP).[170] In the beginning, there was very little assistance from Moscow for either pro-Soviet group. The assistance that was given came in the form of protecting CPSU property rights in Latvia. Arguably, it may be that Gorbachev was unwilling to support hardliners who believed that it was his reforms that allowed the erosion of the status quo to occur. Furthermore, communication between the pro-Soviet groups across the Baltic republics was pitifully small.[171] In both cases, the pro-Soviet factions of the communist party failed to mobilise an effective counter-revolutionary group.

Although the pro-Soviet factions of the republican Parties were incapable of halting the nationalist agenda, there were other organisations linked to the conservative wings that attempted to use collective action as a means to

---

170 Muiznieks, Nils R. 1990. The Pro-Soviet Movement in Latvia. *RFE/RL Report on the USSR* August 24:19-24.

171 The pro-Soviet faction in Lithuania was called *Yedinstvo* (Unity).

maintain the status quo. Not only were these groups focused on stopping the nationalist agenda but also in halting Gorbachev's reforms in the republics. Having underestimated the initial movements for independence, Moscow eventually began trying to impact the course of events. Unable to tap into the Russophonic community sufficiently to mobilise support, Moscow focused its attention onto three overlapping groups: workers and managers in all-Union industries, hardliners within the republican Party, and the military.[172] In Estonia, the Internationalist Movement of the Estonian SSR or Intermovement (*Interdvizhenie*) was created in June 1988 following the removal of the pro-Soviet Party leadership. Also connected to the pro-Soviet faction of the CPE, the United Council of Work Collectives (OSTK) was created to mobilise workers in all-Union enterprises.[173] After the restoration of the pre-Soviet Estonian flag, Russophones participated in their first significant counter-reform protest. On 14 March, 1989, 30-50,000 people assembled in Tallinn to demand the restoration of the flag of Soviet Estonia and the withdrawal of the new language law which made Estonian the key language in government and business. Again in August, there was a strike called by both groups to protest the new electoral residency requirements. Despite the fact that managers and workers were continually paid through the strike, only 5-8% of the workforce supported the action. Overall, both Taagepera and Smith argue that support from the Russophonic community in Estonia for counter-revolutionary groups was quite small.[174]

Likewise, Latvia saw the creation of the International Front of the Workers of the Latvian SSR, or Interfront, in 1988. Muiznieks points to a strong connection between the Interfront and both the LCP and Soviet military.[175] He reports that Alfreds Rubiks, leader of the pro-Soviet faction of the LCP had spoken 'warmly' of the Interfront. The military's involvement was evident from the very beginning when the Interfront's opening congress was held at the Institute for Civil Aviation in Riga, which, despite its name, came under the

172 Muiznieks 1990, 20.

173 Another example of politics evolving along ethno-national lines is that in response to the creation of the OSTK, Estonian workers created the Union of Work Collectives (UWC). See Smith 2002, 48-49.

174 Taagepera 1993, 193; Smith 2002, 56-57.

175 Muiznieks 1990, 21.

auspices of the Soviet military. Former and active servicemen were a large part of Interfront's support base. The military had a significant reason for entering into the counter-revolutionary movement. Although always present, there was an increasing hostility towards what was classified by Latvians as a 'occupying force'. In the same way, there was also a strong resistance to the draft. Furthermore, just as there were moves to curtail the privileges of Party officials, this was also the case for military officers and privileged veterans. Moscow also relied on the military to intimidate the Baltic nationalist movements by increasing the number of military exercises in the region.[176] Action by the Interfront took on the shape of an attempt by over 200 activists to force their way into the Latvian parliament building on 15 May, 1990, in an effort to present their demands, which were to hold a referendum on independence, consultation with the military about the measures touching on service, and rescinding 'unconstitutional' acts.

While Latvia did experience a further radicalisation of the counter-revolutionary movement with the creation of the All-Latvia Salvation Committee headed by Rubiks, pro-Soviet groups in Estonia were much more substantial than in Latvia. The Estonian Russophonic community's further isolation became evident in the creation of the Interregional Council of People's Deputies and Workers of the USSR in the city of Kohtla-Jarve on 26 May, 1990.[177] This organisation was established to create alternative representative and administrative councils, based on the local councils and factories in the predominantly Russophonic north-east. Unsurprisingly, the Interregional Council was dedicated to the preservation of the Soviet federation as it stood. This two-tiered system to take control of government and industry as a means of competing with the Estonian government failed to even achieve a quorum at their first meeting as an organisation. Thus, it was doomed from the beginning from a lack of participation. However, pro-Soviet forces redoubled their efforts to involve Moscow further in their fight to stay the nationalist movement in Estonia.

---

176 Muiznieks also points out that MVD troops (Ministry of Internal Affairs) and the KGB also played a large part in supporting counter-revolutionary organisations. See 'The Pro-Soviet Movement in Latvia', 1990, 21-23.

177 See especially Kionka, Riina. 1990. 'Integral' and Estonian Independence. *RFE/RL Report on the USSR* July 28:20-21, but also Lieven 1993, 193; and Smith 2002, 56.

The 'Integral Commission' was created on 2 July, 1990, by the USSR Council of Ministers when they decreed the establishment of a 'conglomerate of all-Union enterprises located in Estonia.'[178] In an effort to counter growing Estonian economic autonomy, Integral combined a number of larger organisations into an independent industrial sector that would conduct business directly with the centre rather than going through the Estonian SSR. Kionka argues that Integral shifted the centre-periphery political struggle away from politics and into economics. However, this organisation was more than about economics. It also included educational, scientific, and technological organisations. Moreover, Integral was established to be a parallel government controlled directly by Moscow. It offered social services, insurance schemes and housing projects in addition to political representation. The Estonian government considered it to be nothing more than the continuation of Intermovement, being a bid for power by the military industrial complex. This shift away from the political, however, would further push Estonians away from the Soviets, make them resentful of the 'settler' community, and increase the level of isolation experienced by the Russophonic population in Estonia's north-east corner. Overall, there was a significant overlap of the Interregional Council, Intermovement, Integral, and OSTK, emphasising that the proliferation of counter-nationalist organisations did not necessarily mean the growth in the popularity of the movement.

The final phase was characterised by a change in all of the mechanisms and processes we have discussed so far. With the further democratisation of the political process, the attribution of threats to mobilisation directly from Moscow by the nationalist groups was lower than any time before. As discussed early, the centre had previously maintained control over mobilisational resources. Moscow had partly done this through working within the confines of ethno-nationalism, institutionalised in the federal system. However, Gorbachev's rise to power brought about the introduction of competing power bases in the Soviet political system.

With the rise of both radical and moderate titular nationalist organisations, came a collective effort by hardliners to halt the liberal reforms. Even as the nationalist movements began framing their claims in a more radical fash-

---

178 Kionka 1990, 20.

ion (i.e. independence), there was a growing perception of threat from the pro-Soviet movements. In this sense, the perception of threat had changed shape as the power of liberalisers in the centre increased. The entire Soviet security apparatus was no longer seen as a solitary threat. In the end, this threat was partly marginalised by the inter-ethnic dialogue performed by the more moderate nationalist groups.

In addition, the appropriation of ethnicity as a mobilising issue became reinforced. However, this should not be surprising given the link between Soviet federalism and ethno-nationalism. Before, both the centre and titular cadres were setting the ethnic agenda within the confines of the larger Soviet political agenda. Yet, the liberal reforms reduced the power of the centre to control local events while allowing once titular cadres to reform themselves into nationalist leaders. Those titular cadres who continued to support the policies of the centre were delegitimised in the eyes of the titular group.

Finally, the innovation in collective action changed extensively. Groups became even more particular as to whose grievances they were supposed to serve. The scale of collective action also increased during this phase. Finally, the role of mediation became even more important as the nationalist factions of the communist parties became intermediaries between the titular communities and Moscow. Overall, this phase shows an increasing amount of brokerage, the maintenance of identity boundaries, a shift in claims, and a further radicalisation of claims.

5.7 The Last Days

Several events in 1991 increased the tension between titular and Russophonic groups. Events in Estonia remained far less violent than in Latvia or Lithuania, although they too were relatively peaceful considering the uncertainty of the time. In Estonia, the republic held a poll in February 1991 on the issue of independence. *Izvestia* reported that 82.6% of eligible voters participated in the poll with 77.8% voting yes for independence.[179] Those areas that gave the most favourable response were the mostly Estonian localities of Vil-

[179] *Izvestia*, 1 March 1991.

jandi, Parnu, and Tartu. Vladimer Lebedev, chairman of the Interregional Council, stated that, 'as always, the Russian-speakers population in Tallinn, Tartu, and the Northeast weren't active enough.' However the Russophonic leadership had called for a boycott on the poll, instead expecting to participate in the All-Union referendum in 1991. Unsurprisingly, the referendum results showed a large majority of Soviet citizens favoured the continuation of the USSR.

In Latvia, there were further strikes initiated by Interfront and other pro-Soviet groups, protesting that 'human rights are more important than the rights of nations' and called for the republican government to resign and that the All-Latvia Salvation Committee, should 'take control of the situation.'[180] *Izvestia* reported that protest actions occurred at over 300 state enterprises around the country. The *Saeima* subsequently declared the protests illegal.[181] Several days after the protest, the pro-Soviet leadership acted independently in an effort to sway Soviet policy.[182] They called for the resignation of the Latvian government and denounced the Chairman of the Russian SFSR Supreme Soviet, Boris Yeltsin, as a 'separatist'. Furthermore, in a telegram to Gorbachev, they demanded the recognition of the All-Latvian Public Salvation Committee as the only authority in the Latvian SSR. In addition, they demanded that Gorbachev enforce the constitution of the USSR to protect their 'human rights'. Although these were significant events, it is the attacks by MVD troops, 'black berets', that possibly remains the most memorable in the early part of 1991. On 20 January, MVD troops attacked several buildings belonging to the LPF, killing several people. The failure of Soviet authorities to denounce the violence severely damaged their ability to mobilise the Russophonic community.[183]

On the 19 August, the Soviet interior minister Boris Pugo and the chairman of the KGB Vladimer Kryuchkov, seized power in Moscow in response to the approaching signing of the new Union Treaty.[184] The Estonian Emergency Defence Council and the Estonian Supreme Soviet met to dis-

---

180 *Izvestia*, 17 January 1991.

181 *Izvestia*, 18 January 1991.

182 *Pravda*, 21 January 1991.

183 Lieven 1993, 199.

184 See *Izvestia,* 21 August 1991; and *Nevazisimaya Gazeta,* 22 August 1991.

cuss possible responses to the action in Moscow. Late on 20 August, the Estonian Parliament declared independence through the resolution 'On state independence.' The resolution passed with 69 out of 105 votes, with the Russophone factions voting against independence. Airborne troops from the Pskov division arrived in Tallinn as the coup occurred, but despite occupying the television and radio-broadcasting centre, there were no major conflicts. Although it has caused problems between Estonia and the Russian Federation because of events in Chechnya, much can be made of Dzokhar Dudayev's prevention of bloodshed as the commander of the Soviet military base at Raadi, near Tartu in Estonia. Dudayev denied landing rights to Soviet airborne units sent to settle the wayward Baltic republics. In Latvia, the Latvian Supreme Soviet declared the coup and the state of emergency illegal. Soviet paratroopers responded by destroying the LPF headquarters and the police-training centre. In addition, these same troops attacked the Latvian Republic Council of Ministers building. The LPF subsequently moved underground. At the same time, Interfront did little, but encourage everyone to respect the state of emergency. On 21 August, the Latvian Supreme Soviet adopted a resolution on the 'State Status of the Latvian Republic', which declared the independence of the Latvian SSR. In both cases, Russia was the first state to recognise their independence.

While Lithuania chose the 'zero-option', allowing all permanent residents within the republic to have a choice of whether or not to become Lithuanian citizens, Estonia and Latvia chose to continue with their *de jure* independence claims and restrict those who had not applied to the Citizen's Committees. Needless to say, this hugely affected the Russophonic communities' ability to participate in politics and even in early privatisation schemes.[185] Eventually more legislation would be passed into law restricting who could become citizens and thus who could benefit from citizenship status.

In the end, the relatively peaceful nature of the competing movements was remarkable. There are several reasons why political violence stayed at a minimum. First, the nationalist movements, even in their most radical form,

---

185 See Andersen, Erik André. 1997. The Legal Status of Russians in Estonian Privatisation Legislation 1989-1995. *Europe-Asia Studies* 49 (2):303-316.

were peaceful. This eliminated the reactive nature usually associated with revolutionary/counter-revolutionary relations. The peaceful nature of the nationalist movements may also be put down to being associated with a democratic movement, so that violence would have been counter-productive for the desired ends. Second, the popular fronts encouraged inter-ethnic dialogue. As discussed above, the PFE and the LPF established Russian language versions of their newspapers, such as *Atmoda* in Latvia. Furthermore, the communist parties and the popular fronts established organisations, such as the People's Forum in Latvia, that encouraged communication. Edgar Savisaar, as head of the PFE, continually worked with the Russophonic community as a means to prevent a violent backlash against reforms. Actions like these allowed the Popular Fronts to blur the distinctions between ethnic and civic meanings of what it is to be Estonian or Latvian.[186]

Third, the pro-Soviet groups failed to mobilise a significant part of the Russophonic communities. This could have been the key for counter-revolutionary groups in Latvia where ethnic group parity was so close. Overall, there was a general malaise and apathy amongst the Russophonic communities. Needless to say, the Soviet people were far from experienced with collective action. This 'democratic deficit' left the minority communities without a vehicle to address reforms. There was a general mistrust of the Soviet authorities amongst both the titular groups and Russophonic groups. For the titular groups, this led them to push for sovereignty and eventually independence. For the Russophonic populations, this led many to do nothing, while others supported the popular movements.

However, neither 'malaise', 'apathy' nor 'mistrust' can completely explain the large-scale lack of mobilisation amongst the Russophonic communities. A better answer may be found if we again look at the signals coming from Moscow at the time. Moscow had allowed contested elections, economic autonomy, civil society and encouraged the history debate. In combination with Soviet inactivity in relation to changes in East Germany, Hungary and Poland, these reforms did not encourage individuals within the minority community to protest changes in the status quo. Furthermore, the Russophonic

---

186 Muiznieks, Nils R. 1990. The Latvian Popular Front and Ethnic Relations. *RFE/RL Report on the USSR* October 20:20-22.

community, just as well as the titular communities, knew that reforms were required. They were familiar with the Soviet adage, 'we pretend to work and they pretend to pay us'. The Soviet system was no longer providing the services that were required by the Soviet people.

Collective action in post-Soviet Estonia and Latvia would look remarkably different. Although ethnicity still plays a part in politics, it is not the subject of collective action that it once was. Nevertheless, this dynamic period in time laid the foundation on which the modern independent states are based. Within this chapter, I relied on a general model of mobilisation in an attempt to structure the pro-active and reactive nationalist movements in the traditional sense of collective action. In this way, we can see how ethnonationalism represents a type of politicised ethnicity as well as how structure alters ethnic relations. Next we shall see how titular communities dominated post-restoration politics, causing a change in ethnic relations.

Chapter 6 Politics, Parties, and Governments

Thus far, we have seen how Estonia and Latvia came to the end of their Soviet experience and thus the root of their historical grievances. After the restoration of independence, both states began building anew as well as reconstructing nations. Within this process of nation-building, a large proportion of the minority communities found themselves excluded from this process by structural constraints such as citizenship and language. At the same time, this process was based on a restoration ideology that was derived from the nationalist movements. Thus, these structural disadvantages for the minorities were logical consequences of restoration. This chapter finds that the issue of restoration still remains an important issue across the political spectrum in Estonia, while Latvian political parties have discarded the need for such labels given the elimination of the left-wing as a viable political force. This marks one of the key differences between post-restoration politics in Estonia and Latvia. Furthermore, this chapter finds that the minority political parties did not behave in the way expected, given significant grievances against the state. In essence, we would expect minority political elites to band together to present a united front for change. However, alliances amongst the minority political parties have been weak in terms of Estonia and largely non-existent in Latvia. These characteristics of post-restorationist politics affected the capacity for change in exclusionary minority policies.

Before we look at the main policies that produced such structural disadvantages, let us first focus on the political environment in which these policies were made. In particular, the analysis will focus on political parties, elections, and governments. Consequently, this analysis will give us a greater ability to understand the three most important policies of minority rights: citizenship, language, and education reform. Although the issue of language is a key aspect of contention in all three policy-areas, dividing minority rights policy down into three types allows us to see the specific nuances of minority politics. Overall, this is a political analysis rather than sociological, although these fields are not mutually exclusive. Thus, the following focuses on nation-building governance as a means of witnessing the relationship between ethnicity and structure as well as between the nationalising majority and the national minority.

6.1 Estonian Politics

The issue of minority rights was an important topic in post-restoration politics even more so than during the Soviet era. Tied into this were also other issues such as the extent of restoring the inter-war regime and de-Sovietisation. In this political environment, minority rights often overlapped these other issues. As our interest here is to present an analysis of minority rights policy in Estonia, we need an idea of the political context during which this policy was created and implemented. By looking at the Estonian political spectrum, successive governments, and relevant ministries, we can develop the backdrop on which the issue of minority rights has been played.

The structure of ethnic relations in post-Soviet Estonia was partially shaped by several consequences of the Soviet era. First, the de-legitimised left nearly disappeared from politics leaving much of the Russophone population without representation. With this came the increasing alienation of the non-Estonian community from the Estonian political system. Second, the existence of Soviet troops on Estonian soil for several years after independence heightened Estonian tensions regarding the re-nationalisation of the state. This is just one such reason that more radical policies affecting the rights of the non-Estonian population were favoured by much of the Estonian electorate. Third, the most important aspect of late Soviet politics was the dual power centres within the Estonian community. Both the PFE and the Citizens' Congress argued that they spoke for the Estonian people. From these two organisations came many of the post-Soviet political groupings. Therefore, as Estonia started down its road of renewed sovereignty, the ethnic situation was potentially quite volatile.

As well as declaring itself free from Moscow, the independence resolution allowed for the restoration of sovereignty for the Estonian nation. The concept of restoration denotes two important points. First, restoration acknowledges the Soviet period as a time of occupation. This not only shapes the way that Estonians and the international community think about the past but also sets a precedent for the future as regards not allowing it to happen *again*. Note that political independence was still considered less than assured in these early years with thousands of Russian troops still in Estonia. Second, the legal continuation of restoration allows for the presence of an Estonian 'nation' or community that does not include occupying settlers. Thus, restoration would play a large role in influencing minority policy in such a way as to allow nation-building to be prescribed in non-ethnic terms, while affecting the entire population along ethnic lines. Overall, the nationalist parties' support for restoration is a logical next step following the declaration that the Molotov-Ribbentrop Pact was illegal. If the treaty had no legal basis, this would indicate a continuation of the Estonian state despite its occupation by a foreign actor.

For the most part, support for restoration was divided along the traditional left-right political cleavage. The more nationalist right-wing Congress parties, such as *Isamaa* and ENIP, advocated full restoration of the Estonian nation by adopting the 1920 Constitution. Interestingly, there were even more radical actors than the Congress parties evident when the government prevented the organisation of a coup by a group of émigrés that were pressing for the transfer of power to the government in exile that had been maintained from the beginning of Soviet occupation in Oslo. However, this was too much even for the nationalist Congress parties who were not willing to see their electoral support undermined before the upcoming elections. In addition, several parties with tenuous roots in the inter-war period, such as *Isamaa*, could maintain that their organisations were fulfilling the restoration of independent governance. By pressing for restoration of the inter-war regime, the nationalist parties were attempting to establish an ethnic democracy as a long-term nation-building policy.[187]

As the more moderate parties had distanced themselves from the nationalist parties in the late Soviet period, so did they continue this in the post-

---

187 Smith, Graham, Aadne Aasland, and Richard Mole. 1994. Statehood, Ethnic Relations, and Citizenship. In *The Baltic States: The National Self-determination of Estonia, Latvia, and Lithuania*, edited by Graham Smith. New York: St. Martin's Press.

Soviet political scene. Many in the PFE called for a 'third republic', whereby there would be a break with both the inter-war and communist regimes. The leader of the PFE, Savisaar, was popular among Russian-speakers, which hurt his standing with the predominantly Estonian electorate. Other political parties, like the Moderates, supported the restoration of the inter-war regime with changes that would take into account late twentieth-century concepts of democratic governance. Furthermore, they saw the institutions of ethnic democracy as a temporary solution to integrating the Russophonic community into the Estonian nation, rather than as a permanent policy. Most non-Estonian politicians who had supported independence also backed the centre line of breaking with the pre-Soviet regime, but argued against the complete Estonianisation of the state. In the end, exhibiting considerable electoral support, the congress parties won the renewal issue, in as far as those who had migrated to Estonia since the end of the inter-war republic, and their descendants, were relegated to non-citizen status.

Thus, a renewed Estonia began with the state automatically excluding much of the Russophonic population from the citizenry and possibly many of the benefits that came with citizenship. For example, one such benefit that is most often cited surrounds the allocation of property vouchers. This issue has been thoroughly explored by Erik Anderson, who argues that there was a significant level of discrimination in the distribution of national capital and compensation vouchers.[188] Anderson argues that Russian-speakers received far fewer vouchers than would have been justified given their proportion of the population.[189] The roots of the discrimination, Anderson argues, lies in the Estonian Supreme Soviet Resolution on the Restoration of Inheritance Rights (1990) and the Law on the Bases of Property Reform (1991), whereby special preference was given to compensating Estonians. However, there are several problems with Anderson's conclusions. Of course special emphasis would have been given to Estonians under the rules of 'compensation' since it was they, rather than Soviet migrants, who lost property through the inclusion into the Soviet Union. Furthermore, Anderson treats the non-Estonian population

188 Andersen, Erik André. 1997. The Legal Status of Russians in Estonian Privatisation Legislation 1989-1995. *Europe-Asia Studies* 49 (2):303-316.

189 In the case of Latvia, non-citizens received ten less vouchers. See *Izvestia*, 4 Sep-

at the time of independence as largely a homogenous group. This community in fact consisted of many who had spent less than ten years in Soviet Estonia, falling below the required number of years to receive property vouchers. As Pettai and Hallik argue, there seems to be little evidence that the Estonian government attempted to manipulate privatisation policies as means of discriminating against non-Estonians.[190] Rather, non-Estonians were disadvantaged by the structural circumstances that existed within Estonia at the time of independence. For example, around 25 per cent of non-citizens had been in Estonia for less than ten years. Actually, given the grievances of many Estonians towards what they considered to be an occupying settler community, it is quite amazing that non-Estonians who had not historically lived in Estonia gained anything from the privatisation process.

Yet, if we take Anderson's findings into account with regard to the Estonian government's policies of slowly integrating the Russian-speaking population into Estonian society, it can be argued the privatisation policy should have been geared towards overcoming non-citizen structural disadvantages. Although citizenship was allocated independent of ethnicity, the overlap between Estonian and non-Estonian with citizens and non-citizens was almost perfect in the early years of independence. In this light, Anderson legitimately argues that the lack of any type of affirmative action or positive discrimination in privatisation legislation was by default discriminatory to non-citizens. Most importantly, however, Anderson dispels the myth that exists amongst the majority that non-Estonians, given their connections within politics and the Soviet economy, gained far more from the privatisation process than the titular community.

Such an example as the privatisation process exhibits the complicated nature of ethnic relations in Estonia. Minority politics exist outside the hands of the non-Estonian population. Rather, major political parties have dictated the terms of re-nationalising the state. Thus, to understand the evolution of minority's policies we must first look at the political system. More specifically, let us turn our attention to Estonian political parties.

---

tember 1992.

190 Pettai, Vello and Klara Hallik. 2002. Understanding Processes of Ethnic Control: Segmentation, Dependency and Co-operation in Post-Communist Estonia. *Nations*

Estonian Political Parties

In general, the traditional left-right political cleavage, while existing on paper, meant little in the early years of independence.[191] After the August Coup, the Estonian government quickly reacted to possible threats from the Russophonic community by banning the Communist Party of Estonia and dissolving the United Council of Work Collectives (OSTK). Furthermore, it removed all those in power who had openly supported Boris Pugo and his ill-fated coup. Also, the city council leaders of Narva and Sillamae were dismissed from their offices for refusing to recognise legislation during 1990-91, despite a belated pledge of allegiance to the Estonian state.[192] However, unlike Latvia and Lithuania, the Estonian government allowed them to run for re-election in October 1991, when the old leadership was re-elected.

For the most part, leftist parties were extremely affected first by their perceived connection to the CPSU. There were initially two leftist parties who came from opposite sides of the CPE. The first was 'Secure Home' (*Kindel Kodu*) formed by the reform nationalists in the communist party. Overall, their party platform resembled their former organisation's policies very little. The platform was based on 'security, home, and family'. However, from the other side of the communist party, there was 'Left Opportunity'. While Secure Home did well in the first elections, Left Opportunity failed to garner enough votes to pass the electoral threshold and subsequently dissolved. This made Estonia the first post-socialist state not to have an official successor to the communist party in representation. Regionally, however, the remnants of the CPE were not so easily eliminated, as will be discussed later. Surprisingly, many communists were able to remake themselves overnight spouting a new neoliberal ideology. Thus, what existed was predominantly a struggle between rightist and centrist political parties.

---

and Nationalism 8 (4):505-529.

191 For a review of the origin, formation, and dissolution of Estonian party politics up to the 1999 elections see Kreuzer, Marcus and Vello Pettai. 2001. Formation of Party Systems in Post-Communist Democracies: Comparing Estonia, Latvia and Lithuania. Paper read at Annual Meeting of the American Political Science Association, 31 August - 3 September.

192 Smith, David J. 2002. *Estonia: Independence and European Integration*. London: Routledge, 68.

Besides the lack of a strong left party, party politics in Estonia has looked much the way one would expect given a PR system.[193] The earliest parties derived from the two major nationalist organisations present during the late Soviet period: the Popular Front and the Estonian Citizens' Congress. The Popular Front of Estonia was the leading nationalist organisation in the late Soviet period. Indeed, the Popular Front showed strong electoral support in the 1990 Estonian Supreme Soviet elections. However, the PFE's influence over the nationalist movement began to wane soon afterwards. As should have been expected of an umbrella organisation, the PFE began to dissolve as the Soviet authorities met its demands. The Estonian Social Democratic Party, Rural Centre Party, and a Liberal Democratic grouping were the first factions to break away from the PFE. Eventually, the PFE fell apart and Edgar Savisaar, leader of the PFE, consolidated the remaining bit into the People's Centre Party. The Centre Party has continued to be a significant political force both in parliamentary and local elections. Recently, the Centre Party won the parliamentary elections in March 2003.

Like the Centre Party, the Moderates Union had its roots in the Popular Front. This centre coalition contained the Estonian Social Democratic Party and the Rural Centre Party. One considerable difference between the Moderates Union and the Centre Party was that the former campaigned on a more exclusionist citizenship platform during the 1992 election campaign. The most prominent politician within the Moderates was Marju Lauristin, an important figure in Estonia's nationalist movement. Lauristin had begun working for Estonian independence while in the *Komsomol* at the University of Tartu in the 1970's, had been one of the publishers of the 'Letter of Forty' in 1980, and was a co-founder of the Popular Front. Other than the Moderates, the third party to breakaway from the PFE, the Liberal Democrats, became initial members of the *Isamaa* union.

The nationalist movement had begun with the MRP-AEG grouping calling for the publication of the Molotov-Ribbentrop Pact. With the publication of the secret protocol, the MRP-AEG reformed into the Estonian National Independence Movement (ENIP). As a proto-party within the Citizens' Congress, ENIP continued to push a primordial nationalist line that focused on the ethnic

193 See Chapter IV, Article 60, Section 1 of the 1992 Estonian Constitution.

nature of the Estonian nation. Indeed, ENIP initiated the concept of the Citizens' Congress, which was to be based on the accumulation of information completed by 'Citizen Committees'. Of course, the idea of a continued Estonian citizenry was a key aspect of the restoration strategy. In addition to ENIP, *Isamaa* (Fatherland) was formed as a union between the Christian Democrats, Liberal Democrats, Conservative People's Party, and the Republican Coalition Party. While ENIP was a national party by the time of the 1992 elections, *Isamaa* was still gathering support. The major difference between ENIP and *Isamaa* was the former's even more radical nationalist agenda. David Smith states that many ENIP politicians were even calling for the United Nations to take control of the de-colonisation of the Estonian state. While originally standing as two separate parties, ENIP and *Isamaa* came to be represented in the Fatherland Union or *Pro Patria* in the sixth *Riigikogu*, but did not officially come together as one party until 1997.

After restoration, the Russian-speaking population had rather weak representation in government. Estonian officials fostered a division within the minority community by granting nearly 80,000 Russophones automatic citizenship as well as often co-opting many former opponents of independence such as the Narva and Sillamae City Council leaders.[194] Automatic citizenship was given to those who could prove that they supported the Congress of Estonia from 1989-1991.[195] For this reason, many non-Estonians were able to vote in national elections. Furthermore, following the 1993 Law on Local Elections, permanent residents were allowed to vote in local elections.[196] The first attempt to organise a political party around the issue of ethnicity was actually made by Centre Party leader Savisaar. He organised the Russian Democratic Movement (RDM) as a means of filling the political vacuum left by the disappearance of the communist party. For the most part, the RDM's primary result was to bring together 'new' Russian moderate intellectuals. Smith argues that

---

194 Following the election of the Laar government in 1992, Estonian nationalist deputies implemented a yearly quota on the number of automatic naturalisations, reducing them substantially.

195 See Gelazis, Nida M. 2003. The Effects of Conditionality on Citizenship Policies and the Protection of National Minorities in the Baltic States. In *The Road to the European Union: Estonia, Latvia and Lithuania*, edited by Vello and Jan Zielonka Pettai. Manchester: Manchester University Press, p. 53.

196 *Nevazisimaya Gazeta*, 22 May 1993.

rather than being altruistic, Savisaar was making an attempt to revive his political career after the dissolution of the PFE. The RDM was subsequently fell apart due to infighting.

In preparation for the 1995 electoral elections, two new parties were formed, namely the Estonian United People's Party (*Eestimaa Uhendatud Rahvapartei*, EUPP) and the Russian Party in Estonia (*Vene Erakond Eestis*, RPE), led by Nikolai Maspanov.[197] The EUPP derived from the leadership of the RDM and was considered to be pro-integrationist.[198] The chairman of the EUPP was Viktor Andreyev, who was also Tallinn Deputy Mayor, chairman of the Estonian-Russian Chamber of Entrepreneurs, and a representative of the Chamber of Commerce in Tallinn. Overall, the EUPP was to be as inclusive as possible, including both left and right ideologies in its platform. For the 1995 elections, EUPP focused on less stringent naturalisation laws, the state system of Estonian language instruction normalisation, and better relations with the Russian Federation.

While the EUPP was a pro-integrationist, centre-left group closer to the Centre Party, the RPE was much more pro-Moscow in nature. At its founding, Sergei Kuznetsov, who was a Tallinn City Council member and former Estonian Supreme Soviet deputy, considered his party to be the heir of the Russian National Union of Estonia, which was created by the 'Whites' in 1920 and operated during the inter-war years. In a move that would characterise Russophonic party relations, the two organisations came together to contest the 1995 elections under the 'Our Home is Estonia' (*Meie Kodu on Eestimaa*) coalition. Together, they did what they would not have been able to do alone, pass the electoral threshold.

Likewise, the parties were able to work together as an electoral bloc in the Tallinn City Council, although personality clashes were a regular occurrence. Having said this, the EUPP and RPE were unable to keep the pact together for the 1999 elections. The latter decided to contest the elections themselves while the former remained in co-operation with smaller Russo-

197 I owe a great deal of gratitude to Mel Haung, former reporter for *Radio Free Europe*, for helping me untangle the complicated history of Russophonic parties in Estonia.

198 *Segodnya*, 11 October 1994.

phonic parties. However, only the United People's Party garnered enough votes to clear the electoral threshold.[199]

Subsequently, the Russian Party in Estonia's defeat in the 1999 parliamentary elections as well as a leadership challenge to Maspanov, led the party to decide to work closer with the other Russophonic parties. For the 1999 local elections, EUPP parliamentary deputy Sergei Ivanov led a coalition of Russophonic parties called People's Trust (*Rahva Usaldus*). Unsurprisingly, internal conflicts led to several members leaving and forming the similarly named People's Choice (*Rahva Valik*).[200] What makes it even more confusing is that People's Trust and People's Choice were not divided along party lines but across them. However, while People's Trust was closer to the Reform Party, People's Choice was closer to the leadership of the EUPP and thus to Savisaar's Centre Party. Interestingly, there was a split in the Tallinn City Council election results giving nearly half the seats to the Centre Party and half to a centre-right coalition headed by the Reform Party. Showing where their priorities lay, the two Russophonic parties both supported separate factions with People's Trust allying itself with the centre-right coalition and People's Choice allying with the Centre Party. This led to a 32-32 deadlock on the 64-seat council. The deadlock was broken with two events. First, Leon Tsingisser from People's Choice defected to People's Trust theoretically giving the centre-right coalition a 33-31 majority. However, Yevgeni Kogan, former leader of the pro-Soviet Interfront, maintained a mandate with the People's Trust. This meant that right-wing parties were unwilling to work with the Russophonic organisation even if it meant not having enough seats to govern with a majority. Under pressure, Kogan resigned and People's Trust became the kingmaker in the Tallinn City Council.

This short history of Russophonic political parties in Estonia gives some indication of the political nature of the minority community. The parties involved have worked with each other only grudgingly. Furthermore, cooperation pacts seem to be short-lived. Finally, when it was time for them to pick sides in Estonia's 'second parliament', the Tallinn City Council, the two parties went to opposite corners. Indeed, grievances over state-imposed dis-

199 *Vremya MN*, 10 March 1999.

200 *Izvestia*, 20 October 1999.

advantages, although often voiced, have not produced a single political party with a realistic chance of challenging public policy.

Estonian Governments

Between the restoration of independence and the first elections, a care taker government was formed with Popular Front leader Edgar Savisaar as head. This was the result of the formation of a coalition consisting of the PFE and Free Estonia (*Vaba Eesti*) after the March 1990 elections to the Estonian Supreme Soviet, where Savisaar was narrowly elected Prime Minister. At the time, the Supreme Soviet held representatives from the Popular Front, Congress Parties (although not *Isamaa*), and the Communist Party. Nationalist representatives far outweighed the pro-Moscow forces in parliament, which is why the Supreme Soviet was able to pass independence resolutions without the threat of a veto.

In general, the first government's approach to the Russophonic community was rather pragmatic. For the most part, nationalist parties attempted to make the population, and in particular the 'selectorate', more Estonian. The Savisaar government tried to walk the fine line between the policies presented by the nationalist parties and that of international organisations such as the Council of Europe and other individual countries in the West. The Savisaar government was by in any event not overly supportive of a more inclusive citizenship policy, although possibly Savisaar himself would have preferred such an outcome in an effort to increase his political popularity amongst potential new voters.

With the support of the Congress parties during the independence negotiations in August came having to compromise over initial transition policies. In the first year of independence, the Congress parties heavily criticised the Savisaar government for not taking quicker action on key issues such as privatisation and property resettlement, not to mention Savisaar's view on citizenship. Savisaar did not only have to worry about pressure from outside the government, but also defections from within. After only several months in the government, Tiit Vahi and Jaak Tamm resigned and subsequently formed the Coalition Party (*Koonderakond*), which marked the beginning of the end of Savisaar's tenure as prime minister.[201] Savisaar requested emergency powers from the Supreme Council in order to tackle the growing economic crisis that had arisen as Estonia broke away from the Soviet bloc. In the first attempt, over two-thirds of the delegates voted against the request, with only the Russophonic faction voting in support of Savisaar. The second vote passed once it was tied to a confidence motion as well as an Estonian Supreme Council emergency powers committee. However, once the Social Democrats pulled out of the coalition, Savisaar submitted his resignation.

Following Savisaar's resignation in January 1992, Tiit Vahi was asked by the Supreme Council to form a new government until new elections could be held in September. The new Prime Minister and Ministers suspended their party affiliations as a means of improving their perceived moral leadership by the Estonian people. The most important event of the Vahi caretaker government was the passing of the Estonian Constitution in June 1992 by referendum. Importantly for this study, the citizenship criteria in the constitution were partly shaped by the Council of Europe's criticism of the earlier Estonian Citizenship Law passed in February 1992. The constitution itself, however, only laid out the basic framework for citizenship criteria. Most importantly, there was no attempt to immediately bring the large number of people who had recently become stateless into the citizenry. Rather, the citizenship issue would be decided after the *Riigikogu* would sit again after over fifty years.

Seventh Riigikogu

The 1992 election campaigns, as can be imagined, were based on proposed transitional policies for the restored nation. In addition, parties showed potential supporters their platform regarding the large non-Estonian population living in Tallinn and the northeast. Unsurprisingly, those parties who supported quick economic transition and exclusive citizenship did well in the elections. The Moderates came together with *Isamaa* and ENIP to form a government. All three parties benefited from the elections being dominated by nationalist issues. Furthermore, Lennart Meri (*Isamaa*) was elected president in Sep-

---

201 *RFE/RL Newsline,* 'Savisaar Wants Emergency Powers', 13 January 1992; 'Estonian Government Crisis Heats Up', 14 January 1992; 'Pressure Builds on Savisaar', 22 January 1992; and 'Estonian Government Resigns', 23 January 1992.

tember 1992. He immediately asked Mart Laar (*Isamaa*) to form a new government. From 1992 to 1994, the rightist *Isamaa* dominated the ruling coalition and the presidency.

Table 6.1: 1992 Elections[202] (7th *Riigikogu*)

Party	Seats won
Isamaa (Gov)	29
ENIP (Gov)	10
Moderates (Gov)	12
Popular Front Coalition	15
Secure Home Coalition	17
Estonian Citizen	8
Royalists	8
Estonian Greens	1
Estonian Entrepreneurial Party	1

As can be imagined, the new government had a difficult time ahead of them. The Laar government had the unfortunate task of being the first to push through economic and social reforms on the scale that was needed to change Estonia away from its former Soviet self. Several difficulties in particular stand out. As a sign of things to come, the Laar government was required to balance domestic pressure and international pressure over the minority issue. As the government changed its position under Western pressure, many *Isamaa* and ENIP deputies were unhappy with efforts to increase the percentage of non-Estonians in the Estonian citizenry. For example, initially the draft Law on Local Elections (1993) contained provisions for non-citizens to vote and run for office, as the government promised to the Council of Europe. As it came through the *Riigikogu*, deputies voted to remove the provision allowing non-citizens to run for office. Many deputies thought that the government had gone too far to appease Western organisations. Furthermore, the government eventually bowed to Western pressure and allowed Soviet military pensioners to obtain residence permits. During what was known as the 'Aliens' Crisis' in the summer of 1993, non-citizens also stepped up their pressure on the government, with referendums seeking special autonomy for areas in the north-east.[203] The 'crisis' was an important event for the Laar government and ethnic relations in Estonia as a whole. This event will be discussed in Chapter Seven.

In addition, *Isamaa* experienced a major set back when it only won 5 out of 64 seats in the Tallinn City Council elections. As was to be expected, the electorate was not pleased with the pace of progress, not to mention the hardships of shock therapy. To add insult to injury, six liberal democrat deputies broke away from *Isamaa* and formed their own parliamentary faction in November 1993. Finally, President Meri signed a troop withdrawal agreement with Moscow in 1994 without first receiving the approval of the government, as required by the constitution. This clearly circumvented the constitution and alarmed many Estonians who were typically sensitive to authoritarian tendencies. By the summer of 1994, *Isamaa* had very little support amongst the populace. By the end of September, the Laar Government fell to a vote of no confidence after the Moderates pulled their parliamentary support for the coalition.

What followed was another caretaker government established to take Estonia to the next elections to be held in February 1995. President Meri originally chose Sim Kallas to follow Laar with his credentials as head of the Bank of Estonia, yet parliament perceived Kallas to be too similar to Laar. As a compromise, the President chose Andres Tarand from the Moderate coalition to head the 'Christmas cabinet'. Few changes were made to Laar's ministry line-up. Most importantly, Tarand completed a border agreement with Russia following the withdrawal of Russian troops. On his way out, Tarand oversaw the introduction of a new citizenship law that increased the dismay of non-Estonians, as will be seen later.

Eighth Riigikogu

In the lead up to the February 1995 elections, Estonia witnessed the growth of several new parties. The most significant was Sim Kallas' Reform Party, which consisted of the former liberal democrat faction in *Isamaa* as well as a

---

202 Source: http://www.cspp.strath.ac.uk/estelec.html (Page accessed 7 May 2002).

203 *Izvestia*, 20 July 1993.

few defectors from other centrist parties. The election campaigns were markedly different from the first elections as they focused more on economics than the ethnic state of the nation. A key change in 1995 came when *Isamaa* and ENIP came together to form the Fatherland Union or *Pro Patria*. Even with combined efforts, the Fatherland Union failed to win a significant number of seats.

Table 6.2: 1995 Elections (8th *Riigikogu)*

Party	Seats
KMU (Gov)	41
Estonian Reform Party	19
Estonian Centre Party (Gov)	16
Fatherland Union (*Isamaa* and ENIP)	8
Moderates	6
Our Home is Estonia	6
Right Winger's Party	5

The biggest winner in these elections was a coalition consisting of the Coalition Party (formerly the Popular Front Coalition), three smaller agrarian parties, and the Association of Pensioners and Families, with 41 seats. This electoral pact was known as the KMU (*Koonderakonna ja Maarahva Uhendus)* Union. President Meri asked leader of the KMU, Tiit Vahi, to form a government. The KMU Union came together with Savisaar's Centre Party to form a coalition. The Coalition Party would have been obvious partners with the Reform Party but there was tension between it and the agro-parties within the KMU. Evidently, the coalition was weak from the beginning since there were clear policy differences between the Coalition Party and the agrarian parties, not to mention Vahi's reluctance to work with Savisaar.[204] Rather than a nesting of policy initiatives, the KMU Union was nothing more than a tactical electoral pact.

Once more, these elections show an even greater lack of consolidation around ethno-cultural identities. Although Our Home is Estonia did make it into parliament with 6% of the vote, non-Estonian citizens were just as likely to vote for the Centre Party, the Coalition Party, or 'Justice' (*Oiglus*). In relation to the Centre Party, at this point a governing coalition member, Savisaar made his connections early after independence with the creation of the RDM. The Coalition Party, on the other hand, represented the former Communist managerial class. Such a party can be found in many other post-socialist states that made a change from command economics to free market principles overnight. *Oiglus* replaced 'Left Opportunity' as the former Communist Party list, which again failed to reach the 5 per cent threshold. This centre-left political spectrum shows some indication of where Russophones placed their vote in the 1995 election. Thus, despite the anxiety that produced the 'Aliens' Crisis' in 1993 as well as the more stringent citizenship law that was making its way through parliament, Russophones did not find it necessary to support the political parties that were dedicated solely to improving non-Estonian rights. Rather, like titular voters, they were concerned with broader issues. Already by early 1995, ethnicity had considerably lost its appeal as an important issue axis.

The honeymoon for the governing coalition partners was short lived. The relationship between the KMU Union and the Centre Party quickly soured. All of the factions within the ruling coalition became embroiled in a struggle over the issue of agricultural import tariffs. However, the real troubles began when Savisaar was caught in a surveillance scandal reminiscent of Nixon's 'Watergate'. Subsequently, the Centre Party chairman had his Ministry of Interior portfolio withdrawn. At the same time, President Meri was paving the way for the Reform Party, who held 19 seats in the *Riigikogu*, to join the KMU Union in forming a new government. Still, the Coalition Party and its old and new coalition partners were uneasy bedfellows. After the exit of the Centre Party, a nationalist backlash began to affect the government. From within the Coalition Party came the resignation of Endel Lippmaa as Minister of European Affairs over the decision to extend residency applications to non-Estonian military pensioners. Furthermore, the Rural Union, from within the KMU Union, heavily criticised the government over its failure to protect domestic agricultural markets through protective tariffs. On the other hand, the Reform Party continued to bicker with Vahi regarding finance reform.

---

204 Smith 2002, 93.

In May 1996, the Estonian Parliament was considering a law on local elections.[205] The first version of the law stated that those who were running as a candidate for deputy at the municipal level and had been educated in another language had to take an Estonian language test. Russian speaking citizens in the Russophonic areas of Narva and Sillamae were outspoken about their displeasure at the republic's interference in local affairs. It made it worse that the law targeted those individuals that ordinarily were not affected by legislation aimed at non-citizens. Within the Estonian government, there was also dissent, including all of the leftist parties. In the end, the Estonian president rejected the law in its current state and sent it back to parliament. Soon after, the Estonian Parliament made changes easing the requirement for a command of the Estonian language. As a result, a candidate only had to provide a written statement that stated that he or she was competent to the level of fluency. Once in position, if the candidate was discovered to not have a fluent command of Estonian, then he or she could be removed. Overall, there seems to be little change in the law, although it was worded a bit differently. However, it did give the government the choice of whether or not to examine politicians' knowledge of Estonian as opposed to being mandated to do so.

The continued battle between Vahi and the remainder of his coalition began to take its toll. Mart Laar (Reform) refused to enter into an electoral pact with the Coalition Party for the 1996 local elections. Although the Reform Party won the most seats on the Tallinn City Council, the Coalition Party allied itself with the Centre Party and the Russophonic Our Home is Estonia, which led Savisaar into power as Mayor of Tallinn.[206] Through the squabbles of the Reform Party and the Coalition Party, Russophonic politicians and voters were able to punch above their electoral weight. The political situation in Estonia in 1996 showed more or less a Coalition-Reform coalition at the national level, but a Coalition-Centre coalition in Tallinn. Vahi's unwillingness to break the political pact at the city level caused the Reform Party to pull out of the parliamentary coalition, which left the KMU Union without a majority in parliament. Negotiations with the Centre Party produced nothing other than to bring the rightist parties closer to Vahi. Eventually, confronted with unethical

205 *Segodnya*, 23 May 1996.

206 A position that Savisaar still holds following the 2002 local elections.

privatisation allegations as head of the Tallinn City Council from 1993-95, Vahi was forced to resign.

In January 1997, Mart Siimann, deputy chairman for the Coalition Party, was handed the unenviable task of forming a new government. While courting both the Centre Party and the Reform Party, Siimann chose to govern through a minority government. As to be expected, Siimann's minority government could only do so much. Reform, Fatherland Union, Moderates, and the Right-Wingers Party joined together in the 'United Opposition' at the end of 1997.[207] Unable to either call new elections or empower the Government, Siimann slowly worked his way to the 1999 elections. An attempt to institute language proficiency tests for officials was again resumed in the form of a new piece of legislation in November 1998.[208] This time, rather than violate the constitution, the bill stipulated the requirements in the amendment rather than grant the government the ability to define language sufficiency levels. The amendment passed with the United Russian faction voting against the legislation, while the Centre Party and Moderates abstained.

Although the Siimann Government's hands were tied on many issues, it did take the initiative to initiate a State Integration Programme. Estonia had been under considerable pressure to institute such a programme by European organisations. The Vahi government had talked the talk but had failed to put anything substantial into practice. Possibly Siimann would have also done nothing had it not been the case that his minority coalition decided to shore up support by allying itself with the relatively small Progressive Party.[209] Estonian and foreign sociologists had been arguing for the implementation of an integration programme for some time without any progress. With the new political alliance, Progressive Party leader Andra Veidemann became the new Population and Ethnic Affairs Minister. Viedemann decided to tap an obvious

---

207 The Right-Wingers faction was later expelled from the Estonian United Opposition in March 1998. See *RFE/RL Newsline,* 'Estonia's United Opposition Expels Right-Wingers', 25 March 1998.

208 The *Riigikugo* passed the amendment with a vote of 59 to five on 15 December 1998. See *RFE/RL Newsline,* 'Estonian Language Law Amendments Pass in First Reading', 24 November 1998; 'Estonian Parliament Reject Language Requirements for Deputies', 25 November 1998; and 'Estonian Parliament Approves Language Requirements for Deputies', 16 December 1998.

209 Pettai and Hallik 2002, 520.

and easily available source of expertise, the Estonian academic community. Led by Veidemann, the Siimann government established the first programme to promote the integration of the non-Estonian community into titular society. The programme focused on children in particular by improving Estonian language education instruction in schools.[210]

Ninth Riigikogu

The run-up to the 1999 elections was characterised by the electoral negotiations between political parties as was allowed by the recent elections alliance ban[211]. The goal for each party was to maximise its electoral power at least to over the 5 per cent electoral threshold for the smaller parties and ensuring potential coalition partners for larger parties. Before the elections, the political contest broke down into two main groups. On the one hand, the Centre Party allied itself with the Country People's Party, while on the other, the Reform Party co-operated with the Moderates and Fatherland Union. The Centre Party and its associates appealed to 'those who feel they have been left behind by the reforms or who worry that Estonia is turning into a class-based society.'[212] Alternatively, the right-of-centre alliance promised to continue on with laissez-faire reforms and abolish corporate taxes.

At the same time, the two major Russian parties, the EUPP and the Russian Party in Estonia, were bitterly campaigning against one another. Our Home is Estonia had fallen apart previously due to major personality dis-

210 *RFE/RL Newsline,* 'Estonian government seeks to integrate Russian speakers', 5 January 1998.

211 The initial election alliance ban came in November 1999. This legislation banned election alliances but still allowed individual parties within alliances to establish their own caucus separate from that of their political partners. However, in addition to the desire for political consolidation, it was the legislative slowdown that arose from the infighting within political alliances with nearly every individual party holding their own caucus that brought about the ban. The next month, the Centre Party submitted a bill that would establish the principle of 'one list, one caucus'. These changes, in addition to a law requiring that a party must have 1,000 members to become or remain a political party, brought about considerable consolidation before the election. The number of political parties competing in the elections was down to 16 from 30 parties in the 1995 elections. See Cleave, Jan. 1999. Election alliance ban and Estonian politics. *RFE/RL Newsline,* 21 January 1999.

212 Linnart, Mart and Villu Kand. 1999. Estonians vote in third parliamentary poll since independence. *RFE/RL Newsline,* 5 March.

putes. As the election came closer, the campaigns became increasingly hostile. Eventually, the build-up to the elections led to name-calling between the parties. In particular, the EUPP were tagged 'Soviets' while the Russian Party in Estonia were called 'fascists'. Unfortunately for the Russophonic community, the two parties were competing for the same pool of votes.[213] In such a situation, there was a fear that neither of the parties would make the five per cent threshold. Furthermore, of the more than 100,000 ethnic Russian voters, there was some indication that many would vote for mainstream political parties. As it turned out, only one party, the EUPP, received seats in the new parliament.

Although the Centre Party won the election, the right-of-centre alliance just accumulated enough votes to give them a 3-seat majority. The governing coalition consisted of the Estonian Reform Party, the Fatherland Union, and the Moderates. Unfortunately, the 1999 parliamentary elections are also notable for their relatively low rate of voter participation. Overall, turnout was down 10 per cent from the 1995 elections. Mel Huang suggests that there were several reasons for the fall in participation.[214] Huang suggests that circumstances such as complex electoral systems, similar political platforms, campaign burnout, and beautiful weather played their part.

However, the main reason, Huang reports, was the Savisaar or no Savisaar question. As mentioned earlier, Savisaar had experienced several criticisms of his governing style, including being accused of authoritarian tendencies, and his opponents capitalised on this as a means of harnessing votes. Huang argues that those who turned out were those who loved and hated him, while the people who remained away from the polls was the segment of society put off by this polarisation. In the end, only 27 per cent of the electorate voted for the governing coalition. With the Centre Party's election campaigns of a progressive tax system and softer citizenship laws, very little support for the new coalition came from the Russophonic community.

---

213 Georgieff, Anthony. 1999. Estonia: ethnic Russian voters may play key role. *RFE/RL Newsline,* 5 March.

214 Huang, Mel. 1999. Apathy setting in among Estonians? *RFE/RL Newsline,* 17 March.

Table 6.3: 1999 Elections (9th *Riigikogu*)

Party	Seats
Estonian Centre Party	28
Fatherland Union (Gov)	18
Estonian Reform Party (Gov)	18
Moderates (Gov)	17
Coalition Party	7
Estonian Country People's Party	7
Estonian United People's Party	6

The subsequent coalition negotiations produced Mart Laar, from Fatherland Union, as the new prime minister. Despite his party's antagonistic relationship with the Russophonic community, Laar was quick to focus on the socio-economic problems of Estonia's northeast.[215] At this time, President Meri promised to improve the situation of the Russian-speaking population in Estonia in a speech in Helsinki. He also suggested that because of Estonia's increased likelihood of joining the EU, non-citizens would be encouraged to acquire Estonian citizenship.[216] Although scepticism could be seen across Estonian society, many in the Russian-speaking community perceived the move towards Brussels as a move away from Moscow. While this may have increased the 'yes' vote among the Estonian community in the September 2003 referendum, EU membership will do very little to inspire integration.

There were fears that the economic woes of the Russophone community in this region could produce another period of instability as seen during the 1993 'Aliens' crisis'. Although Estonia as a whole was mostly unaffected by the 1998 economic crisis in Russia, the northeast suffered greatly. Before the elections, efforts had been made by the outgoing government to make Sillamae a 'free economic zone'.[217] The economic circumstances of those

215 See especially, Huang, Mel. 1999. Avoiding a Minefield in Estonia's Northeast. *RFE/RL Newsline,* 16 April. For a brief analysis on the effects of Russia's economic problems on the Baltic states, see also Wyzan, Michael. 1999. Baltic States Still Vulnerable to Russia's Troubles. *RFE/RL Newsline,* 25 February 1999.

216 *RFE/RL Newsline,* 'Estonian Update', 5 September 1997.

217 *RFE/RL Newsline,* 'Free Economic Zone Created in Estonia's Northeast', 12 January 1999.

who lived in the northeast are best characterised by the region's unemployment rate at double that of the national level. Shortly after the election, Laar dispatched three ministers – Economics Minister Mihkel Parnoja, Social Minister Eiki Nestor, and Minister without portfolio Katrin Saks – to the region to review the current situation and discuss government plans for development. One such development plan was to restructure the energy industry. It turned out that between 6,000 and 8,000 protesters staged a rally in May to protest the restructuring and its effects on employment opportunities in the region.[218] Huang makes the point that while the Siimann government worked on the issues of integration and language education during the years of relative prosperity, the Laar government did not have that privilege. Furthermore, Huang notes that the 'Aliens' Crisis' occurred during Laar's first tenure as prime minister.

Yet again, voter participation fell from the previous local elections, with 49.4 per cent of eligible voters down from 52.1 per cent in 1996.[219] The turnout for citizens was not much better than that of non-citizens, at 50.9 per cent and 43 per cent respectively. Once again, the Centre Party did quite well in the elections, particularly in Tallinn, winning 21 of the 64 seats on the city council. With neither the Centre Party nor the ruling coalition of the Fatherland Union, Reform Party, and the Moderates, winning enough seats on the city council for a majority, this put the Russophonic People's Trust in the position of king-maker. Despite expectations, the People's Trust decided to ally itself with the ruling coalition rather than Centre Party. The ruling coalition and the People's Trust worked out a three-year agreement giving the latter the position of deputy mayor. The agreement was based on the 'mutual desire to fight corruption' in the Tallinn Administration that had existed under the leadership of the Centre Party. The position of mayor went to the nationalist Fatherland Union. Juri Mois, who had been interior minister after the parliamentary elections in March, filled the position. During his time as interior minister,

218 *RFE/RL Newsline,* 'Large Protest in Northeastern Estonia', 26 May 1999.

219 For coverage of the local elections, see *RFE/RL Newsline,* 'Estonia Holds Local Elections', 18 October 1999; '...While Results Inconclusive in Tallinn', 18 October 1999; 'Russian Party Ensures Ruling Estonian Coalition Local Victory', 25 October 1999; and 'Ruling Coalition Winds Local Seats Throughout Estonia', 25 October 1999.

Mois had called several times for the easing of the residency permit rules and called the citizenship policy 'too inflexible'.[220] This put a Russophonic coalition in the centre of policy decision-making at least at the local level in Tallinn, with a mayor who had previously advocated less stringent citizenship laws.

The following year was marked by new alliances and scandals. Crossing borders, the United People's Party came under fire for signing a co-operation agreement in May with Yevgenii Primakov, head of the Fatherland/All Russia faction in the Russian Duma and former Russian Prime Minister.[221] The agreement was an expansion of an agreement signed in 1999, which stated that the organisations would co-operate in international organisations in dealing with the Russophonic population in Estonia. According to the leader of the EUPP in the *Riigikogu*, the agreement also stated that both parties would work towards bilateral Estonian-Russian agreements. For Estonian officials, the agreements exhibited a lack of loyalty to the Estonian state. Within Estonia, two new political organisations were formed. Several Baltic Russian politicians of various political parties formed the centrist Russian Baltic Party in Estonia.[222] Leaders said that the party would remain free of foreign influences, whether they come from the Russian Federation or the West. It appears that other than its lack of foreign influence, the new party offered little in policy initiatives, with news sources stating that it would deal with the problems of non-Estonians' citizenship, language skills, integration, and socio-economic problems. Party spokesman and Tallinn City Council member Sergei Ivanov stated, 'in Estonia there needs to be a normal, Estonia-centred democratic party that also deals with solving problems of non-Estonians.' The creation of the Russian Baltic Party in Estonia was an attempt by some Russian-speaking politicians to distance the needs of the Russophonic community from leftist politics. The following month, a new union was established between the more traditional Russian-speaking parties, named the Union of

---

220 *RFE/RL Newsline,* 'Estonia's Interior Minister Calls Citizenship Policy 'Too Inflexible'', 30 April 1999; and 'Estonian Interior Minister Calls for Easing Residence Permit Rules', 8 June 1999.

221 *RFE/RL Newsline,* 'Russian Faction in Estonian Parliament Accused of Disloyalty', 30 May 2000.

222 *RFE/RL Newsline,* 'New Centrist Party for Ethnic Russians', 13 June 2000.

Russian Parties of Estonia.[223] The three participating parties were the EUPP, Russian Party in Estonia, and Russian Unity Party. The union was established primarily to counter the Russian Baltic Party in Estonia.

The first scandal was the result of a power struggle among Russian-speaking politicians of the People's Trust faction in the Tallinn administration.[224] Claims were made by the Russian language business paper 'Delovyie Vedomosti' that Sergei Chernov, former ethnic affairs advisor to the city government and thus close to Sergei Ivanov, was a heroin addict with a considerable monthly drug expense. Igor Pisarev then repeated the charges against Chernov and stated that the faction would distance itself from Ivanov. Leaders within the People's Trust acted swiftly instead to say that Pisarev had no right to speak for the faction. Faction spokesman Viktor Lanberg stated that Pisarev had voiced no objections to the appointments when they were made several months before.

The second scandal was also the result of a power struggle within the People's Trust but had the potential to end the ruling coalition in the Tallinn City Council.[225] The subject of controversy was the return to politics of Yevgeni Kogan, a former leader of the radical Interfront that had sat on the Tallinn city council before the 1999 local elections, but stepped down so that People's Trust could join with the other coalition parties. Gennadi Ever of the People's Trust faction contacted Tallinn mayor, Juri Mois, alleging that the People's Trust leader, Sergei Ivanov, had been talking with Kogan about a return to politics. Ivanov denied the charges and Mois responded that he had no reason to distrust his deputy chairman.

While the Russophonic parties were bickering with each other, the government was focusing on how to integrate the large non-citizen population. Specifically, the government approved a new integration programme for 2000-2007 that was meant to increase the integration of minorities into Estonian society.[226] The government allocated about 72 million Kroons ($4.46 mil-

---

223 *RFE/RL Newsline,* 'Three parties of Russian speakers . . .', 27 June 2000.

224 *RFE/RL Newsline,* 'A power struggle among Russian-speaking politicians . . .', 10 July 2000.

225 *RFE/RL Newsline,* 'Feuding Russian Politicians in Tallinn . . .' 16 August 2000.

226 *RFE/RL Newsline,* 'Estonian Government Approves Integration Program.' 20 March 2000.

lion) for various projects, including over half of the resources going to language instruction. However, by the end of the summer, Leeni Simm of the state language department at the Examination and Qualification Centre stated that at least 5000 ethnic Russians were waiting to take the language proficiency test since it had suspended the exams after running out of funding.[227] There was a strong push in particular by young non-Estonians who reported being encouraged by their employers to be fluent in the state language. Eventually, the government took money from the reserve to continue the tests. The government spent a total of 1.85 million Kroons ($112,000) for the exams in 2000.

Viktor Andreyev, leader of the EUPP complained that, 'the concept of integration is only a one-way process, in which the ethnically non-Estonian part of the society would adopt the Estonian language.'[228] Russian-speaking politicians had some reason to be suspicious. The head of the Interior Ministry's department dealing with aliens, Jaak Valge, proposed that those non-citizens 'ill-adjusted and not integrated' into Estonian society could be sent back to their place of origin with financial assistance from the state.[229] However, the government quickly distanced itself from the draft proposal saying that it was 'not a serious proposal.' Prime Minister Laar stated, 'on those papers there is nothing in common with the government's policies.'

Several reports were produced judging the efficiency of the integration programme.[230] The Population Affairs Ministry presented an integration report in October showing that 84 per cent of non-ethnic Estonians living in Estonia considered it their home and 79.3 per cent said that their loyalty was to the Estonian state. On the Estonian side, 86 per cent of respondents said that people of many nationalities can co-exist together in one country, while 75 per cent said that different languages and cultures enrich society. Another report, released the next week by Saar Poll, stated that 18 per cent of non-citizens regarded the former Soviet Union as their homeland, 26 per cent identified with Russia, while 43 per cent saw Estonia as their home.[231] Almost

227 *RFE/RL Baltic States Report*, 7 August 2000.
228 *RFE/RL Baltic States Report*, 7 February 2000.
229 *RFE/RL Baltic States Report*, 1 September 2000.
230 *RFE/RL Baltic States Report*, 29 November 2000.
231 Ibid.

46 per cent of those interviewed wanted to improve their knowledge of Estonian, while 44 per cent stated that they had no intention of even beginning to learn Estonian in the next five years. Similarly, the survey reported that when asked about their desire for Estonian citizenship, only 38 per cent of respondents wanted to attain Estonian citizenship. Finally, the Saar Poll survey reported that economic problems were main reason of discontent among non-citizens. Only 2 per cent of non-citizens cited discrimination on the basis of nationality as the main reason for discontent.

Despite the mixed results of the surveys, the latest parliamentary election that occurred on 2 March 2003 returned no Russophonic parties to the *Riigikogu*.[232] Once again, the EUPP and the RPE did not co-operate for the election. However, it may have made little difference if they had. While the EUPP received 2.24 per cent, the RPE received 1.07 per cent. Thus, even with their combined percentage, they would not have made the electoral threshold. Rather, polls indicate that most Russian-speaking citizens actually voted for the Centre Party or even one of the right-wing parties. The two big winners were the Centre Party and Res Publica, who received the same number of seats. However, Savisaar's victory was short-lived since the eventual coalition leader, Res Publica, refused to work with the Centre Party. Having said this, they also refused to work with the Fatherland Union (or Pro Patria). Thus, as the Estonian parliament stands now, there are no Russophonic parties and the Centre Party is in opposition with an unlikely ally. This is how Estonia stands as it heads towards its titular language transition in the state education system.

6.2 Latvian Politics

The concept of restoration in Latvia tends not to be as tangible as it is for the nation's northern neighbour. Taking the procedure from Estonia, the Latvian national movement also initiated 'Citizens' Committees' as a means of recording 'who' was the Latvian nation. After the restoration of independence,

232 For information on the latest elections see, *RFE/RL Baltic States Report* 'Virtual Tie in Parliamentary Elections', and 'Parliament Has New Look', 26 March 2003.

plans were laid for the election of the Fifth *Saeima*, the fourth having been elected in 1931. Furthermore, the continuation from the pre-Soviet regime was seen as the Latvian Supreme Council re-empowered the 1922 Constitution. Finally, several political parties such as Latvia's Farmer's Union and the Democratic Centre Party were resurrected from the inter-war regime. While the issue of restoration still remains an object of discussion in Estonian political analysis, very little such discourse is seen in Latvia. Nevertheless, the logical conclusions of such an ideology were still readily apparent in the way they shaped citizenship, language, and education policies. Importantly, the impact of democratically responsible political parties played a large role in formulating post-Soviet policies.

Latvian Political Parties

The transition from public inclusion in politics to negotiations behind closed doors was one of the prominent changes in the political process of a newly independent Latvia. In the late Soviet period, it was important for elites to be seen as including the public in forming the strategy for countering Moscow. However, as independence came, elites retreated into such political organisations as *Club 21*, whereby the process of policy-making was hidden from view. Why did Latvian politics change in this way? The Latvian political spectrum splintered after independence because the common cause against the Soviet authorities ceased to exist. In this new environment, umbrella organisations such as the LPF, which were already fragmenting before independence, broke apart to form new political parties. In an openly competitive political system, in which the focus of politics cannot solely be placed on 'decolonisation', political parties were required to develop policy platforms that distinguish them from their political rivals. From this, we can gather that the purpose of the new lack of transparency is not the result of an effort to hide policy decision-making from the public, but rather from potential competitors. Nevertheless, policy-making behind closed doors is reminiscent of Soviet governance and has led some parties to run on a 'transparency' platform.[233]

---

233 Following the October 2002 elections, *Jaunas Laiks* insisted on negotiating coalition agreements in public as a means of making politics more transparent. However, whether or not this will be turned into transparent governance has yet to be seen.

As post-Soviet political parties began to take shape, the role of émigrés became increasingly important. For the most part, émigrés were seen as politically and economically liberal in addition to representing a break from the Soviet leadership. However, their role in Latvian politics did not remain a considerable force. Importantly, being outsiders, while publicly popular, restrained their ability to become insiders in the new post-Soviet leadership. For the most part, the post-Soviet Latvian leadership consisted of members of the former Soviet nomenclature.[234]

From the ashes of the Soviet era organisations, came several political parties representing the full spectrum of politics. In the centre, 'Latvia's Way' (*Latvijas Celš*, LW) was one party in particular that relied on the popularity of émigrés as well as combining much of the domestic political power. Born out of the elite political organisation *Club 21*, Latvia's Way was able to organise popular politicians from the old Soviet and LPF leadership. Primarily, LW relied on a centrist platform of reforms, privatisation, and Western integration. For the next ten years, LW would have a continual political presence in Latvian politics.[235] On the right, the 'Latvian National Independence Movement' (*Latvijas Nacionāla Neatkarība Kustiba*, LNIM) and 'For Fatherland and Freedom' (*Tēvzemei un Brīvībai*, FF) both came from late Soviet era independence organisations. The LNIM, as discussed in chapter four, began several months before the LPF, while For Fatherland and Freedom (FF) organised around the Citizens' Committees. Similar to *Isamaa* and ENIP in Estonia, the two parties on the right contested the first elections separately but combined electoral forces thereafter. In the beginning, the LNIM looked much like LW although with more nationalist rhetoric and far less association with the for-

---

Transparency and anti-corruption were dominant themes in the party's election platform.

234 Steen, Anton. 2000. Ethnic Relations, Elites and Democracy in the Baltic States. *Journal of Communist and Transition Politics* 16 (4):68-87; and Park, Andrus. 1996. The Political Leadership. In *The Baltic States: The National Self-Determination of Estonia, Latvia and Lithuania*, edited by Graham Smith. New York: St. Martin's Press.

235 Upon the results of the October 2002 *Saeima* elections, LW failed to pass the electoral threshold and, for the first time since its creation in the early 1990's, did not have a seat in parliament.

mer Soviet leadership. Further to the right still, FF embodied the Latvian restorationist ideology.

On the other side of the spectrum, there was the 'Latvian Social Democratic Worker's Party' (LSDWP), 'Latvia's Democratic Labour Party' (LDDP), and 'Harmony for Latvia – Revival for the Economy' (*Saskaņa Latvijai – atdzimSana tautsaimniecībai*, SLAT). The LSDWP was based on the pre-Soviet social democratic movement and even became a member of the Socialist International in May 1990. For the most part, this was an attempt to distance itself from Moscow. The LDDP was organised by several former reform communists in the spring of 1990. Finally, SLAT, led by Janis Jurkans, campaigned on the issue of granting citizenship to those Russian-speakers who were willing to take an oath to the Latvian state without being required to pass a language and civic test, similar to the Lithuanian naturalisation policy. Jurkans had been the first Foreign Affairs Minister for a brief period of time after independence but was removed for his liberal attitude toward citizenship.[236] Since restoration, leftist politics has had very little influence over governance on the national level in Latvia.[237]

There were several parties that existed outside the tidy left/right political spectrum. The 'Latvian Green Party' (*Latvijas Zaļa Savienība*, LZS) continued on from the VAK environmental movement in the late Soviet period. Several pre-Soviet parties reformed with varying degrees of success. Three such parties were the Latvian Farmer's Union, Democratic Centre Party, and the Christian Democratic Union. Finally, the Latvian Communist Party (LCP) regrouped in the 'Equal Rights Movement' (*Ravnopravie*), which at first maintained a strong link to conservative communist circles.[238] Throughout the 1990's, Sergejs Dimanis, who eventually left Latvia to live in Russia, led the party. As the party's name suggests, Equal Rights primarily campaigned on the rights of Russian-speakers in Latvia. However, the party is also a tradi-

236 See *Nezavisimaya Gazeta*, 29 October 1992.

237 After the October 2002 elections, Jurkans led the second largest faction in the *Saeima*, 'For Human Rights in a United Latvia' (FHRUL). He is also president of the 'People's Harmony Party', a member of the coalition.

238 The Communist Party of Latvia was banned on 24 August, along with the Interfront, Council of Work Collectives, Council of War and Work Veterans, and the Komsomol. *RFE/RL Report on the USSR* 'Anti-independence Organisations Suspended', 26 August 1991.

tional leftist party in relation to economic policies. Yet the open relationship with Moscow in its early days has severely limited its appeal to Latvian voters.

After the departure of Dimanis, Tatijana Zhdanok became the leader of Equal Rights.[239] Interestingly, she also led the pro-Soviet Interfront during the late Soviet period. Professionally a former mathematics professor, Zhdanok had nothing to do with the Communist Party hierarchy, although she was a member. She has been something of a controversial character since the restoration of Latvian independence. Over the years she has had to fight several battles. In 1996, she was finally awarded citizenship after the naturalisation office tried to block her request. The naturalisation office's attempts to deny her citizenship not only came from the fact that her communist party history made her politically undesirable, but also because of challenges to her family history. Specifically, she qualified for Latvian citizenship through a grandmother that was originally from Rezekne in eastern Latvia. However, Zhdanok's grandmother was not in Latvia in 1940, instead having gone to study in St. Petersburg before the First World War. On the other hand, her grandmother's family were living in Rezekne at the time of the first Soviet invasion. In addition to her family history, Zhdanok alleges that anti-Semitism played a part in the attempted rejection. Second, she lost the legal battle that removed her from the Riga City Council after she refused to renounce her communist party past. She was elected in 1997 and removed by the Central Electoral Commission in 1999. Zhdanok was removed because she had remained a Party member after 13 January 1991, which goes against the Law on Election's stipulations for public officials. Subsequently, she has taken the Latvian government to the European Court of Human Rights 'over infringement of her rights to free and democratic elections, as to [her] own opinion and freedom to association.'[240] She was heard by the ECHR on 15 May 2003 and the court ruled on the side of Zhdanok.

Given the limitation placed on Russian-speakers as far as citizenship (and thus voting) was concerned, it is hard to imagine the political expectations of the Equal Rights Movement. It was very likely that Latvia would re-

---

239 Information taken from interview with Dr. Zhdanok conducted by the author on 12 February 2003. See also *The Baltic Times*. 'Most stubborn survivor speaks out', 17-23 May 2001.

main an independent nation. So, what did Equal Rights hope to gain from such a platform? Quite clearly, they would not be admitted into a governing coalition, as this would mean political suicide for the other ruling parties. Possibly, Equal Rights was having difficulty effectively assessing the political situation. For it must have been difficult going from having a monopoly on political power to being nothing more than a small special-interest group. Rather than improve the conditions for Russian-speakers, its conservative pro-Soviet, and later pro-Russian links encouraged the paranoia among much of the Latvian citizenry that exists today and made changes to the aliens policy far less easy to bring about. Although the Equal Rights Movement made their connections to the communist past and present obvious, other parties would be continually burdened with this issue.

Since the initial formation of political parties, there has been an amazing degree of collapse and reformation.[241] Indeed, none of the political groupings that exist within the current Eighth *Saeima* existed in the first post-Soviet parliament. During the time of this study, LW was a constant component of every government in restored Latvia. In addition, both FF and LNIM were a constant factor in consecutive parliaments, though they combined forces in 1997 (Sixth *Saeima*). In preparation for the elections to the Seventh *Saeima*, the People's Party (*Tautas Partija*), led by Andris Skele, was formed as yet another centre-right grouping. Beyond those mentioned, Latvia has seen many parties come and go, such as the ultra-nationalist 'Ziegerists' Popular Movement for Latvia (*Tautas Kustība Latvijai*), 'Saimnieks' Democratic Party (*Demokrātiskā partija Saimnieks*), Latvian Unity Party (*Latvijas vienības partija*), and the New Party (*Jauna partija*). It could be argued that most new democracies would experience such a dynamic component to party politics. However, most Latvians are quite conscious about how this is seen in relation to long-established democracies.

Possibly as result of the Latvian state's unwillingness to allow resident non-citizens the right to vote in local elections, Latvia has not seen the estab-

240 *The Baltic Times*. 'European Court to Hear Zhdanok Out', 27 March – 2 April 2003.

241 See especially Kreuzer, Marcus and Vello Pettai. 2001. Formation of Party Systems in Post-Communist Democracies: Comparing Estonia, Latvia and Lithuania. Paper read at Annual Meeting of the American Political Science Association, 31 August - 3 September.

lishment of 'Russian' parties as in Estonia. Rather, the 'Russian' vote tends to favour left-wing parties. While there are many left-wing political organisations, four stand out because of their participation in the political process, albeit often as permanent opposition. First, 'Equal Rights' continues to exist although on a less substantial level than in the early post-Soviet period. Second, Latvia has a 'Socialist Party' led by the unrepentant communist and former Soviet mayor of Riga, Alfreds Rubiks. Third, joining these two parties in the electoral union For Human Rights in a United Latvia (*Par cilvēka tiesībām vienotā Latvija*, FHRUL) is the 'People's Harmony Party'. However, it seems that FHRUL's time is coming to an end. Both 'Equal Rights' and the Socialist Party are headed by former pro-Soviet, and now pro-Russian, leaders that have been judged by Latvian electoral laws to be unable to run for public office given their political affiliations during the Soviet era. Furthermore, Zhdanok and Rubiks are both against Latvian accession to the EU and NATO. At the end of 2002, FHRUL and 'People's Harmony Party' president Jurkans has decided that the other two parties maintain politically unrealistic goals and has called for a 'new FHRUL'.[242] Of course, Zhdanok and Rubiks accuse Jurkans of selling out for a future place in the government, while Jurkans maintains that he is conforming the party in lines with other European socialist parties in preparation for the European Socialist Conference in 2004.

In March 2001, the LSDWP had considerable success in Riga municipal elections. The party won the most seats in the Riga City Council (14 out of 60). As a result, the LSDWP began coalition negotiations. The FHRUL coalition won 13 seats, while FF/LNIM won 11 seats. Surprisingly, the LSDWP began coalition negotiations with the right-wing FF/LNIM, rather than with other left-wing parties. However, the two parties were unable to agree on terms and thus the election winners turned towards the FHRUL. As a result of the coalition agreement, Bojars was elected Riga mayor and ethnic Russian Sergei Dolgopolov (FHRUL) was elected vice-mayor. However, the 2002 parliamentary election results gave the LSDWP no seats in the Eighth *Saeima*, whereas they had held 12 seats by the end of the previous parliament. More than likely, many Latvian voters decided to punish the LSDWP for co-

---

242 See Johnson, Steven C. 2003. EU, NATO help break left-wing bloc. *The Baltic Times*, 16-22 January, 4; and *Chas*, 8 January 2003.

operating with the partly pro-Moscow FHRUL. Nevertheless, the Riga City Council position is important for the Russophonic community since the LSDWP/FHRUL coalition has the ability to affect such policies as the reform of language in Riga's schools.

Overall, Latvian party politics is rather convoluted, yet coming to terms with the process means that we can better understand minorities policy in Latvia. The one mitigating factor in the policy-making process has been the stress placed on EU and NATO membership. Consecutive governments have had to walk the fine line between satisfying domestic concerns while negotiating with Western organisations. In order to better understand the role of politics on the minority policy-making process, let us turn to an analysis of post-restoration governments.

Latvian Governments

After the restoration of independence, the Latvian Supreme Council (elected in March 1990) maintained its role as the main legislative body until elections were held in 1993. The transitional government made several important decisions. Initially, the Supreme Council recognised an updated version of the 1922 Constitution. Following this, the deputies approved an amended Electoral Law originally passed in 1922.[243] Most importantly for this study, the Supreme Council decided to not legislate citizenship or major language policies, but rather work with what had been passed in the late Soviet period. Legislators found it more appropriate to wait until after the 'period of constitutional legitimacy'

Fifth Saeima

Like Estonia, Latvia continued its pre-Soviet republic not only by recognising an updated version of the inter-war constitution but also by naming the first post-Soviet parliament the 'fifth' *Saeima*. An example of the 'updating' method of appropriating inter-war legislation, like nearly every other former communist state holding their first elections, every political viewpoint was represented in the election. The parliamentary elections included 874 candidates

---

243 One considerable amendment was an electoral threshold of 4 per cent, later raised to 5 per cent.

representing twenty-three election coalitions, political parties, and organisations.[244]

Table 6.4: 1993 Elections (5th *Saeima*)

Party	Seats
Latvia's Way (Gov)	36
Latvian National Independence Party	15
Harmony for Latvia – Revival for the Economy	13
Latvian Farmers' Union (Gov)	12
Equal Rights Movement	7
For Fatherland and Freedom	6
Latvian Christian Democratic Party	6
Democratic Centre Party	5

As to be expected, the campaign centred on political and social nation-building. Even with the 4 per cent rule, eight parties received seats in the fifth *Saeima*. As a result, LW and the Farmers' Union came together to form a minority coalition by four seats, led by Valdis Birkavs (LW). Similar to Latvia's most recent election in 2002, most cabinet positions went to those from the dominant coalition partner, Latvia's Way.[245] From the beginning, LW had stressed their intention to take Latvia into Europe. Some politicians were even talking of joining the EU and NATO early after the restoration of independence while many in Latvia thought this unrealistic. Thus, almost from the beginning of the nation-building project, pro-European leaders were in power. The Latvian electorate would continue to send pro-European/Western parties into power.

Despite the early co-operation, the Fifth *Saeima* set a precedent for parliaments to come with several parliamentary groupings breaking down. Most importantly, the coalition between LW and the Farmer's Union began to fall apart in July 1994, shortly after President Guntis Ulmanis (Latvian Farmers'

---

244 For a brief review of the 5th Saeima elections, see Bungs, Dzintra. 1994. Latvia: Transition to Independence Completed. *RFE/RL Research Report* 3 (1):96-98.

245 Einers Repse, after winning the 8th Saeima elections in October 2002 with his New Era (Jaunas Laiks) party, has been continually criticised in the Latvian press for wanting to 'control' ministerial positions.

Union) vetoed an initial version of the 1994 Citizenship law.[246] More specifically, the Farmer's Union withdrew its support from the governing coalition. President Ulmanis then nominated Andrejs Krastins (LNIM) to form a new government. However, Krastins failed to get enough votes to approve his new government. President Ulmanis then turned to Maris Gailis (LW) to form a new government with the Farmer's Union and LNIM. In addition to the coalition fracture, SLAT split into two groups with the People's Harmony Party being the only viable result. Relegated to permanent opposition, this made little impact on policy-making.

Several important events occurred during the time of the Fifth *Saeima*. The most important for this study was the passage of the 1994 Citizenship Law in its amended form after President Ulmanis refused to promulgate the law under pressure of Western states and organisations. Citizenship policies will be discussed in full later. Furthermore, by this time the debate between proponents of economic gradualism and 'shock therapy' was won by the latter. In particular, Einars Repse, as head of the Bank of Latvia, 'religiously' followed the International Monetary Fund's (IMF) policies of strong currencies, market forces, and private property.[247] Any illusions that the population was disgruntled over the negative impact of 'shock therapy' were shattered as the electorate would continue to place centre-right parties in power. Additionally, largely to do with the work of Latvia's Way, Latvia became a member of the Council of Europe and an 'associate member' of the European Union in the early part of 1995. Finally, Latvia signed the Council of Europe's Framework Convention for the Protection of National Minorities on 11 May 1995, although it has yet to be ratified.

Sixth Saeima

Resting on these events, political parties began to prepare for elections to the Sixth *Saeima*. Once again, a large number of parties competed in the elections on 30 September and 1 October 1995. Other than the success of two

---

246 Under the Latvian constitution, the president only has so much power to stop legislation once it has left the parliament. Once the president returns the bill to the *Saeima*, legislators can then decide not to change it. The president then has no other choice than to promulgate the legislation.

247 Pabriks and Purs 2002, 94-95.

populist parties, 'Saimnieks' and the 'Ziegerists', Latvians again favoured the centre-right. Interestingly, the elections produced eight independent deputies.[248] Given this, it is rather unsurprising that President Ulmanis chose independent Andris Skele to form a governing coalition. Latvian parliamentary politics went from one extreme to the other.

After the elections, the parliament split into two separate camps: the right-wing National Bloc and the Leftist National Conciliation Bloc.[249] Both camps tried to form governments but failed by narrow margins. As a result, a compromise candidate for prime minister was sought by President Ulmanis after the first two candidates could not muster enough support to establish a coalition.[250] This compromise candidate was the independent Andris Skele. In the Fifth *Saeima*, Birkavs had arranged a minority government with LW and the Farmer's Union.

Table 6.5: 1995 Elections (6th *Saeima*)

Party	Seats
'Saimnieks' Democratic Party (Gov)	18
Latvia's Way (Gov)	17
Popular Movement for Latvia – 'Ziegerists' (Gov)	16
For Fatherland and Freedom (Gov)	14
Latvian National Independence Movement (Gov)	8
Latvian Unity Party (Gov)	8
United List – Farmers Union and Christian Democrats (Gov)	8
People's Harmony Party	6
Latvian Socialist Party	5

In the next parliament, Skele formed a majority ruling coalition with seven members: 'Saimnieks', LC, 'Ziegerists', FF, LNIM, Latvian Unity Party, and the United list. Left out of the coalition were the People's Harmony Party and the Latvian Socialist Party, typically favoured by Russophone voters. At the

248 By the end of the Sixth *Saeima*, there were seventeen independent deputies, five of them coming from the temporarily defunct socialist party.

249 *Nevazisimaya Gazeta*, 11 October 1995.

250 *RFE/RL Newsline,* 'Third Candidate for Latvian Premier Nominated', 15 December 1995; and 'Latvian Parliament Approves New Government', 22 December 1995.

time of his political appointment, Skele was also chairman of the Latvian Shipping Company and had previously been acting Agriculture Minister in 1993. In the end, the leftist 'Saimnieks' broke ranks to join the governing coalition. Eventually, a clash between Skele and the 'Saimnieks' led to the fall of the first government at the end of 1996. Having said this, there is little surprise that the Sixth *Saeima* was not the most stable given the coalition arrangement. The breakdown in the government came about because Skele refused the new candidate for the finance portfolio nominated by the 'Saimnieks'. Considering the candidate, Vasilijs Melniks, inappropriate for the post, Skele resigned. Once again, Skele was put forward to form a new coalition that greatly resembled the previous one.[251] The major difference was the reshuffling of the education and finance portfolios between FF and the 'Saimnieks'. In the end, Skele's government would fall again, but he personally would be the casualty this time.

As in many other post-communist states, corruption has been a reoccurring theme in Latvian transition politics. In particular, the grey area between government and business is considered to be greater than its northern neighbour. In the *1998 Transparency International Corruption Perceptions Index*, Latvia shares the rank of 71 with Pakistan, while Estonia has a rank of 26, sandwiched between Japan and Costa Rica.[252] In 1997, the Skele Government fell victim to a corruption scandal.[253] In particular, the allegations of

251 *RFE/RL Newsline,* 'Further Discussions on New Latvian Government', 27 January 1997; 'Skele Re-nominated as Latvian Prime Minister', 30 January 1997; and 'New Latvian Government Announced', 13 February 1997.

252 As a precondition for EU acceptance, consecutive Latvian governments have attempted to tackle the problem. Overall, there have been improvements in the level of corruption. In the *2002 TI Corruption Perceptions Index*, Latvia's rank had improved to 52, although with Estonia and Lithuania still seen as less corrupt. Anti-corruption campaign promises played a major role in the 2002 parliamentary elections and is seen to be one of the reasons that *Jaunas Laiks* won the election and why Skele's *Tautas Partijas* came in third.

253 Definitely, support for the government was not universal. Nearly a month earlier, the government survived a no-confidence vote in the *Saeima* over an allegation that the government had not abided by a provision of the Law on Agriculture stating that subsidies should amount to 3 per cent of the annual budget. With a vote of 50 to 16 and 2 abstentions, the survival of the Skele government was not actually in danger. See *RFE/RL Newsline,* 'Latvian government survives no-confidence vote', 17 May 1997

corruption prompted several ministers to resign, including ministers of agriculture, culture, health care, and transportation.[254] Some of the ministers were accused of violating the Law on Anti-Corruption by not reporting all of their assets and business activities when filling out income declarations, while others were guilty of holding positions outside the executive. In response to the allegations, Skele appeared on nationwide television to express his 'great concern about the political situation in Latvia' in that it was producing a 'new and privileged group of people' who did not find it necessary to work within the law.[255]

Several days later, Skele held a press conference where he stated that his government would soon propose a 'detailed plan', but refused to elaborate.[256] Evidently, the 'detailed plan' was his resignation.[257] In part, his neutrality is what made him an attractive prime minister in the beginning. Skele's increasing political influence led the seven coalition partners to reconsider his neutrality and, eventually, to seek a replacement.[258] Over the previous two years, Skele had experienced several accusations such as misappropriating funds and having 'undemocratic tendencies'. Furthermore, he oversaw several shady financial deals involving the privatisation of state-owned properties. Although the Prosecutor-General's Office failed to press charges against Skele or any of his ministers, these allegations would come back to haunt him.[259]

Finance Minister Guntars Krasts (FF) replaced Skele as Prime Minister in August.[260] Just before the dissolution of the Skele Government, FF and LNIM joined together to officially become a formal party (FF/LNIM). Together, they stressed their desire for a tougher citizenship law and the repatriation of

---

254 At the same time, the Minister of Internal Affairs resigned over a fatal accident at a fire-fighters' show on June 28.

255 *RFE/RL Newsline,* 'Latvian prime minister on corruption scandal', 19 June 1997.

256 *RFE/RL Newsline,* 'Latvian premier on government crisis', 21 July 1997.

257 *RFE/RL Newsline,* 'Latvian premier resigns', 28 July 1997.

258 See especially, Zvagulis, Peter. 1997. Government Crisis in Latvia. *RFE/RL Newsline,* 29 July.

259 In particular, Skele's connection to allegations of corruption has been seen as the reason why his party has not been welcomed into the governing coalition after the 2002 elections.

260 *RFE/RL Newsline,* 'New Latvian Government confirmed by parliament', 8 August 1997.

aliens. Combined, the FF/LNIM became the second largest party in the *Saeima*, with 17 seats. President Ulmanis stated in August that he wanted the number of aliens in Latvia to reduce from 30 per cent of the population to 10 per cent.[261] However, he did not say how this was to be done, whether it was by repatriation or encouraging aliens to assimilate.

As in Estonia, the pressure from both domestic and international actors to liberalise the citizenship and language policies began to increase around this time. In particular, with the Latvian government attempting to join both the EU and NATO, the West had a considerable amount of leverage. At the end of 1997, the People's Harmony Faction in the *Saeima* put forward an amendment to the Citizenship Law that would have resembled the December 1998 amendment in Estonia.[262] In both cases, the EU, primarily through the OSCE High Commissioner on National Minorities, maintained a constant dialogue on the issue of the naturalisation of stateless children. The change would have meant that citizenship would have been granted to all state-less children that had been born since independence. The proposed amendment was soundly defeated in the *Saeima*. One of the conditions on forming the ruling coalition after the 1995 elections was the provision that the government would not attempt to change the citizenship law.

In March 1998, Riga experienced two sizable demonstrations by predominantly Russian-speakers.[263] The first event included between 2,000-2,500 individuals who protested outside Riga City Hall. The demonstration was organised by the Russian-language newspaper 'Panorama Latvii'. In their 2 March issue, the newspaper asked, 'How should unwanted increases in the rates charged for municipal services be conducted?' Latvian police responded since it was an unlicensed demonstration and blocked traffic near government buildings. Over criticism of how the police acted, Latvian authorities stated that the police department was only doing their job and that most of the officers that responded were also members of the Russophonic community. The impetus for the protests came from many pensioners' inability to pay for services. Under municipal statutes, those who do not pay rent and

261 *RFE/RL Newsline,* 'Latvian Roundup', 27 August 1997.

262 *RFE/RL Newsline,* 'Latvian Parliament rejects amendments to citizenship law', October 1997.

municipal services for three months can be evicted. Although the laws were not meant to be ethnically discriminating, they had the same effect. While many Latvian pensioners have the price of services lowered because they are single or have many children, pensioners who live alone but do have children are not allowed lower service rates. This especially affects Russian pensioners since many of them have children that live in Russia and therefore do not qualify under the statute. Reactions to the protests and police responses in the domestic arena were limited to the Socialist Party urging Prosecutor General Janis Skrastins to conduct a 'thorough' investigation and determine if the police had violated Latvian Law. In addition, the Mayor of Riga, Andris Berzins, said that the police had acted 'absurdly' and were to blame for the incidents.

The second event was somewhat overshadowed by the unfortunate outcome of the first demonstration.[264] The second demonstration targeted issues of a political nature rather than economic. For example, participants demonstrated against 'overly strict citizenship rules and official discrimination' against the Russophonic community. The second demonstration was actually authorised, unlike the first event. In fact, the Interior Minister, Ziedovanis Cevers, briefly met with the protesters to hear their concerns and receive a petition. Most importantly, the second demonstration passed without incident. While the second demonstration received little attention internationally, the first event sparked a diplomatic war-of-words between the Latvian Government and the Russian Federation.[265]

That summer, the *Saeima* finally passed amendments to the 1994 Citizenship Law. However, this did not come without a price to the government. The FF/LNIM planned a referendum requiring the electorate to judge the change in the law. The referendum however resulted in a majority of voters favouring liberalisation of the naturalisation process.[266] Since the referendum, the citizenship issue has been less contentious and even may have led to the

263 *Kommersant Daily*, 6 March 1998; and *Nevazisimaya Gazeta*, 5 March 1998.

264 *RFE/RL Newsline,* 'Russian-speakers rally again in Riga', 18 March 1998.

265 Goble, Paul. 1998. Trapped by Democracy? *RFE/RL Newsline,* 18 March.

266 *Noviye Izvestiya*, 6 October 1998.

issue of 'social integration' being less important in the run-up to the 2002 elections.[267]

Seventh Saeima

The lead up to the elections was greatly overshadowed by the Referendum. Similar to the referendum result, most of the previous ruling coalition parties did well.

Table 6.6: 1998 Elections (7th *Saeima*)

Party	Seats
Latvia's Way (Gov)	21
People's Party	24
For Fatherland and Freedom (Gov)	17
People's Harmony Party	16
LSDWP	14
New Party (Gov)	8

The consolidation in electoral results was the most remarkable about the 1998 election. Where nine parties began in the *Saeima* after the 1995 elections, only seven parties made it over the five per cent electoral threshold in 1998.[268] For the time being, Vilis Kristopans of Latvia's Way established a minority coalition with the New Party and the FF/LNIM.[269] Both the New Party and the Social Democratic Alliance were new parties who received seats in the seventh *Saeima*.

267 See Nils Muiznieks, former director of the Latvian Centre for Human Rights and Ethnic Studies and current Latvian Minister for Social Integration, at *Policy.lv*.

268 However, with the consolidation of TB and LNNK as well as the fragmentation of several parties, only seven parties finished in the sixth *Saeima*. In the end, there were seventeen independent parliamentary deputies.

269 Up to this point, Latvia's Way had been in all three post-Soviet parliaments. The party was often referred to as the 'king-maker' in Latvian politics. However, it failed to clear the 5 per cent threshold allowing it seats in the eighth *Saeima* (2002 elections). Notice also the balanced nature of the minority coalition established under the centre Latvia' Way, the left-of-centre New Party, and the right-of-centre Fatherland Union.

Kristopans avoided the pitfalls of a minority government by signing a co-operation agreement with the Social Democrats (LSDWP) in February 1999.[270] As to be expected, the FF/LNIM opposed the idea, but eventually came around when conditions had been set on the degree of co-operation. Under the conditions, the Social Democrats received the agricultural portfolio, placing Peteris Salkazanovs in the seat of Agricultural Minister. In addition, Kristopans agreed to complete pension reforms by 2001, increase the minimum wage, and boost spending on education and research. In return, the Social Democrats could neither vote against nor abstain from any government-sponsored legislation. Likewise, they could also not support opposition-sponsored legislation. Finally, the Social Democrats agreed not to submit any bills related to the budget or taxes without the support of the new Co-operation Council. Although the Social Democrats have received considerable support from the Russophonic community in Latvia, it was limited in its ability to apply pressure to the government to liberalise the naturalisation and language laws further. In particular, the FF/LNIM held the threat over Kristopans' head that they would seek a coalition with the People's Party if their policy issues were not addressed properly.

The early part of 1999 saw more demonstrations and potentially explosive marches. The Equal Rights movement organised a march to mark the anniversary of the pensioners' rally the previous year.[271] The interior ministry feared that extremists would use the occasion to provoke disturbances. The Russian-language media played a major role in encouraging participants with a call for 'leftists' to turn out in order to continue the 'fight for the defence of their rights.' Nevertheless, participation was quite low and the rally occurred without incident. The result of the rally suggests that general attitudes towards ethnicity had been moderated since the referendum on amendments to the Citizenship Law the previous October.

Another controversy came about surrounding Latvian Soldier's Day. Traditionally, the day of remembrance for those who had fought fell on 16 March. However, veterans of the Latvian Waffen SS are also commemorated

---

270 Cleave, Jan. 1999. A New Leftist 'Coalition Party' in Latvia? *RFE/RL Newsline,* 18 February.

271 *RFE/RL Newsline,* 'Latvian 3 March rally takes place without incident', 4 March

on 16 March as the day they first fought against the Red Army in 1943. The Equal Rights faction in parliament proposed changing the date of the Latvian Soldier's Day in order to disassociate it with the Nazi campaign. The proposal to move the day was defeated narrowly in the *Saeima*. The confrontation between mostly ethnic Russians and the Latvian police the previous year led to fears that, once again, both left and right wing extremists on both sides would use the SS veterans' march as a means of triggering confrontations between ethnic groups. Again, the march went ahead without incident. Paul Goble argues that all actors involved showed considerable restraint.[272] The Latvian Government announced that no official could take part nor could members of the Latvian military. Furthermore, the mostly ethnically Russian counter-demonstration occurred with considerable 'dignity'. The counter-demonstration denounced the march itself but did not attack the Latvian state. Officials participating at the counter-demonstration also denounced the demonstration by extreme Russian nationalists, who floated a portrait of Joseph Stalin from balloons. The outcome of the 1999 Latvian Soldier's Day event offers more reason to suggest that events the previous year had led to better ethnic relations.[273]

The Kristopans Government continued the integration programmes of the previous government. Specifically, Kristopans called for a public discussion on the 'integration of society' in a draft proposal on several issues such as education, language, culture, and naturalisation. At the same time, the *Saeima* voted down a bill that would have allowed non-citizens to form political parties. The bill was proposed by the new left-wing coalition 'For Human Rights in a United Latvia' (FHRUL) in parliament. While only the People's Harmony Party occupied seats in the Saeima, the other two partners, 'Equal Rights' and the Socialist Party, held seats on the Riga City Council. Furthermore, the *Saeima* once again began considering an amendment to the Language Law that would require private sector employees to learn the state language. All parties except for FHRUL supported the amendment's passage in

---

1999.

272 Goble, Paul. 1999. A Disaster That Didn't Happen. *RFE/RL Newsline,* 22 March.

273 Additional protests occurred in Riga regarding the NATO air strikes against Yugoslavia in late March. While the majority of the estimated 100 protesters were ethnic Russians, the event lacked an ethnic component.

its second reading. On the other hand, Kristopans called for changes in the amendment before its third and final reading. He argued that the issue of language in the private sector should only be regulated in cases of national security, territorial integrity, or public safety. However, Kristopans would not be in the position of prime minister by the time of the final reading.

In June, a returned émigré, Vaira Vike-Freiberga, was elected Latvia's head of state in a rather controversial presidential election.[274] Anatolijs Gorbunovs was the favoured candidate representing Latvia's Way going into the election. Gorbunovs did have political handicaps resulting from his Soviet-era part as the Ideological Secretary of Latvian Communist Party. However, it was the perception by much of the populace and many political parties that Gorbunovs was an unwilling frontman for political forces, namely Latvia's Way, which wanted to increase their control over the nation's political and economic structures. Gorbunovs went out in the fourth round. Strange political bedfellows, the Latvian Social Democratic Workers' Party, the FF/LNIM, and the People's Party came together to support the independent Vike-Freiberga. Early in the election, there were allegations of attempted vote-buying on behalf of Latvia's Way as well as against Vike-Freiberga. Although untainted by the vote-buying allegations, the presidential election crisis signalled the end of the Kristopans Government.

Latvia's Way experienced the first decision of national import to have been made against its will. As a result, new negotiations began between the People's Party, the FF/LNIM, and Latvia's Way to form a new government. While the New Party expressed its desire to work with the new coalition, the LSDWP continued once again in opposition. Less than a month after the presidential elections, Vike-Freiberga asked Skele to form a new government. This time, rather than an independent, Skele was the leader of the People's Party. In the end, all three of the non-coalition parties voted against the formation of the new government.

However, Skele's third time as prime minister was rather short-lived: nine months.[275] Indeed, Skele had made uncomfortable relationships among

274 Zvaners, Martins. 1999. Presidential Election Remakes Latvia's Political Landscape. *RFE/RL Newsline,* 30 June.

275 See especially, Zvaners, Martins. 2000. Skele Loses Job In Privatization Struggle.

his coalition partners during previous governments. There was disagreement between Skele and FF/LNIM over the changes to the 1999 Language Law in order to appease European organisations. Yet the main reason was an inter-coalition battle over who would control the Latvian Privatisation Agency (LPA). In particular, the LPA was established to determine the sale of large-scale industrial holdings such as Latvijas Gaze and Latvenergo. Additionally, the LPA would determine the sale of state-owned shares of the large shipping company Ventspils NAFTA, a traditional power-base for Latvia's Way. The beginning of the end occurred when Skele fired Economics Minister Vladimirs Makarovs (FF/LNIM) for interfering in the privatisation process. With the breakdown in the coalition as well as a no-confidence vote scheduled by the opposition, Skele resigned. President Vike-Freiberga, after courting both current Bank of Latvia President Repse and Ingride Udre (New Party), chose Riga Mayor Andris Berzins (LW) as the new prime minister. The new coalition included Latvia's Way, the People's Party, the FF/LNIM, and the New Party.

Under the new government, two issues dominated minority public policy: local voting for non-citizens and the implementation of the 1999 language law. Unsurprisingly, Latvian non-citizens had not been granted the right to vote in local elections. Unlike in Estonia, where only permanent residents can vote in local elections, a group of non-citizens were trying to persuade the government to allow some 500,000 non-citizens to vote. As was to be expected, the governing coalition was unwilling to consider the issue. In response, the non-citizen group began collecting signatures in order to force the Latvian Central Commission (electoral commission) to place the question on a ballot in a referendum. Prime Minister Berzins stated on Latvian State Radio that the proportion of non-citizens would have to be much lower in order to allow them to participate in local elections.[276] However, he did concede that, given the current naturalisation rate, non-citizens could be 'granted voting rights in the elections after the next one'. Similarly, President Vike-Freiberga stated that the right to vote should only apply to citizens. There are many 'liberal' democracies where non-citizens do not have the right to vote.

RFE/RL Baltic States Report 1 (13).

276 *RFE/RL Baltic States Report* 'Local voting for non-citizens surfacing as issue', 7 June 2000, 1(20).

However, the large proportion of society that has been excluded from citizenship and thus politics is not seen in those same countries.

Despite the disenfranchisement of the minority community, voters who wanted to see a change in minority policies made a significant mark on the most recent elections. In terms of vote proportion, the October 2002 elections saw FHRUL receive 25 seats out of 100, one less seat than the election winner New Era. FHRUL's success was the largest capture of seats so far by a party representing the Russophonic community in Latvian national elections. Significantly, the result of over 18 per cent suggests that there are ethnic Latvians who sympathise with a more liberal stance on citizenship, language, and education as well as left-wing politics in general.[277] However, despite personality clashes between the leaders of the two successful moderate right parties, Repse (New Era) and Skele (People's Party), it seemed a more likely outcome that they would form a government before either party would negotiate with FHRUL. As it turned out, both FHRUL and the People's Party make up the opposition in the new Eighth *Saeima*. Understandably, most Latvian political parties find it difficult to work with a party that is seen as pro-Moscow. Although FHRUL has continually repeated its loyalty to an independent Latvian state, party leaders also have not gone out of their way to disassociate themselves from the Russian Federation. For example, just before the 2002 parliamentary elections, party leader Jurkans met with Vladimir Putin while in Moscow meeting with the Duma's deputy secretary; a meeting that many international observers have stated seems strange considering Jurkans' political position. Many in Latvia believe that working with FHRUL in local government was the downfall of the Latvian Social Democratic Workers' Party.

The election of the new party New Era as well as the inability of Latvia's Way to obtain five per cent of the vote means that many parliamentary deputies, who have worked with regional and international organizations over Latvia's minority community, will be outside the eighth *Saeima*. Latvia's Way, in particular, had been a member of all three governments since independence

277 It is important to note that the other left-wing party competing in the elections, the Latvian Social Democratic Workers' Party, did not get over the 5 per cent threshold allowing seats in the *Saeima*.

and had continually held some posts such as Minister of Foreign Affairs.[278] Further pressure to liberalize the citizenship and language laws may come from the negotiations between Latvia and its current partners in accession negotiations – the EU and NATO. However, the Latvian Human Rights Committee argues that neither organization has the "legal instruments nor special assessment procedures nor expertise in this field, while negotiations at the level of political bargaining are hardly effective."[279] Indeed, many current members of these institutions continue to have their own problems with minority communities.

Latvia's post-Soviet social policy has been largely a product of history and is unlikely to change under the new parliament. Understandably, Latvians see the state as the protector of the Latvian language and culture. Furthermore, many Latvians still have resentment over the years of Sovietisation, and the Russophonic community often pays for it politically, although not economically. Both of these facts continue to govern social policy. While the Latvian government has encouraged integration, the result of the latest elections may discourage many non-citizens from seeking citizenship. As Latvia seeks to join the "West", it still has an important socio-political problem with which to deal.

6.3 Conclusion

As stated earlier, the purpose of this discussion was primarily to become familiar with the political systems in Estonia and Latvia. From this, we can go on to look at the individual policies that have most affected the minority community. These policies were constructed within the political environments just described. At this stage, it may be helpful to compare and contrast the Estonian and Latvian political environments. The concept of restoration became an important mobilising force in both states during the late Soviet period. In Estonia, restoration still remains an important political issue as it relates to

278 Up until the 2002 elections, Latvia's Way had been referred to as the 'king-maker'. In fact, the party was one of the few constants in post-Soviet Latvian politics.

279 *Minority Issues in Latvia*, 15 October 2002, (57): http://www.friends-partners.org/partners/rpiac/lhrc/en/main.phtml.

political legitimacy. In Latvia, on the other hand, while there is an importance placed on tying current political actors to the nationalist movements, restoration is not a dominant political issue. Why is this the case? It may be that the political spectrum in Estonia is much broader than in Latvia and thus restoration is an easy, often indefinable, concept with which Estonian parties brand their platforms. In Latvia, the left predominantly revolves around the Russian-speaking population and has little effect on policy-making, while centre-right parties look much the same, only distinguishable by their popular leaders. In the Latvian case, political authority has less to do with the past. Having said this, as we shall see, both countries are quite similar in how they have interpreted restoration for their early citizenship policies.

Furthermore, both states have a similar record in relation to the decline of the popular fronts and rise of the nationalist parties after independence. Political actors within the popular fronts no longer had a common platform on which to stand once independence was achieved. While the PFE actually made it into the first post-Soviet Estonia parliament, the LPF did not in Latvia. Nevertheless, the PFE was in its last days and the Centre Party would rise from its ashes. Although the current Latvian prime minister has his roots in the LPF, there was not a similar Latvian political party. Similarly, both countries experienced high electoral support for centre-right nationalist parties in the first post-Soviet elections, although they were much more successful in Estonia. However, while the right-wing parties fell from grace in the second elections, Latvia's nationalist parties held on to approximately the same number of seats. As stated before, Latvia did not experience a shift to the left like Estonia because there was no viable alternative. Despite the differences, minority policy in both states remained consistent, as we shall see.

The response to this policy by the minority community in the political arena has been different in the two countries. We should expect that as the minority community experiences perceived discrimination, minority political elites would unite as a means of having the largest effect on the policy-making process. In Estonia, the minority community originally came together in the RDM, then the Our Home is Estonia coalition, and later the EUPP. Interestingly, as the citizenship law was reformed in 1997 and the language law in 1998, the two major Russian parties, the EUPP and the RPE, have been unable to co-operate as the conflict between People's Trust and People's Choice exhibits.

However, in Latvia, there was a lack of unity in the beginning. In particular, SLAT and the Equal Rights Movement were elected to the fifth *Saeima* as separate parties. Likewise, SLAT's successor, the People's Harmony Party, as well as the Latvian Socialist Party did not run on the same electoral ticket in 1995. Finally, in 1999, only the People's Harmony Party was able to receive seats in parliament. During this time, there was co-operation amongst these parties, which traditionally represent the minority community, in local councils. However, the unity in national politics did not come until after the 1998 elections in the form of FHRUL, which received the second largest amount of votes in the 2002 elections. It is interesting to see that increased co-operation came after the revised Latvian citizenship law in 1998, indicating that unity in Latvia is the result of electoral strategies rather than a reaction to discrimination. Furthermore, as has been discussed above, the FHRUL in Latvia may be going the same way as the People's Trust/Choice debate in Estonia following the People's Harmony Party's decision to leave the coalition in local government.

Finally, Estonia differs from Latvia in the structural disadvantages established under the electoral laws. Specifically, much of the minority in Estonia was able to vote at least in local elections in Estonia because permanent residents were allowed under the electoral law. In Latvia, this was not the case. Not only were permanent residents not allowed to vote in local elections, but also the Latvian citizenship law would deny much of the minority community the opportunity of gaining citizenship until after 2000. Thus, at least at the local level, Russian-speakers in Estonia had much greater say in general public policy. Of course, the ratio of titulars to minorities means that Estonia is far more Estonian than Latvia is Latvian. Thus, Estonia can afford to allow local voting for permanent residents as it is less likely to disrupt the nation-building process where Latvia politicians were far more unwilling to take the risk. Overall, much of these similarities and differences can be seen in the citizenship, language, and education laws in the two states. With an understanding of the political context under which these policies have been made, we may better understand the structural limitations placed on the minority communities and thus the overall political relationship between the titular majorities and the national minorities.

Chapter 7 Minority Policies

In addition to the everyday relationship between majority and minority, these groups have interacted also within the political system. As is to be expected, the majority groups have had much greater control over the lives of minorities than the other way around. Given the political opportunity structure in both states, minorities have had little input into the policy-making systems. In this chapter, we shall see three examples of how the majority-group-dominated political systems have affected relations between the titular and minority communities. These policy areas are citizenship, language, and education. While the two countries' policies are quite similar, there are some significant differences. Furthermore, it is important to point out that language is the one issue central to the naturalisation and education issues. Let us first turn to Estonia and citizenship.

7.1 Estonian Citizenship Policy

As stated earlier, the issue of citizenship was a subject of debate between moderate and nationalist independence movements.[280] Within Estonia, there were three different perspectives on the issue of citizenship. First, Russophonic politicians, mostly from the Narva and Sillamae City Councils, argued for an inclusive citizenship policy, allowing for all permanent residents to become citizens. Second, radical nationalists such as ENIP and later *Isamaa* were firmly against allowing 'colonists' to become citizens. In some cases, members actually contemplated establishing repatriation programmes. A logical conclusion of the restoration ideology was giving automatic citizenship only to those were citizens, or descendants, of the earlier independent Estonia (before 1940). In fact, the Citizens' Committees were established for accumulating evidence on who made up the Estonian citizenry. Although the

280 See Kionka, Riina. 1991. Who Should Become a Citizen of Estonia? *RFE/RL Report on the USSR* 3 (39).

implications of this argument meant the citizenship would be broken down along ethnic lines, the criterion was not ethnically based. Finally, the moderate nationalists from the collapsed Popular Front supported allowing citizens to have the option of choosing Estonian or Soviet citizenship. For those who were willing to give their loyalty to an independent Estonia, no other conditions would be required for citizenship. Savisaar argued that this was a way to recognise those in the Russophonic community who had supported the independence movement.

However, both the Russophonic and moderate nationalists' proposals were unrealistic, given the grievances of the Estonian people over the illegal nature of the Soviet occupation. Furthermore, Russian troops were still stationed in Estonia, making the non-Estonian population seem larger than it was in actuality. Finally, it was perceived by many Estonians that Russophones would not be loyal to an independent Estonia, but rather to attempts to rebuild the USSR or to the Russian Federation (at the time a realistic perception). For this reason, Estonians were understandably unwilling to give the rights of citizenship to those who did not fulfil the citizenship requirements proposed by the radical nationalist parties.

Although citizenship policies had their roots in the 1938 Citizenship Law, the first modern policy came in 1990. In July, the Estonian Supreme Council passed an immigration law that matched the more stringent policies proposed by the Congress Parties.[281] In particular, the law instituted yearly immigration quotas and restrictions on temporary and permanent residency.[282] Importantly, the 1990 Immigration Law and the 1940 amendments to the 1938 Citizenship Law set the precedence for the 1992 Citizenship Law. Estonia wasted little time after the restoration of independence in passing a new citizenship law set on the *jus sanguinis* principle.[283] In other words, citizenship automatically applied only to those who were citizens before June 1940 and their direct descendants. The remaining part of the population would have to be processed through a naturalisation service. Similar to other

281 *RFE/RL Daily Report*, 'Estonia Passes Immigration Law', 6 July 1990.

282 The yearly immigration quotas are more significant than they may appear in hindsight. At the time, few would have imagined that independence was little over a year away.

283 *RFE/RL Newsline,* 'Estonian Citizenship Law Passed', 27 February 1992.

nations' naturalisation procedures, applicants would have to take an oath of loyalty to the Estonian state, demonstrate competence in the Estonian language, and will have been required to permanently reside in Estonia since the passing of the resolution on independence in March 1990. In effect, the law broke Estonian society into two groups. The citizenry primarily comprised ethnic Estonians. On the other hand, the second group of non-citizens were predominantly Russian-speaking Slavs, although not all Russian. Moderates were willing to support the citizenship law as a short-term solution while more nationalist forces saw it as a means of nationalising the state for the long term.

Anxieties were heightened with the passage of the 1993 Law on Aliens.[284] The law stated that those who held Soviet passports had to submit new applications for residency within one year. Of course, the problem with being required to work through an application procedure is the possibility that you may be rejected. The failure to submit an application would lead the government to consider the Soviet passport holder an illegal immigrant and make deportation possible. Most controversial, the government failed to make a distinction between short and long-term residents. It made little difference if you were born in Soviet Estonia or had immigrated to the republic in the last days before independence. Furthermore, only temporary five-year permits were to be granted. This meant that someone with a resident permit could never be quite sure if the next application might be rejected. Additionally, the Law on Aliens gave Soviet passport holders less than a year to register for non-citizen status. Finally, the law left many terms vague and thus open to interpretation.

The minority community had been building up towards a showdown with the government starting with industrial strikes in 1992. Indeed, the heavily industrial, all-Union northeast was badly affected by shock therapy policies. For the most part, non-Estonians were mostly employed in medium to heavy industry propped up by the Soviet regime. When the Soviet Union collapsed, so did most of these unprofitable factories. This left the Russophonic communities in Narva, Tallinn, and Sillamae coping with the bulk of the overall de-

---

284 *RFE/RL Newsline,* 'New Estonian Law on Foreigners', 22 June 1993. See also *Izvesti*, 8 May 1997.

clines in Estonian industrial production. In addition, they suffered rampant unemployment problems and the collapse of monetary circulation. All of this was compounded by the citizenship problem. In response, the leaders of the Narva trade unions planned a two-hour industrial strike.[285] The strike committees in Narva, Sillamae, and Tallinn began their two-hour strike on the 23 April. Their demands were for a Joint Commission of the Estonian Parliament with representation for the city councils of Narva and Sillamae, trade unions, and the nearly defunct Russian Democratic Movement. Unfazed, the Estonian government only promised to hold future negotiations.

However, with the passage of the Law on Aliens, non-Estonian politicians felt that this was their time to act, although there was little that they could do. The events that followed became known as the 'Aliens' Crisis'. Again, politicians in the northeast called for better representation and access to policy-making in Tallinn. As was to be expected, the Laar government was unsympathetic. In response to the government's inaction, the Narva and Sillamae City Councils chose to hold a referendum for autonomy within the Estonian Republic.[286] The question asked was, '[D]o you want [area name, i.e. Narva] to have the status of territorial autonomous entity within the Estonian Republic?'[287] This brings us back to the discussion in Chapter Two regarding institutions and democracy. Autonomy in Idu-Virumaa would have represented a change from constitutional neutrality to a consociational approach. However, such an approach leaves out the large minority community in Tallinn. Furthermore, greater autonomy in the northeast would challenge Estonia's level of 'national integrity'.

The planning of the referendum did have one immediate effect. The Estonian government responded by revoking the promise of simplifying the naturalisation procedure. In Narva, 57.4% of eligible voters went to the polls and more than 97% supported the move for autonomy. In Sillamae, 61% of the eligible population participated and 98% chose autonomy. Aleksandr Maksimenko, Sillamae City Council Chairman, said 'autonomy is the only peaceful means to bring laws that discriminate against the Russian-speaking

285 *Nevazisimaya Gazeta*, 23 April 1992.
286 *Segodnya*, 16 July 1993.
287 *Nevazisimaya Gazeta*, 17 July 1993.

population into conformity with democratic norms.'[288] Rather than actually press for autonomy, the Narva City Council Chairman, Vladimer Chuikin, stated that the results of the referendum would give weight behind future talks. However, there is very little indication that the referendums did anything except harass the Laar government and prolong revisions of the naturalisation procedures.[289]

Despite international pressure such as recommendations of the OSCE High Commissioner, there was very little support for changes to the rights of non-citizens. The Laar government had already allowed permanent residents the right to vote in local elections as well as allowing military pensioners the privilege of obtaining permanent resident permits.[290] Needless to say, his party (*Isamaa*) was not pleased. The Estonian Government did concede one change in an amendment passed in June 1994 that allowed a one-year extension to the registration deadline imposed by the Law on Aliens. However, the legalistic ambiguities in the law, such as the failure to define the term 'lawful source of income', were not made more specific. Smith argues that these ambiguities existed in the first place so that the Government could appease Western organisations while at the same time allowing the political administration to interpret the law in the most conservative sense.[291] However, the Estonian Parliament signed a revised Law on Aliens that took into account the recommendations of the OSCE and the Council of Europe.[292]

The events that led to the 'Aliens' Crisis', as well as the crisis itself, can easily be construed as the result of historical and current grievances between the Estonians and the Russophones. Historically, Estonia was a colony within the Russian Empire and then forced to become a Soviet Republic within the Soviet Union. Obviously, there was resentment amongst many Estonians against the vestiges of their former Soviet rulers. Also, there were at that time widespread feelings of helplessness and betrayal within the Russophonic community as they were predominantly excluded from citizenship. However,

---

288 *Izvestia*, 20 July 1993.

289 *RFE/RL Newsline,* 'Reactions to Referendums in Estonia', 20 July 1993.

290 *Nevazisimaya Gazeta*, 22 May 1993.

291 Smith, David J. 2002. *Estonia: Independence and European Integration*. London: Routledge, 86.

292 *RFE/RL Newsline,* 'Estonian Parliament Amends Law on Aliens', 9 July 1993.

evidence suggests that rather than a clash between ethnic groups, where there was an extremely low level of violence, it was rather a crisis for the Laar government. Laar was forced to play a two-level game in which he balanced the governing coalition's nationalist agenda with the need for Western integration. Both components were seen as survival strategies for the Estonian nation. The more 'Estonianised' the state, the greater level of trust amongst the populace. Also, the greater level of integration, the less likely the West would be willing to tolerate the loss of Estonian sovereignty again.

The Law on Aliens remained practically the same until August 1998 when, under Population and Ethnic Affairs Minister Andra Veidemann, the law was changed to allow spouses and children of citizens not to be restricted by annual quotas.[293] Under the 1993 Law on Aliens, only 0.05 per cent of the population could apply for permanent residency in a given year. The changes also applied to citizens of EU countries, among others. The changes really only affected those non-Estonians who had married an Estonian but had not yet received permanent residency, the number of which was few. However, this small change does show that the Estonian government was actively reviewing policy.

On the other hand, the *Riigikogu* passed an amendment to the Law on Aliens that would allow non-citizens to apply for permanent residence permits in July 1997.[294] Specifically, the amendment was aimed at those who had applied for temporary residence permits before 12 July 1995. It was estimated that this would affect some 200,000 non-citizens, most of whom were Russian-speaking. Notably, the opposition Fatherland Union opposed the amendments. Yet the government remained vigilant in restricting residence permits for nine Russian reserve officers because they 'posed a threat to Estonia's security'.[295] The government drew this conclusion because the men could have been called to active duty for Russia. However, the situation was

---

293 See *RFE/RL Newsline*, 'Estonian Government Adopts Amendments to Aliens Law', 12 August 1998. This was not completely the case. An amendment was passed in January 1995 to extend the residence requirements from 3 to 6 years. To the chagrin of the rightist parties, this did not apply to those already living in Estonia before the restoration of independence. See *Segodnya*, 20 January 1995

294 *Segodnya*, 28 June 1995.

295 *RFE/RL Newsline,* 'Estonia Refuses Residence Permits to Nine Russian Reserve Officers', 23 July 1997.

even more complicated because all nine of the former Soviet servicemen were married to Estonian citizens.

The cabinet rejected calls by Russian deputies of the Estonian Parliament to amend the citizenship law to allow stateless children, invalids, and spouses of Estonian citizens to become naturalised without being required to pass the language exam.[296] In fact, a change in the citizenship law to grant citizenship to stateless children who were born after 26 February 1992 came in December.[297] Notably, the Fatherland Union and People's Party were the primary antagonists against the amendment. Despite their fears, only 222 applications for citizenship for children of stateless parents had been submitted by the beginning of 2000.[298] A broader integration policy was drafted by the Estonian government in February aimed at reducing the number of stateless persons and improving the knowledge of Estonian among all aliens.[299] The government stressed the need for the public to play a key role in debating and approving the programme.

By 1998, the Russian Embassy estimated that approximately 125,000 Russian citizens were living in Estonia.[300] A Russian Citizens Union of Estonia had existed for some time, although the Russian government had withheld the exact numbers of Russian citizens living in Estonia. In March, a Russian Citizen's League was established and was officially registered in June.[301] The League's creation signalled a conflict within the Russophonic community in Tallinn, where it had split from the unofficial Tallinn Union of Russian Citizens. On the condition that such organisations remain apolitical, the chairman, Vladimir Lebedev, stated that the League would focus on social, economic, and humanitarian issues.

---

296 *RFE/RL Newsline,* '...Turns Down Request to Ease Citizenship Law', 7 January 1998.

297 The *Riigikogu* voted 55 to 20 to change the citizenship law on 8 December 1998. See *RFE/RL Newsline,* 'Estonian Parliament Passes Amendments to Citizenship Law', 9 December 1998.

298 *RFE/RL Newsline,* 'As of the end of 1999 . . .', 31 January 2000.

299 *RFE/RL Newsline,* 'Estonian Government Approves Integration Principles', 11 February 1998.

300 *RFE/RL Newsline,* 'Embassy Says 125,000 Russian Citizens in Estonia', 8 January 1998.

301 *RFE/RL Newsline,* 'Russian Citizen's League Registered in Estonia', 29 June 1998.

The year 2000 was also characterised by changes and difficulties in accommodating non-citizens. At the beginning of the year, the Estonian government eased the procedure for non-citizens attempting to renew their residence permit.[302] The government decided that applicants would not need to provide proof of residence and income any longer. Over 200,000 residence permit renewals were expected that year. Despite the changes, the Estonian Institute of Human Rights reported that government red tape, rather than discrimination, was the primary hindrance for minorities exercising their rights.[303] Furthermore, the government approved the automatic awarding of citizenship to graduates of Russian-language secondary schools who successfully completed courses in Estonian language and citizenship.[304] Moreover, the *Riigikogu* passed an amendment to the immigration law that exempted the immediate family of Estonian citizens from the annual immigration quota.[305]

7.2 Estonian Language Policy

In 1989, the Estonian Supreme Soviet pushed through a language law making Estonian the sole language in the Estonian SSR and required all public officials to learn Estonian in three years up to the level of C (basic working knowledge).[306] Importantly, the law also ensured the continued use of Russian, which angered many Estonians. Before the 1989 language law, Russian was the required language for public officials and the Estonian language was optional. The new law made both languages a requirement. The 1989 language law would stand for almost ten years, well past the disappearance of the Estonian SSR. Interestingly, the language law would be used as a bench mark for the formulation of several other minorities policies, the most important of which was the 1992 citizenship law.

---

302 *RFE/RL Baltic States Report* 'Government Eases Residence Permit Renewals', 31 January 2000.

303 *RFE/RL Baltic States Report*, 8 May 2000.

304 *RFE/RL Baltic States Report*, 3 April 2000.

305 *RFE/RL Baltic States Report*, 17 April 2000.

306 Taagepera, Rein. 1993. *Estonia: Return to Independence*. Boulder, CO: Westview Press, 148.

As time progressed, language requirements increasingly became a detriment to the Russian-speaking community. Despite reforms, there still existed pressure from the Estonian state to enforce language requirements for government officials. In May 1997, the state prosecutor dismissed four Russian-speaking district attorneys in the northeast of the country for insufficient knowledge of the state language.[307] Two days later, the Justice Ministry called for the prosecution of two Russian-speaking judges in the highly Russophonic cities of Narva and Kohtla-Jarve for insufficient Estonian and false language proficiency certificates. That same month, the Estonian government banned the use of Soviet-era passports used by many in the Russophonic community as their main source of identification. The ban came with the introduction of alien passports that are valid for international travel. Leaders in the Russophonic community complained that the alien passports bestow a second-class citizenship status onto non-citizens.

At the same time, the *Riigikogu* continued to concentrate on the issue of language in politics and the services sector.[308] In November 1997, legislators passed amendments to the 1989 language law that required parliamentary deputies and local government officials to prove knowledge of the Estonian language if they had not had at least basic grammar schooling in Estonian. The previous law, passed by national communists in the Estonian Supreme Council in 1989, called on all public officials and service personnel to be conversant in Estonian within three years. The most controversial part of the new amendment was an extension of the service issue under the 1989 Language Law. The new language law allowed the government to regulate the use of the Estonian language in the service sector. However, President Meri refused to sign the amendment into law on the basis that it would give the executive

307 *RFE/RL Newsline,* 'Estonia Cracks Down in Russian-Speaking Officials with Poor Knowledge of Estonian', 12 May 1997.

308 *RFE/RL Newsline,* 'Estonian Parliament Amends State Language Law', 20 November 1997; 'Estonia's Russian Speakers Appeal to President over Language Law', 24 November 1997; 'Estonia's Meri Refuses to Promulgate Amended Language Law', 5 December 1997; 'Estonian Parliament, President Meri Disagree over Language Law', 19 December 1997; 'Estonia's Meri Again Refuses to Sign Amended Language Law', 5 January 1998; and 'Estonian Court Rules Language Law Changes Unconstitutional', 6 February 1998.

too much power to discern whether or not deputies had a sufficient level of Estonian.

Furthermore, Meri argued that the amendment allowed the government to overstep its responsibilities by defining the obligations of the individual. In addition, Meri argued that it would disrupt the balance between the executive and the legislature by giving the government the ability to evaluate and determine the level of proficiency of deputies and local officials. The level of proficiency was already dictated in the constitution. Prior to his rejection of the amendment, the Co-ordination Council of Russian-Speakers' Organisations in Estonia appealed to the president on the basis that the proposed changes of the language law were aimed at restricting Russophonic business activities and would inevitably hinder the integration of Russian-speakers into Estonian society. After Meri's refusal, the *Riigikogu* again returned the amendment to the president. Again, the president refused to promulgate the legislation. Following the second rejection, the Supreme Court found the amendment to be unconstitutional.

The amendment to the language law allowing the government to enforce language proficiency for public officials was signed into law on New Year's Eve in 1998.[309] The government did not wait long before enforcing the changes. The new year would bring unemployment to some 300 policemen who were dismissed after it was deemed by the government that they had not acquired a sufficient level of Estonian. The government argued that the dismissals came primarily because of the need of structural reform, rather than to lay off workers. A police spokesperson said that once the dismissed officers became Estonian citizens, they would be allowed back into the police force. Note that the dismissals did not come in a time of redundancies but rather at a time when there were many vacancies in the force.

Language proficiency was again the key issue for the government in February. The *Riigikogu* passed another amendment to the language and tax laws requiring those working in the services sector to be proficient in the Es-

309 *RFE/RL Newsline,* 'Meri Signs Legislation on Language Requirements for Deputies', 4 January 1999; and 'Some 300 Policemen Sacked in Estonia Over Language, Citizenship Requirements', 8 January 1999.

tonian language.[310] The subsequent promulgation of the amendment by President Meri brought about outrage from parties representing the Russophonic community. Two notable cases were the Russian Party in Estonia and the United People's Party. While the former pleaded to the President not to approve the changes, the latter issued statements to both the EU and OSCE to pressure the Government into revoking the promulgated legislation. The new language law regulations were enacted in July. The government hesitated before implementing the regulations in the private and medical sectors. Furthermore, four ethnic Russians, from the Centre Party and the United People's Party, resigned from the presidential roundtable on ethnic minorities citing the amendments as part of the impetus.[311] The four Russians represented the only Russian-speaking members of the 21-strong consultative body. For this reason, their departure had maximum effect on the meaning of the group. Furthermore, the departures had an important political effect since parliamentary and local elections were to be held that year.

In August 1999, the Narva City Council began considering actions that would make Russian the official language of public administration.[312] Narva, located on the Estonian border with the Russian Federation, has provided constant support for Russian language rights. Nearly 86 per cent of the population in the city speak Russian as their native language. Under Article 52 of the Estonian Constitution, in localities where the language of the majority of residents is not Estonian, local governments may use the language of the majority of those living there. Officials in Narva had earlier considered a proposal in 1995 to make Russian the official language of public administration, but the Estonian government conveniently failed to follow up the request. Population Minister Katrin Saks responded by saying that she was unaware of any problems associated with residents speaking Russian in Narva, although she had experienced difficulties speaking Estonian while in the city.

---

310 *RFE/RL Newsline,* 'Estonian Parliament Approves Amendments to Language Law', 10 February 1999; 'Estonian President Promulgates Amendments to Language Law', 15 February 1999; and 'Estonian Government Enacts Language Law Regulations', 28 July 1999.

311 *RFE/RL Newsline,* 'Four Quit Estonia's Presidential Round Table on Ethnic Minorities', 22 February 1999.

312 *RFE/RL Baltic States Report*, 17 August 2001.

Furthermore, she stated that it was more important to ensure that officials were fulfilling their responsibilities under the language law, under which they are required to be able to speak fluent Estonian, before such a proposal could be considered.

In the new century, language was again a topic of discussion on the national level. In particular, officials within the ruling coalition began to reconsider the language segment of the election law stating that candidates were required to speak fluent Estonian.[313] In October, senior delegates from Fatherland Union, Moderates, and Reform Party proposed an amendment changing the law. 'The amendments would abolish the requirement that candidates for these offices know enough Estonian to be able to understand legislative language and other texts; report on issues on the agenda; and express their opinions, ask questions, and communicate with voters.' Proponents of the change argued that it would convince the OSCE to end its ten-year mission by the High Commissioner on National Minorities. Unsurprisingly, the Fatherland Union faction chair in the *Riigikogu*, Tiit Sinissaar, went against the ruling coalition motion by opposing the amendment. Oddly, he was to find strange company as the amendment went through the legislative process. By 7 November, the *Riigikogu* passed the first reading of the bill. While foreign minister Ilves spoke in favour of the amendment, the Centre Party came out against the changes stating that it would jeopardise the position of Estonian as the state language. However, the Pro Patria faction was quick to point out that they had put bills in motion that would officially establish Estonian as the working language of the *Riigikogu* and all state councils. Finally, by a slim margin, the Constitutional Commission voted to support the amendment to abolish state language requirements.

7.3 Estonian Education Policy

Overall, language is the key ethnic marker distinguishing Estonians and Slavs. The need to reform the education system is a natural nation-building

313 *RFE/RL Baltic States Report*, 'Pro Patria Opposes Removing Language Requirement From Election Law', 1 November 2001.

project working through language. Gellner argues that 'the limits of the culture within which [individuals] were educated are also the limits of the world within which they can, morally and professionally, breathe. A man's education is by far his most precious investment, and in effect confers his identity on him.'[314] With this in mind, we can see why the Estonian and Latvian governments are keen to reform the education system and we should see this as part of their nation-building projects. Furthermore, this should explain why the Russophonic community, especially although not exclusively in Latvia, has resisted the change. Looking back, Estonia has had the most pragmatic approach to education reform.

Following the controversial Law on Aliens, the Estonian parliament also passed an education law in the summer of 1993.[315] The law stated unrealistically that Estonian was the official language of instruction in all schools although other languages could be used at elementary level. More controversially, the law stated that all students would be taught in the state language (Estonian) by 2000. The law was originally passed on 16 July, but President Meri returned the law to the parliament because of reported 'inconsistencies in the text'. Eventually, the law was passed in September. Almost immediately afterwards, the Estonian Minister of Culture and Education Paul-Eerik Rummo stated that he would try to submit amendments to the law by the end of year changing the language transition deadline from 2000 to 2005. He also stated that he thought the language of instruction should be left to the local authorities and that foreign actors might be encouraged to support alternative language schools. Despite Rummo's intentions, the year passed without changes to the law.

It was not until 1997 that the *Riigikogu* voted to change the deadline by which all Russian-language high schools would have to adopt Estonian as the language of instruction.[316] The date was moved from 2000 to 2008. Opponents of the change argued that the delay would be counter-productive in relation to integration. Furthermore, the delay in promoting the Estonian lan-

314 Gellner, Ernest. 1983. *Nations and Nationalism.* Oxford: Blackwell Publishers, 36.

315 *RFE/RL Newsline,* 'Estonia Passes Amended Education Law', 16 September 1993; and 'Amendments to Estonian Education Law', 21 September 1993.

316 *RFE/RL Newsline,* 'Estonian to Keep Russian-Language Schools Beyond 2000', 11 September 1997.

guage makes it more difficult for Russian-speakers to enter into higher education. However, the government also introduced 'state-language teachers' into schools that have Russian language as the main language of instruction as a means of facilitating the language transition.[317] The Russian-language daily *Estonia* collected 10,000 signatures for a petition calling for the continuation of Russian-language secondary education after the 2008 deadline.[318] Representatives of the Russophonic community, including editor-in-chief of *Estonia* Vladimer Velman, met with President Meri to express their concerns.

The type of language strategy that is being gradually introduced into Estonian schools as means of teaching the state language at a young age is referred to as 'immersion'. The technique means that first, young children are taken from their home environment and introduced to the state language. Second, the children are eventually re-introduced to their mother-language. Although immersion would seem a logical strategy in the context of Estonian integration, the technique is not without its critics.[319] Research done in Canada, where immersion has been used for some time, suggests that children are more likely to develop learning difficulties. As it stands now, the Canadian government has given $1,400,000 to the Language Immersion Centre in Tallinn. Unlike the eventual transitions in the educational systems, this immersion programme is voluntary.[320]

7.4 Latvian Citizenship Policy

Until 1991, all of the Latvian pro-independence groups, except the Latvian National Independence Movement, proposed an inclusive citizenship policy similar to that which Lithuania used after independence. With independence

---

317 *RFE/RL Newsline,* 'Estonia's Russian Schools to Get 'State-Language Teachers'', 6 November 1997.

318 *RFE/RL Newsline,* 'Estonian President Meets Russian Minority Representatives', 26 September 1997.

319 Genesee, F. 1984. Beyond bilingualism: social psychological studies of French immersion programs in Canada. *Canadian Journal of Behavioural Science* 16 (4).

320 See Wilson, Duncan. 2000. *Minority Rights in Education: Lessons for the European Union from Estonia, Latvia, Romania and the former Yugoslav Republic of Macedonia.* Stockholm: Swedish International Development Co-operation Agency, 20-38.

framed in such a way, a significant part of the Russian-speaking population supported Latvian independence from Moscow. Latvian sociologist Brigita Zepa estimates about 26% of the Russophonic community supported Latvian independence in 1990.[321] In addition, in the 1990 republican elections, Rudenschiold argues that ethnic Russian voters mainly voted for ethnic Latvian candidates.[322] These two examples give evidence of how the choice to support either the struggle for independence or the maintenance of the status quo was not based on ethnicity alone.

Nevertheless, nearly all of the more moderate Latvian nationalist groups, such as the LPF, chose the more exclusive citizenship policy as well as more conservative initiatives on language and education. In the struggle for political legitimacy in the eyes of Latvian voters, moderate groups had to show their credentials as protectors of the Latvian nation. Kolstø also argues that there was a certain provocation by the Russophonic community among conservative communist elements particularly within the Russian military.[323] Furthermore, he adds that because of the complex nature of the citizenship question, Latvian politicians delayed having to deal with the problem by proposing ever more conservative nationalist policies.

Paving the way for Latvia's post-Soviet aliens' policies, the Latvian Supreme Council passed the resolution 'On the Renewal of the Republic of Latvia's Citizens' Rights and Fundamental Principles of Naturalisation' in 1990. The law stated that despite the illegal occupation of Latvia by the Soviet Union, the Republic of Latvia had not ceased to exist. Logically, this meant that there still existed a Latvian citizenry that had either lived in Latvia before the occupation or were descendants of pre-war Latvian citizens. The Citizen's Committees were particularly important in designating who was to be within this citizenry. This meant that all those who had arrived in Latvia since the occupation that did not fit into one of these two categories were aliens. In fact, these aliens were seen as an occupying community facilitating the continued occupation of Latvia by the Soviet Union in the same line as the Portuguese

321 Zepa, Brigita. 1992. Social Thought in the Transition Period: the Dynamics of Latvian and Foreign Points of View. *Latvijas Zinatnu Akademijas Vestis* 2:23.

322 Rudenschiold, Eric. 1992. Ethnic Dimensions in Contemporary Latvian Politics: Focusing Forces for Change. *Soviet Studies* 44 (4):609-639.

323 Kolstø, Paul. 1995. *Russians in the former Soviet Republics*. London: Hurst.

population in Mozambique or the British community in Kenya. Similarly, as has been discussed before, much of this 'settler' population had actually lived in Latvia for their entire lives. Therefore, at this stage, the Latvian citizenry was defined by the criteria of 'who was here first?', rather than either a civic or ethnic definition. The result however, combined with nation-building policies, resembled an ethnic definition. Like Estonia, Latvia was able to manoeuvre between civic and ethnic notions of citizenship, although 'balancing' seems to best characterise the politics of minorities policy after independence.

Although the 1990 'Renewal' resolution stated that the naturalisation process for non-citizens would start in 1992, it did not begin until 1995 following the 1994 Citizenship Law. Both TB and LNNK wanted annual quotas to be included in the new citizenship law. The argument for quotas was based on the idea that newly-stateless persons would rush into the naturalisation process, overwhelming the state bureaucracy. Others argued that the quotas were set to establish yet another barrier to a multi-ethnic citizenry. Despite the complaints, parliament passed the initial version of the citizenship law. However, President Ulmanis refused to promulgate the law and returned it to the *Saeima*. Taking the president's lead, the law was amended and subsequently passed. In the end, the Citizenship Law required that the naturalization process contain three parts. The first two remain requirements for citizenship currently.

First, prospective citizens would be required to pass a Latvian language test as evidence of fluency. Whereas both languages are in the Indo-European family of languages, Latvian is a Baltic language while Russian is an Eastern Slavic language. Although there are some overlaps in grammar and an occasional basic word, being able to speak Russian offers little to no help in learning Latvian. Of course, the ability to learn another language is largely a factor of time and resources. Those already out of the educational system found it difficult to devote the time to learning or improving another language. Furthermore, non-citizens had to turn to private language instruction, which was expensive. Understandably, the language test has been an intimidating obstacle to many potentially loyal citizens.

Second, applicants would be required to pass a test regarding Latvian history and culture. The test consists of both multiple-choice and essay questions. An example of a question relating to Latvian culture may be 'What is the celebration of Jani characterized by?' A history question could be 'What was the crusaders' attitude towards the local beliefs in the thirteenth century?' Questions on Latvia's laws are also included, such as 'who appoints judges?' Some questions have received criticism from such groups as the British Helsinki Human Rights Group when they allude to immigration during the Soviet period, such as 'How did the proportion of Latvians among the inhabitants of Latvia change during the years of Soviet power?'[324] Overall, civic history tests are not unusual to naturalization programs.

Finally, and most controversially, the law stated that different segments of the population would have a specific time period in which to register for citizenship, generally referred to as 'naturalization windows'. Andrejs Pildegovics, Foreign Policy advisor to the Latvian President, stated that the 'window' system was actually promoted by OSCE High Commissioner on National Minorities Max van der Stoel as a compromise between the quota system and an open application system.[325] The naturalization application process would work in stages. For example, immediate members of a citizen's family could apply for citizenship in 1995, while those non-citizens who were born in Latvia would be able to apply in the period from 1996 to 2000. Those born outside Latvia would need to wait until 2001 in order to apply for citizenship. Despite the fact that some non-citizens were well integrated before independence, they still were required to wait for years in order to take the language and history tests. At the same time, some non-integrated aliens who would not be prepared for the naturalization process in such a short time were expected to apply quite early. 'By applying collective rules to the citizenship issue Latvian authorities alienated many potential loyal citizens and discredited the Latvian legal system in the eyes of many residents.'[326]

---

324 For a critique of the naturalisation programme in Latvia see British Helsinki Human Rights Group. 2000. 'Nationalism and Citizenship in Latvia' *East European Human Rights Review* 6, 1-31.

325 Information taken from interview with Mr. Pildegovics on 14 December 2002.

326 Pabriks, Artis and Aldis Purs. 2002. *Latvia: the Challenges of Change*. London: Routledge, 87.

Why did the Latvian government continue on a more conservative path? First, the constitutional amendments passed in 1992 stated that the fifth *Saeima* would only sit for two years. Therefore, parties within the ruling coalition were already preparing for new elections in 1995. This implies that parties in the ruling coalition would be unwilling to take a stand on such controversial legislation. Second, the minority coalition (48 seats) was required to continually negotiate with other parties, such as the more conservative TB and LNNK, in order to pass legislation. Third, the relationship with the Russian Federation was often contentious. As will be discussed more fully in Chapter Eight, the Russian government's foreign policy towards Latvia produced a great sense of unease amongst the titular community. Fourth, similar to the views taken by Latvian political organisations earlier, being conservative with minority policies was a 'spoon full of sugar' to the bitter medicine of economic reform. Finally, the ruling coalition had no intention of enlarging the 'selectorate' with voters who would more than likely not enlarge their own respective electoral base. Domestically, the political incentives to liberalise citizenship and language laws were non-existent. Internationally, the incentives from the West would, for the most part, come later.

During the time between the citizenship law and its eventual reform, the government reduced the waiting period for re-sitting the naturalisation period. The six-month waiting period was halved to three months. Furthermore, the government implemented a sliding scale for those paying for naturalisation fees. While most would have their fees halved from 30 Lats to 15 Lats, some would have their fees waived altogether. Although these changes would not have made a large impact on the number of people naturalised in 1997, a total of 2,994 people were naturalised in Latvia in that year compared with 3,999 for the previous two years combined.[327]

Indeed, as in Estonia, the pressure from both domestic and international actors to liberalise the citizenship and language policies began to increase several years later. In particular, with the Latvian government attempting to join both the EU and NATO, the West had a considerable amount of leverage. At the end of 1997, the People's Harmony Faction in the *Saeima* put forward an amendment to the Citizenship Law that would resemble the

---

327 *RFE/RL Newsline,* 'More People Naturalised in Latvia in 1997', 9 January 1998.

December 1998 amendment in Estonia. In both cases, the EU, primarily through the OSCE HCNM, maintained a constant dialogue on the issue of the naturalisation of stateless children. The change would have meant that citizenship would have been granted to all stateless children that had been born since independence. The proposed amendment was soundly defeated in the *Saeima*. One of the conditions on forming the ruling coalition after the 1995 elections was the provision that the government would not attempt to change the citizenship law.

At the beginning of the next year, both President Ulmanis and Prime Minister Krasts were willing to talk about changing the citizenship law in order to allow for the naturalisation of all stateless children born in Latvia since 1991. However, the Fatherland Union remained firmly against liberalising the citizenship law. When another attempt to amend the citizenship law on behalf of stateless children was defeated in February, the coalition's co-operation council began to show differing views. In particular, both LW and *Saimnieks* were in favour of 'finding a solution to the issue.' At a party conference, the Fatherland Union stated that it would exert 'all political efforts' in their resistance to any changes in the citizenship law. At the same time, the *Saimnieks* faction was drafting a bill that would automatically grant citizenship to stateless children born in Latvia since independence.

Shortly after the protests in Riga in 1998, the Latvian Government began drawing up a detailed plan for promoting the integration of Russian-speakers in Latvia.[328] Foreign Minister Birkavs (LW) stated that the programme's goals were to prevent the emergence of a 'two-community state on Latvian territory.' Birkavs also stated that the initiation of such guidelines supported the Latvian Government's foreign policy initiative of integrating into the EU. The Foreign Ministry's release of the guidelines led to the establishment of a working group to offer advice on revising the citizenship law. Such a system of promoting dialogue between the ruling parties was seen as a necessary step in maintaining the coalition. The working group was given just two weeks in which to offer proposed changes. In the end, three proposals were put forward. The first proposal stated that all non-citizens born in Latvia be

328 *RFE/RL Newsline*, 'Latvia to Draw Up Guidelines for Integrating Russian-Speakers', 19 March 1998.

granted citizenship by 2001. The second proposal stated that people who came to Latvia as minors be included among those granted citizenship by 2001. Finally, the last proposal stated that the naturalisation windows would be abolished.

The governing coalition eventually agreed on amendments to the citizenship law. The agreed proposal stated that all children born after independence could receive citizenship once they became 16 and passed a language proficiency test. The parents will have needed to live in Latvia legally for at least five years. The working group also supported partially abolishing the naturalisation windows in order to have all non-citizens born in Latvia naturalised by 2001. Other non-citizens would be allowed to apply for citizenship after that date. Once delivered, however, the working group began vacillating on whether or not to keep the clause stating that children born in Latvia since independence would have to wait until they were 16 and passed a language test before applying. For the most part, delegates of the Fatherland Union stated that they would only support the changes if the age limit and the language test were included. However, delegates from Latvia's Way came out against the Fatherland Union's stance, arguing that it was 'too vague and unconcrete'. Latvia's Way chairman, Andrejs Pantelejevs, argued for the abolition of the naturalisation windows and the unfettered granting of citizenship to children born in Latvia since independence. On 6 May, Krasts' government approved the more liberal proposal, against his own party's wishes.

However, the *Saeima* approved the more conservative proposal, in principle, on 20 May. The conflicts among the ruling parties led to the Democratic Party Saimnieks resigning from the governing coalition. By 3 June, the *Saeima* had both proposals sitting before it. In preparation for the parliamentary vote, President Ulmanis came out in favour of revising the citizenship law in line with international norms and standards, meaning without age limit or language proficiency tests. With assistance from *Saimnieks*, Latvia's Way, the National Reform Party, and the Farmer's Union/Christian-Democrats faction, the *Saeima* approved the amendments presenting the more liberal proposal. As expected, the Fatherland Union and the For Latvia Party voted against the amendment. The final amendment, passed in its third and final reading, eliminated naturalisation windows, granted citizenship for children after independence if their parents request it without the age or language limitations, and simplified the language tests for people over 65. Responding to the amendment's success in parliament, Prime Minister Krasts argued that rather than help, the changes would not encourage integration.

The Fatherland Union, having lost their fight against the more liberal amendment to the citizenship law, began obtaining signatures in order to hold a referendum to rescind the amendment.[329] The nationalist party needed to collect signatures of 10 per cent of voters in order to hold a referendum. Once the signatures were gathered, the referendum was planned for 3 October. The Latvian citizenry was split down the middle regarding support for the changes to the citizenship law. On the one side, there were the ruling coalition parties, minus the Fatherland Union, as well as several opposition parties such as *Saimnieks* and the People's Harmony Party. On the other side, there was the Fatherland Union, the For Latvia Party, and several cultural organisations such as the Baltic Unity Organisation, the Latvian Education Association, the Artist's Union, and the Theatre Association. The question posed in the referendum asked whether or not the voter supported repealing the recent amendments to the language law. The referendum was rejected with a result of 53 per cent to 45 per cent. Paul Goble argues that this was something of a turning point in Latvian politics in relation to the non-citizen population. Rather than making token efforts towards the integration process, the Latvian Government and society now had the obligation to make this process work. In other words, this was the only path that Latvia could follow after the amendment to the citizenship law and the approval of the changes by the referendum.

The new government began restructuring administrative organs in an effort to cope with the changes in the citizenship law. The cabinet approved changes in the naturalisation department in order to deal with the expected increased number of citizenship applications submitted on behalf of stateless children. The Latvian Government also created regulations for dealing with the increased number of applications that came with the removal of the natu-

329 *Kommersant Daily*, 6 March 1998; and *Noviye Izvestiya*, 6 October 1998. See also *The Baltic Times* 'Ready, set, sign: Referendum campaign starts July 20', 9 July 1998 (116).

ralisation windows. Over 3000 applications were submitted within six months of changing the naturalisation procedure. At the same time, the Ministry of Education and Sciences started a labour dispute by planning the termination of 88 teachers that had failed to pass the highest state-language certificate by the end of 1998. Another 53 teachers were given permission to obtain the certificates by 1 June 1999. The teachers involved taught at Russian-language schools and therefore did not experience the pressure to earn a certificate. The government was working with legislation approved before its time in power. The Minister of Education, Guntis Vasilevkis, stated that the law had been approved in December 1996 stating that teachers who had not received their education in the Latvian language must obtain the highest state-language certificate.

7.5 Latvian Language Policy

In the 1989 Language Law adopted by the Latvian Supreme Council, bilingualism became an official policy with the same treatment given to Latvian as Russian had received for years. The law also stated that there would be a three-year transition period in which Russian-speakers in the public sphere would begin to learn Latvian depending on their occupation. For example, a doctor would be required to know more Latvian than a tram attendant. Once the transition period was over, Russian was dropped as an official language despite the fact that around 30-35 per cent of the population used Russian as its first language. Despite finding the conservative citizenship policy unfair, Aldis Purs and Artis Pabriks argue that the language policy was quite justified.[330] They argue that there was no reason to treat the Russian language as a lingua franca within the Latvian state since the political unit that it represented, the USSR, no longer existed. Instead, they argue that the continuance of such a bilingual policy would have maintained an 'actual linguistic inequality in Latvia.' However, this would only be the case if bilingualism would be maintained while at the same time not improving the knowledge of Latvian among Russian-speakers.

---

330 Pabriks and Purs 2002.

The language policies initiated during the popular movement and first few years of independence can be broken down into two types. The first type was an environmental approach to re-nationalising the cultural environment. Such an initiative came in the form of the *Place Name Commission* with the purpose of restoring and maintaining the names of historically significant locations. Similarly, the interim Council of Ministers passed a resolution on the 'Naming and Renaming of Railway Stations, Ports, Airports, and Geographic Objects.' There was also a law 'On Additions to the Latvian Code on Administrative Violations Concerning Official State Language Issues,' which dictated the responsibilities of organisations and persons in cases of language law violations. Furthermore, ministers passed the law on 'Official State Language Usage in Titles and Information' later that year. The second type of language policy was focused on social interaction. The 1989 Language Law and the subsequent amendments in 1992 determined the way in which the government interacted with the public and vice versa.[331] These types of policies were about more than renationalising the cultural environment. Instead, these policies encouraged the renationalising of society as a whole. The assumption on the part of the titular community was that if you were to remain in Latvia, you would have to integrate at least to a certain degree, although assimilation was voluntary. Integration denotes a level of retaining one's additional cultural identity while developing a common social framework on which to relate to the rest of society and the government. Both types of language policies were important to the titular community. However, the political consequences of the environmental type were not nearly as important for the Russophonic population as the social type.

After the 1992 amendments to the 1989 Language Law, little changed in relation to language policy. As the move towards a conscious programme of integration developed, the government once again focused on the issue of language.[332] This occurred in 1997-98 in the last months of the Sixth *Saeima*. Prime Minister Krasts voiced his frustration when he argued that the liberalisation of the citizenship law might not have influenced Russian-speakers to

---

331 *RFE/RL Newsline,* 'Russia Criticises Revised Language Law', 15 April 1992.

332 *RFE/RL Newsline,* 'Latvian Premier Urges Public Discussion on Integration of Society', 11 March 1999.

integrate into Latvian society. There is evidence that this may not be the case, however. A poll carried out by Baltu Datu Nams in August and September 1998 showed that some 70 per cent of non-citizens wanted to improve their Latvian language skills. As to be expected, those who already spoke Latvian at an intermediate level were the most keen to improve their language skills. On the other hand, those respondents who did not speak any Latvian were the least likely to want to improve their Latvian. Many respondents cited their age, financial problems, and lack of practice as reasons for not improving their Latvian. Although the amendment to the citizenship law may not have instigated the poll's result, it does exhibit a trend towards at least linguistic integration. For many though, the integration process was not moving fast enough. As a last parting shot, the outgoing seventh *Saeima* passed a law calling for Latvian to be the sole language of instruction in public schools. Some schools would be all-Latvian by 2004, while privately-funded schools and some special institutions would be allowed to maintain Russian language instruction. As in the Estonian case, the problem was finding the resources to support preparing Russophonic children for the change. Again, we see integration by generational replacement as the least contentious way of avoiding two societies in one state.

By 1999, as in Estonia, legislators began attempting to regulate the use of Latvian in the private sphere.[333] A bill was passed in February that allowed businesses to terminate employees who had insufficient knowledge of the Latvian language. The Russian language press in Latvia came out strongly against the promulgation of the bill by the president. In particular, *SM*, *Panorama Latvii* and *Biznes & Baltija*, were the primary instigators in provoking outrage in the Russophonic community. The largest concern with the changes to the labour code stemmed from businesses being responsible for determining language proficiency. On the one hand, businesses know best what level of proficiency is needed for that particular industry. On the other hand, this policy is open to misuse and could have been used to violate worker's rights. After accusing the Russian language media of over-reacting, President Ulmanis returned the bill to the *Saeima* for reconsideration. The bill would have to wait until a new president was elected.

---

[333] *Segodnya*, 26 March 1999.

One of Vike-Freiberga's first acts as president was to veto the amendments to the language law after it passed its third and final reading. The amendment was passed overwhelmingly in July by a 73 to 16 vote. The president argued that there were seven points that needed to be made 'legally precise'. By returning it to the *Saeima*, the amendment was sent to a parliamentary committee for review. Although the amendment's legal precision may have been under question, it was vetoed to satisfy several international actors such as the OSCE, the Council of Europe, and the European Commission. The coalition parties, however, disagreed over the timing of passing a new amendment.[334] While the People's Party wanted to adopt the amendment by November, the Latvia's Way and Fatherland Union factions wanted to wait until 2000. The amendment finally passed and was promulgated by the president in December with the changes that resembled the plans of Kristopans regarding mandatory knowledge of Latvian in the national security and public safety industries.[335]

The implementation of the 1999 language law began nearly six months after the law was promulgated in December. The criticisms by the Russophonic community were not specifically directed towards the language law, but rather at draft government regulations on the law's implementation. The law was specifically aimed at language proficiency for professional employment and the spelling of transliterated non-Latvian names into Latvian. The Russian-language newspaper *Chas* argued that the government was attempting to launch language discrimination in the labour market. There were legitimate fears that many non-Latvians would lose their job when the regulations took into affect. The Russian-language media did have a special interest in the government's implementation of the law since its employees were particularly under threat. For example, editors and proof-readers would be required to know the highest level of Latvian required by the state, although it would fall outside the scope of their occupation.

Furthermore, the leftist faction in the *Saeima*, as well as several NGO's promoting equal rights for ethnic Russians, used such phrases as calling

334 *RFE/RL Newsline,* 'Latvian Coalition Partners Disagree on State Language Law', 19 August 1999.

335 *Kommersant Daily*, 2 September 1999.

people to 'mass resistance actions' and 'civil disobedience'. Demonstrations were held on 10 and 13 July. The first demonstration was held in front of the Latvian Cabinet of Ministers building. Demonstrators brought along a mock bomb sitting atop a map of Latvia with Russian and English slogans to liberalise the language law. The second demonstration was held in Riga's Esplanade Park where demonstrators reiterated their protests against the government's intrusion into the labour market. Despite the demands for change in the media and acts of collective action on behalf of Russian-speakers, the government approved the regulations for the implementation of the language law on 22 August with consent from Western organisations and governments.

7.6 Latvian Education Policy

Within the Latvian Constitution (as amended in 1998), ethnic minorities, which are not defined in the document, 'have the right to preserve and develop their language and their ethnic and cultural identity.' During the Soviet era, education was only offered in Latvian and Russian. In the post-Soviet era, education has been seen as the most effective integration strategy. As in Estonia, there was an initial acceptance that minority language instruction would need to be maintained. However, this was to be part of a transitional process whereby at the end, all state-funded schools would be Latvian language schools. As the revised citizenship law was in essence based on integration by generational replacement, education in the state language would be a logical supplemental policy to the same effect. This transition though would take some time. In 1993, the Latvian Foreign Minister Georgs Andrejevs told a UN delegation that Latvia offers education in sixteen different languages.[336]

The Latvian parliament has passed two laws that define the current transitional process in state-funded schools. In 1998, as the sixth *Saeima* was coming to an end, deputies passed a new school language law 64 to 4.[337] The law called for Latvian to become the sole language of instruction in state-

[336] *RFE/RL Newsline,* 'Education in 16 Minority Languages in Latvia', 18 February 1993.

[337] *RFE/RL Newsline,* 'Latvian Parliament Passes School Language Law', 30 December 1998.

funded schools by 2008. The law also stated that some schools would become state-language schools by 2004. It also allowed privately funded schools to maintain Russian as the language of instruction. Second, the *Saeima* passed the Law on General Education in 1999, which allowed for state-language programmes to be accompanied with education of the minority language as well as minority language instruction in such subjects related to cultural identity (i.e. literature). Unfortunately, the law does not guarantee access to minority language education, but simply 'allows' for it. Rather, the decision is that of the Latvian Ministry of Education. The law also defined the gradual process that was to take place until 2008. Most importantly, the law stated that all instruction after a student's tenth year would be in the state-language by 2004.

On the eve of the first deadline, the school language transition is not without its critics. The Russian-language press has been quite active in 2003 running articles discussing and condemning the elimination of Russian as a language of instruction. Second, the Latvian Human Rights Committee has also criticised the changes. In an interview with the author, the Committee's Secretary General Alexei Dimitrov, argued that bi-lingual education is the only policy that can insure integration and respect minority rights.[338] However, he expressed the fear that the Latvian Ministry of Education is not prepared for the transition and thus, could damage students' education. Also, Dimitrov suggested that it would be unrealistic to expect Russian-speaking children to speak Latvian to Russian-speaking teachers. While he encouraged bi-lingual education, he argued that if parents wish their children to have an all Latvian-language education, it should be their choice. The education laws have taken this choice away. Finally, Latvian sociologist Brigita Zepa has argued that the deadline should be delayed and more resources should be put into methods of bilingual education.[339] She went on further to imply that the Ministry of Education has implemented a Soviet-style five-year-plan for bringing about the transition. Overall, she added that the education policy might actually cause more conflict by exacerbating existing tensions surrounding language.

338 Interview with the author in Riga, 10 January 2003.

339 Johnson, Steve C. 2002. Risks of Reform. *The Baltic Times*, 5-11 September, 18.

Despite the criticisms, politicians have little political incentive to reform the transition period.

7.7 Conclusion

The construction and evolution of the citizenship policies of both states are quite similar. On the one hand, both states have similar naturalisation requirements such as language proficiency and civic tests. On the other hand, Latvia began by implementing a system of naturalisation windows whereby segments of the non-citizen population would be allocated a certain time in which to become naturalised as a means of avoiding a rush towards citizenship. Likewise, both states developed and eventually reformed their citizenship laws at similar periods in time. As we shall see, Estonia and Latvia both experienced a considerable degree of external pressure to reform their citizenship laws at similar times. Both states have continually argued that they have constructed naturalisation policies that meet normal democratic standards. However, rarely have other democracies had to face such international pressures from their inception.

Second, regarding language, the laws are also similar. Both states have completely titularised the public sphere while entering into some areas within the private sphere. Unlike the citizenship laws, the language laws were based on new legislation passed at the end of the Soviet period. Estonia and Latvia differ in their initial Language Laws, both passed in 1989. Estonia eliminated Russian as an official language of the Soviet Republic altogether. However, it did allow for a three-year transition phase for all public officials. Even this was not enough for Estonian nationalists. On the other hand, the Latvian 1989 Language Law introduced official bilingualism. Yet, within the legislation we can see that there is little difference between the two laws, since the Latvian Language Law also establishes a three-year transition period. In both cases, the argument for favouring the titular language over Russian was the creation of an integrated society.

This again brings us back to the earlier discussion of 'national integrity' or stateness in Chapter Two. On the one hand we see that language laws could encourage a stronger sense of nation, leading to a stronger democracy. On the other hand, the language legislation eliminates any possibility of a multicultural approach to group-rights. Importantly, subsequent attempts to change the language laws to interfere in the private sphere have been rejected by the relative Heads of State. Thus, it could be argued that group-rights are maintained since there is no 'cost' to maintaining Russian for Russophones, but there is a 'cost' for not being able to speak the titular language. This would be the important distinction between integration and assimilation.

Finally, the education laws in Latvia are much stricter than in Estonia. The Estonian law allows for forty per cent of a student's instruction to be in the minority language. On the other hand, the Latvian law will approach 100 per cent by 2008. The fear in the minority communities is that their cultural identity will be lost with the eventual total use of the titular languages in education. This does not mean however that minority languages will not continue to be taught. Perhaps a greater issue, one of which the Russian language media has not highlighted, is that Estonian and Latvian children are no longer being required to learn Russian. Instead, many are choosing to learn English. Already, it is not unusual to see youth in Latvia speaking English with one another. In effect, the costs of bilingualism have been transferred from the titular communities to the minority communities.

It is important to note that the resistance against the changes to the titularisation of the education system in both countries are not coming from the Ukrainian or Belorussian schools, but rather the larger and more numerous Russian schools. This highlights the role of Russian-language media as important mobilising forces. Such a review of the media goes beyond the scope of this research project. In the end, the delays in implementing such changes have been a matter of practical concerns. Both countries find themselves struggling to hire enough state-language teachers while applying resources to the new curriculum. Of the citizenship and language policies, little is expected to change. We have yet to see if it will be the same for the education policies.

Chapter 8 Russia as the External National Homeland

There is a natural cultural connection between Russia and the Russian-speaking minority communities in Estonia and Latvia. Not only is there a basic cultural connection but also often a hereditary relationship due to Soviet immigration. On the one hand, the twenty-five million Russians living in the other former Soviet republics in the other former Soviet republics became an additional means of Russian foreign policy. On the other, the Russian-speaking populations became an easy political issue with which to challenge the new Russian government with not doing enough. In addition, as the 'red-brown' opposition increased its pressure on the Kremlin, the Russian government in turn eventually increased its pressure on the Baltic governments to reform their nation-building policies. From this, there have been countless claims of 'human rights abuses', 'ethnic cleansing', and even 'genocide' from government and opposition forces. Moscow attempted to influence Baltic minority policies in two ways: bilaterally and multilaterally. Bilaterally, the Russian government linked other issues such as borders and troop withdrawal to force the Baltic states to reform. Multilaterally, Moscow worked within the context of international organisations such as the UN and the Council of Europe. In this way, we can see Russia's role as Brubaker's 'external national homeland' to Estonia and Latvia's 'national minorities'. In this chapter, we can see the nexus at work from the side of the external national homeland.

In this context, this chapter first gives a brief overview of post-Soviet Russian politics. This will allow us to appreciate the domestic side of the impetus for Russian foreign policy towards Estonia and Latvia. Second, while we have already seen how Russia has defined the Russian-speaking communities in relation to the nation, we look at how the minorities define themselves. Interestingly, we have seen that Russia's attempts to define these communities are no less convoluted than the academic definitions presented in Chapter Three. Third, this chapter will look at the border and troop withdrawal issues as they have been inextricably linked to the 'human rights' issue. Again, we bring forward Keohane's foreign policy tool of issue-linkage to understand Moscow's relation to the Baltic states. Finally, and most importantly, we will analyse the relationship between Russia and the two northern Baltic states in the context of the Russian-speaking minority from 1991-2001. Hopefully, by laying out these four sections, we will able to better understand the role of the external national homeland.

Does Russia see itself as an external national homeland? As has been the case in academic literature concerning the Russophonic minority communities in the former Soviet republics, the Russian government had a difficult time defining what it means to be Russian. However, the question of definition for the Russian people has been an ongoing issue from the Christianisation of Russia, defeat of the Golden Horde, and Peter the Great's defeat of the 'Streltsy', all the way to the fall of the Romanovs and the subsequent Soviet project. With the perpetual identity crisis among Russians (are we Western, Eastern, or something in between?), it is not hard to believe that defining Russians outside Russia would be a complex task.

Much like many scholars, often the definition was taken that best suited the purpose at hand. Neil Melvin offers an insightful analysis of three definitions used by different organs within the Russian government throughout the early 1990's.[340] They are the 'ethnic', 'Slavic-European', and linguistic-cultural definitions. Within each definition, Melvin presents several terms used to categorise the group of people of whom they were trying to protect. Within the ethnic definition, *rossiianin* has been used to denote members of the 'Russian' population without specifically discussing citizenship. For instance, in February 1993, the Russian Council of Nationalities voted to create a 'Standing Commission for the Affairs of Russians (*rossiianin*) and other Ethnic Groups Native to Russia.'[341] However, the term's original context lay outside ethnic criteria, and simply indicated a citizen of Russia. Interestingly, we see here a term that originally constituted a civic characterisation but has changed to an ethnic one. Additionally, the Russian government has often used the term *etnicheskie rossiyane*, meaning ethnic Russian. Again, the

340 Melvin, Neil J. 1994. *Forging the New Russian Nation: Russian Foreign Policy and the Russian-Speaking Communities of the Former USSR*. London: Royal Institute of International Affairs, 17-22.

341 *RFE/RL Newsline,* 'Standing Commission for Russian Affairs to be Created in Council of Nationalities', 25 February 1993.

definition does not necessarily refer to those who are, or potentially could become, citizens of the Russian Federation.

The Slavic-European definition is by far the vaguest. Included in this definition is the term *sootechestvennik* (compatriot), which may have been heard among Baltic minority politicians in the early years of independence although not likely among the general population. Additionally, pundits in Russia would use terms such as *nashi* or *nash narod* (our people), *russkodumaiushee naselenie* (Russian-thinking community), and the even broader *rossusko orientirovannoe naselenie* (Russian-oriented people). As is often done among ethnic groups, albeit usually under considerable pressures, elites define the group by casting the widest net possible. Melvin makes the point that often such vague definitions were useful since there were differences among the Russophone communities in each of the former Soviet republics. In this way, the Russian government ensured that all of the former Soviet republics felt the pressure to ensure certain circumstances for its Russian-speaking community.

Finally, the linguistic-cultural definition includes *russkoyazychnye*, or more popularly *russofony*, as a term used in some government documents often specifically aimed at Western organisations to indicate Russian-speaking. Both the Slavic-European and the linguistic-cultural definitions rely on the basis that Russian was the *lingua franca* during Soviet times and that Russia is the successor state of the Soviet Union. Overall, Melvin makes the point that, 'although considerable numbers of Russian politicians have been more than willing to speak out about the need to protect Russian populations in the former Soviet republics, it is rather unclear exactly whom they wish to protect.'[342] Interestingly, Baltic minorities tend to refer to what would have been their nationality in their Soviet passport. Thus, Russians most likely refer to themselves as *russkii*.

This chapter will concentrate on the role of the external national homeland and the *russkie*. In our case, this is the Russian Federation. Russia fits into this position because political elites, both in the government and the opposition, have continually claimed this role for themselves. While the Baltic states have been rebuilding nation-states, so has the Russian Federation.

342 Melvin 1994, 17.

Thus, we should expect some kind of contention to arise given the number of Russian-speakers in Estonia and Latvia. Furthermore, Russian political elites have also had to play the two-level game in which they balance international issues (compatriots in the 'near abroad') with their own political success.

8.1 The External National Homeland and Nationalising States

Initially, the relationship between nationalising forces in the Baltic states and Russia was good. In fact, the RSFSR was the first state to recognise the independent states. The Russian nationalist movement was personified in Boris Yeltsin. One of the most significant events in the Russian nationalist movement was when Yeltsin was elected to the Russian Supreme Council in March 1990. He was subsequently elected deputy speaker. At the same time, elections in the Baltic republics produced Supreme Councils that were led by nationalist popular fronts. Yeltsin was quick to encourage the nationalist movements in the Baltic republics. He met with popular front leaders as early as July 1990. Lubova Zile argues that Yeltsin recognised that the independence of the Baltic republics would mean a significant step towards the collapse of the Soviet system in Russia.[343] Indeed, Gorbachev was quick to try and limit Yeltsin's influence by attempting to ensure that all of the current Soviet republics remain in the Soviet Union through signing a new Union Treaty, which never came to be. In effect, Gorbachev's actions were counter to both Yeltsin's and the Baltic popular forces' attempts to gain independence.

As the Baltic states become more resolute about their independent status in the international system, Moscow turned up the heat through the use of Interior Ministry troops in early 1991. Alarmed by Soviet actions, Yeltsin called an emergency session of the Russian Supreme Soviet on 12 January in order to formulate a resolution that would denounce the Interior Ministry's attacks. Following this, the relationship between the Baltic republics and Russia became stronger. For example, Latvia and Russia signed a co-operation

343 Zile, Lubova. 2001. Baltic-Russian Co-operation during the Restoration of Independence (1990 until the 1991 Putsch). In *The Baltic States at Historical Crossroads*, edited by Talavs Jundzis. Riga: Latvian Academy of Sciences, 457.

agreement on 14 January reinforcing the independence movements in both republics. Having said this, the pact was criticised by the Latvian Citizen's Committee as being against the interests of Latvian citizens.

Continued support was forthcoming from Yeltsin throughout the summer and was brought to a head when the State Extraordinary Circumstances Committee attempted to take control of the Soviet apparatus in a coup. After both Estonian and Latvian Supreme Councils passed independence declarations, Yeltsin signed a decree recognising the independence of the Baltic republics three days after the attempted coup. Although the good relationship lasted a bit longer while the Soviet Union took its last breath, Estonia and Latvia would soon be the favourite objects of criticism as a new Russian Federation began trying to continue its influence on the 'near abroad'.

The relations between the Russian Federation and the Baltic states are best summed up by the fact that Russia has apologised to Finland for the Winter War, to Poland for events at Katyn, but not the Baltic states for fifty years of occupation.[344] Thus, on the side of Estonia and Latvia, by default Russia recognises the incorporation of the Baltic states in the Soviet Union as legitimate. Although the occupation may be a fact of history that the modern Russian Federation feels is not connected to it, the lack of recognition is a major psychological block to considerable improvements in Estonian/Latvian-Russian relations, as well as maintaining a certain level of paranoia of disloyalty of ethnic Russians by titular communities. It is in this context that the first ten years of Baltic-Russian relations rest.

Russian post-Soviet foreign policy has been based on placing other states into one of two categories: the 'near abroad' and everyone else. The 'near abroad' policy represented a Russian version of the Monroe Doctrine whereby the Russian Federation would maintain an active interest in the region that it considered to be most important: the former Soviet Union. One way in which the Russian Foreign Ministry actively attempted to maintain considerable influence in former Soviet states was through the manipulation of the Russian 'diaspora', approximately 25 million people at the time of the

---

344 Lejins, Atis. 2001. Baltic-Russian Relations: A Reassessment. In *The Baltic States at Historical Crossroads*, edited by Talavs Jundzis. Riga: Latvian Academy of Sciences, 505.

1989 Soviet Census. However, in order for this policy to work, the Russian government needed to prevent an inflow of 'Russians' back into Russia. In this respect, there have been considerable differences between the repatriation of Russians from Central Asia as opposed to those of Baltic states. Furthermore, the Russian government would need to invest in Russian communities to produce an economic environment friendly to minorities. Finally, the Russian government would promote the continued Russification of titular elites through receiving higher education in Russian or even going further to be educated in Russia. However, this final point was all but impossible to force on the Baltic states who were quite conscious of promoting their domestic education institutions, not to mention the distrust that still exists between the titular governments and the Russian Federation. These three policies were first espoused by Sergei Karaganov in 1992 and came to be known as the Karaganov Doctrine.[345]

However, as Igor Zevelov points out, Russian foreign policy objectives in this area have primarily failed.[346] In particular, he argues that the Russian Foreign Ministry has been in many cases far more practical in action than in rhetoric, as well as ineffective in pressing its demands on states in the 'near abroad'. Quite often, economic interests were prioritised over issues of 'compatriots'. In the end, despite threats to the contrary by some leading politicians such as Vladimir Zhirinovsky, deploying military and economic levers to force compliance was fairly unrealistic.

Possibly the lack of success of Russian policy to 'protect compatriots' in former Soviet republics partly relies on these communities' differing relationship with Russia. Melvin presents the assumption made by many in Moscow that Russophones in the 'near abroad' do have some special link to Russia. Yet he fails to question the validity of such links. Edwin Poppe and Louk Hagendoorn take a closer look at the types of identification between Russians in the former Soviet republics and the Russian Federation.[347] They find that the identification between minority community and Russia is on the one hand

---

345 Ibid., 514-515.

346 Zevelev, Igor. 1996. Russia and the Russian Diaspora. *Post-Soviet Affairs* 13 (3):265-284.

347 Poppe, Edwin and Louk Hagendoorn. 2001. Types of Identification among Russians in the 'Near Abroad'. *Europe-Asia Studies* 53 (1):57-71.

often multi-layered, while on the other primarily limited to an older generation. More specifically, they found that only Moldova presented a result of more individuals identifying with Russia than with the successor state. In other post-Soviet states, they found that individuals were more likely to identify with the republic in which they lived rather than with the Russian Federation or Soviet Union. From this we can conclude that Moscow's ability to influence policies in the Baltic states is lessened as the relationship between the national minority and the external national homeland becomes ever more one-sided on the part of the latter.

Bearing this in mind, the status of the Russian-speaking communities in the 'near-abroad' has been an important issue in post-Soviet Russian politics. From these identities, we can gather that the Russian Federation is an external national homeland in the context of this study. Before we move on to the 'human rights' issue, we first need to see how Russia has attempted to link other issues, such as troop withdrawal and border agreements, to the status of Russian-speakers in Estonia and Latvia.

8.2 Troop withdrawal

Indeed, as the previous section indicates, the relations between the newly nationalising states and the external national homeland were not a consequence of long standing animosities but rather a 'consequence of recent Russian dominance and current steps by the titular nationalities to reconstruct political, economic, and sociocultural hegemony.'[348] As early as 1992, the relations between the now sovereign nations took a turn for the worse. Four main inter-connected issues would come to dominate relations: economics, troop withdrawal, borders, and most importantly for this study, the treatment of 'Russian' minorities.

In order to understand Baltic-Russian relations in this context, we need to spend some time on how these factors played a part in deteriorating relations between the nationalising states and the external national homeland.

---

348 Chinn, Jeff and Robert Kaiser. 1996. *Russians as the New Minority: Ethnicity and Nationalism in the Soviet Successor States.* Westview Press: Boulder, 280-281.

The source of the greatest contention was understandably the 128,000 Russian troops stationed in the Baltic states.[349] However, by August 1992 there were approximately 60,000 troops remaining with 12,000 in Estonia and 28,000 in Latvia. Numbers tended to naturally reduce since new soldiers were not replacing those that had ended their tour of duty. For example, in response to Russia's failure to deliver 125,000 tons of flour and cereals as stipulated in a 1991 economic agreement, Estonia stopped supplying these same goods to the Russian troops that were stationed there.[350] On the other hand, the Russian troops played a different role in Latvia. In January 1992, the Russian army allocated 100,000 tons of diesel fuel and 50,000 tons of gasoline for the Latvian public transport system.[351] However, this did not preclude the Latvian government from wanting the Russian troops withdrawn as much as the Estonians.

At first, Russia argued that it would need until 2000 in order to withdraw all troops from the Baltic states. However, Estonian Prime Minister Tiit Vahi was quick to reject the Russian proposal. Vahi argued for the withdrawal of troops from Estonia before the end of 1992.[352] Yet the Russian government's greatest means of exerting pressure on the Baltic states was the continued delaying of talks on the troop withdrawal question. There is little doubt that Russia wanted to drag out the withdrawal as long as possible as a means of retaining some influence over the Baltic states. Major General Vladimir Lopatin even argued for leaving some Russian troops in the Baltic states for 'mutual defence'. As to be expected, the Baltic governments considered this to be out of the question.

Russia's primary argument for delaying the withdrawal of Soviet troops to Russia was the lack of housing available. Although the lack of housing could not substantiate a long drawn-out removal of troops from the Baltic region, it was another tactic used by the Russian government to deny a sudden removal. A far more convincing reason is the need for Moscow to continue to dominate a perceived area of influence during a time of changing world politics. From the beginning, the Baltic governments made no secret of their de-

349 *Pravda*, 9 January 1992.

350 *RFE/RL Newsline,* 'Estonia Cuts off Flour for 'Russian' Troops', 8 January 1992.

351 *Izvestia*, 17 December 1992.

sire to join NATO. Russia's delaying tactics in removing troops were a response to expansive Western influence and eventual NATO enlargement. While trying to engage with the West, Moscow could not legitimise this holding action as simply power politics in the post-Cold War era. Thus, the very real, but easily completed, housing issue was Russia's excuse for maintaining troops in the Baltic states.

In response, Estonia, Latvia, and Lithuania, at a meeting of deputy foreign ministers on 5 February agreed to help build housing if Russia paid the costs.[353] Latvian Supreme Soviet Chairman Anatolijs Gorbunovs went even further by suggesting to the European Parliament that the West should invest in housing for the troops so that the withdrawal could be completed more quickly.[354] His Russian counterpart and Yeltsin opponent, Ruslan Khasbulatov, arguing that the Latvian government should not have discussed the subject at an international forum, quickly denounced this. He also argued that it was Russia's responsibility and that the Russian government would fund the withdrawal. Finally, Khasbulatov argued that more understanding was required from the Baltic states since the existence of Soviet troops in the region was not propagated by the current Russian leadership and was a result of historical circumstances common to both Russia and the Baltic states.

After a meeting between Russian and Latvian experts over the troop withdrawal issue, Latvian Minister of State Janis Dinevics stated that Russia was using 'subtle and not-so-subtle' tactics of delaying a final agreement.[355] Based on this, the Latvian government tried once more to internationalise the situation by calling for representatives from Estonia and Lithuania as well as from Western countries. The Latvian Ministry of Defence noted that Russia was negotiating for automatic citizenship rights for retiring officers in addition to allowing them to become owners of the housing that they currently occupied. Russia's continued negotiations were not accompanied by proposed deadlines for the withdrawal of troops. In response, the Baltic governments

---

352 See *Nezavisimaya Gazeta*, 8 May 1992; and *Izvestia*, 17 December 1992.

353 *RFE/RL Newsline,* 'Baltic Foreign Ministries Coordinate Policy Towards Russia', 10 February 1992.

354 *Izvestia*, 17 December 1992.

355 *Nevazisimaya Gazeta*, 29 October 1992.

threatened to once again internationalise the issue through the OSCE.[356] In April, during the third round of talks on the troop issue between Latvia and Russia, Russian negotiators argued that they were unwilling to set a deadline for the removal of troops while servicemen and their families were being mistreated.

The failure to submit a proposed deadline may have represented Moscow's willingness to bargain itself a 'permanent presence' in the Baltic states. As discussed earlier, shortly after independence, Russia had divided the world into two spheres: the far-abroad and the near-abroad. The Baltic states were clearly within the latter given their geographic location as well as their historical legacy as being part of the Russian Empire and later the Soviet Union. In talks between the Russian Federation and Estonia in June 1992, Russian delegates had made this very clear to the Estonian delegation.[357] Progress towards a solution to the troop problem was further compounded when the commander of the CIS border guards told Lithuanian officials that he considered Lithuania's border with Poland to be Russia's border.[358] Furthermore, a draft Russian position paper was released to the press by Estonian officials stating that Russian troops should remain permanently and be funded by the Baltic states in return for security.[359]

From June, the issues of troop withdrawal and 'human rights' became officially linked as Russia attempted to internationalise the case for Russians living in Estonia and Latvia in international forums. This is not to say that there was not a strong relationship between the two as used by Russia before. The Baltic states had claimed previously that the Russian Government was using the 'human rights' issue as a way of assuming a 'position of force' for the continued troop withdrawal negotiations.[360] Russian Foreign Minister Andrei Kozyrev proposed the linkage during a meeting between the Russian

---

356 *Rossiiskaya Gazeta*, 16 April 1992.

357 *Nevazisimaya Gazeta*, 8 July 1992.

358 At the same time as the discussions to remove Russian troops were taking place, it was discovered that the military was actually secretly bringing more troops into Estonia and Latvia as replacements for troops previously stationed in the Baltic states. See *RFE/RL Newsline,* 'Russia Bringing in More Troops', 10 June 1992.

359 *Nevazisimaya Gazeta*, 8 July 1992.

360 *RFE/RL Newsline,* 'Estonia Rebuffs Russian Claims', 21 July 1992.

and Baltic governments on 6 August.[361] Kozyrev linked the two issues again in a meeting with the Danish Foreign Minister in October and stated that, '[w]e are prepared to resort to the most far-reaching, tough, radical measures, but within the framework of international law.'[362]

Yeltsin also made a statement in October shortly after Russian officials signed a troop withdrawal agreement with Lithuania saying that no agreements relating to troop withdrawal will be made until Estonia and Latvia provide greater 'minority rights' for Russians.[363] Despite these events, at a hearing of the Human Rights Commission of the Russian Supreme Soviet on 28 November, Chairman of the Supreme Soviet Defence and Security Committee Sergei Stepashin stated that the Russian government did not link the two issues either officially or unofficially.[364] Yet a month later, the Russian delegation to the North Atlantic Co-operation Council proposed a link between the two issues, but later rescinded the proposal after negotiations between Estonian and Russian officials.[365]

By April 1993, Russians in the Baltic states were feeling the negative effects of the continued presence of troops. In response, the Russian Citizens' Association in Latvia took issue with the linkage between the prospects of troop withdrawal and the issue of 'human rights'.[366] The association argued that the linkage was Russian 'political propaganda'. They further went on to add that the maintenance of troops was demoralising for the soldiers, and total troop withdrawal could help prevent the disintegration of the Russian military. This is little surprise given that the Baltic troops must have felt like pawns in the hands of a generally uncaring government since the military was suffering heavily from the loss of Soviet-era expenditures.[367]

---

361 *RFE/RL Newsline,* 'Latvia: Kozyrev's Proposals Unacceptable', 14 August 1992.

362 *Nevazisimaya Gazeta*, 29 October 1992.

363 *Izvestia*, 7 October 1992.

364 *Nevazisimaya Gazeta*, 3 December 1992.

365 *Izvestia*, 17 December 1992.

366 *RFE/RL Newsline,* 'Russian Association in Latvia Wants Russian Troops Out', 14 April 1993.

367 For example, see *RFE/RL Newsline,* 'Grachev on State of Russian Army; Withdrawal from Abroad', 9 May 1994.

At this time, there also seemed to be mixed messages coming from Moscow.[368] On 15 April, Yeltsin stated that Russian troops would remain in Estonia and Latvia until the rights of minorities were recognised. Yet just two days before, Kozyrev assured the Dutch Foreign Minister that Russia was not linking the issues of foreign policy and 'human rights'. However, by August, Kozyrev changed tack once more.[369] Addressing the press in Stockholm, he stated that the 'interethnic tensions' in the Baltic states 'have a strong potential for violence'. Therefore, he argued that Russia must wait before withdrawing its troops. Interestingly, Kozyrev made this statement after the 'Aliens' Crisis' in Estonia had lost steam, not to mention that there had been no similar contentious periods in Latvia up to this point. The statement itself was a response to the British and Swedish Prime Ministers' call for a timetable for the withdrawal of troops from Latvia.

By 1994, Russian officials realised that their attempts to internationalise the 'human rights' issue in Estonia and Latvia were being hampered by the Baltic states' ability to internationalise the troop withdrawal issue.[370] The United States Senate shocked Russian officials when Senators attempted to block new US aid to Russia unless it had withdrawn troops from Estonia. Numerous Russian officials produced a barrage of angry responses over the Senate proposal, the harshest coming from former Finance Minister Boris Fedorov who said 'never tell us what we have to do, especially when it concerns our interests.'[371] Nevertheless, post-Soviet political realities as well as Western pressure led the Russian government to decide that it was either unable or at least unwilling to maintain a military presence in Estonia and Latvia. Russia unexpectedly signed a troop withdrawal agreement with Estonia on 26 July where it stated that all Russian troops would be withdrawn by 1 September. Latvia's agreement with Moscow came in a series of meetings between the Presidents of the two nations in April-May 1994. Like the Estonian agreement, Russian troops would be withdrawn by the 1 September deadline, although Russian troops would maintain the Skrunda radar base

368 *Nevazisimaya Gazeta*, 31 March 1993.

369 *Izvestia*, 6 August 1994.

370 See especially *Segodnya*, 13 July 1994.

371 *RFE/RL Newsline,* 'Moscow Denounces US Senate Aid Decision', 18 July 1994.

until 1999. As mentioned earlier, Latvia was required to make the concession of agreeing on social guarantees for retiring Russian officers.[372]

Interestingly, the Baltic states were able to beat Moscow at its own game. While Russia was keen to internationalise the issue of 'human rights' in the Baltic states, Moscow was unwilling to discuss troop withdrawal in an international forum. On the other hand, while the Baltic states were quick to internationalise the troop issue, it did not attempt to prevent third-party observations of the minority issue. With Western governments and organisations unwilling to condemn the Baltic states given the complex nature of the minority issue in the Baltic states, this left the troop issue 'out in the open' for all to see. Moscow's inability to pursue issue-linkage better was partly a result of the ongoing domestic turmoil in Russia between the President and the Duma over the construction of a new constitution. As we can see from the discussion above, there was never a clear dominant policy of *quid pro quo* in Moscow towards the Baltic governments. For example, there was a strong move towards attempting to maintain a dominant position in power politics while instituting a hardline stance for domestic consumption, both among elites and the masses. There is a strong correlation between the resolution of the domestic situation in Russia and the subsequent agreements for troop withdrawal.

The troop-withdrawal issue is important for this study for several reasons. First, the contentious nature of resolving this issue set precedents for Baltic-Russian relations for the next decade. Second, while Russia was unable achieve its primary objective of maintaining a military presence in the Baltic states, it was able to draw a considerable amount of attention to minority issues in Estonia and Latvia. Having said this, prolonging the resolution of the troop-withdrawal issue may have helped set an attitude against the liberalisation of the citizenship and language laws. Third, finally, the troop withdrawal issue sets the background for the discussion on Russia's attempts to change minority policies in the Baltic states.

---

372 For discussion on Baltic-Russian relations see especially Voronov, Konstantin. 2001. The Baltic Policy of the New Russia: A Brief History of the Stormy Decade. In *The Baltic States at Historical Crossroads*, edited by Talavs Jundzis. Riga: Latvian Academy of Sciences.

Finally, we can already see the development of two competing foreign policy stances in Moscow: Atlanticism versus Eurasianism.[373] Atlanticism entails a desire to engage with the West for continued relevance to international politics and encouraging foreign investment. Such engagement has resulted in the Partnership for Peace Programme, despite Russia's wavering attendance in the late 1990's, and its inclusion in the now G8. Eurasianism, on the other hand, is the desire to maintain Moscow's dominant influence in the Eurasian region while continuing its Cold War rivalry with West. An early example would be the Karaganov Doctrine. While the former recognises a change in international politics since the collapse of the socialist regimes in Eastern Europe, the latter views the world in the same Cold War framework as the Soviets. While these two dominant stances influenced Russian foreign policy since the end of the Cold War, there has been little deviation in Moscow's attitude towards the minority situation in the Baltic states, in so far as we have seen divergences in hostility towards NATO and EU expansion but not Russia-Estonia/Latvia relations. However, with this in mind, we move on to another case of issue-linkage: borders.

8.3 Borders

The borders of the independent Baltic states had been set in the 1920 Treaty of Tartu. However, with the beginning of the Soviet Union, the Estonian and Latvian Soviet Republics both lost a considerable amount of land contiguous to the RSFSR in 1944. At the same time, Lithuania actually gained land during the Soviet occupation (the Vilnius region).[374] In Estonia, the disputed territories were both along the western bank of the Narva River as well as the Petseri region (Pechora) in the southeast corner. Latvia's disputed land was the Abrene region (Pytalovo) in the northeast corner, which was the southern half to the former Estonian Petseri region.

---

373 See Lynch, A. C. 2002. The Evolution of Russian Foreign Policy in the 1990s. *Journal of Communist and Transition Politics* 18 (1):161-182; and Shearman, P. 2001. The Sources of Russian Conduct: understanding Russian foreign policy. *Review of International Studies* 27 (2):249-264.

374 For a more in-depth discussion on the border issue, see Lejins 2001.

Upon the restoration of independence, Russia was unwilling to accept a change in borders from that of the Soviet republics. In effect, the Baltic states and the Russian Federation were looking at the issue in two different ways. The Baltic states perceive their post-Soviet independence as de-occupation (restoration) meaning that the independent states, as recognised by Lenin in 1920, still existed throughout the Soviet period. On the other hand, the Russian Federation has viewed Baltic independence as born out of the collapse of the Soviet Union. In other words, the Baltic Soviet Republics 'chose' to become independent states, just as they had 'chosen' to become Soviet Republics. In the same way that the Russian Federation would not attempt to restore the borders of the Russian Empire, the Baltic states would also be required to work with the borders of the Soviet Republics.

While Estonia never formally requested the return of the lost territories (despite Russian media claims to the contrary), the Latvian Supreme Council called for the return of the Abrene region just weeks after the dissolution of the Soviet Union.[375] In fact, one would expect both states to call for the return of the annexed areas as it logically follows the restorationist ideology underpinning both states. However, it may be that the Estonian government found it more practical not to contest areas that had predominantly Russian populations.

Following Latvia's declaration requesting the return of the Abrene area, the Russian Federation Supreme Soviet passed a resolution refuting the return of the annexed area in March.[376] Moscow claimed that Latvia had no historical connection to the area and Riga's January declaration threatened the 1991 Latvian-Russian Treaty, which had yet to be ratified by the Supreme Soviet at this time. Despite the continued crossfire from Riga to Moscow and back regarding the Abrene region, the border issue was far from the most important. Eventually, Latvia followed the Estonian lead and conceded the annexed area to Russia in Pskov in October 1997. Surprisingly, Estonia was unable to formally agree to concede the two regions until March 1999 in St.

375 *RFE/RL Newsline,* 'Latvia Wants Back Annexed Territory', 23 January 1992. See also, *Izvestia*, 16 February 1992.

376 *Izvestia*, 20 March 1992.

Petersburg. In all three cases of the Baltic states, Russia has failed to ratify the border treaties.

The border dispute highlights an important contentious element in the Baltic-Russian relationship: Russia has continued to maintain the official line that the Baltic states voluntarily entered the USSR. Although this is the official line, individual Russian officials have indicated a different view. For example, in July 1993, Russian envoy to Latvia Aleksandr Rannikh and Russian Foreign Ministry official Aleksandr Udaltsov openly stated that the Soviet Union had invaded the Baltic states in 1940.[377] However, they turned this view, previously only held by the Baltic governments, into working for the status quo favoured by Moscow. In particular, Rannikh stated that the 1940 Soviet invasion actually invalidated the 1920 peace treaties. Likewise, Vasilii Svirin, head of the Russian delegation to Estonia regarding border negotiations, argued that the 1920 peace treaties were not valid since the Baltic states had ceased to be subjects of international law after 1940.

The border dispute, similar to the troop withdrawal issue, shows once again Russia's foreign policy at work. Specifically, Russia has used issues like the border treaties as a means of gaining an edge in the bargaining process that is international relations.[378] Although there has not been a direct link made between borders and 'human rights' following Russian statements aimed at Estonia and Latvia, the method of issue-linkage remains an important foreign policy tool. It should be mentioned, that linking issues in this fashion is common to every nation's foreign policy. Thus, this essay is not intended as a criticism of Moscow. Rather, the border issue contributes to a picture of Russia's relations with the Baltic states and will help in discussing how Moscow has attempted to affect minority policy-making in Estonia and Latvia.

---

377 *RFE/RL Newsline,* 'Russian Officials Admit to Soviet Invasion of Baltics', 15 July 1993.

378 *Segodnya*, 15 December 1997.

8.4 The Human Rights Issue

As chapter six illustrated, the controversy over the new nation-building policies started several years before the end of the Soviet project. Almost immediately after the restoration of independence, the Estonian Supreme Council began discussing the issue of citizenship. While Yeltsin remained unwilling to criticise the Baltic states while the RSFSR remained within the USSR, Gorbachev criticised the quick actions of the Estonian government.[379] He stated that some minorities had called upon the Soviet government to defend them. The Estonian government responded by sending a letter to the USSR Ministry for Foreign Affairs requesting evidence of the alleged violations of human rights and denied the allegations. However, the issue of Russians in the near-abroad soon became an important source of political capital for first the so-called red-brown opposition and second the Yeltsin government itself.

For the most part, there are four major actors in Russia formulating a foreign policy towards the Baltic states. First and foremost, the Russian Ministry of Foreign Affairs (MFA) played the lead role in formulating, observing, and implementing Russian foreign policy. In particular, the minister of foreign affairs was at the centre of the ongoing commentary on Russians in the Baltic states. Second, the legislative bodies within the old Soviet system (Supreme Soviet) as well as those of the Russian Federation (Duma and Federation Council) also played a part in making foreign policy primarily in the form of proposed sanctions and hostile resolutions. Third, individual political actors such as President Yeltsin, Ruslan Khasbulatov, Alexandr Rutskoi, Liberal Democratic leader Zhirinovsky, Communist Party leader Zyuganov, and local leaders were also important in affecting foreign policy and domestic public opinion. Finally, the Russian media played an important role in perpetuating anti-Baltic sentiments in Russia as well as portraying a particular picture of Russians living in Estonia and Latvia. These four sets of actors are identified as being primarily involved as making, shaping, and implementing Russia's foreign policy directed at the 'human rights' situation.

Despite the worries over the 'Russian' question in Estonia and Latvia, Russia was still willing to press forward with the interstate treaties that had

---

379 *RFE/RL Newsline,* 'Estonian Diplomatic Note to Moscow', 9 December 1991.

been signed the previous January.[380] While the Russian Supreme Soviet ratified the Estonian-Russian Treaty, they also called on the government to work on resolving the question of citizens' rights in Estonia. Shortly afterwards, officials in Moscow were calling for the ratification of the Latvian-Russian Treaty. Interestingly, the Russian delegation chief Aleksandr Granberg requested that political forces representing Russians in Latvia, such as the Equal Rights movement, send letters to the Russian legislative body backing the ratification. In particular, this had been the case prior to the ratification of the Estonia-Russia Treaty as well. These events give some indication of the ongoing relationship between deputies across borders after the Soviet Union had collapsed, that even to some extent exists today.

However, despite the treaties, relations between the Baltic states and Russia were continually becoming more contentious. Already, Estonia was felling the loss of basic goods that had been set to arrive from Russia, not to mention the controversial citizenship law. Latvia was already under fire for demanding the return of the Abrene region. Even Lithuania, who had set a more liberal citizenship policy and did not come into conflict with Russia over annexed territories, was under the spotlight. There is some indication that officials in Moscow were slow to recognise the lack of contention presented by a restored Lithuania because it had been at the forefront in the Baltic nationalist movements. Furthermore, Lithuania had a remarkable representative in Lithuanian Supreme Council Chairman Landbergis. Recognising that there is security in numbers, the Baltic states began working together in how to best deal with Russian foreign policy.[381] On 5 February, deputy foreign ministers from the three Baltic states agreed to form a permanent working group that would lead towards the formation of a unified policy with Moscow.

In April 1992, the Russian government increased its critique of the nation-building policies in Estonia and Latvia. The Estonian *Riigikogu* had approved a new Citizenship Law that re-established the 1938 Citizenship Law (along with the changes made in 1940) that offered citizenship to those born

---

380 See *Nevazisimaya Gazeta*, 10 June 1992; but also the earlier *RFE/RL Newsline*, 'Russia Ratifies Agreement', 2 January 1992; and 'Latvian-Russian Treaty May Be Ratified in February', 21 January 1992.

381 *RFE/RL Newsline*, 'Baltic Foreign Ministries Coordinate Policy Toward Russia', 10 February 1992.

in Estonia and their descendants. Yet the Russian government did not criticise the changes openly until a CSCE conference in Helsinki on 2 April.[382] No doubt the delay was a result of the law's relatively liberal stance on citizenship allowing anyone who had been resident in Estonia for three years and could pass a language proficiency test to apply for naturalisation. The Russian delegation to the conference stated that the Russian Federation 'reserves the right to use relevant withdrawals from the Baltic states to help prevent conflicts and stabilise the region of central Europe.' At nearly the same time, the Russian MFA sent a letter to the Latvian government complaining of the revisions to the 1989 Language Law.[383] The earlier version placed the Russian language on the same level of Latvian in relation to the state. Before 1989, the Russian language had held a dominant role. With the 1992 changes, Latvian would be the designated language of the state and Russian would be relegated to the status of any other foreign language in Latvia. Latvia's Deputy Foreign Minister Martins Virsis stated that he was puzzled by Russia's efforts to interfere with Latvia's internal affairs. However, rather than making a real effort to protect Baltic Russians from discrimination, it seems that the Russian government was attempting to hide behind the 'human rights' issue as a way of reducing the need for a speedy troop withdrawal from the Baltic states. The Baltic governments made this argument often.[384] This meant both focusing the West's attention on the minorities issue in Estonia and Latvia but also using the troops as a regional stability force. However, this cannot wholly be the case for the 'human rights' issue offered a considerable source of political capital within Russian domestic politics. In fact, Russians in the near-abroad were perfect cannon fodder for the Russian opposition forces.

During the summer of 1992, the Russian Supreme Soviet became much more active in seeking to address the 'human rights' issue. In July, Ruslan Khasbulatov encouraged the Supreme Soviet to review the situation in the Baltic states.[385] Special attention was paid to perceived discrimination

382 *Izvestia*, 27 February 1992.

383 *Izvestia*, 2 April 1992.

384 *RFE/RL Newsline,* 'Russia Accuses Baltics of Disregards for Human Rights', 11 May 1989; 'Latvian-Russian Treaty Discussed', 10 June 1992.

385 *Izvestia*, 2 July 1992. See also *Nevazisimaya Gazeta*, 8 July 1992.

against Russians and Russian-speakers. Interestingly, the issue was taken up in the Commission on Questions of Inter-Republican Relations, a committee within the Supreme Soviet that discussed issues within the Soviet Union rather than relations between the Soviet Union and states in the international community. This indicates the lack of a change in mindset given the collapse of the Soviet Union and the status of the Baltic countries as states rather than Soviet republics.

The results of the initial discussion in the Supreme Soviet were accusations that Estonia, Latvia, and Lithuania were violating human rights and that legislators might impose economic sanctions against the Baltic states if they failed to change their policies. One of two documents passed by the Supreme Soviet called for the UN to discuss the issue during the current General Assembly meeting.[386] The resolution also argued for moves to suspend the Estonian-Russian Treaty that had been signed several months earlier. The second document was entitled 'On Human Rights in the Baltic states', and did little more than condemn the Baltic states for implementing policies that were discriminatory on grounds of nationality and for increasing regional instability. Chairman of the Russian Supreme Soviet's Council of Nationalities Ramazan Abdulatipov stated that the Baltic governments were building 'ethnocentric, not democratic states'. Furthermore, he argued that minorities were being humiliated by being required to know the national language and constitution of the country in order to gain citizenship.

It was the Latvian Foreign Ministry that came out strongly against the discussions in the Russian Supreme Soviet, stating again that Russia was using the issue to prevent the early withdrawal of troops from the Baltic states.[387] Latvia had not, in fact, passed a citizenship law and would not until after the elections of the Fifth *Saeima*. However, at this time Latvia had a foreign minister who was sympathetic to the citizenship issue. Janis Jurkans stated that 'many people came to Latvia from Russia without realising that they had come to a state that was once an independent country. Our duty is

---

386 Ibid.

387 *RFE/RL Newsline,* 'Latvia Rejects Russian Accusations', 24 July 1992.

to understand the fate of these people, who, like we, *are victims of the system.*'[388]

The summer of 1992 also saw the increased appearance of one of the most controversial figures in Russian politics: Russian Liberal Democratic Party leader Vladimir Zhirinovsky. As a populist leader relegated to eternal opposition, Zhirinovsky had the best opportunity to exploit the 'human rights' issue for his own political gain and the government's discredit. During a rally in Ivanograd, situated just across the Estonian border from Narva, Zhirinovsky called the Estonian government 'rabid nationalists' who had made Estonia a 'criminal state' that 'turns the entire population into a nation of thieves.'[389] More alarmingly, he stated that Russian Su-29 bombers would start making 'retribution flights' over Narva, the end result being the death of thousand of Russians who make up the larger part of the city's population. Furthermore, in a speech to reporters on 19 August, the Liberal Democrat leader argued for the reassertion of Russian control over the Baltic states. This was the same speech in which Zhirinovsky discussed the Zionist control over the international system. In a later speech, Zhirinovsky presented another plan to control the wayward Baltics: dismemberment.[390] He argued for the heavily Russian population areas to become parts of the Pskov and Smolensk regions of Russia, but finally decided that returning the Baltic states to 'Moscow's jurisdiction' would be even better.

The Russian MFA, while just as critical, tended to address the problems often without the bellicose language of other actors. In July, the MFA protested the lack of political and representation rights for a large part of the Estonian community.[391] This issue became even more apparent with the Estonian elections in September in which non-citizens were not allowed to vote.[392] Russian Foreign Minister Kozyrev claimed that 42 per cent of the voters were

---

388 *RFE/RL Newsline,* 'Jurkans: Latvia's Citizenship Law not likely in 1992', 11 August 1992; emphasis added.

389 *RFE/RL Newsline,* 'Zhirinovsky Rouses Narva', 14 July 1992; 'Zhirinovsky Speaks Out', 20 August 1992.

390 *RFE/RL Newsline,* 'Zhirinovsky's Views of the Baltic States', 7 December 1992.

391 *Izvestia*, 2 July 1992; and *RFE/RL Newsline,* 'Russia Protests to Estonia', 3 July 1992.

392 *RFE/RL Newsline,* 'Kozyrev Criticises Estonia Over Elections', 23 September 1992; and 'Estonia Rebuts Russian Statement', 24 September 1992.

ineligible to vote based on their nationality, which he argued violated international law. Echoing an earlier demand by the Russian Supreme Soviet, Kozyrev stated that the issue would be discussed at the UN. However, the Estonian Foreign Ministry claimed that the statements made by the Russian government were a threat to the sovereignty of Estonia and were set to intimidate the new *Riigikogu.*

With regard to Latvia, a foreign ministry delegation visit to Riga announced that they found ethnic situation satisfactory for the most part, but took issue with the language law relegating Russian to an unofficial status.[393] Following this, another Russian MFA delegation arrived in Riga to discuss the ethnic situation with members of the government, parliamentary deputies, and individuals within the Russian community.[394] The delegation was invited by the Latvian Foreign Ministry as a way of fostering co-operation amongst the two states.

8.5 Yeltsin versus Parliament

After the Estonian elections in 1992, Russian ongoing commentary on the 'human rights' issue in the Baltic states increased and became even more critical. A Russian delegation to the UN General Assembly warned that the Estonia and Latvian governments were pursuing a path of 'ethnic cleansing', which in current terms seems a bit extreme although the world had not experienced the full impact of the crises in Yugoslavia, Rwanda and Burundi.[395] This statement is important because it shows a more severe analysis of the Baltic situation. Before, only the political mavericks such as Zhirinovsky were using such terms, while the government was discussing discrimination of political and cultural rights. Members of the government had even gone so far to use the term 'apartheid', but 'ethnic cleansing' was surely a turn towards a stronger stand. At the same time, Russian Prime Minister Egor Gaidar, who

---

393 *RFE/RL Newsline,* 'Russian MFA Concludes Human Rights Visit', 17 August 1992.

394 *RFE/RL Newsline,* 'Russian, Latvian Representatives Discuss Human Rights', 27 August 1992.

395 *RFE/RL Newsline,* 'Russian Warns Balts Against 'Ethnic Cleansing'', 30 September 1992.

had before been seen by the Baltics as a moderate democrat friendly to Russia's Baltic neighbours, came out to say that economic sanctions were being considered.

Russian President Yeltsin also stepped up his attacks on Estonia and Latvia. In November, Yeltsin sent a letter to UN Secretary-General Boutros Boutros-Ghali calling on the UN to take measures to help stop the violation of human rights of Russians in Estonia and Latvia.[396] He argued that the discrimination in the Baltic states was contrary to the principles underlying the United Nations. Several weeks later, the president issued the order 'On Questions of Defence of the Rights and Interests of Russian Citizens Outside the Bounds of the Russian Federation'.[397] Interestingly, the order used the term *rossiiskie* (similar in connotation to *rossiianin*) in its reference to the group needing protection. Recognising that disorganisation and uncertainty made it more difficult to press the Baltic states over the 'human rights issue', Yeltsin called on several government agencies to complete co-operation agreements with states in the near-abroad. For example, the order called on the Ministries of Foreign Affairs and Defence to accelerate work on concluding agreements regarding the status of Russian troops.

Towards the end of 1992, several important developments occurred. First, the ultimate opinion maker in Russia, the Russian media, became increasingly anti-Baltic.[398] The Baltic states constantly had to deny accusations such as not allowing Russians to hold jobs and forcing them out of their homes. An opinion poll carried out by the Russian Department of Public Opinion Research in October showed that the three Baltic states were considered to be the foreign countries most hostile to Russia.[399] The respondents were predominantly parliamentarians, military officers, and other influential actors in Russia. Second, there was a growing acknowledgement amongst foreign policy experts in Russia and Russians living in the Baltic states that the increasing contentious Russian foreign policy could make things even more dif-

396 *RFE/RL Newsline,* 'Yeltsin Appeals to UN on Alleged Rights Violations', 9 November 1992.

397 *RFE/RL Newsline,* 'Yeltsin Order on Protection of Rights of Russian Citizens Abroad' 2 December 1992.

398 *RFE/RL Newsline,* 'Landbergis: Russian TV is Anti-Baltic', 19 August 1992.

399 *RFE/RL Newsline,* 'Russians Think Balts Are Hostile', 22 November 1992.

ficult rather than easier for non-citizens.[400] In November, advisors to the Russian Council of Foreign Policy warned against 'exciting passions' over the 'human rights' issue. In Sillamae, in northeast Estonia, 2000 protesters took to the streets calling for increased co-operation with the Estonian government. They also pointed to the difficult circumstances produced by 'outside interference.' Sillamae City Council member Lydia Dolmachova stated that 'we must think in terms of co-operation with the State Assembly and the government. It is important that Estonian authorities not consider us enemies.' Finally, Russian foreign policy was directed at each individual state rather than approaching the Baltic states together.[401] One Baltic politician argued that Russia was 'driving a wedge' between the three Baltic states in order to put the maximum amount of pressure on them. Naturally, the Baltic states would be better able to stand up to Russia if they acted together. Together, these developments characterise where the Baltic-Russian relationship was headed.

An early memorandum submitted at an OSCE meeting of foreign ministers by the Russian FM on 14 December showed a certain amount of foresight.[402] Unsurprisingly, the Russian FM accused Estonia and Latvia of political, economic, and social discrimination against their Russophone communities. Furthermore, he argued against the forceful removal of Russians to Russia. However, he also added that Estonia and Latvia should 'integrate Russians in the native societies while allowing them to preserve their ethnic culture.' This was indeed an interesting statement considering the later integration policies in both states.

In 1993, the Russian MFA continued being the main proponent for changes in Baltic minority policies. In the case of Estonia, the citizenship law was the focus of Russian attention. On the other hand, Latvia had yet to pass a citizenship law. Rather, the 1992 Language Law was the object of contention between Latvia and Russia regarding the minority issue. At the same

---

400 *RFE/RL Newsline,* 'Raised Passions Cause Problems for Russians in Balts', 22 November 1992; 'Estonia's Russians Point to Outside Interference, Want Co-operation with Tallinn', 9 November 1992.

401 *RFE/RL Newsline,* 'Latvian MP: Russia Driving a Wedge Between Balts', 10 September 1992.

402 *RFE/RL Newsline,* 'CSCE, Russia, and the Baltics', 15 December 1992.

time, the Russian government was increasingly conscious of how much the opposition had hijacked the 'human rights' issue.[403] The head of consular service within the MFA, Vasilii Vinogradov, remarked that the lack of a definite policy towards the defence of Russophones in the near-abroad was encouraging the opposition.

Russian Foreign Minister Kozyrev was under increasing pressure as well to maintain demands on the Baltic states to liberalise minority policies. At a meeting of foreign ministers of the Council of Baltic Sea States, Kozyrev likened the plight of Russians in Estonia and Latvia to the events in Yugoslavia.[404] At the same meeting, Kozyrev called for the establishment of a Minorities Commissioner to protect the rights of ethnic minorities in the Baltic states. As was to be expected, the foreign ministers from Estonia and Latvia argued against the necessity of creating such a post. It must be said also that the OSCE held a similar position as Russia, not to mention that Estonia had already invited an OSCE Mission to monitor the discrimination against minorities.

Prior to the Council of Baltic Sea States meeting, Kozyrev had charged the Estonian government with supporting the Estonian Decolonialisation Fund which helped repatriate non-citizens.[405] However, the Estonian government denied the accusations that it had any connections with the group. The government did concede that many Russians were not happy living away from family, not to mention finding themselves living outside their home nation. Indeed, the Estonian Decolonialisation Fund was established to help voluntary repatriation and was closely monitored by the authorities.

Encouragingly, Baltic and Russian representatives agreed on a written accord with the UN Commission on Human Rights.[406] The agreement stated that the governments in Estonia, Latvia, and Russia would stop criticising each other's actions and would co-operate on solving the problems of the Russophone minorities. The accord also acknowledged that all three states

---

403 *RFE/RL Newsline,* 'Problems of Consular Work in 'Near Abroad' Discussed', 25 February 1993.

404 *Izvestia*, 18 March 1993.

405 *RFE/RL Newsline,* 'Estonia Responds to Kozyrev', 2 March 1993.

406 *RFE/RL Newsline,* 'Balts, Russia Agree on Human Rights Co-operation', 11 March 1993.

were victims of the Soviet past. However, the agreement had little effect on the Baltic-Russian relationship.

All three Baltic states were on track to become members of the Council of Europe, but Estonia and Lithuania had progressed at a quicker pace in meeting the requirements for full membership.[407] The Russian government put a great deal of effort into trying to block Estonia's membership. The Russian delegation had earlier blocked the Baltic states admission in 1992.[408] Interestingly, Russia at this time was not a member of the Council of Europe. Kozyrev reiterated his accusations of discrimination against the Russophone minority and argued that Estonia's membership was premature. As was to be expected, the Estonian government perceived Russia's actions as 'interference'. There is good reason to speculate that Russia's 'interference' actually reduced the number of negative votes cast by the parliamentary assembly. Once again, Russia's Baltic policy failed to achieve the desired results.

Within the next month, Estonia would again stand out as the target of Russian foreign policy as tensions within the country flared. As discussed in chapter five, the Estonian 'Aliens' Crisis' arose after the *Riigikogu* passed a Law on Aliens that required all non-citizens to seek residence permits within one year or risk being deported. The law also stated that permanent residents could vote in local elections. Russia responded immediately. Even before the final reading of the legislation was passed, the Russian MFA accused Estonia of 'aggressive nationalism' and warned of an 'interethnic explosion' that could destabilise the region.[409] The day after the law's passage, Russian Deputy Foreign Minister Churkin stated that Russia was preparing a retaliatory package of diplomatic and political measures targeted at Estonia's 'grave violation of human rights'.[410] Churkin also pinned down the fundamental problem with the law. He argued that, by requiring that all non-citizens apply for residency permits, the law was placing Estonia's Russophone population in the position of 'illegal immigrants', a status they already held according to Estonian nationalists.

---

407 *Izvestia*, 12 May 1993.

408 *Izvestia*, 6 July 1992.

409 *RFE/RL Newsline,* 'Heated Exchanges Over Civil Rights in Estonia', 21 June 1993.

410 *RFE/RL Newsline,* 'New Estonian Law on Foreigners', 22 June 1993; 'Russia Considering Sanctions Against Estonia', 23 June 1993.

Kozyrev argued that the West had encouraged the 'violation of human rights' by allowing Estonia to become a member of the Council of Europe.[411] He argued that 'one of its new members is embarking on the path, I am not afraid to exaggerate, of apartheid, as a third of the population is proclaimed foreigners, and of ethnic cleansing, as a third is facing the threat of being driven out of the country.' At the same time, presidential foreign policy advisor Sergei Stankevich, the architect of Russia's post-Soviet foreign policy for the near-abroad, claimed that the Estonia was declaring war on its Russian population and a cold war on Russia.

The condemnation from the Russian government continued.[412] In Russia, the battle between Yeltsin and the Duma was heating up and Estonian authorities pointed to this as the source of Russia's 'interference'. Echoing the earlier claims of Kozyrev, Yeltsin accused Estonia of 'ethnic cleansing' in the style of South African apartheid. The President stated that actions would be taken 'to protect the honour, dignity, and legitimate rights of our compatriots. . .' At the same time, Yeltsin halted the withdrawal of Russia's Baltic Fleet from Estonian ports. Furthermore, the Russian gas provider, Lentransgaz, stopped the daily shipment of 500,000 cubic meters of natural gas. While the commercial director stated that the halt in shipments was due to the way Russians were being treated in Estonia, government officials stated that actually Estonia had failed to pay a $6-million debt. Even economic transactions were being tied to the 'human rights' situation in Estonia.

Subsequently, the Russian Supreme Soviet was set to discuss the option of sanctions on 25 June. It took until 1 July to reach a decision on a resolution dealing with events in Estonia. The Supreme Soviet resolution was passed nearly unanimously with only two abstentions. Overall, the resolution took little action over the Estonian Law on Aliens. The Supreme Soviet gave the government two weeks to implement a package of measures against Estonia, including halting the withdrawal of Russian troops. Finally, the resolution asked the MFA to inform the UN, OSCE, and the Council of Europe of the events in Estonia.

---

411 *RFE/RL Newsline,* 'Russia Sharpens Rhetoric against Estonia', 24 June 1993; and 'Response from Estonian Ambassador', 24 June 1993.

412 *Nevazisimaya Gazeta*, 8 July 1993; *Izvestia*, 10 July 1993; and *Segodnya*, 16 July

At first, Estonian President Lennart Meri decided to wait to sign the Law on Aliens until it had been reviewed by international experts. After taking some suggested changes into account, Meri signed the law on 12 July. However, the changes were not as the Russian government would have wanted them. In essence, a law concentrating on the stateless status of much of the Russophone population was a problem. There were moves in the Russian Supreme Soviet Presidium to denounce the 1920 bilateral treaties with both Estonia and Latvia over the 'human rights' issue. As was to be expected, the Estonian and Latvian foreign ministries criticised the moves. However, more surprisingly, the Russian Foreign Ministry came out against the move, calling it 'nonsensical'. Yet once again, Russian foreign policy had little effect in changing the minority policy in a Baltic State. In the end, events within Russia led attention to be directed away from Estonia.

8.6 The 'Normalisation' of Russian Politics

However, with Yeltsin coming out on top of the political crisis, in February 1994 Russia eventually focused its attention on the Baltic states once more. Russian Deputy Foreign Minister Sergei Krylov denied the Baltic argument that there was a Soviet 'occupation' of the three states in 1940.[413] He stated that the evidence showed that there was a legitimate call for inclusion. Yet more likely, the call for inclusion could not be considered as legitimate since Soviet troops had already occupied the Baltic states before the appeal was submitted to the Soviet authority. Krylov's statement was the result of Estonia's efforts to encourage the UN General Assembly to condemn the Soviet occupation. In addition, a representative of Russia's Liberal Democratic Party went even further. Petr Rozhok claimed that Estonia was ancient Russian territory. He encouraged all Russians to apply for Russian territory. Furthermore, Rozhok encouraged retired military servicemen and officers to form military units as a means of defending their 'honour and dignity.'[414]

1993.

413 *RFE/RL Newsline,* 'Kostikov: There Was No Soviet Occupation of Estonia', 24 February 1994.

414 *Segodnya*, 27 January 1994.

Krylov's statements signal the beginning of an increased focus on the Russians in the near-abroad by the Russian MFA specifically. MFA spokesman Mikhail Demruin stated on 8 February that 'diplomatic measures were not enough.'[415] He discussed a proposal that would offer economic support to the various Russophone communities as well as the establishment of a powerful broadcast system that allow Moscow to communicate with some 25 million Russians. Furthermore, the proposal would allow the Russian government to favour businesses that were owned by ethnic Russians. A special commission set up under Yeltsin's office eventually took up the proposal. The commission favoured the economic component to the proposal but also pressed for dual citizenship.

Less than a week after the proposal was made public, Kozyrev, in an interview for *Newsweek*, condemned once again the 'ethnic cleansing' in Estonia and Latvia.[416] Possibly characterising the lack of results thus far, Kozyrev stated that Russia could not remain 'indifferent' to what was happening near its borders. He also asked the world to pay attention to what was occurring in the Baltic states. The Latvian Foreign Ministry denied the accusations and pointed to the findings of several international organisations concerning its Russophonic community. The Estonian Foreign Ministry argued that Kozyrev's statements were untrue and helped undermine the Estonian-Russian relationship. Furthermore, Estonian Defence Minister Juri Luik stated that the Russian Foreign Minister's remarks played into the hands of the Russian government's opposition.

In the summer of 1993, the 'Aliens' Crisis' in Estonia had dominated Baltic-Russian relations. In 1994, Latvia had an equivalent experience when it passed the citizenship law in June.[417] Estonia had passed a citizenship law in early 1992, which allowed them to avoid the established focus on the 'human rights' issue in the Baltic states. On the other hand, the Latvian Supreme Soviet decided to wait until after the election of the first post-Soviet legislature before discussing the law. Although the passage of the Latvian Citizenship

415 *Newsweek*, 14 February 1994.

416 *Izvestia*, 9 February 1994.

417 *Segodnya*, 11 June 1994; and *Izvestia*, 6 August 1994.

Law did not prove to be domestically contentious on the scale seen in Estonia's northeast, the Russian Federation responded in a similar fashion.

Russian complaints over the law began during the legislative phase. After the second reading, Russian Deputy Foreign Minister Vitalii Churkin criticised the law saying that Russia would use economic leverage to punish Latvia. He stated that 'in conditions when Latvia adopts discriminatory laws, we must be in no haste to sign Russian-Latvian economic agreements'.[418] He further threatened that Russia would cancel Latvia's 'most-favoured-nation' status. Once again, after the law was passed following the final reading, Russian Deputy Minister Sergei Krylov called the law 'inhumane' and purposefully directed at the Russophone community. Krylov also pointed out that the main objection of the Russian government was to the naturalisation quotas. Furthermore, Krylov, echoing Churkin's threats, stated that the fate of any bilateral agreements would remain uncertain. Finally, along with the growing concern over the law from international organisations and human rights organisations, Yeltsin also let his views be known in a letter to Latvian President Ulmanis, complaining of the discriminatory nature of the law.

Alone, the Russian government had little effect on the final revised version of the law. The threats of cancelling bilateral economic agreements did little to improve the situation towards Moscow's objective. In fact, the Baltic states were quickly transferring their trade from Russia to the EU. However, having said this, Russia's impact through international organisations should not be underestimated. The Council of Europe was unwilling to allow Latvia to be a member until they had elected a parliament and passed a citizenship law. Having fulfilled the former condition, the Council of Europe was unhappy with the result of the latter. Similarly, the OSCE was critical of several points within the law, including the yearly naturalisation quota of 0.1 per cent of the Latvian citizen population. On the part of the OSCE, the High Commissioner on National Minorities, Max van der Stoel, encouraged President Ulmanis to send the legislation back to the *Saeima* for revision. In the final version, the law did not include the annual naturalisation quotas but instead included a more substantial system of naturalisation windows that had been present to some degree in the first version to pass the *Saeima*.

---

418 *RFE/RL Newsline,* 'Churkin Critical of Latvia's Draft Citizenship Law', 13 June 1994.

As the EU, Council of Europe, and OSCE were congratulating Latvia on the passage and subsequent promulgation of the revised citizenship law, Russia continued to show its disapproval. Once again, Yeltsin denounced the law. He argued that actually, Latvia had ignored the advice of the Western organisation. Instead, he claimed that the law divided the population into first and second-class citizenship. Furthermore, he argued that Latvia was descending into 'militant nationalism'. Finally, Yeltsin, like several others from within the Russian government, only gave vague descriptions of how Russia would respond to Latvia, once again pointing to the renunciation of economic agreements.

Perhaps revealing Russia's mood, the German Friedrich Ebert Foundation released data from a survey carried out on 615 Russian military officers. In response to a question asking who they considered to be Russia's 'main enemy', 49 per cent gave Latvia as their answer, followed by Afghanistan, Lithuania, and Estonia. Indeed, it is interesting that the Baltic states ranked as high as a nation with which the Soviet Union had recently practically lost a decade-long war.[419]

A main objective of Russian foreign policy since the fall of the Soviet Union was to encourage Russian citizenship within the other post-Soviet states. Within Estonia and Latvia, this policy was having considerable affect on the status of Russians and other minorities.[420] In both Baltic countries, thousands of individuals sought Russian citizenship. In many cases, many within the Russophone communities still had a strong emotional connection to an ethnic homeland. Others in Estonia found that it would be easier to do business with, as well as visit family in, Russia being a Russian citizen and having Estonian permanent residency status rather than the other way around. Many Russophones in Latvia were put off by Latvia's delay in devising a citizenship law, and then by the naturalisation windows that would mean that many would have to wait until after 2000 to begin applying for Latvian citizenship. Other non-ethnically Russian minorities also became Russian citizens. For example, many of the 80,000 Ukrainians in Latvia applied for

419 *Izvestia*, 30 August 1994.

420 *RFE/RL Newsline,* 'Growing Number of Russian Citizens in Estonia', 21 October 1994; 'More Than 60,000 Russian Citizens in Estonia', 7 February 1995.

Russian citizenship before the February 1995 deadline because Ukrainian law stated that individuals have to live in the Ukraine in order to become a citizen.[421] It seems that this follows the logic that being a citizen brings with it a level of security that the stateless status does not, despite the Baltic government's best efforts to prevent such fears.

Furthermore, as chapter six related, Russian citizenship allowed many individuals within the Russophone community to politically organise in a way that would have been impossible without citizenship. In both states, Russian citizens' organisations arose as a means of defending Baltic Russian interests. However, the ability to gain citizenship presented many in the minority communities with a dilemma. On the one hand, Russian citizenship would allow for some political assurances that if all else failed, the Russian government would be obligated to do something. On the other, minority individuals would jeopardise their ability to become citizens of their resident state. For example, the Estonian and Latvian parliament decided to restrict the ability to gain dual citizenship. Dual citizenship can generally only be granted in the case of returning people who had fled the Soviet occupation or were direct descendants of those who had.

This citizenship dilemma led to a split within the Russophone populations. While on one side there are those that have sought Russian citizenship, there are also those that are quite willing to integrate into Baltic society while maintaining their cultural identity. The problem is that each side violates the position of the other. By becoming Russian citizens, minorities perpetuate the 'enemy within' fears that are still apparent in Baltic society, thus making it more difficult for those who wish to integrate. Likewise, those who are willing to integrate can be seen to dilute the ability of the minority populations to defend their interests against a 'titular' government. Of course positions within the Russophonic communities are not this well defined, but the dilemma does represent an ongoing split. Yet over the years, this dilemma has become less the case as far fewer stateless persons are seeking Russian citizenship since the barriers to Baltic citizenship had lessened.

---

421 *RFE/RL Newsline,* 'Many Ukrainians in Latvia to Take Russian Citizenship', 30 June 1994.

8.7 Effective Foreign Policy?

So, how well was the Russian government able to use the Russian citizens to help complete its foreign policy objectives? For the most part, very poorly. Clearly, Russian citizens would be unable to affect policy-making through the electoral process. This is less the case in Estonia where permanent residents are able to vote in local elections. The Russian strategy of encouraging Russian citizenship was based on the idea that the Russian Federation would have an increased moral responsibility to protect the interests of its own citizens as opposed to an often-vague notion of 'compatriots'. However, as long as the majority of residents either remained stateless or became citizens of either Estonia or Latvia, the Russian policy would have little practical effect.

After the Russian reactions to the 1993 Law on Aliens in Estonia and the 1994 Citizenship Law in Latvia, the verbal exchanges across borders dramatically decreased. Overall, the relationship between Russia and the Baltic States changed. This occurred for several reasons. First, several international organisations were observing the 'human rights' issue in Estonia and Latvia, with the most important being the OSCE High Commissioner and permanent missions. The Russian Federation often discredited its own position towards the Baltic states by consistently being more radical than European institutions. As we have seen in this chapter, when Estonia or Latvia adopted the suggestions of such officials as the High Commissioner, Moscow still protested that the changes did not go far enough. Thus, while vesting the OSCE and Council of Europe with the authority to investigate the claims of 'human rights violations' in Estonia and Latvia, Moscow consistently called for more radical solutions. In the end, with the continually watchful eye of international organisations and the lack of dramatic events to arouse critical commentary from Moscow, the Russian position stagnated.

Second, domestic politics within Russia had also changed. Yeltsin had come out on top of the 1993 crisis, and a new constitution had been passed placing a considerable amount of power into the hands of the president. While Yeltsin consolidated power, especially after the 1996 presidential elections, the divergence in foreign policy goals continued. While Atlanticists were attempting to engage the West through cordial relations, the Eurasianists maintained a hard stance towards the US and NATO.[422] Russian foreign policy during the years of Yeltsin was characterising by policies from both camps. Without a clear and consistent voice, Russia's ability to influence minority policy in Estonia and Latvia without the backing of European institutions, and thus Western governments, was slim indeed.

Finally, Moscow had larger problems to deal with while it could save face through rhetoric alone in relation to the Baltic states. Although the 'human rights' issue in Estonia and Latvia remained important, the opposition in the Duma (primarily the Communist Party) turned to the deteriorating state of the country in general. This became even more the case after the economic collapse in the late 1990's. Another example of the transfer of attention came when the Russian government fell into a war in the secessionist republic of Chechnya in December 1994, established a peace agreement, only to recommit to military operations. Combined, this change in Baltic-Russian relations produced a more pragmatic and often mundane relationship, although there were still the occasional contentious remarks made on all sides.

Looking back, we can see that Russian-Estonian relations had already begun to warm by 1997.[423] In April, Russia gave a cordial signal to Tallinn by allowing Estonians and Russian residents living near the Russian border to have multi-entry visas.[424] Furthermore, the tone from the Russian Foreign Ministry also became less harsh. In May, Russian Foreign Minister Yevgenii Primakov stated that Russia was looking for 'cloudless relations' with Estonia, but pointed out that the minority and border issues was still a problem.[425] However, rather than condemn Tallinn, as had been done often in the past, Primakov stated that he was looking for increased dialogue between Estonia and Russia as well as increased co-operation with OSCE regarding Estonia's Russian-speakers. In a meeting between the Estonian and Russian Ethnic

---

[422] The most frequent complaints have come from the Duma, but as the Kremlin has often pointed out, Parliament's position is not necessarily the Government's position. See especially *The Baltic Times*, 'Russia steps up its anti-NATO campaign', No. 139, 17 December 1998.

[423] *RFE/RL Newsline,* 'Are Estonian-Russian Relations Warming?', 28 August 1997.

[424] *RFE/RL Newsline,* 'Estonian-Russian', 23 April 1997.

[425] *RFE/RL Newsline,* 'Russia Wants 'Cloudless Relations' with Estonia', 26 May 1997.

Affairs Ministers, Russia again urged increased dialogue as a means of solving the minority issue. Estonia stated that it would speed up integration.

The relationship between Tallinn and Moscow had changed. Despite Russia's calls for dialogue, Estonian politicians still considered the minority issue to be an internal matter. However, despite this stand on the issue, Estonia would still be beholden to international agreements it had signed relating to the membership criteria of Western organisations. On 15 July 1997, the European Commission announced that it was recommending that Estonia begin accession negotiations. Indeed, the EU began to increase pressure on Estonia to solve several outstanding problems relating to the Russian-speaking minority. In the end, the EU could withhold membership without policy changes, although it would be difficult to imagine that it would ever come to this point. On the other hand, Russia had lost much of its leverage on Tallinn. Russian troops were withdrawn by September 1994. The border issue, although still unresolved, remained static without any further demands in years.

At the same time, there was a growing link between Baltic security and the minority issue. In a letter to the Latvian president, Yeltsin stated that the treatment of the Russophone communities was the 'decisive factor' in Russian-Latvian relations.[426] Nearly a month later, Yeltsin stated that Russia would reconsider its relations with NATO if the security alliance expanded to include former Soviet Republics.[427] The Latvian Foreign Ministry responded to Yeltsin's remarks by saying that each country had a sovereign right to choose a security system.

In September 1997, the Latvian government passed a law restricting the use of foreign-published textbooks. Of course, the greatest impact was seen in the Russian language secondary schools, where many of the textbooks had been printed in Russia. The problem was that it was difficult to find a sufficient supply of Russian language textbooks published in Latvia. Interestingly, while Moscow Mayor Yurii Luzhkov announced that the city council

---

426 *RFE/RL Newsline,* 'Yeltsin on Russian-Latvian Relations', 22 April 1997.

427 *RFE/RL Newsline,* 'Latvia Responds Angrily to Yeltsin's Comments on NATO Accord', 21 May 1997.

would begin sending textbooks to Russian-speaking students in the near-abroad, Latvia was not on the list.[428]

In 1998, Lithuanian parliamentary chairman Vytautas Landsbergis argued that Russia was waging a cold war against the Baltic states. He argued that the Russian objective was to create the impression that the Baltic states' fate rested solely with Moscow. Interestingly enough, this statement was made when Baltic-Russian relations were at their least contentious since the restoration of independence. However, as NATO and EU membership became more likely, Russia again stepped up the pressure on the Baltic states to reform their minority policies. Similar to the Council of Europe episode years earlier, Russia was attempting to stall, in the case of EU membership, and prevent, in the case of NATO membership, while remaining outside those institutions itself. Overall, Russia's 'cold war' with the Baltic states seems to have been short-lived and ineffective. As the following chapter will discuss, the EU, through the OSCE, was already applying pressure on Estonia and Latvia to reform its citizenship policy.

Despite Landsbergis' claim, it seemed that Moscow was unable to even have a consistent Baltic foreign policy. For example, the Russian government and Duma were at odds over the minority issue in Estonia.[429] In early February, a Russian FM spokesperson stated that the main obstacle to Estonia joining the EU was the nation's 'colonial' attitude toward minorities. The Foreign Ministry stated that although it was interested in seeing Tallinn find a 'civilised' solution to the minority issue, it did not oppose EU membership. However, the tone of a Duma delegation to Estonia was much different. The delegation stated that the citizenship issue in Estonia was an internal affair, although they would like to see everyone born in Estonia granted citizenship. Furthermore, the head of the delegation Yelena Mizulina stated that situation of the ethnic Russians in Estonia was not nearly as dramatic as the Russian press had portrayed. Finally, Oleg Mironov, a member of the Communist faction in the Duma, argued that those minorities that had failed to seek Estonian or Russian citizenship were 'to a certain extent to blame for their problems.'

428 *RFE/RL Newsline,* 'Luzhkov Says Moscow Will Provide Textbooks for Russians Abroad', 10 October 1997.

429 *RFE/RL Newsline,* 'Russia Accuses Estonia of 'Colonial' Attitude', 6 February 1998;

However, in the case of Latvia, the Government and the Duma agreed that the status of Russian-speakers was a major problem.[430] Viktor Chernomyrdin, Russian Premier, argued that it was 'unacceptable for people living in the middle of Europe at the end of the twentieth century to be humiliated the way Russians are in Latvia.' Chernomyrdin also stated that the status of Russian-speakers in Latvia was the priority issue in Russian-Latvian relations. Keep in mind that at this time, the majority of Russian-speakers were still unable to apply for citizenship because of the naturalisation windows. Yet having said this, the Latvian Department of Naturalisation estimated that 121,000 non-citizens who were able to apply for naturalisation in 1997 failed to do so.[431]

Although Russia's rhetoric directed at Estonia continued to be contentious, particularly over the introduction of language requirements for elected officials, the verbal contest between Riga and Moscow increased. As stated in a previous chapter, the Riga police physically stopped an unsanctioned protest held predominantly by Russian pensioners regarding the price of utilities. Moscow pounced on the issue.[432] Both Yeltsin and Foreign Minister Yevgenii Primakov argued that the Riga police action violated the human rights of the protesters. The president further cancelled preliminary talks on establishing a meeting between Yeltsin and Ulmanis. The Russian FM called on the international community to condemn the actions of the police. The Latvian FM responded by saying that the Russian officials were making highly biased, and thus presumably misleading, comments about the demonstration. Prime Minister Guntars Krasts said that Russia might have even helped stage the rally, a charge the Russian government quickly denied.

Also that March, the Russian Federation Council (upper house) passed a non-binding resolution that called on the government to freeze trade and economic ties if the discrimination against Russian-speakers in Latvia continued.[433] Moscow Mayor Yurii Luzhkov stated that the Latvia authorities were

---

'Russian Duma Delegation in Tallinn', 23 February 1998.

430 *RFE/RL Newsline,* '. . . Warns Latvia's Ulmanis Over Russian Minority', 26 January 1998.

431 *RFE/RL Newsline,* 'More People Naturalized in Latvia in 1997', 9 January 1998.

432 *Nevazisimaya Gazeta*, 7 March 1998 and *Noviye Izvestiya*, 11 March 1998.

433 *Nevazisimaya Gazeta*, 21 March 1998

'permitting genocide and discrimination against our *former* compatriots.'[434] The mayor then argued that Russian-speakers were being used as slaves. Although there is no evidence that the Russophonic community was suffering from genocide, across the board discrimination, or being treated as slaves, this did not stop Russian politicians and the press from using the event to 'play to the crowd.' As Paul Goble argues, it is comforting to see a government that is responsive to the public mood, for that is what democracy should be about.[435] However, the populist rhetoric may easily go too far and become especially dangerous in transitioning societies. Nevertheless, the event and its subsequent aftermath changed the trajectory of bilateral relations. Furthermore, it put Latvia firmly under the spotlight of the Russian politicians, press, and populace.

The subsequent effects of the 3 March event left Russia and Latvia in a standoff, in which both sides were unwilling to back down. The Russian Foreign Minister even went so far as to say that Latvians 'have finally aroused the bear'.[436] However, Primakov tempered his statement by saying that Russia was simply asking that Latvia abide by the recommendations of the OSCE. Even after the Latvian *Saeima* passed a more liberal citizenship law, the Russian government was not pleased, although the OSCE was satisfied. The Russian Deputy Foreign Minister stated that several of the points within the new law left it unclear how sincere the Latvian government was in considering reform.[437]

With the defeat of the referendum that would have appealed the changes to the citizenship law, Latvians signalled their desire for increased integration and thus a general acceptance of the non-titular communities. As Goble points out in another article, the defeat of the referendum offered a challenge to the Russian government.[438] For the most part, the new citizenship law and the subsequent approval by the Latvian electorate removed the primary contentious issue between the two states. Furthermore, it went a long

---

434 Emphasis added.

435 Goble, Paul. 1998. Trapped by Democracy? *RFE/RL Newsline,* 18 March.

436 *RFE/RL Newsline,* 'Primakov Says Moscow Won't Back Down', 29 April 1998.

437 *RFE/RL Newsline,* 'Russian Official Picks Holes in Latvian Citizenship Amendments', 27 August 1998.

438 Goble, Paul. 1998. The Latvian Challenge. *RFE/RL Newsline,* 6 October.

way to ending the campaign targeted at Latvia since the March pensioners' rally. Finally, as Goble states, 'Russian efforts to advance Moscow's influence in Latvia will need to find a new direction'. Interestingly, it did not take long to reinvent the issue.

At first, there did seem to be some change in Russia's relationship with Latvia. For example, former St. Petersburg Mayor Anatolii Sobchak stated after a visit to Latvia in October that he saw no evidence to suggest any hostilities between titulars and non-titulars in Latvia.[439] He said, 'I am starting to comprehend that to a great extent [the problems of the Russian-speaking minority are] an object of political speculation. The parties use it to raise their political capital. In real life, I did not find even a trace of hostility or opposition between Latvians and Russians.' However, it must be said that even Sobchak, who was at the time being investigated by the Russian Prosecutor-General on four incidents of bribery, may have had his own score to settle with the Russian government.

Although the issue of citizenship was largely settled in Latvia, the Russian government found fault with the new education and language laws. The education law passed on 29 October 1998 began the phasing out of Russian in state-run schools. The Russian Foreign Ministry called the new law discriminatory and against international norms.[440] Over a year later, the *Saeima* passed a new language law, which regulated the use of language in the public sphere and specific private industries related to health and safety.[441] The Russian Foreign Ministry went so far as to ask the EU not to consider Latvia for membership.[442] However, both the EU and OSCE praised Latvia on the new legislation.

---

439 *RFE/RL Newsline,* 'Sobchak Comments on Interethnic Relations in Latvia', 19 October 1998.

440 *The Baltic Times* 'Russia steps up criticism of Latvia: Estonia also suffers barbs from Moscow', No. 129, 8 October 1998; and 'Russia sends mixed signals to Riga' No. 129, 10 December 1998.

441 The Russian Duma passed a resolution condemning the first draft of the language law while it was being debated in the *Saeima*. However, that draft was still passed but returned due to European pressure. See *RFE/RL Newsline,* 'Russian State Duma Passes Anti-Latvian Legislation', 22 November 1999.

442 *RFE/RL Newsline,* 'Latvia Receives Praise for Language Law, But Russia Slams It', 12 December 1999.

Despite the complaints over the education and language laws, the diplomatic mood between the Russian government and Riga had settled since the defeat of the October 1998 citizenship referendum. However, the Russian Duma continued to press the issue. In May, the Duma passed a bill on sanctions again Latvia over the 'violation of the rights of ethnic Russians living in Latvia.'[443] The legislation imposed economic sanctions by banning any trade deals with the Latvian government and any private entities that were not Russian citizens. The bill further banned exports to Latvia and non-humanitarian imports. Latvian PM Kristopans responded by saying that the Russian Duma failed to understand the process of democracy. In the end, however, the bill got passed after its second reading but was stifled after opposition within the Russian government.

On the other hand, Russian relations with Estonia had considerably improved. One of example of good-natured relations came when the Estonian Population and Nationalities Minister Andra Veidemann, credited with devising the Estonian integration programme, meet with Russian Nationalities Affairs Minister Ramazan Abdulatipov.[444] On 20 January 1999, the two ministers signed a document that allowed for co-operation in ethnic policies and the increased exchange of information. Another example came when Estonian President Lennart Meri stated that, despite the fact that the leaders of the two countries had not met since 1994, relations were improving.[445] He stated that the legal foundations on which bilateral relations were based were very strong. President Meri subsequently became co-chairman of the Estonian-Russian Intergovernmental Commission.

One bump in the new Estonian-Russian relationship came when the *Riigikogu* passed an amendment to the Law on Foreigners that placed more restrictions regarding residency permits. The Russian Duma claimed that the amendment opened the way for the deportation of Russian military pensioners. The Duma further stated that the amendment was passed 'to force persons whose native language is Russian to leave'. However, the OSCE Mis-

443 *RFE/RL Newsline,* 'Kristopans Slams Russian Duma Bill on Sanctions', 21 May 1999.

444 *RFE/RL Newsline,* 'Estonia's Viedemann in Moscow', 21 January 1999.

445 *RFE/RL Newsline,* 'Estonian President Sees Improved Relations with Moscow', 6 April 1999.

sion to Estonia backed the changes and argued that the amendment established the way for the removal of those who had agreed to leave and live in housing built for them with foreign assistance, but had not done so.[446]

While Estonia's relationship with Russia seemed to be improving, the relations between Riga and Moscow became worse.[447] In an interview with the BBC in May 2000, Latvian President Vaira Vike-Freiberga stated that recent Russian statements opposing the expansion of NATO in the Baltic area had caused Latvia to be increasingly concerned about Russia's 'new military doctrine.' She went on to say that any attack on Latvia would be the same as an attack on the EU and NATO. This was surprising given that Latvia was a member of neither. Nevertheless, the Russian FM released a statement two days later calling the statements of the Latvian president 'unprecedented in their anti-Russian tone and following the worst traditions of the Cold War.'[448] The statement went on to accuse the Latvian president of using the Russian military doctrine as a way of deflecting attention away from the inter-ethnic situation in Latvia.

Interestingly, the road to NATO membership for the Baltic states was argued to go through Moscow. Throughout the post-Soviet period, the Russian government continually stated that it would not appreciate NATO's expansion to include former Soviet republics. Many in the West believed that Moscow had the diplomatic ability to stop the Baltic states becoming members.[449] Clearly, Baltic NATO membership is not beholden to Moscow's whim since the flags were raised at NATO Headquarters on 2 April 2004.

In 2001, Russia maintained the same policy of rhetoric without corresponding action. The Chairman of the Russian Duma Foreign Affairs Committee Dmitrii Rogozin stated in February that Russia needed a new policy towards Estonia.[450] He stated that Russia should come to know Estonia better. Furthermore, he stated that he acknowledged Estonia's right as a sovereign

---

446 *RFE/RL Newsline,* 'OSCE Mission in Estonia Backs Policy on Ex-Russian Officers', 4 November 1999.

447 *RFE/RL Baltic States Report* 8 May 2000 1 (16).

448 Russian Foreign Ministry statement released by the Russian Embassy in Tallinn, 3 May 2000.

449 See Goble, Paul. 2000. A De Facto Veto? *RFE/RL Baltic States Report* 1 (22).

450 *RFE/RL Newsline,* 'Call for New Russian Policy towards Estonia', 16 February 2001.

state to determine whether or not it wanted to become a member of NATO. However, the following day, Rogozin made a statement whereby he was forced to drop his prepared list of military steps that Russia would take if Estonia did join the security pact.[451] In addition to Rogozin, Russian Communist Party leader Zyuganov argued that the Estonian government was destroying the nation's north-eastern region populated predominantly by Russians.[452] He called on the government to protect the Russian 'compatriots' through the use of economic sanctions. In October, Estonian PM Mart Laar stated he doubted any further improvement in relations with Russia.[453]

8.8 Conclusion

Indeed, towards the end of 2001, Moscow continued to raise the ethnic issue in Estonia and Latvia.[454] Russian Foreign Minister Igor Ivanov told the OSCE HCNM Rolf Ekeus that Moscow remained concerned about the status of Russian-speakers. At the Congress of Compatriots in October, Moscow Mayor Luzhkov claimed that the attitude towards ethnic Russians in Estonia and Latvia was 'blatant apartheid'. Yet at the same time, representatives of the three Baltic states were meeting to discuss Russian Baltic Foreign Policy.[455] The Baltic parliamentarians condemned Russia's statements comparing the Baltic states to the Balkans and agreed that more co-operation was needed in order to counter Russian efforts to hinder domestic policy. In the end, the Russian policy in the Baltic region was similar to what it had been in the beginning: a lot of talk and very little action. Having said that, is this not the nature of diplomacy?

---

451 *RFE/RL Baltic States Report* 'Rogozin Calls for New Russian Approach to Estonia', 12 March 2001.

452 *RFE/RL Baltic States Report* 'Russian Communist Pledges Help to Ethnic Russians', 19 February 2001.

453 *RFE/RL Newsline,* 'Estonian Premier Doubts Improvement in Relations with Russia', 29 October 2001.

454 *The Baltic Times* 'Russia grumbles as OSCE pulls out', No. 286, 16 December 2001.

455 *RFE/RL Baltic States Report* 'Baltic Parliamentarians Condemn Russian Statements', 16 October 2001.

This chapter was particularly directed at the external national homeland within our own metaphorical 'nexus'. We can claim that the Russian Federation is an external national homeland because there is every indication that the Russian political elites, as well as the general Russian population, see themselves in the role of guaranteeing the protection of the Russian-speaking communities in the 'near abroad'. Furthermore, minority leaders in Estonia and Latvia maintained links to Moscow in the beginning, although this has lessened over time. However, as time progresses, we should expect that the Russian Federation will no longer be able to maintain the role of external national homeland for several reasons.

First, as the Baltic states become EU member-states, we should not expect to see a hardening of the nationalist policies but rather the opposite. Thus, the fodder for protest of the Russian Foreign Ministry will no longer be available. Second, in general, the Russian-speaking communities in Estonia and Latvia are doing far better socially and economically than their 'compatriots' in Russia. For example, both Estonia and Latvia have experienced continued economic growth, while the Russian economy collapsed in 1998. Thus, the typical 'human rights' argument will bring less domestic political gains. Third, assuming that there will not be a resumption of radical nationalist policies, the minority communities will identify less with the cultural motherland. Indeed, this is as an expected by-product of the integration programmes. Finally, the Russian Federation will simply no longer be able to perform this role in the future, because of a general inability to change European policies from outside of the EU, in addition to an expected unwillingness as the potential returns to such protests are reduced. This is not to say that 'compatriots' in the 'near abroad' may not be an easy foreign political issue with which to gain political capital, but rather this will be focused away from the Baltic states. Hopefully, as this occurs, the often-contentious relationship between Moscow and the Baltic states will change.

Chapter 9 The Baltic States and Europe[456]

Of the fifteen post-Soviet nations, the Baltic states have come the furthest in European integration. The increasingly close relationship with Europe is predominantly based on Baltic democratic development and market transition.[457] At the same time, questions of cultural-linguistic identities in Estonia and Latvia in particular have remained an important issue in restoration politics. Several scholars have proposed that stringent social policies have led the two northern Baltic states towards ethnic democracies rather than liberal democracies.[458] On the other hand, Lithuania has escaped this label by instituting more liberal social policies from the beginning, such as an inclusive law on citizenship.

By expanding on Brubaker's 'nexus' metaphor, we can see that several forces are at work in affecting the development of social policy in Estonia and Latvia.[459] First, traditional political parties have catered to the 'selectorate' by instituting more stringent minority policies. By minority policies, we mean those policies relating to the minority community created within the larger po-

456 An early version of this chapter was published as Galbreath, David J. 2003. The Politics of European Integration and Minority Rights in Estonia and Latvia. *Perspectives on European Politics and Society* 4 (1):35-54.

457 For an earlier review of national identity and foreign policy in the Baltic states, see Misiunas, Romuald. 1994. National Identity and Foreign Policy in the Baltic States. In *The Legacy of History in Russia and the New States of Eurasia*, edited by S. Frederick Starr. Armonk, New York: M. E. Sharpe, Inc. Misiunas primarily looks at the Baltic states relationship with international actors concerning citizenship and boundary issues.

458 See in particular Smith, Graham. 1996. The ethnic democracy thesis and the citizenship question in Estonia and Latvia. *Nationalities Papers* 24 (2):845-64. For an opposing view see, Pettai, Vello. 2000. Competing Conceptions of Multiethnic Democracy: Debating Minority Integration in Estonia. Paper read at European Consortium for Political Research, Joint Sessions Workshop on 'Competing Conceptions of Democracy in the Practice of Politics', April 14-19, at Copenhagen, Denmark. For a general discussion on ethnic democracy see Smooha, Sammy. 1990. Minority Status in Ethnic Democracy: the status of the Arab minority in Israel. *Ethnic and Racial Studies* 13 (3):389-413.

459 Brubaker, Rogers. 1996. *Nationalism Reframed: Nationhood and the National Question in the New Europe*. Cambridge: Cambridge University Press.

litical establishment traditionally controlled to a large extent by the majority community. Second, national minorities have attempted to affect policy-making through traditional democratic channels.[460] The minority composition of Estonia and Latvia at the end of the Soviet era was 38.5 per cent and 48 per cent respectively, giving rise to the term 'Russian question'.[461] Third, as self-styled external national homeland, the Russian Federation has played a significant part in affecting social policy development.[462] Finally, Western organisations have consistently applied pressure on the two Baltic governments to liberalise social policies. Overall, this chapter will illustrate a new 'European context' of minority politics. More specifically, this chapter examines the linkages between minority policies and European integration.

Grievances of the titular communities were largely expressed in social policies after the restoration of independence. Importantly, the European Union (EU), Council of Europe (CoE), and the Organisation for Security and Co-operation in Europe (OSCE) have had a significant effect on social policies in the Baltic states. Much of the minority policy evaluation has come through the OSCE High Commissioner on National Minorities (HCNM) and the deployment of OSCE long-term observer missions in Estonia and Latvia. With the expected enlargement of the EU and NATO, we see a further change in the international system whereby states are beholden to international organisations in return for access to foreign markets and collective security. In this way, we see a new definition of Europe unfolding before us. Europe today is debating the merits of cohesion, multiculturalism, and the place for national identities. The relevance of these issues makes Estonia and Latvia unique and timely case studies.

---

460 The OSCE does not maintain a legal definition of 'national minorities'. However, we can determine that a national minority constitutes a significant part of the population while maintaining a separate national identity.

461 Numbers based on the 1989 Soviet census, taken from Smith, Graham, ed. 1996. *The Baltic States: The National Self-determination of Estonia, Latvia, and Lithuania.* St. Martin's Press: New York, 7.

462 See Demuth, Andreas. 1997. Post-Soviet Minorities on the Fence: Ethnic Russians between Estonia, the Russian Federation, and the international community. Paper read at Theoretical and methodological issues in migration research: interdisciplinary, intergenerational and international perspectives, at University of Utrecht.

9.1 Organisation on Security and Co-operation in Europe

Nearly from the beginning, the Baltic states had shown their desire for further integration with the West. The most important organisations would be those that would ensure Baltic independence in the future such as NATO, EU, and the Council of Europe.[463] However, one organisation in particular became the primary facilitator for greater European integration: the OSCE. The OSCE became the 'eyes and ears' of other regional organisations, not to mention the United Nations.

As the Soviet Union began to show stress fractures, the Conference on Security and Co-operation in Europe (CSCE, forerunner of the OSCE) gathered in Paris in November 1990 to mark the end of the Cold War.[464] Even before the breakdown of the Soviet Union, the Baltic states were already a subject of discussion.[465] In fact, the Baltic states had formally applied to the OSCE three times previously without success. As expected, opposition to the Baltic states' participation came from Moscow. Little would change until the 1991 August Coup and the restoration of Baltic independence. Soon afterwards, the Baltic states were official members of the OSCE. OSCE involvement in the Baltic states was immediate. One of the dominant issues of Baltic-Russian relations was troop withdrawal and borders as portrayed in chapter seven. Initially, the new Russian Federation was unwilling to work within the framework of the OSCE, claiming that it was a bilateral problem. However, given little choice by the EU and United States, Russia entered into OSCE-sponsored negotiations.[466] The catch was that, as the previous chapter indicated, Russia tied the removal of troops and border treaties with the status of the Russophone communities in Latvia and Estonia. Although the

---

463 For example, all three Baltic states signed association agreements 12 June 1995, while Estonia and Latvia submitted accession applications 24 November 1995 and 13 October 1995 respectively. Deksnis, E. B. 2001. Baltic Accession to the European Union: Challenge and Opportunity. In *Baltic Accession to the European Union: Challenge and Opportunity*, edited by T. Jundzis. Riga: Latvian Academy of Sciences.

464 The CSCE became the Organisation for Security and Co-operation in Europe at the 1994 Budapest meeting. Since the majority of the time frame studied here is beyond 1994, I use the latter name of the organisation.

465 Kionka, Riina. 1990. The CSCE and the Baltic States. *Report on the USSR*, 17-19.

OSCE had been closely watching the ethnic situation in the Baltic states, Russia's move increased the pressure for the Estonian and Latvian governments to adjust the trajectory of current social policies affecting the large non-titular communities.

Pressure from European organisations began immediately after independence. Many feared that both nations, although Estonia more probably than Latvia, would experience violent clashes between ethnic groups as happened in Moldova. Estonia's Russophone enclaves in the northeast of the country were a particular worry.[467] However, both situations remained remarkably non-violent. After the Baltic states became OSCE members little more than a month after independence, the organisation began putting pressure on Estonia and Latvia to modify their nation-building policies.

As soon as the late 1980's, the CSCE realised that the state of majority/minority relations in Europe could be a destabilising factor in the region. The Copenhagen Document (1990) stresses the importance of liberal democracy and the role that human rights plays within such a system of governance.[468] More specifically, the document stresses the need to resolve issues of 'National Minorities' within the democratic process. Section IV 32 defines several key rights of national minorities. They are:

- the free use of the minority language in both the private and public sphere (32.1)
- the establishment of educational, religious and cultural institutions (32.2)
- the establishment and maintenance of contacts between themselves and their national homeland (32.4)

Section IV 33 states that 'states will protect the ethnic, cultural, linguistic and religious identity of national minorities on their territory and create conditions for the promotion of their identity.' At the same time, the document also

466 *Izvestia*, 8 May 1992.

467 For an argument linking ethnically concentrated areas and conflict, see especially Horowitz, Donald L. 1981. Patterns of Ethnic Seperatism. *Comparative Studies in Society and History* 23:165-195; and id., 1992. Irrendentas and Secessions: adjacent phenomena, neglected connections. *International Journal of Comparative Sociology* 13 (1):118-130.

468 *Copenhagen Document* (1990): http://www.osce.org/docs/english/1990-1999/hd/cope90e.htm

stresses the need to interpret these rights as not to harm the integrity of the state.[469] Strategically, the Copenhagen Document fails to define a 'National Minority'.

Also in 1990, the Charter of Paris sets out to influence a 'new era of democracy, peace and unity'.[470] With the collapse of the Berlin Wall a year earlier and the realisation that the end of the Cold War was near, the Charter stresses the importance of Human Rights, democracy and the rule of law. As a whole, the Charter says far less about the rights of national minorities than does the Copenhagen Document. In fact, national minorities are only discusses twice. First the document states:

> We affirm that the ethnic, cultural, linguistic and religious identity of national minorities will be protected and that persons belonging to national minorities have the right [to] freely express, preserve and develop that identity without any discrimination and in full equality before the law.

Second, the Charter reaffirms its commitment to protect the rights of national minorities and ties the observation of such rights to the creation and maintenance of democratic institutions. Furthermore, it assigns a future date to discuss the role of national minorities within Europe's 'human dimension'.

The product of that meeting was the 1991 Geneva Meeting of Experts on National Minorities.[471] Interestingly, both the United Nations and Council of Europe had representatives at the meeting. The main point of the report is the recognition of the role of democracy for protecting the rights of minorities and mitigating potential conflict.
Section II of the report states:

> This [democratic] framework guarantees full respect for human rights and fundamental freedoms, equal rights and status for all citizens, including persons belonging to national minorities, the free expression of all their legitimate interests and as-

---

469 Ibid. Section IV 37.

470 *Charter of Paris* (1990): http://www.osce.org/docs/english/1990-1999/summits/paris90e.htm.

471 *Geneva Meeting of Experts on National Minorities* (1991): http://www.osce.org/docs/english /1973-1990/other_experts/gene91e.htm.

pirations, political pluralism, social tolerance and the implementation of legal rules that place effective restrains on the abuse of governmental power.

In relation to this study, the report offers three specific suggestions, among others, for the promotion and protection of national minority rights. First, elected bodies and assemblies for national minority affairs are seen as a way to promote interest articulation. Second, the Report promotes 'adequate types and levels' of education in the language of the national minority based on the level of density of the population within a given region of the state. Note that the Report leaves 'types and levels' ambiguous. Having said this, the Report recognises that there are many different forms of governance in the OSCE region and being too specific would fail to recognise these differences. Finally, the Report suggests that the member-state fund the teaching of the national minority language to the majority community in 'regions inhabited by persons belonging to national minorities.' As a caveat to the suggestions, the report 'note[s] that not all ethnic, cultural, linguistic or religious differences necessarily lead to the creation of the national minorities' While undoubtedly true, the experts leave a way-out for infringing states who can simply claim, as Estonia and Latvia have done, that their Slavic communities are not 'national' minorities.

Armed with these documents and reports, the OSCE implemented two methods of observing and influencing the ethnic situation in the OSCE region. The first, and most well known, was the HCNM. Under Max van der Stoel, the HCNM tended to work behind the scenes in an effort to effect policy changes.[472] This was often done through personal correspondence between the High Commissioner and relevant ministers. Through 'quiet diplomacy', the HCNM could avoid over-dramatising the situation or specific events. The High Commissioner's official mandate was set out in the 1992 Helsinki Document, which established the office as an early warning mechanism.[473] Sub-section 11b states that 'the High Commissioner will assess at the earliest possible stage the role of the parties directly concerned, the nature of the tensions and

---

472 Kemp, Walter A. 2001. *Quiet Diplomacy in Action: The OSCE High Commissioner on National Minorities*. The Hague: Kluwer Law International.

473 *Helsinki Final Act* (1975): http://www.osce.org/docs/english/1990-1999/summits/helfa75e.htm.

recent developments therein and, where possible, the potential consequences for peace and stability within the [OSCE] area'. Additionally, section 26 establishes the role of the High Commissioner as an independent third party that can facilitate co-operation and reconciliation among conflicting parties. The document encourages the HCNM to seek communication with member-state governments as well as 'representatives of associations, non-governmental organisations, religious and other groups of national minorities directly concerned and in the area of tension . . .' Importantly, Section 34 encourages the High Commissioner to communicate its recommendations to the member-state governments while allowing for a public response from the state.

Much of what the High Commissioner has become is based on the character of the first occupant of the position. A former Dutch Foreign Minister, Max van der Stoel chose to 'promote dialogue, confidence, and co-operation' through what Kemp has referred as 'quite diplomacy'. Rather than stated in the Helsinki Document or the subsequent 1996 Lisbon Document, which again reaffirmed the role of the HCNM within the OSCE, the behind-the-scenes nature of the High Commissioner was a technique of van der Stoel. Interestingly, his successor Rolf Ekeus has maintained this style of intervention. Needless to say, the ability of the High Commissioner to remain at times unpublicised has allowed for a greater impact as an impartial, yet quiet, diplomat. This impartiality allows the OSCE to work as a third party mediator while the confidentiality helps the High Commissioner mediate sensitive issues without the fear of sensationalism and misrepresentation. Having said this, Max van der Stoel still remains one of the most well-known foreigners in Estonia and Latvia.

With the creation of the post of High Commissioner and the active role of its holder, three additional documents were produced to help qualify his duties based on the overlapping themes of education, identity and political participation. This elaboration came about through the Foundation on Inter-Ethnic Relations. The Foundation was established in 1993 as a non-governmental organisation for the support of the HCNM, based on expert participation. The experts consulted were academics from several European countries including the United Kingdom, Hungary and Norway. The first document was the *Hague Recommendations Regarding the Education Rights of National Minorities*.[474] Set within the context of the Universal Declaration of Human Rights, the purpose of the Hague Recommendations was an 'attempt to clarify . . . the content of minority education rights generally applicable in the situations in which the HCNM is involved.'[475] The recommendations overwhelmingly stress the need for mutual bilingualism, which has consistently been eroding since the Baltic restoration of independence.

In 1998, the Foundation produced the *Oslo Recommendations Regarding the Linguistic Rights of National Minorities*.[476] The experts involved in the construction of this document included academics outside of Europe as well as one Latvian. The Oslo Recommendations are grounded in the International Covenant on Civil and Political Rights. In particular, the former focuses on the rights of the national minority to use their language within their own community. It addresses personal names and the use of language in religion, non-governmental organisations, the media, economic life and in relation to the state. For example, section 15 states that

> in regions and localities where persons belonging to national minorities live should ensure that these persons have, in addition to appropriate judicial recourses, access to independent national institutions, such as ombudspersons or human rights commissions, in cases where they feel that their linguistic rights have been violated.

The Oslo Recommendations afford the High Commissioner a benchmark by which standards for the use of language is measured. Importantly, the Recommendations detail the responsibility of member-states to their own national minorities in regards to language rights.

Finally, the *Lund Recommendations on the Effective Participation of National Minorities in Public Life* were released in 1999.[477] Up to this point the

---

474 *Hague Recommendations on the Education Rights of National Minorities* (1996): OSCE HCNM recommendations are available at http://www.osce.org/hcnm/documents/recommendations/.

475 Ibid.

476 *Oslo Recommendations Regarding the Linguistic Rights of National Minorities* (1998)

477 *Lund Recommendations on the Effective Participation of National Minorities in Public Life* (1999).

High Commissioner had been quite active in areas where the effective participation of national minorities was limited. The Lund Recommendations relied on a much larger and international base of experts. The document is based on the premise that 'effective participation of national minorities in public life is an essential component of a peaceful and democratic society'.[478] Specifically, the document focuses on national minority participation in central government as well as at regional and local levels. Nationally, section 6 says that 'states should ensure that opportunities exist for minorities to have an effective voice at the level of the central government. . .' In the case of national, regional and local participation, the document recommends several mechanisms such as reserving a certain number of seats in the national legislature, allocating some cabinet and court positions, agenda-setting influence in relevant ministries and, finally, participation in the civil service. Finally, the document stresses the potential for forms of self-governance. This follows a general within other European institutions such as the EU to encourage power-sharing. Once again, the Lund Recommendations are set within the context of international agreements such as the United Nations Charter and the Council of Europe's Framework Convention for the Protection of National Minorities.

While the three recommendations do refine the High Commissioner's responsibilities, they do not define the concept of a 'national minority'. They do recognise that the HCNM is most often involved in areas where an ethnic/national group is a majority in one state, while being a minority in the other state. The purpose of not strictly defining 'national minority' is useful for the OSCE as it allows for a wider investigation of alleged discrimination of participating countries. However, it also allows member-states to deny that their minorities are 'national' minorities and thus, his remit does not apply to that state.

The second method employed by the OSCE was the long-term missions to Estonia and Latvia.[479] In general, the aim of the missions was to help the governments draft legislation that would meet OSCE and international standards. However, the missions also became used as human rights moni-

---

478 Ibid., Section 1.

479 *Nevazisimaya Gazeta*, 19 December 1992.

tors in relation to the effects of previous legislation. The OSCE Mission to Estonia was deployed in February 1993. Officially, the Estonian government requested the mission, although according to Zaagman, Estonia was pressed into the request by the US government.[480] The OSCE Mission to Latvia was deployed in November 1993. This mission was the result of a recommendation by a Special Representative of the OSCE Chairman-in-Office. The two missions, while similar, had slightly different mandates. On the one hand, the OSCE Mission to Estonia had a general mandate to encourage communication and stability between the titular and minority community. On the other hand, the OSCE Mission to Latvia was sent to address the citizenship issue as well as to be at the disposal of the Latvian government for expert advice. While the Estonian mission's mandate required that it work with the HCNM, the Latvian mission had no such requirement. However, the OSCE Mission to Latvia did have the ability to co-operate with the High Commissioner as well as other OSCE institutions. Despite the differences in mandate, the two missions tended to concentrate on similar issues (e.g. citizenship and the status of military pensioners). Both the HCNM and the long-term missions played an overwhelming part in shaping social policy over time.

OSCE Relations with Estonia and Latvia

Russia's continued efforts to tie the troop withdrawal issue to the 'human rights' situation in the Baltic states led Estonia to encourage international organisations to monitor the ethnic situation. In December 1992, the OSCE sponsored a team of experts to investigate the Russian allegations of 'human rights' violations.[481] Furthermore, at a meeting in Stockholm that month, foreign ministers decided to recommend the creation of a 'mission' to Estonia in order to increase the integration process. Importantly, the Estonian government welcomed the idea. Indeed, international investigation was an important part of Estonia's way of dealing with Russian foreign policy. Headed by Klaus Tornudd, the six-member OSCE mission to Estonia established offices in Tal-

---

480 Zaagman, Rob. 1999. *Conflict Prevention in the Baltic States: the OSCE High Commissioner on National Minorities in Estonia, Latvia, and Lithuania.* Flensburg, Germany: European Centre for Minority Issues, 90.

481 *RFE/RL Newsline,* 'CSCE Human Rights Team to Estonia', 22 November 1992; 'CSCE, Russia, and the Baltics', 15 December 1992.

linn, Kohtla-Jarve, and Narva in February.[482] The mission immediately established communication with trade unions, businesses, public organisations, and individuals as a means of monitoring ethnic tensions. The Estonian Foreign Ministry welcomed the mission calling it a 'historic step'. Estonian Foreign Minister Trivimi Velliste remarked that the mission would 'provide the world with additional information about Estonia and its policies'.[483]

Following the creation of the HCNM the previous year, correspondence between the High Commissioner and the Baltic States (even Lithuania at first) began in April 1993.[484] In his letter to the Estonian Foreign Minister, Trivimi Velliste, van der Stoel acknowledged that he was 'fully aware of the fact that there is no convincing evidence of systematic persecution of the non-Estonian population since the [restoration of independence].' The High Commissioner points out that the Estonian government was attempting to implement two contradictory policies in relation to the minority community. On one hand, the Estonian government implemented a policy of integration through the importance placed on the knowledge of the titular language. On the other, the Government attempted to assure a privileged status for the 'Estonian Population'. From this, we must assume that he is referring to an ethnic category rather than one based on citizenship. He argues that not only will the latter policy violate several Estonia's 'international obligations' but also cause increased friction between Tallinn and Moscow. In this way, we can see how the High Commissioner works within his mandate of preventive diplomacy to moderate potential conflict both internally and internationally. From his discussion based on his observations in Estonia, the High Commissioner offers thirteen recommendations. For the most part, the focus is on the integration of non-citizens into Estonian society with special emphasis placed on children and diffusion of information. Finally, he calls for the creation of a 'National

482 *RFE/RL Newsline,* 'Estonia Welcomes CSCE Mission', 16 February 1993.

483 Ibid.

484 CSCE, 23 April 1993, Communication No. 124, Prague, Secretariat of the Conference on Security and Co-operation in Europe; see also Sarv, Margit. 2002. Integration by Reframing Legislation: Implementation of the Recommendations of the OSCE High Commissioner on National Minorities to Estonia, 1993-2001. *Working Paper 7*, edited by Wolfgang Zellner, Randolf Oberschmidt and Claus Neukirch. Hamburg: Centre for OSCE Research.

Commissioner on Ethnic and Language Questions'. Eventually, the EU would take up the campaign to encourage Estonia to install such an arbiter.

In the response, the Estonian Ministry of Foreign Affairs judged the High Commissioner's analysis as 'fair and accurate'. Relating to the above suggestion of a National Commissioner, the Estonian Government proposed further investigation into the creation of such a post although the constitution allowed for the creation of an ombudsman post. While reaffirming the commitment to the protection of the elderly and disabled, the response does not refer to the High Commissioner's recommendation that children born in Estonia who would otherwise be stateless be given citizenship. This would not be settled until the 1997 amendment to the Law on Citizenship. Overall, the message from the Estonian Government is that rather than discriminating against non-Estonians, post-Soviet policies are aimed at redressing the disadvantages of the Soviet policy of Russification. In this context, we can see the difficult position of the High Commissioner. While addressing yesterday's discriminations today will include further discrimination tomorrow, the Estonian Government's policy of nation-building made a distinction based on citizenship rather than ethnicity. Of course, this begs the question of whether the Law on Citizenship was not restored with a discriminatory objective in mind.

In the lead up to the 6 April letter to the Latvian Ministry of Foreign Affairs, the High Commissioner met with the Latvian Supreme Council Chairman Anatolijs Gorbunovs in order to discuss the ethnic situation in January 1993.[485] Similar to his statement to the Estonian government, van der Stoel told Gorbunovs that he had not observed any violations of human rights of non-Latvians. In his letter of recommendations to Latvian Foreign Minister Georgs Andrejevs, the High Commissioner notes that 93% of non-Latvians have lived in Latvia for more than sixteen years. From this he concludes, as surely did the Latvian government, that there will not be a mass exodus of non-citizens. In fact, much of the letter and the recommendations are similar to that sent to Tallinn, which reflects the similar conditions in the two countries. However, the High Commissioner looks at the need for a new citizenship law in Latvia. As discussed in an earlier chapter, the Latvian Congress of

485 *RFE/RL Newsline,* 'CSCE Commissioner on Minority Rights in Latvia', 22 January 1993.

People's Deputies were to wait until a new parliament was elected before a adopting a new citizenship law. Finally, he also suggests the creation of an office of National Commissioner on Ethnic and Language Questions, which Latvia failed to do until the Latvia First Party came into Parliament after the 2002 elections when the post of the Integration Minister was established.

In the a responding letter, the Latvian Government rejected the creation of the special minister stating that 'we would like to mention that the existing system of human rights protection in Latvia has not been exhausted and provides, in our opinion, sufficient avenues for problem-solving in this area.'[486] While conceding that the lack of a Citizenship Law is a problem, the response addresses virtually no other points found within the High Commissioner's recommendations. Rather, the Latvian Government simply states that the 'conclusions and recommendation are carefully being examined by the respective Government institutions of Latvia.'

In the summer of 1993, the passage of the Estonian Law on Aliens led to the 'Aliens' Crisis' (see chapters five and six) whereby the Russian-speaking community demanded greater rights through protests and a referendum on autonomy.[487] This 'crisis' became a defining moment for the OSCE. Although the events were more of a crisis for the Laar government than between ethnic communities, the HCNM made several trips to Estonia within just a few weeks in an effort to foster negotiation between the government and the northeast. Max van der Stoel's visit to Estonia began with being stopped by nearly 6,000 protesters in the city of Sillamae to protest the Law on Aliens while on a trip from Tallinn to Narva. Once in Narva, the High Commissioner met with the city council, who told him that they were willing to hold a referendum rather than using more contentious actions as such strikes or blocking roads. Subsequently, the Estonian Chancellor of Justice Erik-Juhan Truvali ruled that holding the referendum would be unconstitutional.

Following the High Commissioner's visit, van der Stoel sent his findings

---

486 For additional information on the OSCE High Commissioner in Latvia, see Dorodnova, Jekaterina. 2002. Challenging Ethnic Democracy: Implementation of the Recommendations of the OSCE High Commissioner on National Minorities to Latvia, 1993-2001. *Working Paper 10*, edited by Wolfgang Zellner, Randolf Oberschmidt and Claus Neukirch. Hamburg: Centre for OSCE Research.

487 *RFE/RL Newsline*, 'CSCE High Commissioner in Estonia', 1 July 1993.

and recommendations in a letter to the Estonian president Lennart Meri.[488] In the letter, the High Commissioner addresses concerns over the law that provided the context for the 'Alien's Crisis'. While recognising that much of the content of the Law on Aliens matches other European states, van der Stoel criticises several controversial parts. Most of the recommendations refer to clarifying ambiguous parts of the legislation such as 'employment or other lawful income sufficient to support himself or herself'. Furthermore, the recommendations address Article 12, Paragraph 4 that restricts residency for any who had served in the armed forces. Recognising that this would place many minority families at risk of expulsion, the High Commissioner recommends that the law address only those who have been decommissioned after July 1991. Near the end of the letter, van der Stoel says, 'the main purpose of my comments is to suggest amendments, which, in my view, without affecting the structure and many of the provisions of the law, would help considerably to remove the tensions which have arisen about its content.'

While addressing the concerns of non-citizens in the northeast, the OSCE also encouraged the Estonian Government to seek several changes in the law. However, there was very little support in the predominantly Estonian nationalist Mart Laar Government after it had bowed to CoE pressure over allowing permanent residents the right to vote in local elections, as well as allowing military pensioners the privilege of obtaining permanent resident permits. The Estonian Government did concede one change in an amendment passed in June 1994 that allowed a one-year extension to the registration deadline. However, the legalistic ambiguities, such as the failure to define the term 'lawful source of income', continued.

Despite the amendment to the law, the Narva and Sillamae city councils did not cancel the planned referendum. In his third visit to Estonia in a space of a few weeks, the High Commissioner met with political elites in the northeast. More specifically, Max van der Stoel met with the Mayors of Narva and Sillamae, Vladimer Chuiken and Aleksandr Maximenko, in order to assuage fears and persuade the city councils to cancel the referendums. In another letter less than a fortnight later, the High Commissioner traded his expert 'hat'

488 OSCE, 1 July 1993, Letter to President of the Republic of Estonia, OSCE High Commissioner on National Minorities, Tallinn.

for his diplomatic 'hat' by facilitating the exchange of information between the Estonian government and the Russophonic communities in Narva and Sillamae.[489] The letter followed a meeting with the Estonian president and the prime minister as well as representatives from the northeast. On the Estonian side, the government assured that their policies did not amount to attempts of mass expulsion nor plans for permanent exclusion from citizenship. Also, 'the Government of Estonia, even though considering the referendums planned in Narva and Sillamae as illegal, will not use force to prevent them from being held.'

On their part, the minority representatives offered three assurances. First, they said they would play a constructive role in the dialogue with Tallinn. Second, the City Councils of the northeast stated they would abide by the ruling of the National Court on the decision of whether or not the referenda are legal. Finally, and most importantly, the minority representatives stated that 'they will fully respect the Constitution and the territorial integrity of Estonia.' While it is hard to judge the consequences of this exchange, we can argue that attempts to assure the Estonian government that there was not a concerted effort to harm the Estonian Republic must have been helpful in negotiations. In fact, as we have seen since, the minority communities in the northeast were not operating from a position of strength and little way of articulating their grievances otherwise.

During his visit, the High Commissioner negotiated an agreement between the Narva and Sillamae City Councils and the Estonian Government.[490] As an indication of the weak position of the city councils, together they issued a letter to the High Commissioner requesting that he 'urgently' return to Estonia to help break the intransigence of the Estonian Government. Evidently, the letter stated that the Estonian Government refused to discuss certain issues agreed upon in the earlier agreement, such as speeding up the issue of auxiliary regulations for obtaining Estonian citizenship, residence permits, and aliens' passports.

---

489 OSCE, 12 July 1993, Statement of the High Commissioner on National Minorities, OSCE High Commissioner on National Minorities, Tallinn.

490 *RFE/RL Newsline,* 'CSCE Commissioner Invited to Estonia', 28 September 1993.

Latvia's year was much less contentious than in Estonia. The High Commissioner's next letters came in December.[491] The HCNM's main concern was the state of the draft citizenship law that had first been discussed in 1992.[492] Realising that an overly conservative citizenship law would not bode well for Latvia's democratic transition and that a liberal citizenship like that seen in Lithuania was politically unrealistic, he presented a 'third option'. This included a language test, a civic exam, and an oath to the Republic of Latvia. The object that was most alarming was Article 9 of the draft Citizenship Law, which would implement annual naturalisation quotas. He argued that the annual quotas would cause considerable uncertainty among the stateless population. 'This uncertainty, moreover could possibly last for many years, even for persons who have been living in Latvia for a long time or have been born in Latvia, and for persons with a sincere willingness to integrate in Latvian society.'[493] Rather than the annual quotas, the High Commissioner proposed the controversial 'window' system, which would allow different categories to apply for citizenship with all who wish it to be able to apply by 1998. Although assuaging the fears of the more nationalist elements in the Latvian governments, the window system itself was less than ideal, as discussed in Chapter Six.[494] Following the High Commissioner's recommendations, the Citizenship Law was revised and promulgated including the 'window' system.

In February 1994, OSCE representatives once again participated in efforts to ease the minority issue in Estonia.[495] The High Commissioner returned to attend roundtable talks on ethnic minority issues, also attended by Estonian Foreign Minister Juri Tuik, Population Minister Peeter Olesk, and a representative of President Meri Ants Paju. Furthermore, van der Stoel met with Prime Minister Laar and the head of the Citizenship and Migration Department Mart Piiskop to discuss similar issues. Also that month, the head of

---

491 OSCE, 10 December 1993, Letter to the Latvian Minister of Foreign Affairs, Reference No. 1463/93/L, OSCE High Commissioner on National Minorities, The Hague.

492 *Segodnya*, 28 June 1994.

493 OSCE, 10 December 1993, Letter to the Latvian Minister of Foreign Affairs, Reference No. 1463/93/L, OSCE High Commissioner on National Minorities, The Hague.

494 Pabriks, Artis and Aldis Purs. 2002. *Latvia: the Challenges of Change*. London: Routledge.

495 *RFE/RL Newsline,* 'CSCE High Commissioner in Estonia', 14 November 1994; 'CSCE Representative on Human Rights in Estonia', 23 February 1994.

the OSCE mission to Estonia, Lahelma, reported that the mission had found no evidence of human rights' violations, but 'only minor shortcomings, typical of many other democracies.'[496] Lahelma also urged the government to issue internationally recognised travel documents for stateless persons. Additionally, he requested that the government increase funding for Estonian language courses in the minority communities.

By the time the next letter arrived from the High Commissioner, Estonian commentators had accused van der Stoel of working 'for', rather than 'on', national minorities. The letter on 9 March 1994 addresses this problem immediately.[497] He then moved on to discuss the implementation of the Law on Aliens passed the year before. The Law gave non-citizens a year from the passage of the legislation to register for residency. The letter indicated that a large section of the minority population had yet not registered. The High Commissioner proposed extending the deadline by six months has to give the 400,000 that had not registered time to do so.

Interestingly, van der Stoel met with Russian Foreign Minister Kozyrev at the end of March.[498] Kozyrev stated that the Russian Federation would continue to press for minority rights for Russian-speakers in the 'near abroad'. He also stated that he hoped that Western states would support the plight of the Russian-speakers once troops had been withdrawn from the Baltic states. The High Commissioner's willingness to meet with a Russian official exhibited an additional dimension of the HCNM's role. It gives support to the use of Brubaker's 'nexus' structure in analysing nationalising states and national minorities. Within two months, the High Commissioner met with representatives of the 'nationalising state', 'national minority', and the 'external national homeland'.

Following the withdrawal of Russian troops from Estonia (August 1994), the High Commissioner released a statement that he agreed with the OSCE mission's report that had found no evidence of any violations of human rights.[499] He also reiterated the requests of the mission to fund Estonian lan-

496 Ibid.

497 OSCE, 9 March 1994, Letter to the Estonian Minister of Foreign Affairs, Reference No. 3005/94/L, OSCE High Commissioner on National Minorities, The Hague.

498 *RFE/RL Newsline*, 'Kozyrev Warns Baltic States', 30 March 1994.

499 *RFE/RL Newsline*, 'CSCE Commissioner: Human Rights Observed in Estonia', 9

guage courses in minority communities, and issue residence to Russian military retirees as well as travel documents for non-citizens. Van der Stoel's statement indicates an expected level of co-operation amongst different bodies of the OSCE within Estonia. Although both the HCNM office and that of the OSCE missions are connected through the OSCE Office for Democratic Institutions and Human Rights (ODIHR), each had their own mandate in addition: at the HCNM was a permanent organ within the OSCE while the missions were *ad hoc* attempts to influence domestic policy.

Later that year, the High Commissioner wrote to discuss the Law on Citizenship's residence and language requirements.[500] The High Commissioner sent the letter when the *Riigikogu* was about to read the law for the second time. Again, the problem was ambiguities in the legislation. Specifically, the High Commissioner advised that the Law date the residency requirements from 30 March 1990. Furthermore, referring to assurances by the Estonian PM Mart Laar, the letter advised against 'prohibitive' levels of citizenship required for naturalisation. In July, Laar stated, 'As far as the requirements for citizenship are concerned, the Government intends to take concrete steps i*n the near future* to ensure that the recommendations made on this subject by the High Commissioner on National Minorities last April will be put into effect. Directives will be issued to ensure that the language requirements will not exceed the ability to conduct a simple conversation in Estonian and the requirements will be even lower for persons over sixty and invalids.'[501] In response to the High Commissioner's letter, the Estonian Government addressed his concerns with another letter pointing out that Article 29 of the draft legislation ensured that the residency requirements be dated from 30 March 1990. Of the concerns over language, there was no mention.

In regards to Latvia, the High Commissioner requested similar provisions for promoting the integration of non-Latvians into Latvian society.[502] Specifically, he called on Western nations to help fund language training cen-

---

September 1994.

500 OSCE, 8 December 1994, Letter to Estonian Minister of Foreign Affairs, Reference No. 3053/94/L, OSCE High Commissioner on National Minorities, The Hague.

501 Ibid.

502 *RFE/RL Newsline,* 'CSCE and UN Officials on Human Rights in the Baltic States', 19 September 1994.

tres for Russian-speakers. Furthermore, he also appealed for the creation of radio and television programmes that would help Russian-speakers to learn the Latvian language. Finally, the High Commissioner recommended that Latvia establish a citizenship law that would alleviate much of the uncertainty among the non-Latvian community.

Unlike Estonia, Latvia waited until after a new parliament was elected in 1993 before passing a new citizenship law, as discussed in chapter 6. Despite the High Commissioner's earlier objections, the draft 1994 Law on Citizenship laid out three requirements, as discussed above. First, the government would institute a language examination ensuring that new citizens would have fluent Latvian skills. Second, citizenship applicants would be required to take a history and civics test. Finally, the law would enforce annual quotas, limiting the number of new applicants. In his visit to Latvia in January 1994, the High Commissioner stated that he supported the language requirements for naturalisation, which is a normal part of citizenship tests in the rest of Europe.[503] However, he disagreed with the more controversial plan to issue citizenship on a quota basis. In essence, the High Commissioner recommended that citizenship be offered on the three conditions of the draft law without the quota restrictions to those who did not constitute a clear threat to the Latvian state.[504] However, van der Stoel did not fully recommend the granting of citizenship unconditionally to all those wanted it. As a compromise, the High Commissioner put forward 'naturalisation windows' to better control the naturalisation process.

Despite the OSCE's objections to the original draft, the Latvian Parliament passed the legislation. However, Latvian President Ulmanis refused to promulgate the law and it was returned to parliament. Eventually, the quotas were dropped from the legislation, although the other three points were adopted in July 1994. Although the OSCE was unable to influence a large change in the 1994 Law on Citizenship, it was able to encourage legislators to drop the most egregious component. In the end, it may have been important to discourage the use of quotas in principle, but there was little need in

---

503 *RFE/RL Newsline,* 'CSCE Commissioner in Latvia', 10 January 1994.

504 *RFE/RL Newsline,* 'CSCE Commissioner on Latvia's Draft Law on Citizenship', 7 February 1994.

reality. The rush of non-citizens to seek naturalisation did not occur. The naturalisation windows barred many from applying citizenship and hurt future attempts of integration. Once Latvia had created a citizenship law that largely fitted the expectations of the OSCE and other regional institutions, the High Commissioner recommended that Latvia be admitted into the CoE.[505] Important for the sake of estimating the effect of the HCNM on Latvia's relationship with European institutions, Van der Stoel's opinion did matter.

Furthermore, the OSCE missions played a large role in recommending changes that would mirror international norms to the national governments.[506] Not only did the OSCE attempt to influence legislative negotiations in both Estonia and Latvia, but they also monitored the implementation of the naturalisation policies.[507] In both states, the OSCE missions monitored citizenship examinations, even going so far as to sit in on naturalisation examinations. Furthermore, the OSCE made on-site inspections to ensure that residence permit applications were being processed following the relevant policies. Although the missions would not take up individual cases, the OSCE would look into 'patterns of rigid or arbitrary administrative practices and discusses these findings with the Government.'[508] Finally, the OSCE went even further by becoming involved in activities relating to titular language training for non-citizens in Estonia and Latvia.[509]

Once the citizenship laws were established in both countries, since they were at least partially formed around the recommendations of the HCNM, the High Commissioner turned his attention to the residency and naturalisation process. In April 1995, van der Stoel made a two-day visit to Tallinn to meet with Foreign Minister Riivo Sinijarv.[510] The High Commissioner was primarily

505 *RFE/RL Newsline,* 'CSCE Commissioner Favors Latvia's CE Membership', 12 September 1994.

506 See Zepa, Brigita. 2001. *Towards a Civil Society - 2000.* Riga: Baltic Institutes of Social Sciences, 31-33.

507 Zaagman 1999, 20-24. Estonia passed a new citizenship law in 1995, which raised residency requirements and civic knowledge as well as prohibiting any new Estonian citizen from holding the citizenship of another state. See Smith 2002, 93.

508 Zaagman 1999, 20.

509 Individual European nations also funded language programs. For example, see *RFE/RL Daily Report*, 'Finland Provide Funds for Latvian State Language Program', 27 August 1999.

510 *RFE/RL Newsline,* 'OSCE Human Rights Commissioner in Estonia', 27 April 1995.

concerned about the small number of applications for residency permits amongst the non-citizen community. As is typical of citizenship legislation, a substantial period of permanent residency is required before an individual can be naturalised. Thus, the lack of residency applications was not only an immediate problem (i.e. illegal status), but also would affect future rates of naturalisation and integration.

In the same month, the Estonian Citizenship Law came into force. After following its implementation for several months, the High Commissioner sent a letter to Tallinn regarding the Law.[511] The High Commissioner wrote, 'I have noted that, even though there are a number of easy questions amongst those which can be asked during these examinations, there is also a considerable number which even persons with a university education might find difficult to answer.' However, the problem was furthered since prospective citizens have to answer in Estonian, thus requiring a much higher level of the indigenous language than the Law would suggest otherwise. While the language test was established to prove an applicant's ability to perform a 'simple conversation' in Estonian, the civic examination required more.[512] For example, as the letter notes, the language test at the time required knowledge of 2500 words, where generally the knowledge of 2000 is considered roughly fluent. The High Commissioner states, 'to many linguists the knowledge of 800 words of a language is sufficient to conduct a simple conversation.'

The Estonian Government responded with their own letter detailing several legislative changes that addressed many of the High Commissioner's comments.[513] First, the Estonian Government enlarged the number of people who could apply for alien passports. The Government also appealed to the High Commissioner for assistance in encouraging other OSCE states to recognise the passports for foreign travel. Second, the Law on Public Service was changed in order to extend the deadline from which non-citizen civil servants could not be employed by the state. The extension was for one year. Finally, regarding language, the letter defends the civic examination portion of

511 OSCE, 11 December 1995, Letter to the Estonian Minister of Foreign Affairs, Reference No. 1340/95/L, OSCE High Commissioner on National Minorities,The Hague.

512 See the letter of 8 December 1994, President Meri's comments.

513 Estonian Minister of Foreign Affairs, 7 February 1996, Letter to the OSCE High Commissioner on National Minorities, No. 6/10680, Tallinn.

the naturalisation process. In particular, the Foreign Minister argues that since the candidates are given copies of the constitution and Citizenship Law during the examination, the applicant should not have a problem. The argument is based on the prospective citizen being able to understand the question, but ignores whether or not the citizen can understand the two documents. The High Commissioner promptly sent a letter to the members of the Permanent Council of the OSCE to accept the alien passports for travel documents.[514]

Following a similar letter to Latvian officials, the Latvian Government exhibited a pro-active approach to the naturalisation issue in a responding letter.[515] In particular, Foreign Minister Birkavs described the publication of an informative book to assist applicants for naturalisation entitled 'The Basic Issues of Latvian History and the State Constitutional Principles'. However, it must be noted that the information was published in Latvian with only Russian summaries at the end of each chapter. Additionally, Birkavs reported a 50% reduction in the naturalisation fees for students aged 16 to 20. This also included a similar reduction for orphans, which seems a bit harsh given that their access to income would be negligible. Unfortunately, this came at a time when the budget for the Naturalisation Board was severely cut by the Government.

In October 1996, the High Commissioner again visited both Estonia and Latvia. In the subsequent letter to Estonian Foreign Minister Siim Kallas, the High Commissioner focuses on the 'considerable delays' in the process for providing residence permits and alien passports.[516] He warns that such delays will continue to encourage non-citizens to seek alternative (mainly Russian) citizenship when available. Interestingly, the responsorial letter states that the Estonian Government's interests are best served by reducing the number of stateless individuals and thus this 'should not be viewed as a

---

514 OSCE, 14 February 1996, Letter to the Members of the Permanent Council of the OSCE, Reference No. 1996 314/Bis/96/L, OSCE High Commissioner on National Minorities, The Hague.

515 OSCE, 14 March 1996, Letter to the Latvian Minister of Foreign Affairs, Reference No 516/96/L, OSCE High Commissioner on National Minorities, The Hague.

516 OSCE, 28 October 1996, Letter to the Estonian Minister of Foreign Affairs, Reference No. 1084/96/L, OSCE High Commissioner on National Minorities, The Hague.

negative development.'[517] More importantly, the High Commissioner indicates his alarm that the Estonian Government at the time was unwilling to apply the CoE's Framework Convention for the Protection of National Minorities to non-ethnic Estonians who were *Estonian citizens.*[518] He argues, 'the Framework Convention was drafted with the aim to transform to the greatest possible extent the political commitments adopted by the (OSCE) into legal obligation . . . As far as the Framework Convention itself is concerned, article 6 (1) does explicitly refer to all persons living on the territory of a state.' As discussed earlier, the CSCE Copenhagen Document on the Human Dimension resembles many of the commitments within the Framework Convention, as the High Commissioner points out. This interpretation by the Estonian Government was based on there being no definition within the Framework Convention or in international law. This interpretation will be discussed in more detail below.

During a similar visit to Latvia in October 1996, the High Commissioner discussed the large non-citizen community with Foreign Minister Birkavs and President Ulmanis.[519] In his comments following the visit, the High Commissioner pays particular attention to the low numbers that had applied for citizenship since its adoption in 1995.[520] Some elements within the Latvian Government at the time estimated that there would be a mass rush to apply for naturalisation. As in Estonia, quite the opposite occurred. With the 'windows' system in place rather than annual quotas, the naturalisation process was spread over seven years. In the High Commissioner's view, there was no evidence to suggest that the Latvian Government needed to continue with institutional constraints on the number of applicants. He states, 'I hope therefore that due consideration will be given to the abolishment of the window system', the very mechanism that he had helped to create. In his response, Birkavs states that any negotiation over amending the Citizenship Law would be delayed since 'political difficulties remain in this regard.'[521]

---

517 Estonian Minister of Foreign Affairs, 27 November 1996, Letter to the OSCE High Commissioner on National Minorities, Reference No. 1/19028, Tallinn.

518 *Framework Convention for the Protection of National Minorities* (1995): http://conventions.coe.int/Treaty/EN/Treaties/Html/157.htm

519 *RFE/RL Newsline,* 'OSCE Commissioner Visits Latvia', 9 October 1996.

520 OSCE, 28 October 1996, Letter to the Latvian Minister of Foreign Affairs, Reference No. 1085/96/L, OSCE High Commissioner on National Minorities, The Hague.

521 Latvian Minister of Foreign Affairs, 24 December 1996, Letter to the OSCE High

A year later, the High Commissioner criticised the history component of the naturalisation test in response to the fact that only 4 per cent of those who were eligible to apply for citizenship did so. He stated that most citizens of the Netherlands would fail similar questions relating to Dutch history and law. Latvian Naturalisation Office Director Eizenija Aldermane argued that the history test was not 'too complicated'. Arguing that only a small percentage of those eligible to apply have actually sought information, she stated that non-citizens were more likely not entering the naturalisation process because they were trying to avoid military service.[522] On the other hand, People's Harmony Party Leader Janis Jurkans agreed with the High Commissioner arguing that it impeded the integration of non-citizens.

The last public letter from the High Commissioner is a detailed eight-page set of observations and recommendations.[523] In fact, the letter begins with a concluding character noting the correspondence since 1993. The letter is broken down into three sections. First, the High Commissioner comments on the policies of the Siimann Government regarding minorities. He compliments the Government on the provision to change the Law on Aliens to extend the availability of permanent residence permits to temporary permit holders. He also marks the important introduction of the Minister for Inter-Ethnic Affairs, as discussed in Chapter Six. However, the introduction of a ministerial post rather than an ombudsman, as the High Commissioner had suggested in 1993, produced a fear that many of the issues important to the OSCE would be unattended by the post. Furthermore, the creation of a ministerial post rather than an ombudsman meant that the position would not be independent.

Second, the letter focuses on the naturalisation process. Looking back to the introduction of the Citizenship Law, the High Commissioner finds a clear failure to absorb the non-citizen population. With numbers released by the Citizenship and Migration Board of Estonia, the letter finds that by 1997,

---

Commissioner on National Minorities, Reference No. 31/1003-7767, Riga.

522 See *RFE/RL Newsline,* 'OSCE Says Latvia's Naturalization Test Too Complicated', 8 April 1997, and 'Latvian Official Respond to OSCE Criticism of Citizenship Test', 10 April 1997.

523 OSCE, 21 May 1997, Letter to the Estonian Minister of Foreign Affairs, Reference No. 359/97/L, OSCE High Commissioner on National Minorities, The Hague.

only 6,225 of a population around 210,000 of non-citizens had received citizenship. Even more worryingly, many of those who had become citizens in 1996 and 1997 were actually children who did not have to pass any tests if one parent was a citizen or the child was orphaned or adopted by a citizen. Citing a UNDP survey, the High Commissioner finds that the main impediment to increased naturalisation was the language test. Nevertheless, he argues, 'I have come to the conclusion that, after various changes have been made in the test, a level of knowledge is now required which cannot reasonably be considered as being too high.' With this, there is the recognition of the establishment of the Language Training Centre the year before. In addition, he takes issue with the civic test that would be difficult to answer, despite the applicants had access to copies of the Constitution and Citizenship Law.

Finally, van der Stoel looks at the rights of children where neither of the parents are Estonian citizens. According to the High Commissioner, the Estonian Government had previously argued that Article 7 of the Convention on Rights of the Child 'would not have any practical consequences for Estonia because most stateless children have as parents former USSR citizens who have the option of acquiring the citizenship of the Russian Federation.' However, the High Commissioner does not find this a valid argument. He argues that Article 7 'cannot be made dependent upon the possible exercise of an option available to the parent.' As the letter points out, the availability of Russian citizenship is not a 'duty' but a 'right'. Finally, the letter argues that the best interests of the child are not protected if he/she is required to become a citizen of a foreign state. The High Commissioner points the Law on Citizenship of Finland, which resembles the Estonian Law. The Finnish Law also delegates citizenship on the basis of heredity, 'but an exception is made for stateless children.' He argues, 'in my view, the Convention of the Rights of the Child does not oblige Estonia to grant Estonian citizenship automatically to children born in Estonia who would otherwise be stateless.' Rather, it gives parents the right to apply for citizenship on behalf of their child. Overall, these recommendations laid the groundwork for the revised Citizenship Law that year.

Latvia's turn under the spotlight came in the same month.[524] The High Commissioner attempted to reverse the trend of continued low levels of naturalisation. He considers the fact that military service and visa requirements for travel to Russia may be important stumbling blocks to naturalisation. However, he finds that the primary impediment to naturalisation is the language requirement. Importantly, he called for international assistance 'in achieving the aims of the National Programme for Latvian Language Training' (i.e. financial assistance). Furthermore, he recommended the review of the civic exam in order to make it easier. He argued that despite the fact that over 90% of applicants pass the test, this does little to promote the insecurity within the stateless community. Interestingly, he criticises particular questions in the test. Specifically, he argues 'I wonder whether it is really necessary for candidates for citizenship to know what Swedish educational policy was like in Vidzeme in the seventeenth century . . .' Finally, the High Commissioner presented similar arguments about the rights of children in Latvia. As in Estonia, the High Commissioner's views would be adopted in Latvia's amended Citizenship Law.

Setting the naturalisation issue to one side, the HCNM turned towards the issue of language. In particular, there was controversy over the use of language in the public and private sphere. Both Estonia and Latvia had electoral laws stating that parliamentary deputies and local officials were required to have fluent titular language skills. In Estonia, the OSCE had continually complained about the aspect of the election law disallowing non-Estonian citizens the right to become elected officials if they did not have the ability to communicate fluently in Estonian. The law overwhelmingly affected non-Estonian citizens who lived in the predominantly Russophone areas in the Northeast. The High Commissioner argued that citizens should be given certain rights regardless of their ethnic background. Van der Stoel argued that it was 'up to the voters to decide whether they want to elect to the parliament somebody who is not fluent in the Estonian language.'[525] In June 2000, based

---

524 OSCE, 23 May 1997, Letter to the Latvian Minister of Foreign Affairs, Reference No. 376/97/L, OSCE High Commissioner on National Minorities, The Hague.

525 *RFE/RL Daily Report*, 'Van der Stoel Again Criticizes Estonian Language Requirements for Deputies', 11 January 1998. See also, 'OSCE Again Points to 'Deficiencies' in Estonian Language Law', 27 April 1999.

on recommendations by the OSCE Mission to Estonia as well as the HCNM, Tallinn changed the 1994 election law, Article 26, Section 26, stating that electoral candidates had to be proficient in the State Language.[526]

In the 1989 Language Law adopted by the Latvian Supreme Council, bilingualism became an official policy with the same treatment given to Latvian as Russian had received for years. The law also stated that there would be a three-year transition period in which Russian-speakers in the public sphere would begin to learn Latvian depending on their occupation. For example, a doctor would be required to know more Latvian than a tram attendant. Once the transition period was over, the 1992 Law on Language dropped Russian as a co-official language despite the fact that around 30-35 per cent of the population used Russian as a first language.

Attempts to change the Law on Language to regulate the use of language in the private sphere began in 1997. After the Citizenship amendment debates, centre-right forces in the government and parliament began drafting new legislation that would allow the Latvian Government the ability to determine language proficiency levels in the private sphere. Again, the major European players jumped into action.[527] The OSCE, Council of Europe, and the EU stressed that this would be a violation of many of the international conventions Latvia had signed. Again, the HCNM became the primary voice urging reconsideration.[528] His diplomatic offensive began with a trip to Riga in January 1999. Van der Stoel argued that the draft legislation would 'over-regulate' language in the private sector. He concluded his visit stating, 'it is possible to have meaningful laws on language that perform the function of promoting and protecting the Latvian language while at the same time choosing regulations in conformity with international law.'[529]

Following the High Commissioner's recommendations, the minority Kristopans Government called for changes in the amendment that would only regulate language in cases of national security, territorial integrity, or public

526 *RFE/RL Daily Report*, 'Changes to Estonian Language Law Praised by EU', 27 June 2000.

527 *Nevazisimaya Gazeta*, 7 February 1998.

528 *RFE/RL Daily Report*, 'OSCE Official Wants Latvians Language Law to Meet International Norms', 14 January 1999.

529 *RFE/RL Daily Report*, 'Van der Stoel in Latvia', 25 May 1999.

safety. Showing a lack of party discipline, the amendment passed with help from deputies within the ruling coalition without the recommendations of the Prime Minister in July 1999. President Vaira Vike-Freiberga returned the legislation to parliament complaining that it had several legalistic ambiguities, although many saw the veto as bowing to Western pressure. In fact, Olafs Bruvers, head of the State Human Rights Office was quite open about accommodating the recommendations of the High Commissioner in the changed amendment. [530] The changed amendment finally passed in December 1999 with the changes that resembled the plans of the government regarding national security and public safety, and was subsequently promulgated by the president.

Clearly, the HCNM and the long-term missions were not able to influence large-scale policy revision at the beginning of the independence period. However, the OSCE in particular did facilitate a positive outcome in four ways. First, the High Commissioner and the long-term missions were able to provide a normative direction for policies related to minorities. Second, the long-term missions provided 'on-the-ground' information, which eliminated the need to filter political rhetoric. Third, the OSCE was able to lend an ear to the minority communities who often felt as though their governments were not listening. Finally, the OSCE was able to act as informer and mouthpiece for the EU, Council of Europe, and other regional institutions. The OSCE Missions to Estonia and Latvia ceased on 31 December 2001.[531]

Why did the OSCE missions, and thus the only on-the-ground operations of any European institution, close in 2001? According to the OSCE mission heads, Estonia and Latvia had implemented changes in their minority policy to the degree deemed necessary by OSCE and European standards. Peter Semneby, head of the last mission to Latvia, stated that 'the OSCE's permanent council in Vienna had been impressed by President Vaira Vike-Freiberga's recent commitment to table legislative amendments that would scrap Latvian language requirements for people standing for public office.'[532] Likewise, the last head of the OSCE mission to Estonia, Doris Hertrampf, ar-

530 *RFE/RL Baltic States Report*, 16 August 2000.

531 *The Baltic Times* 'OSCE closures boost EU and NATO hopes', No. 288, 20 December 2001.

gued that Estonia's decision to scrap language requirements for election candidates had completed the reforms that her office was supposed to monitor. Despite the missions closure, Semneby stated that the reforms were 'processes that require constant efforts - there will always be more to do.'[533]

While there has been little substantive evidence, it is hard to believe that closure of the missions were not a result of pressure by the EU and NATO. Clearly, the closure of the missions was required before Estonia and Latvia could become members of either of the organisations. Both Tallinn and Riga believed that the closing of the missions was a step to larger membership. The European Commission *Regular Reports* on Estonia and Latvia acknowledged the closures as justified, having come to the conclusion that little needed to be changed a year earlier.[534] In an interview with the author, Latvian Social Integration Minister Nils Muiznieks, who was head of the Centre for Human Rights and Ethnic Studies at the time, stated that both NATO and Western governments had a big influence on the mission closures.[535] He stated that the US Government was the main opponent to the missions since it prevented NATO expansion. However, according to the Minister, NATO did want the reforms to take place that the OSCE and EU recommended. He stated that NATO's concerns were pragmatic rather than a desire to see liberal minority policy. NATO was more worried about the reform of the security services and the vetting procedures for access to sensitive materials once the Baltic states became members. Muiznieks stated that the EU and NATO were equally important in bringing about the closure of the missions.

Contrary to the Latvian Minister's remarks, Sander Soone at the Estonian Foreign Ministry stated in an interview with the author, that NATO had nothing to do with the OSCE mission closures.[536] Soone stated, 'NATO as an

---

532 Ibid.

533 Ibid.

534 See Commission of the European Communities, *2001 Regular Report on Estonia's Progress towards Accession* and *2001 Regular Report on Latvia's Progress towards Accession*. EU Regular Reports can be accessed at http://europa.eu.int/comm/enlargement/index_en.html.

535 Interview with the author at the Latvian Ministry of Social Integration (Riga), 5 January 2004.

536 Interview with the author at the Estonian Ministry of Foreign Affairs (Tallinn), 12 January 2004.

organisation never had anything to do with the mission, its presence or its removal.' He argued that while the US Government applied pressure to the OSCE to remove the missions, the EU was far more influential in bringing about the decision to close. The European Union member countries, along with the US Government, supported the closure of the missions. Importantly, he argued that while the EU actually followed the OSCE missions, NATO was unconcerned. Rather, it was important that Estonia should look like stable, secure prospective member-state to the EU countries. Following a similar line, Andzeys Vilumsons of the Latvian Ministry of Defence, also in an interview with the author, stated that NATO had little to do with the OSCE mission closures, but also pointed to the pressure of the US Government.[537] Furthermore, he also pointed to other EU members such as Sweden as being key proponents of their removal. While there are some discrepancies over the external influences to bring the missions to a close, the probability that the US Government did intercede on Estonia and Latvia's behalf looks rather certain.

Most definitely, the OSCE's combined efforts did not come without a backlash.[538] Among Baltic politicians, the OSCE was often considered to be unfairly interfering in internal state affairs. In addition came the claim that the High Commissioner was only acting in response to dramatic claims from Moscow or was an agent of Russian imperialism. Often, as the face of the OSCE in Estonia and Latvia, van der Stoel received undue attention for his efforts to persuade Baltic politicians to work on the basis of consensus. Furthermore, the long-term missions were considered to be too intrusive and ill-aimed in their mission. For example, in May 1999, Estonian President Lennart Meri argued that the OSCE Mission to Estonia should be re-organised into an educational centre 'to help Estonia overcome the burden of its Soviet past.'[539] Externally, the Russian Federation often argued that the OSCE was unwilling to listen to voices within the Russophonic community and not forceful enough in its ability to persuade policy revision.[540]

---

537 Interview with the author at the Latvian Ministry of Defence (Riga), 8 January 2004.

538 *RFE/RL Baltic States Report*, 27 June 2000.

539 *RFE/RL Daily Report* 'Meri Recommends Reorganization of OSCE Mission', 7 May 1999.

540 *The Baltic Times*, 'Russia Grumbles as OSCE Pull-out', No. 286, 16 July 2004.

Despite the perceived intrusion, European organisations have been able to allow the Baltic states to develop policies that reinforce their sense of nation while making Estonia and Latvia's road to European integration easier. The evolution of social policy in the Baltic states gives some indication of the European organisations' commitment to cohesion, co-operation, and multiculturalism. Nevertheless, European integration has remained largely an elite-led process. People in Estonia and Latvia still have many questions regarding increased integration. While collective security arrangements remain fairly popular among titular communities, it is not difficult to find voices arguing that their nation has exchanged rule by Moscow for rule by Brussels.

9.2 European Union

From the beginning of the post-Soviet era, the Baltic governments made EU membership a primary policy goal. The politicians of this early time must be applauded for their optimism, as the idea of actually becoming a part of the EU seemed to be a long time away. However, now we are witnessing the beginning of Estonia and Latvia's membership in the EU. No doubt, the path to EU membership has been difficult given the standards set by the accession criteria. Politicians are often required to set aside electorally significant policies for the sake of promoting EU-required reforms. Furthermore, the Copenhagen Criteria affected every policy area including minority policy. For Estonia and Latvia, the handling of their large Russophonic, predominantly stateless, communities would be a major hurdle to overcome for EU membership. Having said that, this does not mean the minority issue was the most important policy area in regards to EU membership. Rather, the EU is first and foremost an economic institution, while the battle between intergovernmentalists and supranationalists remains predominantly in the background when it does not touch economic or financial policy. Importantly, many in the minority communities recognise this and distrust the EU project because they feel that Brussels had been unwilling to press for truly liberal reforms that would halt the perceived discrimination currently in the area of language.

As Duncan Wilson states, 'ensuring respect for minority rights among the pre- accession countries has had questionable results.'[541] Within the Copenhagen criteria, there is only the quite ambiguous requirement that countries respect and protect minorities. Although a part of the Copenhagen criteria, passed by the European Commission in 1993, the minority protection clause was left out of the Amsterdam Treaty, which made the Copenhagen criteria EU law. Thus, the EU left out a fundamental legal basis on which to encourage the protection of minorities in potential new member-states. This is not to say that minority protection is not an important part of the accession criteria. In fact, the European Commission does monitor how potential member-states observe this requirement within the terms of the Charter of Fundamental Rights of the European Union. The lack of a standard definition of minority means that the European Commission must use internationally agreed standards on the protection of minorities as a means of monitoring minority policies.

Although the minority protection clause was left out of the Amsterdam Treaty, a 'Race Equality Directive' is part of the *acquis communautaire* (the body of EU law that must be incorporated into domestic law).[542] This European Council directive did not come into force until 2003, but there was no doubt that it is already being applied as a standard. The directive rejects discrimination based on racial or ethnic grounds and 'therefore performs a vital function in ensuring the aims of integration to benefit all sectors of society.'[543] Not only does the directive require that states combat discrimination, it also requires governments to be proactive in their evaluation of direct and *indirect* discrimination.[544] The directive also requires that the party that is accused of discrimination hold the burden of proof, under which the body will have to

---

541 Wilson, Duncan. 2000. *Minority Rights in Education: Lessons for the European Union from Estonia, Latvia, Romania and the Former Yugoslav Republic of Macedonia*. Stockholm: Swedish International Development Co-operation Agency: www.right-to-education.org.

542 European Union, 29 June 2000, Council Directive 2000/43/EC, Council of the European Union: http://europa.eu.int/infonet/library/m/200043ce/en.htm

543 Wilson 2000, 16.

544 Russian-speakers in Estonia and Latvia are often most likely to suffer as the result of indirect discrimination. That is discrimination that is rooted within a system not necessarily directly targeted against minorities.

prove that their acts do not present a discriminatory impact. Other than the political component of the Copenhagen criteria, which has been undercut by its absence from the Amsterdam Treaty, the European Union has few structural assurances for the protection of minorities. Nonetheless, the European Commission was able to set the standard that was required before a country was invited to join the EU. However, the Commission is not necessarily a consistent body.

EU Relations with Estonia and Latvia

As was to be expected, the Baltic states' first encounters with the EU were economic in nature. Within six months after the practical restoration of Baltic independence, both Estonia and Latvia had signed trade and co-operation agreements with the EU.[545] The agreements allowed for the elimination of trade barriers on many goods but not on more traditional manufactured goods and agriculture. Importantly, the trade and co-operation agreements initiated the relationship between the European organisation and the Baltic states. We should even be able to date the Baltic states' road to EU membership to when the agreements were signed. However, questions over minority issues may have even affected these economic agreements when the European Parliament (EP) delayed its vote.[546] British MEP Gary Titley stated that the vote on the accord with Estonia was delayed because of concerns over the constitutional referendum, citizenship law, and election law. On the other hand, EP Secretariat officials stated that the delays were due to 'purely technical' matters.

Indeed, on-the-ground observations made by the EU were few and far between in comparison to the OSCE, nor did the EU have a long-term mission to any of the Baltic states. However, there were some such visits to the Baltic states in order to observe the minority situation. For example, an EP delegation visited Latvia in April 1993 in order to make an assessment of the

545 Latvia signed the agreement on 4 February 1992 while Estonia did 27 February 1992. Incidentally, Lithuania was the first to sign the accord on 31 January. See *RFE/RL Newsline,* 'Latvia Initials EC Trade Pact', 6 February 1992, 'Estonian-EC Trade Accord', 2 March 1992.

546 *RFE/RL Newsline,* 'EC Talks About Balts', 16 September 1992.

validity of the claims made by politicians in Moscow.[547] However, the delegation found no evidence 'for the recent accusations by Russian President Boris Yeltsin and other Russian leaders of massive and grave violations of human rights in Latvia.'

As both states began the road towards European integration, the pressure on the governments to liberalise their social policies relating to minorities increased. With the growing relationship with the EU after 1995, officials in Brussels began applying greater pressure on Estonia and Latvia. Overall, the EU largely worked through the OSCE missions and the HCNM to monitor the status of national minorities in the Baltic states.[548] However, Brussels also maintained communication on social policies through the EU Commissioner for Central and Eastern Europe. In 1997, EU Commissioner Hans van den Broek stressed that legislation in Estonia would need to be changed in order to give greater independent oversight to the way social policies were implemented.[549] In particular, Estonia, unlike Latvia and Lithuania, had been unwilling to appoint an ombudsman to oversee minority and non-citizen complaints, as discussed earlier.[550] Tallinn was unwilling to create the ombudsman institution because it would overlap with the office of the Legal Chancellor.

Despite Estonia's unwillingness to appoint an independent arbitrator for minority complaints, it was the first of the three Baltic states to be recommended for EU membership in July 1997, along with the Czech Republic, Hungary, Poland, and Slovenia.[551] In particular, Estonia was the most advanced economic reformer among post-socialist states. By implementing strict fiscal policies and attracting foreign investment, Estonia was able to begin the road to membership nearly two years before Latvia and Lithuania. With the changes in social policy, both the OSCE and the EU became more

547 *RFE/RL Newsline,* 'Europarliament Delegation in Latvia, Lithuania', 14 April 1993.

548 *RFE/RL Daily Report*, 'OSCE Says Latvia's Naturalization Test Too Complicated', 14 April 1993.

549 *RFE/RL Daily Report*, 'EU Official Urges Legislative Changes in Estonia', 16 April 1997.

550 For a discussion of the ombudsman institution in the Baltic states, see Dreifelds, Juris. 2001. Divergent Paths of the Ombudsman Idea in the Baltic States. In *The Baltic States at Historical Crossroads*, edited by Talavs Jundzis. Riga: Latvian Academy of Sciences.

551 *RFE/RL Daily Report*, 'Why Estonia rather than Latvia or Lithuania?', 30 July 1997.

pleased with Estonia's performance. In March 1998, British Foreign Secretary Robin Cook stated that he saw no obstacle for Estonia joining the EU over the Russophone minority.[552] In fact, with Estonia following the recommendations of the OSCE and the Council of Europe, officials in Brussels became increasingly relaxed about Estonia's entry.[553]

The EU continued to try and persuade Estonia to allow citizenship for stateless children. The Estonian Government had rejected calls in the past by Russian deputies to amend the citizenship law to allow stateless children, invalids, and spouses of Estonian citizens to become naturalised without being required to pass the language exam.[554] However, the Estonian government was unable to deny efforts of the OSCE and the EU to change the citizenship law. Furthermore, there was growing desire within the Estonian population for a more liberal stance on citizenship, especially dealing with children. In fact, a change in the citizenship law to grant citizenship to stateless children who were born after 26 February 1992 came in December 1997.[555] Notably, the Fatherland Union and People's Party were the primary antagonists against the amendment. Despite their fears, only 222 applications for citizenship for children of stateless parents had been submitted by the beginning of 2000.[556] Changes in the citizenship law to allow stateless children born after the deadline followed the earlier efforts of the Government's integration programme which focused on youth education.

Latvia's efforts to gain fast-track status for EU Membership continued to be delayed, despite the fact that it had signed the European Social Charter in

---

552 *RFE/RL Daily Report*, 'UK's Cook Sees No Obstacle for Tallinn over Russian Minority', 31 March 1998.

553 An additional issue that further limited progress towards EU membership was the policy of capital punishment in both states. Eventually, both states repealed the death penalty. Brennan, Neil J. 1998. European integration and human rights' cultures in Eastern Europe: the EU and abolitions of capital punishment. *University of New Brunswick Law Journal* 47:49-84.

554 *RFE/RL Daily Report*, '...Turns Down Request to Ease Citizenship Law', 7 January 1998.

555 The *Riigikogu* voted 55 to 20 to change the citizenship law on 8 December 1998. See *RFE/RL Daily Report*, 'Estonian Parliament Passes Amendments to Citizenship Law', 9 December 1998.

556 *RFE/RL Daily Report*, 'As of the end of 1999 . . .', 31 January 2000.

1997.[557] Although it can be argued that Latvia had not been as successful in their market transition as Estonia, the former was not far behind. Much of the controversy relating to Latvia's inability to progress on the road to European Integration surrounded the stringent 1994 Law on Citizenship. As negotiations over drafting a new citizenship law began in late 1997, the European pressure began to build.[558] In fact, the negotiations gained much attention from the OSCE, EU, NATO, Council of Europe, the Baltic Council, and individual Western states.[559] Despite disagreements in the government amidst controversy over an alternative more conservative amendment, the Latvian Parliament passed a new amendment to the 1994 Citizenship Law in late June 1998. The final amendment eliminated the 'naturalisation windows', granted citizenship for children after independence without age or language limitations, and simplified the language tests for people over 65. The controversy increased as the more nationalist parties gathered enough signatures to hold a referendum on the approval of the new changes to the citizenship law in October. Through the success of the amendment in the *Saeima* and the referendum, Latvia marked a major turning point in relation to its future of European integration.[560]

The conditionality of the European Union is seen in the European Commission's *Regular Reports* on proposed member-states. The Reports were part of the EU's reform initiative *Agenda 2000* that was formulated at an Intergovernmental Conference in Amsterdam in 1997 and further developed at the 1998 Luxembourg European Council.[561] Concentrating on agricultural and financial reform, the document also mandated that regular reports would be made to the Council, 'reviewing the progress of each Central and East European applicant state towards accession in the light of the Copenhagen

---

557 *RFE/RL Daily Report*, 'Latvia Signs European Social Charter', 30 May 1997.

558 *Izvestia* 26 August 1997.

559 *RFE/RL Daily Report*, 'EU Wants Riga to Act Quickly on Citizenship Law'; and 'Germany Reportedly Backs Changes to Latvian Citizenship Law', 20 April 1998. See also 'Baltic Council Head Urges Latvia to Amend Citizenship Law', 14 May 1998; 'Council of Europe Slams Latvia Over Citizenship, Death Penalty . . .', 19 May 1998; 'Latvia's Birkavs Urges Lawmakers to Comply with OSCE Recommendations', 2 June 1998; and 'NATO Chief Urges Latvia to Change Citizenship Law', 19 June 1998.

560 See *The Baltic Times* 'No amendments, no EU?', No. 188, 23 July 1998.

criteria.' There were two main methods of evaluation employed in the Reports.[562] First, the EU Commission reviewed candidate country legislation required to meet the Copenhagen Criteria. Second, the Reports concentrated on implementation and the state-capacity to meet membership requirements.

The Reports are important because they 'indicate the main trends and results in the field of minority protection within the [Central and East European States].'[563] The reports have four main characteristics. First, they pay special attention to the minority situation in Estonia and Latvia. Second, the Reports judge the success of adopting the *acquis*, primarily based on the candidate countries' economic transition rather than the level of political adoption. Thirdly, the Reports were not meant to delay the enlargement process especially for the original six (Poland, Hungary, Czech Republic, Slovakia, Slovenia and Estonia). Finally, as Hughes and Sasse rightly point-out, the Reports consist of various reports from a variety of sources from the OSCE to NGOs. 'The lack of transparency in the process of compilation by the EU makes it impossible to measure the relative weight of each of these inputs.'[564]

Hughes and Sasse find that the 'Reports do not systematically assess the structure and operation of institutional frameworks or policies for dealing with minority groups.'[565] While the Reports do illustrate the lack of 'hard' law in relation to minority rights, it must be remembered that regimes are usually based on 'soft' laws and thus we should not expect the minority rights regime in Europe to be different. Most importantly, the Reports illustrate the role and conclusions of European experts. While Hughes and Sasse see the Report's concentration on the OSCE and Council of Europe as a weakness, an epistemic communities approach allows us to view the Reports as exemplifying community co-ordination to further policy implementation.

The first Reports were delivered to the European Council at the end of 1998. The reports have four objectives. First, they describe the relationship

---

561 *Agenda 2000* (1998).

562 Hughes, James and Gwedolyn Sasse. 2003. Monitoring the Monitors: EU Enlargement Conditionality and Minority Protection in the CEECs. *Journal of Ethnopolitics and Minority Issues in Europe* (1):16. (www.ecmi.de).

563 Ibid., 14.

564 Ibid., 15.

565 Ibid.. 16.

between the applicant countries at the Union in relation to the Europe Agreement. Second, the Reports analyse the status of 'democracy, rule of law, human rights, and the protection of minorities'. Note that the Reports do not refer strictly to 'national' minorities, as neither do the Copenhagen Criteria. Third, the Commission assesses the economic conditions of the applicant countries. Finally, the Reports assesses whether the applicant country will be able to accept the obligations of membership. In this capacity, the Commission Reports offer an important perception of political and economic events in Estonia and Latvia.

The 1997 Opinion on Estonia's application for EU membership set the backdrop for the first Report in 1998. The Opinion came to the conclusion that the 'measure to facilitate the naturalisation process and to better integrate non-citizens including stateless children and to enhance Estonian language training for non-Estonian speakers are considered a short-term priority.'[566] Within the 1998 Report on Estonia, little has changed in that year.[567] In Section 1.2, there is a direct reference to using the OSCE as a benchmark for minority protection. The Report argues, 'it is regrettable that the Parliament has not yet adopted the amendments to the Citizenship Law which would align it with OSCE recommendations and facilitate naturalisation of stateless children.' While it recognised moves within the *Riigikogu* to change the citizenship law, the Commission expressed regret over the delays to the amendments. The failure to amend the Citizenship Law was a key detriment to Estonia's efforts to join the EU. However, the Report did concentrate on several efforts to increase the integration of minorities. Special attention was paid to amendments to the 1993 Law on Aliens, the rejection of conservative amendments to the State Language Law and the extension of the existing minority language education system established in a restricted form in the Basic and Secondary Schools Act. Not only did the EU recommend changes, but also donated significant sums of money to improve Estonian language skills amongst the minority community through the PHARE programme. As we have seen before, the pressure of the EU and the OSCE would soon led

566 Commission of the European Communities, *1997 Opinion on Estonia's Application for EU Membership.*

567 Commission of the European Communities, *1998 Regular Report on Estonia's Pro-*

Parliament to change the Citizenship Law in line with many changes for which Estonia is praised.

It must be said that the Regular Reports were largely concerned with Estonia's ability to meet the political and economic terms of the Copenhagen Criteria, rather than the status of minorities, possibly for good reason. By 1998, the status of minorities in the Baltic states was unlikely to cause regional instability. Nevertheless, the EU does pay attention to the treatment of minorities in the report within the Political Criteria sections. In this context, the 1999 Report on Estonia congratulates the *Riigikogu* for passing the amendment to the Citizenship Law concerning the naturalisation of stateless children.[568] On the other hand, the Commission condemns the 1999 Language Law, which restricted access of non-titular speakers in the political and public sector. The Report views the Law as 'a step backwards and should be amended.'[569] Thus, the short-term priorities of the Accession Partnership had been only 'partially met.' By 2000, the Regular Report does not include criticisms of Estonia's handling of the minority situation. The Commission compliments the change in the Language Law, use of the Ombudsman to address complaints, and the instillation of the national programme for integration. The Report concludes that the short-term political criteria have been 'met to a large extent.'[570] By the time of the 2001 Report, the Commission states that 'Estonia continues to implement concrete measure for integration of non-citizens'.[571] The EU had ended its dialogue over the minority issue.

Latvia's relationship with the EU proceeded in much the same way. The first Regular Report was issued at the end of 1998.[572] Of most concern, the Report points out that Latvia has failed to ratify the Framework Convention for the Protection of National Minorities and the European Social Charter. In addition, the Report points out that the naturalisation process has been too

---

gress towards Accession.

568 Commission of the European Communities, *1999 Regular Report on Estonia's Progress towards Accession.*

569 Ibid., 16.

570 Ibid., 89.

571 Commission of the European Communities, *2001 Regular Report on Estonia's Progress towards Accession.*

572 Commission of the European Communities, *1998 Regular Report on Latvia's Progress towards Accession.*

slow. The Commission blames this specifically on the inclusion of the 'window' system into the 1994 Law on Citizenship. However, the Report does recognise that changes of the Law on Citizenship had occurred in 1998 with the amendments and subsequent referendums. In conclusion, both the short and medium-term goals concentrate on the acquisition of Latvian skills by minorities.

Subsequent reports concentrated on the ability of the naturalisation service to process applicants. The 1999 Report stated, 'the major outstanding problem in the first half of 1999 concerned the capacity of the Naturalisation Board and its branches to receive and process the increasing numbers of requests within the necessary time limits.'[573] Furthermore, the documents reports, 'Latvian now fulfils all recommendations expressed by the OSCE in area of citizenship and naturalisation . . . Latvia fulfils the Copenhagen political criteria'. The 2000-2001 Reports review the process of change in relation to the naturalisation system as well as language legislation.[574] Most importantly, however, the Commission points out the problems that come with transitioning from a parallel to a single education system. The problem is largely as it stands today; there are not enough 'State' language teachers to implement the changes. Surprisingly, little is said about the effects of the changes on the ability to learn of minority children once the education system is reformed. While the minority issue was and is important for the EU, other issues such as corruption and the criminal just system were far more important.

Although the EU has not been as active as the OSCE in its pressure on Estonia and Latvia to adopt more liberal minority legislation, the voice of Brussels carries the greatest weight of any of the regional institutions. In September 2003, Estonia and Latvia voted to become members of the EU. The 'No' campaigns in both states had considerable support. Even though the electorates continued to put parties in power that favour European integration, the argument that there is little difference between the EU project and the Soviet project was dramatically pronounced. Unfortunately, such an ar-

---

573 Commission of the European Communities, *1999 Regular Report on Latvia's Progress towards Accession.*

574 Commission of the European Communities, *2000 Regular Report on Latvia's Progress towards Accession*; and *2001 Regular Report on Latvia's Progress towards Accession.*

gument obscured more than it revealed given that economically, the two projects could not be farther apart. Needless to say, the Baltic states became members of the EU on 1 May 2004, only a month after coming under the NATO collective security umbrella. In looking at the actions of the EU from 1991-2001 in relation to Estonia and Latvia, Brussels has had a substantial impact on the citizenship and language policies of both states.

9.3 Council of Europe

Membership of the CoE was a natural foreign policy objective of Estonia and Latvia. Not only is it an important organisation within Europe, but also membership is closely related to a nation's prospects of EU membership. The CoE contains many institutional devices in which to insure the rights and protection of minorities. Although not as persistent as the HCNM under Max van der Stoel, the CoE has been far more scrutinising of Baltic minority policies. First, Council of Europe Parliamentary Assembly delegations have often visited Estonia and Latvia in order to monitor the minority situation. Furthermore, through the office of the OSCE HCNM, the Council of Europe maintained a constant review of the evolution of social policy in the Baltic states.

Also, there are several treaties relating to the rights and protection of minorities within the auspices of the Council of Europe. Most notable is the Framework Convention for the Protection of National Minorities (Framework Convention). Interestingly, as Wilson points out, the Framework Convention is 'the only binding multilateral treaty on minority rights, which makes no attempt to define to whom it applies.'[575] Nevertheless, the Framework Convention does offer a normative framework on which to base the treatment of national minorities. For example, Article 4, subsection 1 states:

> The Parties undertake to guarantee to persons belonging to national minorities the right of equality before the law and of equal protection of the law. In this respect, any discrimination based on belonging to a national minority shall be prohibited.[576]

575 Wilson 2000, 10.

576 *Framework Convention for the Protection of National Minorities* (1995).

Article 5 is more specific and takes into account the need for cohesion within the state (i.e. integration programmes). It states:

1. The Parties undertake to promote the condition necessary for persons belonging to national minorities to maintain and develop their culture, and to preserve the essential elements of their identity, namely their religion, language, traditions, and cultural heritage.
2. Without prejudice to measures taken in pursuance of their general integration policy, the Parties shall refrain from policies or practices aimed at assimilation of persons belonging to national minorities against their will and shall protect these persons from any action aimed at such assimilation.

Importantly, since the next major step towards the titularisation of the state will be through the educational system, the Framework Convention lays out the rights of national minorities. Article 13 states:

1. Within the framework of their education systems, the Parties shall recognise that persons belonging to a national minority have the right to set up and to manage their own private educational and training establishments.
2. The exercise of this right shall not entail any financial obligation for the Parties.

Thus, the Framework Convention approves the withdrawal of instruction in the minority language within state-funded schools, while allowing for the establishment of private minority language schools. Interestingly, the Latvian 1998 Education Law allows for public funding to be provided to private schools. However, the law also discriminates against schools that do not practice instruction within the national language (Latvian). Nevertheless, although arguably discriminatory, the Education Law does not violate Article 13. Having said this, the Framework Convention does require that governments maintain the teaching of minority languages to the national minority under Article 14.

There is little doubt that the rights of minorities are an important issue across Europe. For this reason, the Framework Convention is a vital document laying the foundations for the protection of national minorities under the auspices of the CoE. While Estonia has signed and adopted the Framework

Convention, Latvia has signed but rejected the agreement on three separate occasions in the *Saeima*.[577] Furthermore, there seems little initiative under the current Repse Government to approve the Framework Convention at any time in the near future. According to the Latvian Human Rights Committee, the parliamentary debates reveal several reasons why the framework could not be approved, including that the law of Latvia already provides for such protection and terms such as 'national minority' are too ambiguous. [578]

Another reason may be that it is potentially politically unpopular amongst the largely titular electorate to be seen favouring the Russian-speaking community (although the Framework Convention could hardly be considered discriminatory towards Latvians). However, it seems to me that the main reason is that the Latvian Constitution states that only the near-extinct Finno-Ugric Livonian is a native language other than Latvian. Other languages such as Russian and German are considered to be alien. Thus, this begs the question once again, what is a national minority? In the case of Latvia, could Slavs be a minority but not a national minority? The Latvian constitution and subsequent legislation (i.e. 1999 Language Law) seem to imply this is the case. From this perspective, the Framework Convention hardly applies to Latvia. On the other hand, if approved, Europe could see things another way. Nevertheless, since Latvia has signed the Framework Convention, it is required to abide by the Convention in accordance with the 1969 Vienna Convention on the Law of Treaties, which states that a country must not act in a way that violates the agreement between the act of signing and ratification.

While Chapter Two illustrated how institutional solutions in the domestic arena could insure minority protection, the Framework Convention shows that states can insure minority protection through committing themselves to international benchmarks. Most recently on 6 May 2004, the Latvian government again rejected the move to ratify the Framework Convention by refusing to

---

577 The Latvian *Saeima* refused to approve the Convention in May 2000, March 2001, and September 2002.

578 Dimitriov, Alexei and Boris Koltchanov, eds. 2002. *Report on the Implementation of the Framework Convention for the Protection of National Minorities*. Riga: Latvian Human Rights Committee.

send it to committee for consideration.[579] Both Estonia and Latvia have stated that the Framework Convention is an unnecessary document since minority protection has been enshrined in domestic legislation. These two case studies illustrate the relationship between domestic and international solutions to minority protection. In the Estonian case, the Framework Convention was ratified with the additional reservations listing 'traditional' national minorities, which did not include the largely stateless community. Latvia, on the other hand, was the only state to enter the EU without having ratified the Framework Convention. The latter case study illustrates a greater tension between domestic and international sources of minority protection. The Latvian government's policy towards the stateless community tends towards integration through Latvian language acquisition. This is at odds with Articles 9, 10 and 11 of the Framework Convention that deal with giving and receiving information from the government, the most visible example would be street signs. While there are clear legal discrepancies between domestic legislation and international codes of practice, Latvian Minister for Integration Muiznieks has argued that 'the problem is political, not legal.' In the end, almost nothing would change with ratification.[580] However, it is the political will even to make the motion that is lacking most evidently in Latvia.

In addition to the Framework Convention, there is also the European Convention for the Protection of Human Rights and Fundamental Freedoms (1950) that lies within the CoE.[581] Although an important document that attempts to ensure basic human right in Europe, it makes very little reference to group rights (i.e. minorities). On the other hand, this European Convention has been tied directly to the United Nations Minority Declaration which does not only target 'national' minorities, but all minorities.[582] Furthermore, Article 19 of the Framework Convention directly asserts that it is subject to the limita-

579 See *The Baltic Times*, 'Government Fails to Ratify Minorities' Convention', 13-19 May 2004.

580 Ibid.

581 *European Convention for the Protection of Human Rights and Fundamental Freedoms* (1950): http://www.pfc.org.uk/legal/echrtext.htm.

582 Gilbert, G. 2002. Jurisprudence of the European Court and Commission of Human Rights in 2001 and Minority Groups, Sub-Commission on the Promotion and Protection of Human Rights. In *54 Session, Working Group on Minorities,* 8 Session 27-31 May 2002. E/CN.4/Sub.2/AC.5/2002/WP.2, 24 May, 6.

tions of the European Convention. Thus, theoretically, the Framework Convention could be a document insuring the protection of all minorities rather than only national minorities.

There are other agreements under the Council that address minority rights, such as the European Charter on Regional and Minority Languages, but have little practical effect. Nonetheless, the Council of Europe has played an important part in moving Latvia towards liberal democratic governance. While the CoE maintained its own observation of Estonia and Latvia throughout the 1990's, it also worked with the OSCE and the EU to fulfil its objectives. A review of its relationship with Estonia and Latvia will further illustrate how the CoE has influenced minority's policy in the Baltic states.

CoE Relations with Estonia and Latvia

At the same time that the Baltic states were signing trade agreements with the EU, the Council of Europe Secretary General Catherine Lalumière visited Estonia and Latvia.[583] In Estonia, the Secretary General spoke out for the exclusionist stand the government took on the minority issue. She acknowledged 'that there exist long-lasting liberal traditions towards the minorities in Estonia'. Interestingly, she followed this with 'I understand that giving the right to vote to all Russian people living in Estonia could jeopardise Estonia's identity'.

Likewise in Latvia, Lalumière expressed her support for the stand taken in draft citizenship guidelines in the Latvian parliament to require sixteen years of residency before a non-citizen could be naturalized, hardly within the standards of Europe. In a meeting with Latvian Supreme Council's Commission on Human and Nationality Rights, the Secretary General argued that Latvia's position was understandable since the Russian minority did not fit the 'traditional' concept of a national minority since it was above ten per cent. Overall, the Secretary General hardly exhibited the spirit of liberal governance as typically exhibited by the Council. However, it is possible she saved her 'liberal' approach for evaluating Estonia and Latvia's economic reforms.

583 See *RFE/RL Newsline*, 'Lalumière: Estonia Does Right by Minorities', 20 February 1992; 'Lalumière in Latvia', 19 February 1992; and 'Lalumière Understands Latvian Situation', 21 February 1992.

Unlike Secretary General Lalumière, members of the Council of Europe Parliamentary Assembly took a much harsher stand in a visit to Estonia in October 1992.[584] In particular, the group criticized the Estonian Government for not allowing non-citizens to vote in national elections held the previous month. The former Deputy Speaker of the *Riigikogu* was surprised to find that even the delegation's conservative members were critical. Notably, this was still at a time when Estonia was waiting to become a Council of Europe member.

In the lead up to the Baltic states becoming members of the Council, pressure was put on the organisation to delay the entrance of Estonia and Latvia. Latvia's entrance was delayed until after it could show that it had held 'free and fair' elections. As the vote on Estonian membership came in 1993, the Russian Foreign Ministry continually lobbied the Council to reject Estonia's membership on the basis of human rights violations.[585] Russian Foreign Minister Kozyrev even sent a letter to Lalumière calling Estonia's membership 'premature', citing 'discrimination' against Russian minorities. It must be noted that Russia was not a member of the Council of Europe at this time. As an indication of Russia's powers of persuasion in the Council, Estonia was admitted just two days after Lithuania on 13 May with only 3 delegates not voting for Estonian membership.[586]

At this point, Latvia remained the last Baltic state not to be a Council member. On 15 September, a delegation of experts headed by the Council's Secretariat Director Hans Peter Furrer came to analyse the draft citizenship law in the *Saeima*.[587] The delegation met with both parliamentary factions and Russophone leaders. Furrer called on the Latvian Parliament to pass a citizenship law that relied on the principles of human rights. Parliamentary deputies went ahead with the first draft of the citizenship law that passed its second reading on 9 June 1994.[588] Afterwards, Latvia's State Minister for Human Rights Olafs Bruvers stated that the Council of Europe was not happy with the present state of the legislation. As was to be expected, the quota system

584 *Izvestia*, 7 October 1992.
585 *RFE/RL Newsline*, 'Council of Europe and the Baltics', 12 May 1993.
586 *RFE/RL Newsline*, 'Estonia Admitted to Council of Europe', 14 May 1993.
587 *RFE/RL Newsline*, 'Council of Europe Delegation in Latvia', 16 September 1993.
588 *Segodnya*, 16 June 1994.

was the primary complaint of the Council. Eventually, as the OSCE section illustrated, the Latvian Parliament passed a citizenship law acceptable to Europe. Subsequently, Latvia became a member of the Council of Europe on 10 February 1995 and signed the Framework Convention on 12 May.

After the elections and citizenship laws in both countries, the Council of Europe turned its attention to other matters such as abolishing the death penalty. Estonia ratified the Framework Convention on 7 January 1997.[589] Subsequently, the Council of Europe's Parliamentary Assembly ended its monitoring of whether or not Estonia had met its commitments of becoming a member.[590] The assembly did recommend that Estonia has still not done enough to ensure the naturalisation of the non-Estonian community. The assembly, however, did reject Russia's insistence that the Assembly maintain its observation, based on the Russian Foreign Ministry's statement that Estonia had still not fulfilled its promise to end discrimination.

As required of signatories to the Framework Convention, Estonia constructed a 'state report' of their 'national minority' policies in relation to the individual articles of the treaty. The report concentrates on the rights guaranteed by the Estonian Constitution and the National Minorities Cultural Autonomy Act. The latter is the document that defines 'national minorities' is non-Estonian *citizens* that have a historic place within the territory of the state. For the most part, Estonia finds that it is well within the Framework's provisions. However, the Council of Europe did its own review of the Framework's application through the Advisory Committee; a body of experts established within the treaty.[591] The Committee found that while 'Estonia has made efforts to implement the Framework Convention and to improve intercultural dialogue . . . protection of national minorities is not always addressed in an adequate manner in the legislative process and administrative practice.' Furthermore, the Committee found that the National Minorities Cultural Autonomy Act (de-

589 *RFE/RL Newsline*, 'Estonian Relations with Council of Europe', 8 January 1997.

590 *RFE/RL Newsline*, 'Council of Europe Ends Monitoring of Estonia', 31 January 1997.

591 Council of Europe, *Resolution ResCMN (2002)8*, Council of Ministers: http://www.coe.ee/eng/?op=body&SID=35&BID=77. Rules adopted by the Committee of ministers on the monitoring arrangements under Articles 24 to 26 of the framework Convention for the Protection of National Minorities.

signed in 1925), 'contain(s) elements that are not particularly suited for the present situation of minorities in Estonia . . .' Obviously, more was needed to meet the demands of the Framework Convention.

Not yet a member, Latvia found its commitment monitored by the CoE. By 1998, the Council of Europe added its voice to the European organisations calling for changes in Latvia's citizenship law.[592] The Council of Europe's Parliamentary Assembly monitoring committee head Terry Davis stated that 'after seven years of independence, Latvia has not yet managed to successfully integrate its non-citizens.' He further pointed out that the stateless status of many children was worrying as well as insistence on a fluent knowledge of Latvian for employment in the private sector. In November, the Council of Europe's Parliamentary Assembly openly stated that the EU had not included Latvia for fast-track membership in the past because of Riga's failure to integrate the Russophone community.[593]

Following the changes to Estonia and Latvia's citizenship laws, the Council of Europe became less of a voice for Europe in the Baltic states. As an example of the Council's satisfaction, the president of the Council of Europe's Parliamentary Assembly Lord Russell Johnston stated that he had seen no evidence of discrimination against the Russian-speaking population in Estonia's northeast. However, it must be pointed out that Lord Johnston seemed to looking for social discrimination rather than that resulting from policy (i.e. the policies the Council of Europe had been criticising from the beginning of the Baltic states restoration). Yet he did state, 'I'm not an expert in this field...'[594]

By 2000, the Council of Europe, although still an important institution for the region, became less visible in relation to the minority issue. Since the restoration of independence, the Council was an effective institution in moderating nationalising policies in Estonia and Latvia. Primarily, the Council of Europe's Parliamentary Assembly was the main instrument of influence. Similar to the OSCE, the Council of Europe's recommendations were influential

592 *RFE/RL Newsline*, 'CE Slams Latvia over Citizenship Law, Death Penalty...', 19 May 1998.

593 *RFE/RL Newsline*, 'Decision on Latvia Linked to Russian-Speakers' Situation?', 5 November 1998.

594 *RFE/RL Newsline*, 'CEPA Head Praises Estonia's Language Policy', 13 May 1999.

primarily because of the importance put on EU membership. In effect, a satisfied Council of Europe meant a ticket on the fast-track route to Brussels.

9.4 Other Actors

As we have seen in the discussion of the OSCE mission closures, there were additional peripheral actors that monitored and often affected minority policy in Estonia and Latvia. In this section we shall consider three such actors: the United Nations, NATO and Western governments. They are peripheral actors in these cases because their attempts to influence minority policy were either relatively low level or their efforts were not overtly publicised. In all three cases, Estonia and Latvia could not have been high on their agenda because of the Baltic states' geographical location, lack of conflict and overall success of democratic reforms. Other Central European states like Poland and Hungary were far more important to the Europeans and the Americans. Throughout the 1990's, there were far more pressing matters in the Former Yugoslavia and other areas of the Former Soviet Union. Furthermore, Estonia and Latvia's democratic transition has been quite remarkable given its authoritarian past. Nevertheless, the Baltic states have gained significant attention from several actors of which this study requires more discussion. First, we begin with the United Nations.

Similar to the other organisations examined in this section, UN involvement with Estonia and Latvia relating to the minority issue began to become far less frequent as time went on. This is little surprise given the ethnic crises that were occurring elsewhere in Europe and around the world at this time. The UN continued to maintain a much more general observation of events in the Baltic states through the UNDP.[595] However, on two occasions, other bodies within the UN criticised Latvia specifically. In August 1999, the UN Committee on Racial Discrimination criticised Latvia's treatment of its minority community.[596] In particular, the Committee targeted the slow naturalisation

595 See the UNDP Annual Reports on Estonia and Latvia: http://www.undp.org/annualreports/.

596 *RFE/RL Newsline*, 'UN Committee Criticises Latvia's Treatment of Aliens...', 30 August 1999.

process, although it should be pointed out that by this time inactivity by the non-citizen population was equally as much the problem as the naturalisation process. Finally, the Committee argued that Latvia should continue to provide education in minority languages. The second circumstance came in November 2001 when the UN Human Rights Committee criticised the language proficiency regulations for public office.[597] The Committee recommended that the state should only verify the authenticity of the language certificate rather than the candidate's actual proficiency. The Latvian State Language Board subsequently changed the law to reflect the recommendations.

Remarkably, the UN did not maintain a critical review of the minority situation in Estonia and Latvia. Rather, multiple observations of the circumstances by the UN Human Rights Committee concluded with a satisfactory report. Why was this the case? Although international law is a starting point for European human rights conventions, European law has gone further with developing a liberal stand on rights in general. Furthermore, unlike the EU and the Council of Europe, the UN may have lost much of its power of persuasion once the Baltic states became members. Yet, this did not prevent the OSCE, of which the Baltic states also became members almost immediately after the August Coup, from being an effective liberal organisation. Of course the objectives of the UN are much more narrow and far ranging than the European institutions discussed here. Finally, in relation to many places in the world, including within many liberal democracies, the minority situation was not terribly egregious although it had the potential to become far worse. In the end, as the last example indicated, the UN did have some degree of influence over the minority policy evolution in Estonia and Latvia.

The Baltic states' relationship with NATO began before Russian troops had been withdrawn.[598] In February 1994, both Estonia and Latvia enrolled in

---

597 *RFE/RL Newsline*, 'Government Accepts Changes in Language Regulations Required by UN Committee', 5 December 2001.

598 For a review of the relationships between NATO, Russia and the Baltic States, see Jundzis, Talavs. 2001. The Baltic States, NATO, and the European Security and Defense Indentity. In Baltic Accession to the European Union: Challenge and Opportunity, edited by T. Jundzis. Riga: Latvian Academy of Sciences; and Lievan, Anatol and Dmitri Trenin, ed. 2003. Ambivalent Neighbors: the EU, NATO and the Price of Membership. Washington, D.C.: Carnegie Endowment for Peace; and Yesson, Erik. 2001. NATO, EU and Russia: Reforming Europe's Security Institutions.

the Partnership for Peace Plan. While NATO saw this as part of the stabilisation of the region, the Baltic states saw the signings as a step towards membership. On the part of Estonia and Latvia, consecutive governments were elected who supported NATO membership. Estonia's first government, headed by *Isamaa*, set the membership process in motion. Similarly in Latvia, Latvia's Way maintained an aim towards NATO membership, not only in the first government, but continued to do so by maintaining control of the foreign ministry until October 2002. The Baltic governments have never made a secret that NATO membership was more important than EU membership.

There is little evidence to suggest that concern over minority policies in the Baltic states came directly from NATO headquarters. Rather, we should look at individual member-states. Most importantly, the Clinton and Bush Administrations would have carried a significant amount of weight. For example, the US-Baltic Partnership was established in 1998.[599] At its inaugural session, the US Secretary of State Strobe Talbott stated that the US Government supported NATO and EU membership of the Baltic states. Importantly, as a member of the OSCE, the US Government would have been aware of the events in the Baltic states. In addition to the US, the Nordic states would have also been keen to see Baltic European integration. All four states have been primary sources of foreign direct investment in Estonia and Latvia. Often, the four states have come at the integration issue from slightly different directions. While Denmark, Sweden, and Finland are relatively new member-states, and thus redirected the focus of EU enlargement towards the Baltic States, Norway falls outside the EU. Similarly Norway and Denmark are NATO members while Sweden and Finland are not. While the Scandinavian countries have historical links to what was Livonia, Finland is linguistically and culturally tied to Estonia. Bearing this in mind, we should expect that not only have the Nordic states promoted Baltic membership in NATO and the EU, but also they have sought liberal reform in exclusionary policies. This has had its greatest effects on the Social Integration programmes in both states.

European Foreign Affairs Review 6:197-221.

599 *The Baltic Times*, 'Talbott reaffirms Baltic moves to the West', 16 July 1998.

9.5 Conclusion

This chapter completes the revision of the 'nexus' metaphor and his shed light on international sources of domestic policy in Estonia and Latvia. Overall, this chapter indicates that European institutions such as the OSCE, EU and the Council of Europe have had a large influence over the policy-making process and policy evolution. In the case of the OSCE, the HCNM was vigilant with the pressure applied to Tallinn and Riga. In general, the High Commissioner maintained that the Baltic states would need to live up to the international agreements that they themselves had signed. Furthermore, the long-term missions to Estonia and Latvia also played an important part by observing prospective legislation as well as the implementation of policy. In both countries, the OSCE played a part in effecting the outcome of the citizenship laws, language laws, and election laws.

Likewise, the EU also influenced the policy process. This study indicates that the EU was more effective after the citizenship laws were passed. After this point, many of the other organisations began to relent as either the Baltic states had become members or the organisations were required to turn their attention elsewhere. The EU's effectiveness was derived mainly from the appeal of membership sought by the two countries. The primary instruments of observation within the EU were the European Parliament and the European Commissioner for Central and Eastern Europe. In particular, EU influence was best seen in the citizenship law reforms and language laws of the late nineties. It is important to note that this section shows only a small part of policy directives sent from Brussels for EU membership. Indeed, the Copenhagen Criteria go far beyond the scope of minority rights. Once in the EU, it will be interesting to see how much Estonia and Latvia can withstand the pressure of the EU to complete further reforms.

The Council of Europe was (and remains) an important promoter of policy that respects European minority standards. The Council of Europe Parliamentary Assembly has played an important role in maintaining influence on Estonia and Latvia even after the two countries became members. In particular, the Council was very effective in pressuring the two governments to change their citizenship laws before their promulgation. This was especially the case with the 1994 Citizenship Law in Latvia. The Council of Europe thus completes an important triumvirate of European organisations. Although the OSCE is less well known amongst the wider European community, the three organisations worked well together in providing a foundation for regional stability and propagating politically liberal ideals. Although three separate organisations, as they are treated in this section, the OSCE, EU, and the Council did rely on each other for observation, information, and practical enforcement that tends to blur the boundaries of where one organisation ends and another begins.

Finally, other actors have also played a part, albeit less intense than the European institutions. The United Nations was concerned with the minority situations in both countries, but has little capacity to affect policy-making. Similarly, NATO must have been aware of the situation given its ability to draw the Baltic states and the Russian Federation into rhetorical conflict. As an organisation, NATO has no capacity to consistently monitor events on the ground in Estonia and Latvia. However, like the EU, it could work through the monitoring devices of the OSCE. Individual member-states of NATO and the EU would have also had an interest in minority policy in the region. The combination of the institutions and their constituent states would have been a significant international influence on domestic policy in Estonia and Latvia.

Chapter 10 Conclusion

Currently, Estonia and Latvia are either about to pass or have passed several important thresholds. Domestically, both states are pushing through school language reforms with Latvia hoping to complete the first phase in 2004. Although evidence indicates that the minority communities are unhappy with the changes, there has been little in the way of organised protest against the school reforms. This is little surprise given the minority communities' inability to shape policy since the restoration of independence. The latest elections in both countries leave the minority community without clear representation on the national level. The Estonian Centre Party and the Latvian FHRUL have been relegated to permanent opposition, while the latter has come apart.

Internationally, the Baltic states joined NATO and the EU in April and May 2004, respectively. In all three cases, NATO membership was always more important than membership in the EU. EU membership will give the Baltic states open access to European markets even more than allowed under the previous co-operation agreements. At the same time, Baltic industries will also be more vulnerable given the elimination of trade barriers. Having said this, the Baltic states continue their path towards democratic institutions first begun with their membership in the Council of Europe. In particular, there is still the question of whether or not EU membership will continue to influence liberal reforms of exclusionary minority policies. It may be too much to assume that EU membership will be a positive influence where countries such as France and Belgium still refuse to sign key minority protection treaties. At the same time, NATO membership places the Baltic states under the American-led collective-security umbrella, which has so ruffled the feathers of Moscow. Indeed, NATO membership is seen by most within the titular communities as the only way to ensure the continued sovereignty of the three Baltic nations.

The continued nation-building projects and the large predominantly Russian-speaking minority communities have determined the path to the current state of politics, both domestic and international. Many other Central and

East European countries are experiencing very similar processes and hurdles. In this context, Estonia and Latvia have been important case studies of minority politics in post-socialist transformations. In order to fully appreciate the process of minority politics, we have to go beyond traditional majority/minority group dynamics. Brubaker's 'triadic nexus' gives us a starting point by recognising the importance of the external national homeland, which in our case is the Russian Federation. Yet, the application of the nexus metaphor leaves out one key actor (or rather actors) that so greatly affects domestic and international politics in the contemporary international system: international institutions.

As a means of testing this hypothesis, the book has used Estonia and Latvia as cases. In the context of our understanding minority politics, this book has looked at the roles of nationalising states, national minorities, the external national homeland, and regional/international organisations within these two case studies. Several important points can be made from this study. The post-restorationist nation-building project was largely a result of historical grievances perceived on the part of the titular communities. The loss of independence, the indignity that followed and the influx of emigrants from other areas of the Soviet Union meant that titular politicians would attempt to (re)build a nation that would change the ethnic power structure to benefit the titular communities. In this way, titular political elites created a political structure that greatly limited the ability of the minority communities to affect policy-making. As a result, the Russian-speaking communities in Estonia and Latvia had little impact on policies dealing with the creation of the 'nation' and the application of national 'markers' such as language. Finally, the Russian-speaking communities, as a result of the structural disadvantages of the political systems, were unable to consistently and competently challenge these policies through collective action, including successful political coalitions.

Events in Estonia and Latvia indicate that the natural external national homeland had very little positive impact on the minority policy-making process and implementation. Rather, Moscow often made the situation worse for minorities living in the two countries by confirming the fears of the titular communities and alienating an entrepreneurially competent minority community. Additionally, regional and international organisations influenced the policy-making process and implementation. Predominantly, the actors were the European Union, Council of Europe, and the OSCE. On the other hand, we must note that other organisations such as the United Nations and NATO as well as Western governments also may have influenced domestic policy. While these conclusions are overall conclusions, we need to also review the comparative nature of this study. In particular, this chapter will highlight the similarities and differences between the Estonian and Latvian experience.

10.1 The Nationalising State and the National Minority

Throughout this study, Estonia and Latvia have proved to be quite compatible case studies. One reason in particular has been there similar historical circumstances. Both countries comprise much of what was Hansa Livonia, while Lithuania experienced very little, if any, German influence. Despite changing from Hansa German rule, to Swedish, to Russian, much of the historical experience of the two nations is similar. Furthermore, both the Estonian and Latvian national awakenings were inspired by the larger German equivalent. In fact, the German elite were often the driving force behind this rise in national consciousness. Following the dissolution of the Russian Empire and the subsequent establishment of the Soviet Union, Estonia and Latvia found themselves, for the first time, sovereign states.

Like much of Central and Eastern Europe, Estonia and Latvia were the true losers of the Second World War. Despite the Nazi invasion of the Soviet Union, thus nullifying the non-aggression pact, Soviet forces permanently occupied the Baltic states. Although Moscow claimed, as many still do, that the Baltic states voluntarily entered into the USSR, there is little question that this was done through force, and thus was not voluntary. Up to this point, there had been a Russian-speaking population within both states, which is little surprise since they were a part of the Russian Empire. However, it was the subsequent Soviet policies of relocation that brought the majority of today's Russian-speaking communities. The Baltic peoples had been decimated by the war and subsequent Soviet repression and collectivisation policies. In addition to the policy of relocation of 'more trustworthy' Russians as a means of settling any moves for independence, the growth of heavy industry in these largely agricultural republics brought a large migration of predominantly Russian-speakers.

The majority of Russian-speakers in Estonia and Latvia arrived before 1964, although there was a continual troop rotation. This means that by the time of the restoration of independence, there was a significant portion of the Russian-speaking community that had been born in the Soviet Baltic republics. By the end of the Soviet Union, Soviet Latvia was just barely majority Latvian, while Riga still has a shade more Russians than Latvians. Interestingly, there is a prominent difference between the minority communities in Estonia and Latvia as a result of the type of industry. While Estonia saw the growth of heavy industry and oil-shale mining, Latvia experienced a growth in specialised industries including weapons manufacturing. Thus, the Russian-speaking community in the former was much less well educated than in the latter. What effect has this had on inter-ethnic relations? Partly, the pro-Soviet forces in Latvia were significantly more organised than their Estonian counterparts in the late Soviet period. However, a more intellectual Russian-speaking community in Latvia has not produced a considerable threat to the Latvian state as was feared. Nor has the rather 'working class' Estonian northeast been easily roused into collective action.

Following the restoration of independence, the titular majorities constructed their minority policies similarly. In both cases, the Communist Party was made illegal and any supporters of the Moscow August 1991 Coup were barred from politics, if not tried in court. The new status of the communist party significantly impaired the minority populations' ability to respond to the new changes in an organised way. Furthermore, both the first post-Soviet elections brought to power conservative nationalist parties, which had a large impact on nation-building. In subsequent elections, the centre-right continued to be in power, although the centre-left Centre Party remained electorally popular and thus often held some sway in the Estonian *Riigikogu*. In Latvia, the centre-right Latvia's Way became the one constant element in every ruling coalition, as well as parliament, until 2002. Other than the centre-left *Saimnieks*, the Latvian ruling coalitions were alliances amongst right-of-centre parties. This is not to say that Russian-speaking voters would not vote for centre-right parties, but rather centre-right parties are least likely to see a political gain in liberalising naturalisation, language, or education policies.

In regard to the national minorities, there are also considerable differences. In Estonia, the Communist Party apparatus did not survive the first elections in 1992. Thus, the traditional political representation of the Russian-speaking community had disappeared. Begun by Savisaar, the RDM was formed as a more moderate, non-communist political organisation that would occupy this vacuum. However, this organisation hardly got started before it practically became ineffective. Following this, several Russian political parties were born such as the EUPP and the RPE. The two parties came together in the 'Our Home is Estonia' coalition to compete in the 1995 elections, where it won six seats. Subsequent moves to maintain co-operation amongst Russian political parties has produced few results. For example, the practical extensions of the EUPP and the RPE, the People's Trust and People's Choice, have been quite hostile to each other. In the latest elections, the majority of the Russian vote went to Savisaar's Centre Party.

In Latvia, the former communist party apparatus existed in the Latvian Supreme Soviet for some time until elections were held nearly two years after the restoration of independence. The LSP and the Equal Rights Movement were the two main far-left parties representing Russian-speakers. On the other hand, the People's Harmony Party represented a more moderate left-wing party. As a result of the 1993 elections, the LSP failed to receive any seats. In 1995, of the three parties, Equal Rights failed to receive enough votes. By the 1998 elections, only the People's Harmony Party received any seats in the *Saeima*. Subsequently, the three parties came together in the form of the FHRUL and did well in the 2002 elections. During 1991-2001, the three major parties representing the Latvian Russian-speaking community continued to compete for the same pool of votes, while at the same time, more traditional left-wing parties such as the LSDWP also took their share.

In both Estonia and Latvia, there have been very few signs of co-operation. Interestingly, while Estonian Russian parties co-operated in the 1995 elections, the electoral co-operation amongst such parties in Latvia falls outside this study's time-period. Furthermore, this co-operation was only a temporary political strategy in both cases. Both Our Home is Estonia and the FHRUL in Latvia collapsed shortly after the respective elections. Why was there such a lack of co-operation? There may be several possible answers. First, the Russian-speaking communities did not feel sufficiently aggrieved over the minority policies to the extent that elites would find power in co-operation. However, according to traditional theories of ethnic politics, we should have seen a greater political consolidation of the Russian-speaking communities if for no other reason than the Russian-speaking vote was so small. Second, there would have been little practical advantage in co-operating since titular parties were unwilling to work with minority parties. Perpetual opposition leaves little ability to affect policy-making although representation is still important. Finally, Estonian and Latvian minority parties are typically dominated by major personalities. This may be the case in Estonia more so than in Latvia, although minority elites in the latter have not been quick to join forces. Although the lack of co-operation is significant, the ability of the national minorities to affect policy-making was severally weakened by the structure of the political system. Therefore, co-operation would have been unlikely to provide any additional results.

Although interesting if seen separately, this book analyses titular and minority parties simultaneously since they are within the same political system. So, what has been the relationship between the two? In Estonia, minority political parties found no co-operation with any governments. However, after the 1999 local elections, People's Trust helped the Reform Party and its coalition allies take control of the Tallinn City Council for some time. In Latvia, there has been no co-operation in national politics although the LSDWP has co-operated with FHRUL on the Riga City Council only to suffer the consequences in the 2002 parliamentary elections. While there has been very little co-operation amongst minority parties in both states, there has also been very minimal co-operation offered by the titular parties. Once again, such little co-operation is a result of the political structure as defined by the restrictive citizenship and language policies.

10.2 The External National Homeland

Clearly, Russia's attempts to define those Russians living outside of Russia are an important element of constructing the identity of post-Soviet Russia. Quite naturally, we should expect that there would be a link between Russians living in the 'near abroad' and the Russian state. In our case studies, this is the relationship between the national minority and the external national homeland. What is the nature of this relationship and how is it different between Estonia and Latvia? Until 1994, the Russian Federation was directly connected to a large part of the Russian-speaking communities through the continued military presence in both states. After August 1994, the Russian government had few direct links to the national minority communities. Moscow continued to work on their behalf rather than through the minority communities. This was clearly a result of the failure of early post-Soviet foreign policy.

As discussed in chapter seven, the relationship between Russia and the two Baltic states is a good example of issue-linkage. Two such issues were linked to the 'human rights' issue. First, Moscow has used the border agreements as a means of applying pressure to Tallinn and Riga to liberalise their minority policies. In both cases, the Baltic states have lost sizable areas of land despite the agreements of independent Estonia and Latvia with the Soviet Union. While Estonia originally fought the loss of territory, Latvia did not. With the policy of relinquishing land to Moscow, the border agreements became less important issues that could be used to influence the 'human rights' situation in the Baltic region. Despite this, Moscow has yet to conclude border treaties with the two states.

Similarly, the troop withdrawal issue was also a key element within Russia's Monroe-Doctrine foreign policy style following the collapse of the Soviet Union. At first, Moscow proposed maintaining a troop presence in the Baltic states as a means of keeping some control over events. The Baltic governments, for their part, would have none of it. In particular, Tallinn and Riga were able to successfully internationalise the issue. In this case, Western governments and, as a result, Western institutions were keen to see the troops withdrawn. Needless to say, this was impossible to do in the political climate preceding the 1993 political crisis between the President and the Russian Supreme Soviet. After Yeltsin's victory, the troops were pulled out the following year. Importantly, the troops were withdrawn with the Baltic governments failing to concede any liberalisation in their minority policies although there was some acceptance of the permanent residence of military pensioners.

In regard to issue-linkage, the Russian government was unsuccessful in forcing Tallinn and Riga to change the conditions of their large Russian-speaking communities. While the Baltic states successfully internationalised the troop withdrawal issue, the 'human rights' issue was also pushed into a multi-lateral forum despite Estonia and Latvia's statements that this was an internal matter. At the same time, the Russian MFA continued to act on behalf of the Russian-speakers. During specific moments of legislative reform, politicians and officials in Moscow made often-hostile remarks. Even after legislation was changed to meet the recommendations of European organisations, Moscow was still condemning the two Baltic governments.

The major difference between the way Russia dealt with Estonia and Latvia comes in the timing of Moscow's focus on each. Estonia's moment under the spotlight came with the 'Aliens' Crisis' in 1993. In particular, the Russian Government was concerned with the new Aliens' Law. Once the crisis itself began, political pundits from every direction rose to the occasion. The controversy was compounded by the Russian constitutional crisis. On the other hand, Latvia became the subject of Moscow's attention when it began revising its citizenship and language laws towards the end of the nineties. However, the most vehement criticisms came with the unfortunate outcome of the pensioners' protest in March 1998. Having said this, a contentious relationship still exists today between Riga and Moscow, while relations between Tallinn and Moscow have improved marginally.

In both cases, the primary instrument of applying pressure on the Baltic states was the Russian Ministry of Foreign Affairs. Within the MFA, the Foreign Ministers under Yeltsin and Putin played a large role, as to be expected. Furthermore, the MFA worked through the embassies in both countries to continually notify the Baltic governments of Moscow's displeasure. Finally, the MFA worked through European organisations as a means of forcing the Baltic governments to rectify the 'human rights' problem. Most notably, Moscow attempted to halt Estonia and Latvia's membership in the Council of Europe while, at the time, itself remaining outside the institution. Overall, the evidence provided suggests that Russia's 'near-abroad' policy was significantly ineffective when applied to the Baltic states. The most apparent reason is that the Baltic states had moved quickly to place themselves within the institutions of Europe, which would bring its own pressures.

10.3 International Influences

Thus far, we have seen that the titular majorities have maintained significant control over policy-making and evolution, while the national minority communities and external national homeland have been unable to affect such policies. Chapter eight indicates that, in particular, European organisations were able to affect minority policy in Estonia and Latvia. Specifically, European organisations were able to wield such influence for the very reason that membership within European institutions was a sure step to ensuring Baltic independence in the future, not to mention economic growth. Three institutions had the most impact outside the titular majority. They were the Organisation for Security and Co-operation, European Union, and the Council of Europe.

The OSCE was represented in two ways in the Baltic states. First, the office of the High Commissioner on National Minorities took a great interest in the ethnic situation in Estonia and Latvia. For the majority of the time period studied here, Max van der Stoel held the High Commissioner post. The HCNM made frequent trips to Tallinn and Riga in order to help sway policy-makers during times of policy-making. For example, van der Stoel made frequent trips during the formulation and approval of the citizenship laws in the early nineties. Furthermore, the High Commissioner met with all sides including the political leaders of the majority, national minority, and external national homeland. By including all sides, the HCNM went to great lengths to maintain mediation and communication. Second, long-term missions represented the OSCE in Estonia and Latvia. While the HCNM worked hard to affect policy-making, the missions focused on policy-implementation. In both cases, the

OSCE became less intrusive as minority policies were slowly liberalised and democratic institutions were consolidated. At the end of 2001, the OSCE and the two Baltic states decided to end the long-term missions. Likewise, the HCNM has been less visible since the departure of van der Stoel.

The European Union equally had a strong effect on minority policy. From the very beginning, the Baltic states made EU membership a priority and signed co-operation agreements early after the restoration of independence. Despite a lack of specifics as well as the failure to make the minority protection clause in the Copenhagen Criteria binding through EU law, the EU has been quite effective. In particular, the EU has often been the important mechanism by which other organisations have put pressure on the Baltic states. Often working through the OSCE or the Council of Europe, the EU has been vocal during times of policy reform. The primary actors within the EU have been the European Commission and the EU Commissioner for Central and Eastern Europe. In both cases, these actors have routinely monitored the ethnic situation in Estonia and Latvia.

Finally, the Council of Europe has been an extremely important organisation in post-socialist Europe by helping entrench democratic institutions. Most importantly in the area of minority rights, the Council of Europe has formulated the Framework Convention for the Protection of National Minorities. Although Latvia has yet to ratify the framework, Riga is still beholden to its recommendations. Like the OSCE and the EU, the Council has been present at times of policy-making and reform. The CoE did this through the activities of the Secretary General and the Parliamentary Assembly. The Council ended its regular monitoring of the ethnic situation shortly after Estonia and Latvia approved revised citizenship laws. Once again, its power to persuade relied on its close connection to the EU.

While European organisations have played a part in affecting minority policy in Estonia and Latvia, broader international organisations have done far less. This book paid special attention to the role of the United Nations. Overall, the UN had little constructive supervision for the contentious situation. Primarily, the UN concerned itself with the relations between states rather than the policies within Estonia and Latvia. This is little surprise given the nature of the UN Charter. Interestingly, the UN became the organisation through which the Russian Federation and the Baltic states internationalised their issues. For Moscow, the important issue was 'human rights' in the Baltic states. On the other hand, the Baltic states were keen to bring attention to the border disputes and, most importantly, to the troop withdrawal issue. Although the UN may have played little part in affecting domestic policy, it may have very well reduced the potential for conflict in the often-contentious relations between the Baltic governments and Moscow.

10.4 Implications

The book results laid out above generate several theoretical and policy implications. First, how unique are the cases of Estonia and Latvia? This is a key question for the applicability of the analytical scheme for minority politics discussed in the book. At first glance, it would seem that similar conditions exist in many states in Central and Eastern Europe as well as the former Soviet Union. As Yugoslavia collapsed, Serbians became a new minority in all but one of the successor states. It is possible that Baltic recent history would have been far more violent had there been an effort by the Russian government to make a 'greater Russia' following the collapse of the Soviet Union. However, this was not the case and few parallels can be drawn, although we can say that moderation was far more evident in the Baltic region than in the Balkans. Perhaps a better example would be the historical presence of Hungarians in the neighbouring states of Romania, the Former Republic of Yugoslavia and Slovakia. Like the Russian communities in the Baltic states, the Hungarian minority communities are a result of a collapsed empire. In this case, of course it was the Austro-Hungarian Empire. In fact, as chapter three discussed, the issue of minorities in the Austro-Hungarian Empire was of primary importance in relation to its survival. The Hungarian minorities are an important issue in Europe, although EU enlargement means that eventually the Hungarian communities will be able to interact more freely with their own external national homeland, because most of the states concerned will be members of the EU. However, this is not the case for the Russians, Ukrainians, or Belarusian in Estonia and Latvia. These nations are unlikely to become EU member-states in the near to medium term future.[600] Ironically, ethnic Russians will outnumber Estonians and Latvians in the EU once the two nations become member-states.

A similar case to Estonia and Latvia has been seen in the Ukraine and Moldova where Russophones demographically dominate the eastern regions in both cases. The avoidance of conflict in the Ukraine has partly been the result of intense mediations between Ukrainian politicians, Ukrainian nationalists and the Russian Federation. Unlike the two Baltic states, Ukrainian political elites have been unable to push through similar exclusionary policies. Moscow's influence in the Ukraine is far greater than in the Baltic states. Also, the pressure to assimilate in the Ukraine is far less than in Estonia or Latvia given the size of the Russophone communities and their geographical location. On the other hand, Moldova's collapse into largely ethnic conflict centred on what are essentially Romanians and Russians has left the country split down the middle. Romanian nationalists attempted to implement policies that favoured the titular majority. The nationalists in the Trans-Dniestra region, with help from Russian mercenaries and collusion with Moscow, established an independent state within Moldova. Currently, Russian troops as well as the OSCE monitor the status-quo. What makes Moldova different from Estonia or Latvia? A justified answer would require more than could be included here. Nevertheless, the size and concentration of populations, political and geographical distance from the West, differences in historical circumstances and perhaps less attention from foreign investment as well as Western commitments to assist in the transition all provide starting-points for an analysis.

Importantly, Estonia and Latvia have had far different relationships with key international institutions since the collapse of the Soviet Union. The role of institutions such as the EU, CoE, OSCE and NATO has been important for co-ordinating peace in the region. In the same way the OSCE has monitored the ethnic situation in the Baltic states, so has it done in a myriad of states across Europe and Central Asia. The EU has maintained a persuasive influence while states have vied for membership. It is in the EU member-states

---

600 See Lieven, Anatol and Dmitri Trenin, ed. 2003. *Ambivalent Neighbors: the EU, NATO and the Price of Membership*. Washington, D.C.: Carnegie Endowment for Peace.

closest to the Baltic states' interest to maintain peace and stability in the region. Likewise, the CoE has continued to stress the need for democratic institutions. Overall, international organisations are becoming an increasingly important partner in minority issues.

Secondly, what do the situations in Estonia and Latvia tell us about ethnicity and its relationship to politics? Although there is little need to restate this given the events of ethnic violence throughout the world in 1990's, ethnicity remains an important source of social identity. Not only has ethnicity remained important in 'developing' nations but also in industrially advanced nations such as Spain and Britain. Given this, should we expect 'integration' programmes to reduce the level of ethnic salience? The best answer is perhaps. The importance of ethnicity in a society is partly a factor of the salience of competing social identities. So, it may be that Russophones' ethnic identities reduce in importance as their civic identities increase. However, it is possible that EU membership could either enhance or reduce the importance of identity in the Baltic states.

Finally, the growing importance of international organisations has challenged the traditional Westphalian state system. Therefore, international organisations are also altering the study of international relations. What are the implications of this book on approaches to international relations? First, we can see the two-level game at work in both the nationalising states and the external national homeland. In Estonia and Latvia, political elites must satisfy the electorate as well as be beholden to the international agreements they have signed. Similarly, Russian political elites must balance relations with the Baltic states, and thus the West, with the challenges of domestic politics.

How much are international organisations a product of the will of member-states rather than being international actors unto themselves? This is a fundamental question for the future of international relations theory. This book treats international organisations as institutions that both benefit and constrain (potential) member-states to the point that an exclusively state-centred approach would be misleading. Such an approach fails to recognise the influence of international organisations on relations between states. Rather, a liberal approach is far more helpful as it attempts to explain the relationships between the nationalising states, the external national homeland and international organisations. Finally, the book exhibits the need not to underestimate domestic political issues as the impetus for larger international issues.

The increasing influence of international organisations suggests several policy implications. First, states need to consider the expected benefits of membership alongside the possible constraints. Second, governments have to be proactive participants in the constant bargaining of membership in order to maintain considerable degree of sovereignty on such issues as nation-building. Third, the minority communities have to reorganise themselves into electorally significant groups if they wish to have a greater say in policy-making. Finally, European organisations will have to use their influence over domestic policy responsibly. A backlash against Brussels would not bode well for the European Project.

Appendix

A1. Dates of Fieldwork

15 January – 31 January 2002
17 September 2002 – 20 June 2003
3 January 2004 – 20 January 2004

A2. Interviews

Brigita Zepa (January 2002) – Director of the Baltic Institute of Social Sciences

Nils Muiznieks (January 2002) – Director of the Latvian Centre for Human Rights and Ethnic Studies

-Latvian Special Minister for Social Integration (January 2004)

Artis Pabriks (January 2002) – Policy analyst at the Latvian Centre for Human Rights and Ethnic Studies

Andrejs Pildegovics (December 2002) – Foreign Advisor to the Latvian State President

Alexei Dimitrov (January 2003) – Secretary Executive of the Latvian Human Rights Committee

Solveiga Silkalna (February 2003) – Foreign Affairs Advisor to the Prime Minister of the Republic of Latvia

Tatyana Zhdanok (February 2003) – President of the 'Equal Rights' Party

Gary Peach (February 2003) – Editor-in-chief at *The Baltic Times*

Vadim Poleshchuk (May 2003) – Legal advisor/analyst at the Legal Information Centre for Human Rights

Sander Soone (January 2004) – Spokesperson for the Estonian Foreign Ministry

Andzeys Vilumsons (January 2004) – Spokesperson for the Latvian Ministry of Defence

Bibliography

Andersen, Erik André. 1997. The Legal Status of Russians in Estonian Privatisation Legislation 1989-1995. *Europe-Asia Studies* 49 (2):303-316.

Anderson, Richard D., Jr. et al. 2001. *Postcommunism and the Theory of Democracy*. Oxford: Princeton University Press.

Armstrong, John. 1968. The Ethnic Scene in the Soviet Union: The View of the Dictatorship. In *Ethnic Minorities in the Soviet Union*, edited by Erich Goldhagan. New York: Praeger.

Banton, Michael. 1983. *Racial and Ethnic Competition*. Cambridge: Cambridge University Press.

Banton, Michael. 1998. *Racial Theories*. Second ed. Cambridge: Cambridge University press.

Barnes, William A. 1998. Incomplete Democracy in Central America: Polarization and Voter Turnout in Nicaragua and El Salvador. *Journal of Interamerican Affairs* Fall:63-79.

Barth, Fredrik. 1969. *Ethnic Groups and Boundaries: The Social Organization of Culture Difference*. London: Allen & Unwin.

Barth, Fredrik and Donald Noel. 1972. Conceptual Frameworks for the Analysis of Race Relations: an evaluation. *Social Forces* 50:333-348.

Bellamy, Richard. 2000. Dealing with Difference: Four Models of Pluralist Politics. *Parliamentary Affairs* 53 (1):198-217.

Bendix, Reinhard. 1996. *Nation-Building and Citizenship*. Enl. ed. London: Transaction Publishers.

Besançon, Alain. 1981. *The Intellectual Origins of Leninism*. Oxford: Blackwell Publishers.

Brass, Paul R. 1991. *Ethnicity and Nationalism: Theory and Comparison*. London: Sage Publications.

Brass, Paul R. 1992. Language and National Identity in the Soviet Union and India. In *Thinking Theoretically about Soviet Nationalities: History and Comparison in the Study of the USSR.*, edited by Alexander J. Motyl. New York: Columbia University Press.

Bratton, Michael and Nicholas Van de Walle. 1994. Neopatrimonial Regimes and Political Transitions in Africa. *World Politics* 46 (July):453-89.

Bremmer, Ian. 1993. Reassessing Soviet Nationalities Theory. In *Nations and Politics in the Soviet Successor States*, edited by Ian Bremmer and Ray Taras. New York: Cambridge University Press.

Brennan, Neil J. 1998. European Integration and Human Rights' Cultures in Eastern Europe: the EU and abolitions of capital punishment. *University of New Brunswick Law Journal* 47:49-84.

Breuilly, John. 1993. *Nationalism and the State*. Second ed. Manchester: Manchester University Press.

Brubaker, Rogers. 1996. *Nationalism Reframed: Nationhood and the National Question in the New Europe*. Cambridge: Cambridge University Press.

Bunce, Valerie. 1999. *Subversive Institutions: The Design and the Destruction of Socialism and the State*. Cambridge: Cambridge University Press.

Bungs, Dzintra. 1994. Latvia: Transition to Independence Completed. *RFE/RL Research Report* 3 (1):96-98.

Carr, E. H. 1946. *The Twenty Years' Crisis, 1919-1939: An Introduction to the Study of International Relations*. Second ed. London: Macmillan.

Chinn, Jeff and Robert Kaiser. 1996. *Russians as the New Minority: Ethnicity and Nationalism in the Soviet Successor States*. Boulder: Westview Press.

Cleave, Jan. 1999. Election Alliance Ban and Estonian Politics. *RFE/RL Newsline* 21 January 1999.

Collier, David. 1993. The Comparative Method. In *Political Science: The State of the Discipline II*, edited by Ada W. Finifter. Washington, DC: American Political Science Association.

Connor, Walker. 1978. A Nation is a Nation. *Ethnic and Racial Studies* 1 (4):379-388.

Daalder, Hans. 1966. The Netherlands: Opposition in a Segmented Society. In *Political Oppositions in Western Democracies*, edited by Robert A. Dahl. New Haven, Conn: Yale University Press.

Dahl, Robert A. 1989. *Democracy and its Critics*. New Haven: Yale University Press.

Dahl, Robert A. 1998. *On Democracy*. New Haven: Yale University Press.

Dawson, Jane I. 1996. *Eco-Nationalism: Anti-Nuclear Activism and National Identity in Russia, Lithuania, and Ukraine*. London: Duke University Press.

Deksnis, E. B. 2001. Baltic Accession to the European Union: Challenge and Opportunity. In *Baltic Accession to the European Union: Challenge and Opportunity*, edited by T. Jundzis. Riga: Latvian Academy of Sciences.

Demuth, Andreas. 1997. Post-Soviet Minorities on the Fence: Ethnic Russians between Estonia, the Russian Federation, and the international community. Paper read at Theoretical and methodological issues in migration research: interdisciplinary, intergenerational and international perspectives, at University of Utrecht.

Diamond, Larry and Marc F. Plattner. 1994. *Nationalism, Ethnic Conflict, and Democracy*. London: Johns Hopkins University Press.

Dimitriov, Alexei and Boris Koltchanov, ed. 2002. *Report on the Implementation of the Framework Convention for the Protection of National Minorities*. Riga: Latvian Human Rights Committee.

Dion, Douglas. 1997. Competition and Ethnic Conflict. *Journal of Conflict Resolution* 41 (5):638-648.

Dorodnova, Jekaterina. 2002. Challenging Ethnic Democracy: Implementation of the Recommendations of the OSCE High Commissioner on National Minorities to Latvia, 1993-2001. *CORE Working Papers* 10.

Dowley, Kathleen M. and Brian D. Silver. 2002. Social Capital, Ethnicity and Support for Democracy in the Post-Communist States. *Europe-Asia Studies* 54 (4):505-527.

Dreifelds, Juris. 1996. *Latvia in Transition*. Cambridge: Cambridge University Press.

Dreifelds, Juris. 2001. Divergent Paths of the Ombudsman Idea in the Baltic States. In *The Baltic States at Historical Crossroads*, edited by Talavs Jundzis. Riga: Latvian Academy of Sciences.

Dunlop, John. 1993. Russia: Confronting a Loss of Empire. In *Nations and Politics in the Soviet Successor States*, edited by Ian Bremmer and Ray Taras. New York: Cambridge University Press.

Eckstein, Harry. 1975. Case study and Theory in Political Science. In *Handbook of Political Science: Strategies of Inquiry*, edited by Fred I. Greenstein and Nelson W. Polsby. Reading, Mass: Addison-Wesley Publishing Company.

Elman, M. 1995. The Foreign Policies of Small States: Challenging Neorealism in its own backyard. *British Journal of Political Science* 25 (2):171-217.

Erickson, John. 1975. *The Road to Stalingrad*. Second ed. London: Cassell.

Evans, Geoffrey. 1998. Ethnic Schism and the Consolidation of Post-Communist Democracies. *Communist and Post-Communist Studies* 31 (1):57-74.

Furnivall, John Sydenham. 1944. *Netherlands India: a Study of Plural Economy*. Cambridge: University Press.

Furtado, Charles F. and Michael Hechter. 1992. The Emergence of Nationalist Politics in the USSR: A Comparison of Estonia and the Ukraine. In *Thinking Theoretically about Soviet Nationalities: History and Comparison in the Study of the USSR.*, edited by Alexander J. Motyl. New York: Columbia University Press.

Galbreath, David J. 2003. The Politics of European Integration and Minority Rights in Estonia and Latvia. *Perspectives on European Politics and Society* 4 (1).

Galbreath, David J. 2004. Kurp tālāk? Recenzija par Latvijas ārpolitikas pamatvirzienu projektu (iepriekšējo projektu). *Policy.lv*, May.

Geertz, Clifford, ed. 1963. *Old Societies and New States the Quest for Modernity in Asia and Africa*. London: Free Press of Glencoe Collier-Macmillan.

Gellner, Ernest. 1983. *Nations and Nationalism*. Oxford: Blackwell Publishers.

Gellner, Ernest. 1994. *Encounters with Nationalism*. Oxford: Blackwell.

Genesee, F. 1984. Beyond Bilingualism: Social Psychological Studies of French Immersion Programs in Canada. *Canadian Journal of Behavioural Science* 16 (4).

Georgieff, Anthony. 1999. Estonia: Ethnic Russian Voters May Play Key Role. *RFE/RL Newsline*.

Gilbert, G. 2002. Jurisprudence of the European Court and Commission of Human Rights in 2001 and Minority Groups, Sub-Commission on the Promotion and Protection of Human Rights. In *54 Session, Working Group on Minorities, 8 Session 27-31 May 2002. E/CN.4/Sub.2/AC.5/2002/WP.2, 24 May, 6.*

Goble, Paul. 1998. The Latvian Challenge. *RFE/RL Newsline*, 6 October.

Goble, Paul. 1998. Trapped by Democracy? *RFE/RL Newsline.*

Goble, Paul. 1999. A Disaster That Didn't Happen. *RFE/RL Newsline* 22 March 1999.

Goble, Paul. 2000. A De Facto Veto? *RFE/RL Baltic States Report* 1 (22).

Gough, Clair and Simon Shackley. 2001. The Respectable Politics of Climate Change: the Epistemic Communities and NGOs. *International Affairs* 77 (4):329-345.

Gourevitch, Peter. 1978. The Second Image Reversed: the international sources of domestic politics. *International Organization* 32 (4):881-911.

Grugel, Jean. 2002. *Democratization: a Critical Introduction.* London: Palgrave.

Gurr, Ted Robert. 1994. Peoples Against States: Ethnopolitical Conflict and the Changing World System. *International Studies Quarterly* 38:347-377.

Gutmann, Amy. 2003. *Identity in Democracy.* Princeton, N.J.; Oxford: Princeton University Press.

Haas, Ernest. 1986. What is Nationalism and Should We Study It? *International Organization* 40 (3):707-744.

Haas, Peter M. 1989. Do Regimes Matter? Epistemic Communities and Mediterranean Pollution Control. *International Organization* 43 (3):377- 403.

Haas, Peter M. 1992. Introduction: Epistemic Communities and International Policy Coordination. *International Organization* 46 (1):1-34.

Hannan, Michael T. 1979. The Dynamics of Ethnic Boundaries in Modern States. In *National Development and The World System: Education, Economic, and Political Change 1950-1970*, edited by J. W. Meyer and M. T. Hannan. Chicago: University of Chicago Press.

Hardin, Russell. 1995. *One for All.* Princeton: Princeton University Press.

Hechter, Michael. 1974. The Political Economy of Ethnic Change. *American Journal of Sociology* 79 (5):1151-1178.

Hechter, Michael. 1975. *Internal Colonialism: The Celtic Fringe in British National Development, 1536-1966.* London: Routledge and Kegan Paul.

Hechter, Michael. 1978. Group Formation and the Cultural Division of Labor. *American Journal of Sociology* 84 (2):293-319.

Higley, J and R. Gunther, eds. 1992. *Elites and Democratic Consolidation in Latin America and Southern Europe.* Cambridge: Cambridge University Press.

Hjorth, Ronnie. 1994. Baltic Sea Environmental Co-operation: The Role of Epistemic Communities and the Politics of Regime Change. *Cooperation and Conflict* 29 (1):11-31.

Horowitz, Donald L. 1981. Patterns of Ethnic Seperatism. *Comparative Studies in Society and History* 23:165-195.

Horowitz, Donald L. 1985. *Ethnic Groups in Conflict.* Berkeley London: University of California Press.

Horowitz, Donald L. 1992. Irrendentas and Secessions: Adjacent Phenomena, Neglected Connections. *International Journal of Comparative Sociology* 13 (1):118-130.

Horowitz, Donald L. 1994. Democracy in Divided Societies. In *Nationalism, Ethnic Conflict, and Democracy*, edited by Larry Diamond and Marc F. Plattner. London: Johns Hopkins University Press.

Hough, Jerry F. 1997. *Democratization and Revolution in the USSR 1985-1991.* Washington D.C.: Brooking Institute Press.

Hough, Jerry F. and Merle Fainsod. 1979. *How the Soviet Union is Governed.* New York: Harvard University Press.

Huang, Mel. 1999. Apathy setting in among Estonians? *RFE/RL Newsline* 17 March.

Huang, Mel. 1999. Avoiding a Minefield in Estonia's Northeast. *RFE/RL Newsline* 16 April.

Hughes, James and Gwedolyn Sasse. 2003. Monitoring the Monitors: EU Enlargment Conditionality and Minority Protection in the CEECs. *Journal of Ethnopolitics and Minority Issues in Europe* (1).

Huntington, Samuel P. 1991. *The Third Wave.* Norman: University of Oklahoma Press.

Jenkins, J. Craig. 1983. Resource Mobilization Theory and the Study of Social Movements. *American Review of Sociology* 9:527-553.

Jenkins, Richard. 1994. Rethinking Ethnicity: Identity, Categorization and Power. *Ethnic and Racial Studies* (April):197-223.

Johnson, Steve C. 2002. Risks of Reform. *The Baltic Times*, 5-11 September, 18.

Johnson, Steve C. 2003. EU, NATO Help Break Left-wing Bloc. *The Baltic Times*, 16-22 January, 4.

Jubulis, Mark A. 1996. The External Dimension of Democratization in Latvia: The Impact of European Institutions. *International Relations* 13 (3):59-73.

Juska, Arunas. 1999. Ethno-Political Transformation in the State of the Former USSR. *Ethnic and Racial Studies* 22 (3):524-549.

Karl, Terry Lynn. 1990. Dilemmas of Democratization in Latin America. *Comparative Politics* (October):1-21.

Kemp, Walter A. 1999. *Nationalism and Communism in Eastern Europe and the Soviet Union: A Basic Contradiction.* New York: St. Martin's Press, Inc.

Kemp, Walter A. 2001. *Quiet Diplomacy in Action: The OSCE High Commissioner on National Minorities.* The Hague: Luwer Law International.

Keohane, Robert and Joseph Nye. 1977. *Power and Interdependence: World Politics in Transition.* New York: Little Brown.

Keohane, Robert O. 1984. *After Hegemony: Cooperation and Discord in the World Political Economy.* Princeton, N.J.: Princeton University Press.

King, Charles and Neil J. Melvin. 1998. *Nations Abroad: Diaspora Politics and International Relations in the Former Soviet Union.* Boulder: Westview Press.

King, Gary; Robert O. Keohane; and Sidney Verba. 1994. *Designing Social Inquiry.* Princeton, New Jersey: Princeton University Press.

Kionka, Riina. 1990. The CSCE and the Baltic States. *Report on the USSR*:17-19.

Kionka, Riina. 1990. The Estonian Citizens' Committee: an opposition movement of a different complexion. *RFE/RL Report on the USSR* February 9:30-33.

Kionka, Riina. 1990. 'Integral' and Estonian Independence. *RFE/RL Report on the USSR* July 28:20-21.

Kionka, Riina. 1991. Who Should Become a Citizen of Estonia. *RFE/RL Report on the USSR* 3 (39).

Kirch, Marika and David D. Laitin. 1994. *Changing Identities in Estonia: Sociological Facts and Commentaries*. Tallinn: Akadeemia Trükk.

Kitschelt, Herbert. 1991. Resource Mobilization Theory: A Critique. In *Research on Social Movements*, edited by Dieter Rucht. Boulder, CO: Westview Press.

Klandermans, Bert. 1991. New Social Movements and Resource Mobilization: The European and the American Revisited. In *Research on Social Movements*, edited by Dieter Rucht. Boulder, CO: Westview Press.

Kolstø, Pål. 1995. *Russians in the former Soviet Republics*. London: Hurst.

Krasner, Stephen D. 1982. Structural Causes and Regime Consequences: Regimes as Intervening Variables. *International Organization* 36:1-21.

Kreuzer, Marcus and Vello Pettai. 2001. Formation of Party Systems in Post-Communist Democracies: Comparing Estonia, Latvia and Lithuania. Paper read at Annual Meeting of the American Political Science Association, 31 August - 3 September.

Kuper, Leo and M. G. Smith, eds. 1969. *Pluralism in Africa*. Los Angeles: University of California Press.

Kymlicka, Will. 1995. *Multicultural Citizenship: A Liberal Theory of Minority Rights*. Oxford: Clarendon Press.

Laitin, David D. 1998. *Identity in Formation: the Russian-Speaking Populations in the Near Abroad*. Ithaca London: Cornell University Press.

Lapidus, Gail W. 1992. From Democratization to Disintegration: the impact of perestroika on the national question. In *From Union to Commonwealth: Nationalism and separatism in the Soviet republics*, edited by Victor Zaslavsky Gail W. Lapidus, and Philip Goldman. New York: Cambridge University Press.

Lejins, Atis. 2001. Baltic-Russian Relations: A Reassessment. In *The Baltic States at Historical Crossroads*, edited by Talavs Jundzis. Riga: Latvian Academy of Sciences.

Lievan, Anatol. 1993. *The Baltic Revolution: Estonia, Latvia, Lithuania and the Path to Independence*. London: Yale University Press.

Lievan, Anatol and Dmitri Trenin, eds. 2003. *Ambivalent Neighbors: the EU, NATO and the Price of Membership*. Washington, D.C.: Carnegie Endowment for Peace.

Lijphart, Arend. 1984. *Democracies: Patterns of Majoritarian and Consensus Government in Twenty-one Countries*. Westford, Mass: Yale University Press.

Linnart, Mart and Villu Kand. 1999. Estonians Vote in Third Parliamentary Poll since Independence. *RFE/RL Newsline* 5 March.

Linz, Juan J. and Alfred Stepan. 1996. *Problems of Democratic Transition and Consolidation: Southern Europe, South America, and Post-Communist Europe*. Baltimore: Johns Hopkins.

Linz, Juan J. and Alfred Stepan. 1996. Toward Consolidated Democracy. *Journal of Democracy* (April):14-33.

Lustick, Ian. 1979. Stability in Deeply Divided Societies: Consociationalism versus Control. *World Politics* 31 (3):325-44.

Lynch, A. C. 2002. The Evolution of Russian Foreign Policy in the 1990s. *Journal of Communist and Transition Politics* 18 (1):161-182.

Marrett, Cora Bagley and Cheryl Leggon. 1979. Introduction. In *Research in Race and Ethnic Relations*, edited by C. B. Marrett and C. Leggon. Greenwich, Connecticut: JAI Press Inc.

Mason, T. David and David Galbreath. 2004. Ethnicity and Politics. In *Encyclopedia of Government and Politics*, edited by Maurice Kogan and Mary Hawkesworth. London: Routledge.

McAdam, Doug. 1999. Conceptual Origins, Current Problems, Future Directions. In *Comparative Perspectives on Social Movements: Political Opportunities, Mobilizing Structures, and Cultural Framings*, edited by John D. McCarthy Doug McAdam, and Mayer N. Zald. Cambridge: Cambridge University Press.

McAdam, Doug, John D. McCarthy, and Mayer N. Zald, eds. 1999. *Comparative Perspectives on Social Movements: Political Opportunities, Mobilizing Structures, and Cultural Framings.* Cambridge: Cambridge University Press.

McAdam, Doug, Sidney Tarrow, and Charles Tilly. 2001. *Dynamics of Contention.* Cambridge: Cambridge University Press.

McCarthy, John D. and Mayer N. Zald. 1977. Resource Mobilization and Social Movements: A Partial Theory. *American Journal of Sociology* 82 (6):1212-1241.

Medrano, Juan Diez. 1994. The Effects of Ethnic Segregation and Ethnic Competition on Political Mobilization in the Basque Country, 1988. *American Sociological Review* 59 (6):873-889.

Melvin, Neil J. 1994. *Forging the New Russian Nation: Russian Foreign Policy and the Russian-Speaking Communities of the Former USSR.* London: Royal Institute of International Affairs.

Melvin, Neil J. 1995. *Russians beyond Russia: the Politics of National Identity.* London: Royal Institute of International Affairs.

Mettam, Collin W. and Stephen Wyn Williams. 1998. Internal Colonialism and Cultural Divisions of Labour in the Soviet Republic of Estonia. *Nations and Nationalism* 4 (3):363-88.

Mettam, Collin W. and Stephen Wyn Williams. 2001. A Colonial Perspective on Population Migration in Soviet Estonia. *Journal of Ethnic and Migration Studies* 27 (1):133-150.

Misiunas, Romuald. 1994. National Identity and Foreign Policy in the Baltic States. In *The Legacy of History in Russia and the New States of Eurasia*, edited by S. Frederick Starr. Armonk, New York: M. E. Sharpe, Inc.

Moravscik, Andrew. 1993. Preferences and Power in the European Community: A Liberal Intergovernmentalist Approach. *Journal of Common Market Studies* 31 (4):473-524.

Morgenthau, Hans J. 1962. *Politics in the Twentieth Century.* Chicago: University of Chicago Press.

Morgenthau, Hans J. 1967. *Politics among Nations: the Struggle for Power and Peace.* Fourth ed. New York: Knopf.

Mueller, John. 1995. Minorities and the Democratic Image. *East European Politics and Societies* 9 (3):513-522.

Muiznieks, Nils R. 1990. The Latvian Popular Front and Ethnic Relations. *RFE/RL Report on the USSR* October 20:20-22.

Muiznieks, Nils R. 1990. The Pro-Soviet Movement in Latvia. *RFE/RL Report on the USSR* August 24:19-24.

Muiznieks, Nils R. 1995. The Influence of the Baltic Popular Movements on the Process of Soviet Disintegration. *Europe-Asia Studies* 47 (1):3-25.

Muller-Brandeck-Bocquet, Gisela. 2002. The New CFSP and ESDP Decision-Making System of the European Union. *European Foreign Affairs Review* 7:257-282.

Nagel, Joane and Susan Olzak. 1982. Ethnic Mobilization in New and Old States: An Extension of the Competition Model. *Social Problems* 30 (2):127-141.

Nielson, Francois. 1985. Toward a Theory of Ethnic Solidarity in Modern Societies. *American Sociological Review* 50 (2):133-149.

Nogee, Joseph L., and R. Judson Mitchell. 1997. *Russian Politics: The Struggle for a New Order*. Needham Heights, MA: Allyn & Bacon.

O'Donnell, Guillermo. 1996. Illusions about Consolidation. *Journal of Democracy* (April):34-51.

Olzak, Susan. 1989. Contemporary Ethnic Mobilization. *Annual Review of Sociology* 9:355-74.

Olzak, Susan. 1992. *The Dynamics of Ethnic Competition and Conflict*. Stanford: Stanford University Press.

Pabriks, Artis and Aldis Purs. 2002. *Latvia: the Challenges of Change*. London: Routledge.

Pettai, Vello. 2000. Competing Conceptions of Multiethnic Democracy: Debating Minority Integration in Estonia. Paper read at European Consortium for Political Research, Joint Sessions Workshop on 'Competing Conceptions of Democracy in the Practice of Politics', April 14-19, at Copenhagen, Denmark.

Pettai, Vello and Klara Hallik. 2002. Understanding Processes of Ethnic Control: segmentation, dependency and co-operation in post-communist Estonia. *Nations and Nationalism* 8 (4):505-529.

Poppe, Edwin and Louk Hagendoorn. 2001. Types of Identification among Russians in the 'Near Abroad'. *Europe-Asia Studies* 53 (1):57-71.

Przeworksi, Adam. 1991. *Democracy and the Market: Political and Economic Reforms in Eastern Europe and Latin America.* Cambridge: Cambridge University Press.

Przeworksi, Adam and Henry Teune. 1970. *The Logic of Comparative Social Inquiry.* Malabar, FL: Robert E. Krieger Publishing.

Putnam, Robert. 1988. Diplomacy and Domestic Politics: the Logic of Two-Level Games. *International Organization* Summer:427-61.

Ragin, Charles. 1977. Class, Status, and "Reactive Ethnic Cleavages: The Social Bases of Political Regionalism. *American Sociological Review* 42 (3):438-450.

Rawls, John. 1993. *Political Liberalism.* New York: Columbia University Press.

Rogowski, Ronald. 1985. Causes and Varieties of Nationalism: a rationalist account. In *New Nationalisms of the Developed West*, edited by Edward A. Tiryakian and Ronald Rogowski. Boston: Allen and Unwin.

Rothschild, Joseph. 1981. *Ethnopolitics: A Conceptual Framework.* New York: Columbia University Press.

Rudenschiold, Eric. 1992. Ethnic Dimensions in Contemporary Latvian Politics: Focusing Forces for Change. *Soviet Studies* 44 (4):609-639.

Rustow, Dankwart. 1970. Transition to Democracy: Toward a Dynamic Model. *Comparative Politics* 2 (3):337-363

Sarv, Margit. 2002. Integration by Reframing Legislation: Implementation of the Recommendations of the OSCE High Commissioner on National Minorities to Estonia, 1993-2001. *CORE Working Papers* 7 (Hamburg).

Schimmelfenning, Frank. 2001. The Community Trap: Liberal Norms, Rhetorical Action, and the Eastern Enlargement of the European Union. *International Organization* 55 (1):47-80.

Schimmelfenning, Frank. 2002. Liberal Community and Enlargement: An Event History Analysis. *Journal of European Public Policy* 9 (4):598-626.

Schedler, Andreas. 1998. What is Democratic Consolidation? *Journal of Democracy* (April):91-107.

Schmitter, Philippe C. with Terry Lynn Karl. 1994. The Conceptual Travels of Transitologists and Consolidologists: How far to the East should they attempt to go? *Slavic Review* 53 (1):173-185.

Sebenius, James K. 1992. Challenging Conventional Explanations of International Cooperation: Negotiation Analysis and the Case of Epistemic Communities. *International Organization* 46 (1):323-365.

Shafir, Gershon. 1995. *Immigrants and Nationalists: Ethnic conflict and accommodation in Catalonia, the Basque Country, Latvia, and Estonia.* Albany: State University of New York Press.

Shearman, P. 2001. The Sources of Russian Conduct: understanding Russian foreign policy. *Review of International Studies* 27 (2):249-264.

Smith, Anthony. 1991. *National Identity.* London: Penguin Books.

Smith, Anthony D. 1992. Ethnic Identity and Territorial Nationalism in Comparative Perspective. In *Thinking Theoretically about Soviet Nationalities: History and Comparison in the Study of the USSR.*, edited by Alexander J. Motyl. New York: Columbia University Press.

Smith, David J. 2002. *Estonia: Independence and European Integration.* London: Routledge.

Smith, Graham. 1996. The Ethnic Democracy Thesis and the Citizenship Question in Estonia and Latvia. *Nationalities Papers* 24 (2):845-64.

Smith, Graham. 1996. The Resurgence of Nationalism. In *The Baltic States: The National Self-Determination of Estonia, Latvia, and Lithuania.*, edited by Graham Smith. New York: St. Martin's Press.

Smith, Graham. 1999. *The Post-Soviet States: Mapping the Politics of Transition.* London: Arnold Publishers.

Smith, Graham, Aadne Aasland, and Richard Mole. 1994. Statehood, Ethnic Relations, and Citizenship. In *The Baltic States: The National Self-determination of Estonia, Latvia, and Lithuania*, edited by Graham Smith. New York: St. Martin's Press.

Smith, Graham and Andrew Wilson. 1997. Rethinking Russia's Post-Soviet Diaspora: The Potential for Political Mobilization in Eastern Ukraine and North-East Estonia. *Europe-Asia Studies* 49 (5):845-864.

Smith, Graham, Vivien Law, Andrew Wilson, Annette Bohr, and Edward Allworth, ed. 1998. *Nation-Building in the Post-Soviet Borderlands: The Politics of National Identity*. Cambridge: Cambridge University Press.

Smooha, Sammy. 1990. Minority Status in Ethnic Democracy: the Status of the Arab minority in Israel. *Ethnic and Racial Studies* 13 (3):389-413.

Steen, Anton. 2000. Ethnic Relations, Elites and Democracy in the Baltic States. *Journal of Communist and Transition Politics* 16 (4):68-87.

Taagepera, Rein. 1993. *Estonia: Return to Independence*. Boulder, CO: Westview Press.

Tajfel, Henri and John C. Turner. 1986. The Social Identity Theory of Intergroup Behavior. In *Psychology of Intergroup Relations*, edited by William G. Austin and Stephen Worchel. Chicago: Nelson-Hall Publishers.

Tarrow, Sidney. 1998. *Power in Movement: Social Movements and Contentious Politics*. Second ed. Cambridge: Cambridge University Press.

Tarrow, Sidney. 1999. States and Opportunities: the political structuring of social movements. In *Comparative Perspectives on Social Movements: Political Opportunities, Mobilizing Structures, and Cultural Framings*, edited by John D. McCarthy Doug McAdam, and Mayer N. Zald. Cambridge: Cambridge University Press.

Taylor, Dalmas A. and Beatrice F. Moriarty. 1987. Ingroup Bias as a Function of Competition and Race. *Journal of Conflict Resolution* 31 (1):192-199.

Terry, Sarah Meiklejohn. 1993. Thinking about Post-Communist Transitions: How Different are They. *Slavic Review* 52 (2):337.

Tilly, Charles. 1995. Contentious Repertoires in Great Britain 1758-1834. In *Repertoires and Cycles of Collective Action*, edited by Mark Traugott. Durham and London: Duke University Press.

Tishkov, Valery. 1997. *Ethnicity, Nationalism, and Conflict in and after the Soviet Union: The Mind Aflame*. London: Sage Publishers.

Triandafyllidou, Anna. 1998. National Identity and the 'Other'. *Ethnic and Racial Studies* (July):593-612.

Ugur, M. 1997. State-Society Interaction and European Integration: a political economy approach to the dynamics and policymaking of the European Union. *Review of International Studies* 23 (4):469-500.

Unwin, Tim. 1998. Rurality and the Construction of Nation in Estonia. In *Theorising Transition: the political economy of transition in post-commmunist countries*, edited by John Pickles and Adrian Smith. New York: Routledge.

Van de Berghe, Pierre. 1967. *Race and Racism: A Comparative Perspective.* New York: John Wiley.

Voronov, Konstantin. 2001. The Baltic Policy of the New Russia: A Brief History of the Stormy Decade. In *The Baltic States at Historical Crossroads*, edited by Talavs Jundzis. Riga: Latvian Academy of Sciences.

Waltz, Kenneth N. 1959. *Man, the State and War: a Theoretical Analysis.* New York: Columbia University Press.

Waltz, Kenneth N. 1979. *Theory of International Politics.* New York: Random House.

Weale, Albert. 1999. *Democracy.* London: MacMillan Press.

Weber, Max. 1947. *The Theory of Social and Economic Organization.* Translated by A. M. Henderson and Talcott Parsons. New York: The Free Press.

Wendt, Alexander E. 1987. The Agent-Structure Problem in International Relations. *International Organization* 41 (3):335-369.

White, James D. 1996. Nationalism and Socialism in Historical Perspective. In *The Baltic States: the national self-determination of Estonia, Latvia, and Lithuania*, edited by Graham Smith. New York: St. Martin's Press.

White, Stephen. 2000. *Russia's New Politics: The Management of a Post-communist Society.* Cambridge: Cambridge University Press.

Wilder, A. 1986. Social Categorization: Implications for creation and reduction of intergroup bias. In *Advances in Experimental Social Psychology*, edited by Leonard Berkowitz. New York: Academic Press.

Wilson, Duncan. 2000. *Minority Rights in Education: Lessons for the European Union from Estonia, Latvia, Romania and the former Yugoslav Republic of Macedonia.* Stockholm: Swedish International Development Co-operation Agency.

Wyzan, Michael. 1999. Baltic States Still Vulnerable to Russia's Troubles. *RFE/RL Newsline* 25 February 1999.

Zaagman, Rob. 1999. *Conflict Prevention in the Baltic States: the OSCE High Commissioner on National Minorities in Estonia, Latvia, and Lithuania.* Flensburg, Germany: European Centre for Minority Issues.

Zepa, Brigita. 1992. Social Thought in the Transition Period: the Dynamics of Latvian and Foreign Points of View. *Latvijas Zinatnu Akademijas Vestis* 2:23.

Zepa, Brigita. 2001. *Towards a Civil Society - 2000.* Riga: Baltic Institutes of Social Sciences.

Zevelev, Igor. 1996. Russia and the Russian Diaspora. *Post-Soviet Affairs* 13 (3):265-284.

Zile, Lubova. 2001. Baltic-Russian Co-operation during the Restoration of Independence (1990 until the 1991 Putsch). In *The Baltic States at Historical Crossroads*, edited by Talavs Jundzis. Riga: Latvian Academy of Sciences.

Zvagulis, Peter. 1997. Government Crisis in Latvia. *RFE/RL Newsline* 29 July.

Zvaners, Martins. 1999. Presidential Election Remakes Latvia's Political Landscape. *RFE/RL Newsline* 30 June.

Zvaners, Martins. 2000. Skele Loses Job In Privatization Struggle. *RFE/RL Baltic States Report* 1 (13).

Newspapers and Periodicals

RFE/RL Report on the USSR
RFE/RL Newsline
RFE/RL Daily Report
RFE/RL Report on the Baltic States
The Baltic Times
Chas (Latvia)
Izvestia (Russia)
Noviye Izvestia (Russia)
Nevazisimaya Gazeta (Russia)
Pravda (Russia)
Sevodnya (Russia)
Kommersant Daily (Russia)
Rossiiskaya Gazeta (Russia)
Vremya MN (Russia)

Documents

Council of Europe

European Convention for the Protection of Human Rights and Fundamental Freedoms (1950)

Framework Convention for the Protection of National Minorities (1995)

Council of Ministers, *Resolution ResCMN (2002)8*

European Union

Agenda 2000 (1998)

Commissioner of the European Communities, *1997 Opinion on Estonia's Application for EU Membership*

Commissioner of the European Communities, *1998 Regular Report on Estonia's Progress towards Accession.*

Commissioner of the European Communities, *1999 Regular Report on Estonia's Progress towards Accession.*

Commissioner of the European Communities, *2000 Regular Report on Estonia's Progress towards Accession.*

Commissioner of the European Communities, *2001 Regular Report on Estonia's Progress towards Accession.*

Commissioner of the European Communities, *1998 Regular Report on Latvia's Progress towards Accession.*

Commissioner of the European Communities, *1998 Regular Report on Latvia's Progress towards Accession.*

Commissioner of the European Communities, *1999 Regular Report on Latvia's Progress towards Accession.*

Commissioner of the European Communities, *2000 Regular Report on Latvia's Progress towards Accession.*

Commissioner of the European Communities, *2001 Regular Report on Latvia's Progress towards Accession.*

Organisation for Security and Co-operation in Europe

Copenhagen Document (1990)

Charter of Paris (1990)

Geneva Meeting of Experts on National Minorities (1991)

Helsinki Final Act (1975)

Hague Recommendations on the Education Rights of National Minorities (1996)

Oslo Recommendations Regarding the Linguistic Rights of National Minorities (1998)

Lund Recommendations on the Effective Participation of National Minorities in Public Life (1999)

OSCE High Commissioner on National Minorities

Letter to the Estonian, Latvian and Lithuanian Ministers of Foreign Affairs, CSCE Communication No.124

Letter to President Lennart Meri of Estonia (1 July 1993)

Letter to Estonian Minister of Foreign Affairs, Reference No. 3005/94/L.

Letter to Estonian Minister of Foreign Affairs, Reference No. 3053/94/L.

Letter to Estonian Minister of Foreign Affairs, Reference No. 1340/95/L.

Letter to Estonian Minister of Foreign Affairs, Reference No. 1084/96/L.

Letter to Latvian Minister of Foreign Affairs, Reference No. 1463/93/L.

Letter to Latvian Minister of Foreign Affairs, Reference No. 516/96/L.

Letter to Latvian Minister of Foreign Affairs, Reference No. 1085/96/L.

Letter to Latvian Minister of Foreign Affairs, Reference No. 376/97/L.

Letter to the Permanent Council of the OSCE, Reference No. 1996 314/Bis/96/L.

Estonian Government

1989 Law on Language

1990 Law on Immigration

1992 Estonian Constitution

1992 Law on Citizenship

1993 Law on Aliens

1993 Law on Education

Letter to the HCNM from the Estonian Minister of Foreign Affairs No. 6/10680.

Letter to the HCNM from the Estonian Minister of Foreign Affairs No. 1/19028.

Latvian Government

1989 Law on Language

1992 Latvian Constitution

1994 Law on Citizenship

1998 Law on Education

1999 Law on Language

1999 Law on General Education

Letter to the HCNM from the Latvian Minister of Foreign Affairs No. 31/1003-7767

Index

SOVIET AND POST-SOVIET POLITICS AND SOCIETY

Edited by Dr. Andreas Umland

ISSN 1614-3515

1 *Андреас Умланд (ред.)*
Воплощение Европейской конвенции по правам человека в России
Философские, юридические и эмпирические исследования
ISBN 3-89821-387-0

2 *Christian Wipperfürth*
Russland – ein vertrauenswürdiger Partner?
Grundlagen, Hintergründe und Praxis gegenwärtiger russischer Außenpolitik
Mit einem Vorwort von Heinz Timmermann
ISBN 3-89821-401-X

3 *Manja Hussner*
Die Übernahme internationalen Rechts in die russische und deutsche Rechtsordnung
Eine vergleichende Analyse zur Völkerrechtsfreundlichkeit der Verfassungen der Russländischen Föderation und der Bundesrepublik Deutschland
Mit einem Vorwort von Rainer Arnold
ISBN 3-89821-438-9

4 *Matthew Tejada*
Bulgaria's Democratic Consolidation and the Kozloduy Nuclear Power Plant (KNPP)
The Unattainability of Closure
With a foreword by Richard J. Crampton
ISBN 3-89821-439-7

5 *Марк Григорьевич Меерович*
Квадратные метры, определяющие сознание
Государственная жилищная политика в СССР. 1921 – 1941 гг
ISBN 3-89821-474-5

6 *Andrei P. Tsygankov, Pavel A.Tsygankov (Eds.)*
New Directions in Russian International Studies
ISBN 3-89821-422-2

7 *Марк Григорьевич Меерович*
Как власть народ к труду приучала
Жилище в СССР – средство управления людьми. 1917 – 1941 гг.
С предисловием Елены Осокиной
ISBN 3-89821-495-8

8 *David J. Galbreath*
Nation-Building and Minority Politics in Post-Socialist States
Interests, Influence and Identities in Estonia and Latvia
With a foreword by David J. Smith
ISBN 3-89821-467-2

9 *Алексей Юрьевич Безугольный*
Народы Кавказа в Вооруженных силах СССР в годы Великой Отечественной войны 1941-1945 гг.
С предисловием Николая Бугая
ISBN 3-89821-475-3

10 *Вячеслав Лихачев и Владимир Прибыловский (ред.)*
Русское Национальное Единство, 1990-2000. В 2-х томах
ISBN 3-89821-523-7

11 *Николай Бугай (ред.)*
Народы стран Балтии в условиях сталинизма (1940-е – 1950-е годы)
Документированная история
ISBN 3-89821-525-3

12 *Ingmar Bredies (Hrsg.)*
Zur Anatomie der Orange Revolution in der Ukraine
Wechsel des Elitenregimes oder Triumph des Parlamentarismus?
ISBN 3-89821-524-5

13 *Anastasia V. Mitrofanova*
The Politicization of Russian Orthodoxy
Actors and Ideas
With a foreword by William C. Gay
ISBN 3-89821-481-8

14 *Nathan D. Larson*
Alexander Solzhenitsyn and the Russo-Jewish Question
ISBN 3-89821-483-4

15 *Guido Houben*
Kulturpolitik und Ethnizität
Staatliche Kunstförderung im Russland der neunziger Jahre
Mit einem Vorwort von Gert Weisskirchen
ISBN 3-89821-542-3

16 *Leonid Luks*
Der russische „Sonderweg"?
Aufsätze zur neuesten Geschichte Russlands im europäischen Kontext
ISBN 3-89821-496-6

17 *Евгений Мороз*
История «Мёртвой воды» – от страшной сказки к большой политике
Политическое неоязычество в постсоветской России
ISBN 3-89821-551-2

18 *Александр Верховский и Галина Кожевникова (ред.)*
Этническая и религиозная интолерантность в российских СМИ
Результаты мониторинга 2001-2004 гг.
ISBN 3-89821-569-5

19 *Christian Ganzer*
Sowjetisches Erbe und ukrainische Nation
Das Museum der Geschichte des Zaporoger Kosakentums auf der Insel Chortycja
Mit einem Vorwort von Frank Golczewski
ISBN 3-89821-504-0

20 *Эльза-Баир Гучинова*
Помнить нельзя забыть
Антропология депортационной травмы калмыков
С предисловием Кэролайн Хамфри
ISBN 3-89821-506-7

21 *Юлия Лидерман*
Мотивы «проверки» и «испытания» в постсоветской культуре
Советское прошлое в российском кинематографе 1990-х годов
С предисловием Евгения Марголита
ISBN 3-89821-511-3

22 *Tanya Lokshina, Ray Thomas, Mary Mayer (Eds.)*
The Imposition of a Fake Political Settlement in the Northern Caucasus
The 2003 Chechen Presidential Election
ISBN 3-89821-436-2

23 *Timothy McCajor Hall, Rosie Read (Eds.)*
Changes in the Heart of Europe
Recent Ethnographies of Czechs, Slovaks, Roma, and Sorbs
With an afterword by Zdeněk Salzmann
ISBN 3-89821-606-3

24 *Christian Autengruber*
Die politischen Parteien in Bulgarien und Rumänien
Eine vergleichende Analyse seit Beginn der 90er Jahre
Mit einem Vorwort von Dorothée de Nève
ISBN 3-89821-476-1

25 *Annette Freyberg-Inan with Radu Cristescu*
The Ghosts in Our Classrooms, or: John Dewey Meets Ceauşescu
The Promise and the Failures of Civic Education in Romania
ISBN 3-89821-416-8

26 *John B. Dunlop*
The 2002 Dubrovka and 2004 Beslan Hostage Crises
A Critique of Russian Counter-Terrorism
With a foreword by Donald N. Jensen
ISBN 3-89821-608-X

27 *Peter Koller*
Das touristische Potenzial von Kam''janec'–Podil's'kyj
Eine fremdenverkehrsgeographische Untersuchung der Zukunftsperspektiven und Maßnahmenplanung zur Destinationsentwicklung des „ukrainischen Rothenburg"
Mit einem Vorwort von Kristiane Klemm
ISBN 3-89821-640-3

28 *Françoise Daucé, Elisabeth Sieca-Kozlowski (Eds.)*
Dedovshchina in the Post-Soviet Military
Hazing of Russian Army Conscripts in a Comparative Perspective
With a foreword by Dale Herspring
ISBN 3-89821-616-0

29 *Florian Strasser*
Zivilgesellschaftliche Einflüsse auf die Orange Revolution
Die gewaltlose Massenbewegung und die ukrainische Wahlkrise 2004
Mit einem Vorwort von Egbert Jahn
ISBN 3-89821-648-9

30 *Rebecca S. Katz*
The Georgian Regime Crisis of 2003-2004
A Case Study in Post-Soviet Media Representation of Politics, Crime and Corruption
ISBN 3-89821-413-3

31 *Vladimir Kantor*
Willkür oder Freiheit
Beiträge zur russischen Geschichtsphilosophie
Ediert von Dagmar Herrmann sowie mit einem Vorwort versehen von Leonid Luks
ISBN 3-89821-589-X

32 *Laura A. Victoir*
The Russian Land Estate Today
A Case Study of Cultural Politics in Post-Soviet Russia
With a foreword by Priscilla Roosevelt
ISBN 3-89821-426-5

33 *Ivan Katchanovski*
Cleft Countries
Regional Political Divisions and Cultures in Post-Soviet Ukraine and Moldova
With a foreword by Francis Fukuyama
ISBN 3-89821-558-X

34 *Florian Mühlfried*
Postsowjetische Feiern
Das Georgische Bankett im Wandel
Mit einem Vorwort von Kevin Tuite
ISBN 3-89821-601-2

35 *Roger Griffin, Werner Loh, Andreas Umland (Eds.)*
Fascism Past and Present, West and East
An International Debate on Concepts and Cases in the Comparative Study of the Extreme Right
With an afterword by Walter Laqueur
ISBN 3-89821-674-8

36 *Sebastian Schlegel*
Der „Weiße Archipel"
Sowjetische Atomstädte 1945-1991
Mit einem Geleitwort von Thomas Bohn
ISBN 3-89821-679-9

37 *Vyacheslav Likhachev*
Political Anti-Semitism in Post-Soviet Russia
Actors and Ideas in 1991-2003
Edited and translated from Russian by Eugene Veklerov
ISBN 3-89821-529-6

38 *Josette Baer (Ed.)*
Preparing Liberty in Central Europe
Political Texts from the Spring of Nations 1848 to the Spring of Prague 1968
With a foreword by Zdeněk V. David
ISBN 3-89821-546-6

39 *Михаил Лукьянов*
Российский консерватизм и реформа, 1907-1914
С предисловием Марка Д. Стейнберга
ISBN 3-89821-503-2

40 *Nicola Melloni*
Market Without Economy
The 1998 Russian Financial Crisis
With a foreword by Eiji Furukawa
ISBN 3-89821-407-9

41 *Dmitrij Chmelnizki*
Die Architektur Stalins
Bd. 1: Studien zu Ideologie und Stil
Bd. 2: Bilddokumentation
Mit einem Vorwort von Bruno Flierl
ISBN 3-89821-515-6

42 *Katja Yafimava*
Post-Soviet Russian-Belarussian Relationships
The Role of Gas Transit Pipelines
With a foreword by Jonathan P. Stern
ISBN 3-89821-655-1

43 *Boris Chavkin*
Verflechtungen der deutschen und russischen Zeitgeschichte
Aufsätze und Archivfunde zu den Beziehungen Deutschlands und der Sowjetunion von 1917 bis 1991
Ediert von Markus Edlinger sowie mit einem Vorwort versehen von Leonid Luks
ISBN 3-89821-756-6

44 *Anastasija Grynenko in Zusammenarbeit mit Claudia Dathe*
Die Terminologie des Gerichtswesens der Ukraine und Deutschlands im Vergleich
Eine übersetzungswissenschaftliche Analyse juristischer Fachbegriffe im Deutschen, Ukrainischen und Russischen
Mit einem Vorwort von Ulrich Hartmann
ISBN 3-89821-691-8

45 *Anton Burkov*
The Impact of the European Convention on Human Rights on Russian Law
Legislation and Application in 1996-2006
With a foreword by Françoise Hampson
ISBN 978-3-89821-639-5

46 *Stina Torjesen, Indra Overland (Eds.)*
International Election Observers in Post-Soviet Azerbaijan
Geopolitical Pawns or Agents of Change?
ISBN 978-3-89821-743-9

47 *Taras Kuzio*
Ukraine – Crimea – Russia
Triangle of Conflict
ISBN 978-3-89821-761-3

48 *Claudia Šabić*
"Ich erinnere mich nicht, aber L'viv!"
Zur Funktion kultureller Faktoren für die Institutionalisierung und Entwicklung einer ukrainischen Region
Mit einem Vorwort von Melanie Tatur
ISBN 978-3-89821-752-1

49 *Marlies Bilz*
Tatarstan in der Transformation
Nationaler Diskurs und Politische Praxis 1988-1994
Mit einem Vorwort von Frank Golczewski
ISBN 978-3-89821-722-4

50 *Марлен Ларюэль (ред.)*
Современные интерпретации русского национализма
ISBN 978-3-89821-795-8

51 *Sonja Schüler*
Die ethnische Dimension der Armut
Roma im postsozialistischen Rumänien
Mit einem Vorwort von Anton Sterbling
ISBN 978-3-89821-776-7

52 *Галина Кожевникова*
Радикальный национализм в России и противодействие ему
Сборник докладов Центра «Сова» за 2004-2007 гг.
С предисловием Александра Верховского
ISBN 978-3-89821-721-7

53 *Галина Кожевникова и Владимир Прибыловский*
Российская власть в биографиях I
Высшие должностные лица РФ в 2004 г.
ISBN 978-3-89821-796-5

54 *Галина Кожевникова и Владимир Прибыловский*
Российская власть в биографиях II
Члены Правительства РФ в 2004 г.
ISBN 978-3-89821-797-2

55 *Галина Кожевникова и Владимир Прибыловский*
Российская власть в биографиях III
Руководители федеральных служб и агентств РФ в 2004 г.
ISBN 978-3-89821-798-9

56 *Ileana Petroniu*
Privatisierung in Transformationsökonomien
Determinanten der Restrukturierungs-Bereitschaft am Beispiel Polens, Rumäniens und der Ukraine
Mit einem Vorwort von Rainer W. Schäfer
ISBN 978-3-89821-790-3

57 *Christian Wipperfürth*
Russland und seine GUS-Nachbarn
Hintergründe, aktuelle Entwicklungen und Konflikte in einer ressourcenreichen Region
ISBN 978-3-89821-801-6

58 *Togzhan Kassenova*
From Antagonism to Partnership
The Uneasy Path of the U.S.-Russian Cooperative Threat Reduction
With a foreword by Christoph Bluth
ISBN 978-3-89821-707-1

59 *Alexander Höllwerth*
Das sakrale eurasische Imperium des Aleksandr Dugin
Eine Diskursanalyse zum postsowjetischen russischen Rechtsextremismus
Mit einem Vorwort von Dirk Uffelmann
ISBN 978-3-89821-813-9

60 *Олег Рябов*
«Россия-Матушка»
Национализм, гендер и война в России XX века
С предисловием Елены Гощило
ISBN 978-3-89821-487-2

61 *Ivan Maistrenko*
Borot'bism
A Chapter in the History of the Ukrainian Revolution
With a new introduction by Chris Ford
Translated by George S. N. Luckyj with the assistance of Ivan L. Rudnytsky
ISBN 978-3-89821-697-5

62 *Maryna Romanets*
Anamorphosic Texts and Reconfigured Visions
Improvised Traditions in Contemporary Ukrainian and Irish Literature
ISBN 978-3-89821-576-3

63 *Paul D'Anieri and Taras Kuzio (Eds.)*
Aspects of the Orange Revolution I
Democratization and Elections in Post-Communist Ukraine
ISBN 978-3-89821-698-2

64 *Bohdan Harasymiw in collaboration with Oleh S. Ilnytzkyj (Eds.)*
Aspects of the Orange Revolution II
Information and Manipulation Strategies in the 2004 Ukrainian Presidential Elections
ISBN 978-3-89821-699-9

65 *Ingmar Bredies, Andreas Umland and Valentin Yakushik (Eds.)*
Aspects of the Orange Revolution III
The Context and Dynamics of the 2004 Ukrainian Presidential Elections
ISBN 978-3-89821-803-0

66 *Ingmar Bredies, Andreas Umland and Valentin Yakushik (Eds.)*
Aspects of the Orange Revolution IV
Foreign Assistance and Civic Action in the 2004 Ukrainian Presidential Elections
ISBN 978-3-89821-808-5

67 *Ingmar Bredies, Andreas Umland and Valentin Yakushik (Eds.)*
Aspects of the Orange Revolution V
Institutional Observation Reports on the 2004 Ukrainian Presidential Elections
ISBN 978-3-89821-809-2

68 *Taras Kuzio (Ed.)*
Aspects of the Orange Revolution VI
Post-Communist Democratic Revolutions in Comparative Perspective
ISBN 978-3-89821-820-7

69 *Tim Bohse*
Autoritarismus statt Selbstverwaltung
Die Transformation der kommunalen Politik in der Stadt Kaliningrad 1990-2005
Mit einem Geleitwort von Stefan Troebst
ISBN 978-3-89821-782-8

70 *David Rupp*
Die Rußländische Föderation und die russischsprachige Minderheit in Lettland
Eine Fallstudie zur Anwaltspolitik Moskaus gegenüber den russophonen Minderheiten im „Nahen Ausland" von 1991 bis 2002
Mit einem Vorwort von Helmut Wagner
ISBN 978-3-89821-778-1

71 *Taras Kuzio*
Theoretical and Comparative Perspectives on Nationalism
New Directions in Cross-Cultural and Post-Communist Studies
With a foreword by Paul Robert Magocsi
ISBN 978-3-89821-815-3

72 *Christine Teichmann*
Die Hochschultransformation im heutigen Osteuropa
Kontinuität und Wandel bei der Entwicklung des postkommunistischen Universitätswesens
Mit einem Vorwort von Oskar Anweiler
ISBN 978-3-89821-842-9

73 *Julia Kusznir*
Der politische Einfluss von Wirtschaftseliten in russischen Regionen
Eine Analyse am Beispiel der Erdöl- und Erdgasindustrie, 1992-2005
Mit einem Vorwort von Wolfgang Eichwede
ISBN 978-3-89821-821-4

74 *Alena Vysotskaya*
Russland, Belarus und die EU-Osterweiterung
Zur Minderheitenfrage und zum Problem der Freizügigkeit des Personenverkehrs
Mit einem Vorwort von Katlijn Malfliet
ISBN 978-3-89821-822-1

75 *Heiko Pleines (Hrsg.)*
Corporate Governance in post-sozialistischen Volkswirtschaften
ISBN 978-3-89821-766-8

76 *Stefan Ihrig*
Wer sind die Moldawier?
Rumänismus versus Moldowanismus in Historiographie und Schulbüchern der Republik Moldova, 1991-2006
Mit einem Vorwort von Holm Sundhaussen
ISBN 978-3-89821-466-7

77 *Galina Kozhevnikova in collaboration with Alexander Verkhovsky and Eugene Veklerov*
Ultra-Nationalism and Hate Crimes in Contemporary Russia
The 2004-2006 Annual Reports of Moscow's SOVA Center
With a foreword by Stephen D. Shenfield
ISBN 978-3-89821-868-9

78 *Florian Küchler*
The Role of the European Union in Moldova's Transnistria Conflict
With a foreword by Christopher Hill
ISBN 978-3-89821-850-4

79 *Bernd Rechel*
The Long Way Back to Europe
Minority Protection in Bulgaria
With a foreword by Richard Crampton
ISBN 978-3-89821-863-4

80 *Peter W. Rodgers*
Nation, Region and History in Post-Communist Transitions
Identity Politics in Ukraine, 1991-2006
With a foreword by Vera Tolz
ISBN 978-3-89821-903-7

81 *Stephanie Solywoda*
The Life and Work of Semen L. Frank
A Study of Russian Religious Philosophy
With a foreword by Philip Walters
ISBN 978-3-89821-457-5

82 *Vera Sokolova*
Cultural Politics of Ethnicity
Discourses on Roma in Communist Czechoslovakia
ISBN 978-3-89821-864-1

83 *Natalya Shevchik Ketenci*
Kazakhstani Enterprises in Transition
The Role of Historical Regional Development in Kazakhstan's Post-Soviet Economic Transformation
ISBN 978-3-89821-831-3

84 *Martin Malek, Anna Schor-Tschudnowskaja (Hrsg.)*
Europa im Tschetschenienkrieg
Zwischen politischer Ohnmacht und Gleichgültigkeit
Mit einem Vorwort von Lipchan Basajewa
ISBN 978-3-89821-676-0

85 *Stefan Meister*
Das postsowjetische Universitätswesen zwischen nationalem und internationalem Wandel
Die Entwicklung der regionalen Hochschule in Russland als Gradmesser der Systemtransformation
Mit einem Vorwort von Joan DeBardeleben
ISBN 978-3-89821-891-7

86 *Konstantin Sheiko in collaboration with Stephen Brown*
Nationalist Imaginings of the Russian Past
Anatolii Fomenko and the Rise of Alternative History in Post-Communist Russia
With a foreword by Donald Ostrowski
ISBN 978-3-89821-915-0

87 *Sabine Jenni*
Wie stark ist das „Einige Russland"?
Zur Parteibindung der Eliten und zum Wahlerfolg der Machtpartei im Dezember 2007
Mit einem Vorwort von Klaus Armingeon
ISBN 978-3-89821-961-7

88 *Thomas Borén*
Meeting-Places of Transformation
Urban Identity, Spatial Representations and Local Politics in Post-Soviet St Petersburg
ISBN 978-3-89821-739-2

89 *Aygul Ashirova*
Stalinismus und Stalin-Kult in Zentralasien
Turkmenistan 1924-1953
Mit einem Vorwort von Leonid Luks
ISBN 978-3-89821-987-7

90 *Leonid Luks*
Freiheit oder imperiale Größe?
Essays zu einem russischen Dilemma
ISBN 978-3-8382-0011-8

91 *Christopher Gilley*
The 'Change of Signposts' in the Ukrainian Emigration
A Contribution to the History of Sovietophilism in the 1920s
With a foreword by Frank Golczewski
ISBN 978-3-89821-965-5

92 *Philipp Casula, Jeronim Perovic (Eds.)*
Identities and Politics During the Putin Presidency
The Discursive Foundations of Russia's Stability
With a foreword by Heiko Haumann
ISBN 978-3-8382-0015-6

93 *Marcel Viëtor*
Europa und die Frage nach seinen Grenzen im Osten
Zur Konstruktion ‚europäischer Identität' in Geschichte und Gegenwart
Mit einem Vorwort von Albrecht Lehmann
ISBN 978-3-8382-0045-3

94 *Ben Hellman, Andrei Rogachevskii*
Filming the Unfilmable
Casper Wrede's 'One Day in the Life of Ivan Denisovich'
ISBN 978-3-8382-0044-6

95 *Eva Fuchslocher*
Vaterland, Sprache, Glaube
Orthodoxie und Nationenbildung am Beispiel Georgiens
Mit einem Vorwort von Christina von Braun
ISBN 978-3-89821-884-9

96 *Vladimir Kantor*
Das Westlertum und der Weg Russlands
Zur Entwicklung der russischen Literatur und Philosophie
Ediert von Dagmar Herrmann
Mit einem Beitrag von Nikolaus Lobkowicz
ISBN 978-3-8382-0102-3

97 *Kamran Musayev*
Die postsowjetische Transformation im Baltikum und Südkaukasus
Eine vergleichende Untersuchung der politischen Entwicklung Lettlands und Aserbaidschans 1985-2009
Mit einem Vorwort von Leonid Luks
Ediert von Sandro Henschel
ISBN 978-3-8382-0103-0

98 *Tatiana Zhurzhenko*
Borderlands into Bordered Lands
Geopolitics of Identity in Post-Soviet Ukraine
With a foreword by Dieter Segert
ISBN 978-3-8382-0042-2

99 *Кирилл Галушко, Лидия Смола (ред.)*
Пределы падения – варианты украинского будущего
Аналитико-прогностические исследования
ISBN 978-3-8382-0148-1

100 *Michael Minkenberg (ed.)*
Historical Legacies and the Radical Right in Post-Cold War Central and Eastern Europe
With an afterword by Sabrina P. Ramet
ISBN 978-3-8382-0124-5

101 *David-Emil Wickström*
"Okna otkroi!" – "Open the Windows!"
Transcultural Flows and Identity Politics in the St. Petersburg Popular Music Scene
With a foreword by Yngvar B. Steinholt
ISBN 978-3-8382-0100-9

102 *Eva Zabka*
Eine neue „Zeit der Wirren"?
Der spät- und postsowjetische Systemwandel 1985-2000 im Spiegel russischer gesellschaftspolitischer Diskurse
Mit einem Vorwort von Margareta Mommsen
ISBN 978-3-8382-0161-0

103 *Ulrike Ziemer*
Ethnic Belonging, Gender and Cultural Practices
Youth Identitites in Contemporary Russia
With a foreword by Anoop Nayak
ISBN 978-3-8382-0152-8

104 *Ksenia Chepikova*
‚Einiges Russland' - eine zweite KPdSU?
Aspekte der Identitätskonstruktion einer postsowjetischen „Partei der Macht"
Mit einem Vorwort von Torsten Oppelland
ISBN 978-3-8382-0311-9

105 *Леонид Люкс*
Западничество или евразийство? Демократия или идеократия?
Сборник статей об исторических дилеммах России
С предисловием Владимира Кантора
ISBN 978-3-8382-0211-2

106 *Anna Dost*
Das russische Verfassungsrecht auf dem Weg zum Föderalismus und zurück
Zum Konflikt von Rechtsnormen und -wirklichkeit in der Russländischen Föderation von 1991 bis 2009
Mit einem Vorwort von Alexander Blankenagel
ISBN 978-3-8382-0292-1

107 *Philipp Herzog*
Sozialistische Völkerfreundschaft, nationaler Widerstand oder harmloser Zeitvertreib?
Zur politischen Funktion der Volkskunst im sowjetischen Estland
Mit einem Vorwort von Andreas Kappeler
ISBN 978-3-8382-0216-7

108 *Marlène Laruelle (ed.)*
Russian Nationalism, Foreign Policy, and Identity Debates in Putin's Russia
New Ideological Patterns after the Orange Revolution
ISBN 978-3-8382-0325-6

109 *Michail Logvinov*
Russlands Kampf gegen den internationalen Terrorismus
Eine kritische Bestandsaufnahme des Bekämpfungsansatzes
Mit einem Geleitwort von Hans-Henning Schröder und einem Vorwort von Eckhard Jesse
ISBN 978-3-8382-0329-4

110 *John B. Dunlop*
The Moscow Bombings of September 1999
Examinations of Russian Terrorist Attacks at the Onset of Vladimir Putin's Rule
ISBN 978-3-8382-0388-1

111 *Андрей А. Ковалёв*
Свидетельство из-за кулис российской политики I
Можно ли делать добро из зла? (Воспоминания и размышления о последних советских и первых послесоветских годах)
With a foreword by Peter Reddaway
ISBN 978-3-8382-0302-7

112 *Андрей А. Ковалёв*
Свидетельство из-за кулис российской политики II
Угроза для себя и окружающих (Наблюдения и предостережения относительно происходящего после 2000 г.)
ISBN 978-3-8382-0303-4

113 *Bernd Kappenberg*
Zeichen setzen für Europa
Der Gebrauch europäischer lateinischer Sonderzeichen in der deutschen Öffentlichkeit
Mit einem Vorwort von Peter Schlobinski
ISBN 978-3-89821-749-1

114 *Ivo Mijnssen*
The Quest for an Ideal Youth in Putin's Russia I
Back to Our Future! History, Modernity and Patriotism according to *Nashi,* 2005-2012
With a foreword by Jeronim Perović
ISBN 978-3-8382-0368-3

115 *Jussi Lassila*
The Quest for an Ideal Youth in Putin's Russia II
The Search for Distinctive Conformism in the Political Communication of *Nashi,* 2005-2009
With a foreword by Kirill Postoutenko
ISBN 978-3-8382-0415-4

116 *Valerio Trabandt*
Neue Nachbarn, gute Nachbarschaft?
Die EU als internationaler Akteur am Beispiel ihrer Demokratieförderung in Belarus und der Ukraine 2004-2009
Mit einem Vorwort von Jutta Joachim
ISBN 978-3-8382-0437-6

117 *Fabian Pfeiffer*
Estlands Außen- und Sicherheitspolitik I
Der estnische Atlantizismus nach der wiedererlangten Unabhängigkeit 1991-2004
Mit einem Vorwort von Helmut Hubel
ISBN 978-3-8382-0127-6

118 *Jana Podßuweit*
Estlands Außen- und Sicherheitspolitik II
Handlungsoptionen eines Kleinstaates im Rahmen seiner EU-Mitgliedschaft (2004-2008)
Mit einem Vorwort von Helmut Hubel
ISBN 978-3-8382-0440-6

119 *Karin Pointner*
Estlands Außen- und Sicherheitspolitik III
Eine gedächtnispolitische Analyse estnischer Entwicklungskooperation 2006-2010
Mit einem Vorwort von Karin Liebhart
ISBN 978-3-8382-0435-2

120 *Ruslana Vovk*
Die Offenheit der ukrainischen Verfassung für das Völkerrecht und die europäische Integration
Mit einem Vorwort von Alexander Blankenagel
ISBN 978-3-8382-0481-9

121 *Mykhaylo Banakh*
Die Relevanz der Zivilgesellschaft bei den postkommunistischen Transformationsprozessen in mittel- und osteuropäischen Ländern
Das Beispiel der spät- und postsowjetischen Ukraine 1986-2009
Mit einem Vorwort von Gerhard Simon
ISBN 978-3-8382-0499-4

122 *Michael Moser*
Language Policy and the Discourse on Languages in Ukraine under President Viktor Yanukovych (25 February 2010–28 October 2012)
ISBN 978-3-8382-0497-0 (Paperback edition)
ISBN 978-3-8382-0507-6 (Hardcover edition)

ibidem-Verlag / *ibidem* Press
Melchiorstr. 15
70439 Stuttgart
Germany

ibidem@ibidem.eu
www.ibidem-verlag.com
www.ibidem.eu

GPSR Authorized Representative: Easy Access System Europe, Mustamäe tee 50, 10621 Tallinn, Estonia, gpsr.requests@easproject.com

www.ingramcontent.com/pod-product-compliance
Lightning Source LLC
Chambersburg PA
CBHW051711020426
42333CB00014B/937

* 9 7 8 3 8 9 8 2 1 4 6 7 4 *